A HANDBOOK OF
INDUSTRIAL
RELATIONS
PRACTICE

A HANDBOOK OF

INDUSTRIAL RELATIONS PRACTICE

PRACTICE AND THE LAW IN THE
EMPLOYMENT RELATIONSHIP

Edited by **Brian Towers**

Published in association with the
Institute of Personnel Management

KOGAN
PAGE

First published in 1987 by
Kogan Page Ltd,
120 Pentonville Rd, London N1 9JN

Revised edition, 1989

Printed and bound in Great Britain by Billing & Sons Ltd, Worcester

British Library Cataloguing in Publication Data
A handbook of industrial relations practice. —
 Rev. ed.
 1. Great Britain. Industrial relations
 I. Towers, Brian
 658.3′15′0941

ISBN 1–85091–656–X

Contents

Contributors   ix
Foreword to the First Edition   xiii
Introduction to the Revised Edition   xv

PART ONE: THE BACKGROUND

Chapter 1: British Industrial Relations and Trade Unions:
Change and its Consequences   1

Background   2
The Trade Union Crisis   15
Trade Union Responses: Five Strategies   22
Conclusion: The Prospects for the Trade Unions   28

Chapter 2: Industrial Relations in the Public Sector   34

Joint Procedures   36
Pay Determination   40
The Changing Context of Public Sector Industrial Relations   45
Strikes and the Union Response   49
Conclusion   53

Chapter 3: New Technology and Industrial Relations   55

Economic Change, New Technology and Jobs   55
The Management of New Technology   58
Effects on Trade Unions and Workers   65
Conclusion   74

PART TWO: THE PRACTICE OF INDUSTRIAL RELATIONS

Chapter 4: Managing Industrial Relations   81

Changing Styles   82
Cost-effective Industrial Relations: the Elements   84
Perspectives   93

Chapter 5: Negotiations   95

Perspectives on Negotiations   96
Models for Analysing Negotiations   97

The Dynamics of Negotiations 98
Preparations for Negotiations 99
Stages of Negotiations 103
The Trust Factor 109
Training for Negotiations 110
The Future of Negotiating 110

Chapter 6: Collective Agreements **112**

The Nature of Collective Agreements 112
The Contents of Collective Agreements 115
Levels of Collective Agreement 118
Trends: a Strategic Approach to Industrial Relations 122
The Future of Collective Agreements 129

Chapter 7: Industrial Relations Procedures **132**

The Meaning and Extent of Procedures 132
The Merits and Limitations of Procedures 133
Negotiating Procedures 135
Grievance Procedures 139
Disciplinary Procedures 141
Redundancy Procedures 146
Health and Safety Procedures 148
Procedural Checklist 153
Procedural Trends and Developments 154

Chapter 8: Employee Participation **159**

Forms of Employee Participation 160
Team Briefing 163
Quality Circles 167
Joint Consultation 169
Worker Directors 173
Profit Sharing and Employee Share Ownership 176
Conclusion 178

Chapter 9: Managing Professional and Managerial Staff **181**

Who are Professional and Managerial Employees? 181
Recruitment, Selection and Mobility 182
Management Education 184
Human Resource Management 186
Economic Rewards 190
Unionization of Managers 194
Conclusion 195

**Chapter 10: Employee Relations in Small and Medium-
             sized Enterprises**   **197**

What is a Small Firm?   198
Employing People   200
Communications   209
Rules and Regulations   210
Trade Unions   212
Conclusion   214

Chapter 11: Pay and Payment Systems   **217**

Classification of Payment Systems   217
Introducing a Payment System   219
Output-related Systems   221
Measured Daywork   224
Plant or Enterprise-wide Systems   226
Profit Sharing   229
Pay Structures and Job Evaluation   233
Harmonization   242
Trends and Possibilities   245

**Chapter 12: Motives for and Incidence of Seeking
             Single-union Agreements**   **248**

The Extent of Single-unionism   249
Union Recognition Problems   250
Employer Interest in Single-union Agreements   258

PART THREE: THE LAW IN INDUSTRIAL RELATIONS
Chapter 13: Changes in the Law since 1979: an Overview   **265**

Law as Strategy: Reforming the UK Industrial Relations
Culture   265
The Elements of Change   266
Law as Tactics: Effecting Change   268
Labour Law: Main Changes since 1979   270
Employer-employee Relations   274
Industrial Action   281
Trade Union Organization and Activities   286
Conclusion   292

Chapter 14: Ballots, Picketing and Strikes   **300**

Ballots   300
Picketing   306
Strikes   313
Conclusion   316

Chapter 15: Unfair Dismissal and Tribunals   319

Purposes of the Legislation   319
The Law in Practice   319
When is a Dismissal Fair?   325
Special Cases   336
Industrial Tribunals   339

Chapter 16: Other Individual Rights   345

Statutory Employment Rights   345
Contractual Rights   353
Equal Opportunities   356
Rights of Trade Unionists and Non-unionists   359
Health, Safety and Welfare   363

List of Cases Cited   367
Useful Addresses   371
Index   383

Contributors

Brian Towers, editor of *The Handbook of Industrial Relations Practice*, is Senior Lecturer in Industrial Relations at Nottingham University where he has taught trade unionists since 1966. He founded and has edited the *Industrial Relations Journal* since 1972 and has had long practical involvement in industrial relations as an ACAS arbitrator. His research experience, interests and publications have included productivity bargaining, negotiating practice, worker-directors, the arbitrating process and British employment policy. He has extensive academic contacts in the USSR and has researched and taught in the USA as a visiting professor. Currently he is writing a book on trade unions in the UK and the USA.

Greg Bamber is Associate Professor, Graduate School of Management, University of Queensland, Brisbane, Australia. He was previously at Durham University and an ACAS arbitrator. His publications include *Militant Managers?* (Gower, 1986) and, with Russell Lansbury, *International and Comparative Industrial Relations* (Allen & Unwin, 1987), and *New Technology: International Perspectives on Human Resources and Industrial Relations* (Unwin Hyman, 1989).

P. B. Beaumont is Reader in Industrial Relations in the Department of Social and Economic Research at the University of Glasgow. He has been involved in a number of funded research projects, has acted as consultant and adviser to a number of organisations and has held visiting positions at universities abroad. A long standing research interest in public sector industrial relations has resulted in a number of books and monographs on the subject.

Chris Brewster joined the Cranfield School of Management in 1985 where he is Senior Lecturer in Industrial Relations and personnel. He has had substantial experience in industrial relations prior to joining Cranfield and has acted as a consultant to UK and international organisations mainly in the areas of personnel policies (the subject of his PhD) and management training. He is the author of *Understanding Industrial Relations* and *Cost Effective Strategies in Industrial Relations* as well as numerous articles.

Colin Duncan is Lecturer in Industrial Relations in the Department of Business Studies at Edinburgh University. He joined the Department in 1983 following a career in hospital personnel work and as a Research Officer with LACSAB (Local Authorities Conditions of Service Advisory Board). His research interests are in the field of pay and public sector industrial relations and he is the author of the book *Low Pay, its Causes and the Post-War Trade Union Responses*, Research Studies Press, Chichester, 1981.

Derek Fatchett is Labour Member of Parliament for Leeds Central and an opposition spokesperson on Education. Previously he was a Lecturer in Industrial Relations at the University of Leeds and he has written a number of books and articles including *Trade Unions and Politics in the 80s* a study of the 1984 Trade Union Act, published by Croom Helm.

John Gennard is Professor of Industrial Relations and Dean of the Strathclyde Business School. He has written widely on industrial relations and is author of books on white collar unionism, financing strikers, and the closed shop. He is currently writing the official history of the National Graphical Association and is also engaged in a major work on trade union administration and government.

Colin Gill is University Lecturer in Industrial Relations in the Management Studies Group at the University of Cambridge and a Fellow of Wolfson College. He is the Editor of *New Technology, Work and Employment* and is the author of *Work, Unemployment and the New Technology*, Polity Press, Oxford, 1985.

Paul Lewis is Lecturer in Industrial Relations at the University of Leeds. He has substantial practical experience of industrial relations, and has published widely, particularly in the areas of unfair dismissal, redundancy and industrial training. He is a Member of the Industrial Tribunals (England and Wales).

Karl J. Mackie is a Lecturer in the University of Nottingham. He is a barrister and psychologist, reviews editor and law commentary editor on the *Industrial Relations Journal*, and an ACAS arbitrator. He is author of a number of publications in the field of industrial relations law including *Lawyers in Business: and the Law Business*, Macmillan, 1988.

Mick Marchington is Lecturer in the Manchester School of Management at UMIST. His primary research interest is the management of employee involvement; this is now proceeding with the aid of a three year ESRC grant. He is editor of *Employee Relations* and has published widely in the field, including *Managing Industrial Relations*, McGraw Hill 1982.

Ian Roberts is Senior Research Fellow at the Durham University Business School, Small Business Centre. He has had work experience in the shipbuilding industry and is currently researching small firms with special emphasis on industrial relations.

Derek Sawbridge is Senior Lecturer in Industrial Relations and Chairman of the Board of Studies at the Durham University Business School. His work experience has been in coalmining and textiles. He is a deputy chairman of the Central Arbitration Committee and an ACAS arbitrator.

Ramsumair Singh is Lecturer in Industrial Relations at the University of Lancaster. Previously he was a chartered electrical engineer with training and work experience at GEC and Texaco. He has published on third party intervention and industrial disputes and is an ACAS arbitrator.

Ed Snape is Lecturer in Economics at Teesside Polytechnic and an Associate Research Fellow at Durham University Business School. He has previous experience as a school teacher and his research interests include the industrial relations of managerial and professional employment.

P. J. White is Senior Lecturer in Industrial Relations at the University of Edinburgh. He was formerly a civil servant and British Steel Corporation Research Fellow. He has published in a number of journals on a wide range of industrial relations themes and is co-author of books on worker-directors and the role of information in government policy-making.

Foreword to the First Edition

By coincidence I write the foreword eight years after I took up my post in the Advisory, Conciliation and Arbitration Service in 1979, which is when the first *Handbook of Industrial Relations Practice* appeared. Over these years there have been far-reaching changes in the structure of industry and in the environment of work. The impact on the balance, and the conduct, of collective bargaining has, in my view, been profound. Perhaps the most remarkable feature has been the pace and scope of these changes. The need to compete in the market place at home or abroad, often requiring a positive approach to the introduction of technological change, has created a pressure for major modifications to the world of work and to traditional attitudes and practices at all levels of the enterprise. For those in work and in organizations surviving and flourishing in this environment many benefits have accrued.

Despite the scope and pace of these changes, other fundamental tenets of our industrial relations system have held firm. The first of these, in my view, is that although trade unions have lost members in some of the traditional areas where industries have severely retrenched, they have sustained practicable working relationships in many areas of collective bargaining, with some adjustment to plant-level or enterprise-level negotiation and agreements. Some unions have successfully secured membership in new areas of employment although recruitment and recognition agreements have not been easy to achieve.

Second, the concept of individual employment protection by law has been continued and extended in areas such as equal pay and unauthorized deductions from pay. The system has undergone significant modification to such things as qualifying periods, and although there are critics of the tribunal system, the principle of good individual employment practice still broadly holds.

Third, and despite the intrusion of the law in the form of more frequent injunctions and claims for damages, the great majority of businesses and organizations with an established history of collective bargaining continue to value collectively bargained agreements with trade unions and staff associations which include dispute and grievance procedures which are not legally binding. These have persisted and sometimes been extended in the areas where other change has been most rapid.

The tensions created by this changing scene have to be positively and creatively addressed and resolved jointly if all are to benefit. Many issues have been thrown up and vigorously debated: the role of management and trade unions; the organization of work and the workforce; trade union services to individuals; communications and employee participation for the good of the enterprise; the framework for orderly collective bargaining and the role of conciliation and arbitration; payment systems, performance related pay and other reward packages; the effect of the extension of balloting and legal injunctions into the bargaining process; the maintenance of union membership agreements; and many more. One particular area of employment however – the public sector – continues to be beset with conflict. There has been a succession of major public disputes since 1979 and no agreement exists between the various interested parties as to how such conflict may be avoided in the future.

Therefore, in the range of issues addressed in this handbook I identify significant contributions worthy of full consideration by personnel and industrial relations practitioners, whatever their role, be it in management or trade union. Brian Towers has drawn together an impressive group of contributors. Most of them I know and many of them are handpicked members of the ACAS Panel of Arbitrators, selected for their professional competence, integrity, and independent spirit. The others have impressed me with their thorough approach to the subject. Like ACAS their views and work will not be beyond critical comment or analysis but I am certain that they will be worthy of study.

Dennis Boyd
Chief Conciliation Officer
ACAS
London
August 1987

Introduction to the Revised Edition

The first edition of this handbook was published in the autumn of 1987. It has clearly met a need judging by the level of demand and this encouraged the publisher to decide to bring out this revised, second edition in paperback.

Much has happened in British industrial relations even in the short period since the first edition. The Employment Act became law in 1988 and this statute has been fully absorbed by the authors in making their revisions. In particular the Act removed the remaining legal props supporting the closed shop.* It therefore seemed sensible to replace the chapter on this theme in favour of a more viable alternative. It almost chose itself; that is a chapter by the same author on single-union agreements, especially those with 'no-strike' clauses, which have attracted much attention and comment in trade union, employer, government and academic circles. What is needed now is a cooler, more detached, analytical appraisal. This is the approach of Chapter 13.

The Employment Act also introduced a new provision which allows individual trade union members the freedom not to be bound by a lawful ballot in favour of strike action. This controversial change is fully discussed throughout the handbook. Perhaps even more controversial is the government's Draft Statutory Code of Practice on Trade Union Industrial Action Balloting (which was published on 3 November 1988 by the Department of Employment with representations invited up to 3 February 1989), and its more significant provisions are discussed in the text.

The new edition has also provided an opportunity for the authors to remove illustrative material which has become dated. It is particularly the case with the first two background chapters which have been combined into a single chapter somewhat shorter than the sum of its earlier parts. This new chapter takes account of recent developments in the trade unions, not least the possibility that they are reaching the low point of their decline and may even begin to look forward to a modest revival. But if there is a silver lining the dark cloud has surely thickened with the expulsion of the EETPU at the 1988 Bournemouth Congress. The circumstances and consequences of the

---

* The Government has also recently announced its intention to abolish the closed shop completely.

expulsion feature in a number of chapters, but especially the first chapter and the new contribution on single-union agreements.

Yet in spite of the necessary changes to content, this edition retains the features and style of the first which were so well received. Hence it remains a handbook of *industral relations* (ie recognizing the still existing primacy of collective bargaining despite the post 1979 changes) but takes account of the new approach of human resource management where it has influenced personnel management (notably Chapters 5 and 7). Chapter 11 also adopts the term 'employee relations' as more 'appropriate to actual style and practice in smaller enterprises.

All the authors, as in the first edition, write in an even-handed way. This is as it should be, especially since most of them are ACAS arbitrators. The handbook is intended for practitioners, be they in companies, trade union offices, government departments or town halls. It also has a strong following – from the evidence of sales – in universities, polytechnics, business schools and colleges. It is hoped that this cheaper, second edition will more closely fit the pockets (in both senses!) of this wider market.

Finally, may I once again thank the contributors to this handbook for the efficiency with which they have approached the task of revision and the publishers for the speed with which they have got it into print. For this second edition I have again had the advantage of the co-ordinating and editing skills of the *Industrial Relations Journal*'s managing editor, Pam Arksey. For her contribution I was especially grateful at a difficult time.

Brian Towers
Editor

Industrial Relations Journal
University of Strathclyde 1989

Part One:
The Background

Chapter 1

British Industrial Relations and the Trade Unions: Change and its Consequences

Brian Towers*

Since the return of the Conservatives to government in 1979, British industrial relations has been pushed, pulled and re-shaped by a combination of external and internal influences which some would see as the beginning of a process of change and adaptation which cannot be reversed, particularly since the re-election of the Conservative Party to government in the summer of 1987. Much of the discussion has focused upon the dramatic decline in trade union membership associated with a battery of powerful, negative influences such as the persistence of high levels of unemployment and major changes in the composition of the labour force. Others counter the significance of *nationally-measured* membership decline and point to the relative stability of day-to-day industrial relations and trade union influence at workplace level. Thus, as the Advisory, Conciliation and Arbitration Service has observed concerning developments in 1986:

> '. . . cases in which companies withdrew previous negotiating or consultative rights remained very much the exception. Overall, where trade union membership was well-established it remained so and collective bargaining and consultative machinery continued to be the major means through which employers and employees dealt with each other.'[1]†

While it is important to recognize that long-established institutions and patterns of behaviour *can* be quickly, even suddenly, transformed, it is

* The author is grateful to Karl Mackie and Ram Singh for helpful comments on successive drafts of this chapter.
† ACAS repeated this observation for 1987[2] but for the first time added some comment on 'derecognition' of trade unions by employers. Recognition and derecognition are discussed later (pp 7–8).

more likely in relatively stable, complex societies that change will be both slow and piecemeal. Additionally, industrial relations in Britain – perhaps more than in most other comparable countries – has strong links with its past which gives it an inbuilt resistance to reform and reformers. It is therefore important to take account of these characteristics if the present industrial relations situation is to be adequately understood and evaluated, and the impact of changes is not to be exaggerated. At the same time there is evidence that the pressures for change – which have accelerated under the present Government – are having an influence which seems more than transitory and all indications suggest that this influence will in some degree survive the present Government.

This chapter has two purposes. Firstly, to outline those changes in the economic and political background to industrial relations, some of which have been dramatic, that have taken place since 1979. Secondly, to describe the impact of these changes on the trade unions, how they are responding to the changes and including an assessment of their future prospects.

Background

Changes in those factors which have had a direct influence upon British industrial relations since 1979 can be described and discussed under three headings: changes in the economy, changes in employment, and increasing government intervention. Such headings are of course devices of convenience given the complexity of the relationships between them. Changes in employment are partly determined by economic change and government intervention both influences, and is influenced by, developments in the economy and employment. Nor should 1979 necessarily be seen as marking a decisive break with the past since current trends and present policies, even legislation, had their origins many years earlier. These important analytical and historical considerations cannot be discussed here but at least they should be borne in mind.[3]

The Economy

The long postwar boom of the Western economies began to lose momentum in the late 1960s, a process accelerated by the 'oil shocks' of 1973 and 1979 and complemented by widespread deflationary and tight money policies – especially after 1979. In the UK the unemployment rate,* which had only exceptionally been above 2 per cent for more than 20 years, after 1967 began its long upwards drift reaching 5 per cent in 1976 and staying there until 1979. Then it doubled in three years and touched 12 per cent in

---

* Comprehensive employment, unemployment and consumer price data is published monthly in the Labour Market Data section of the official *Employment Gazette* from which these and subsequent figures are taken. The *Gazette* is cited in the references.

1985. Early in 1986 unemployment began to fall and in 1988 reached 9.5 per cent with the underlying trend still downwards.

In output terms* Gross Domestic Product (GDP) grew by 16 per cent between 1979 and 1987. This, over the whole period, compared unfavourably with the growth in the Organization for Economic Co-operation and Development (OECD) as a whole of 25 per cent but, since 1983 and especially since 1985, there has been a marked improvement in British performance. Growth and labour productivity have both accelerated to 3–4 per cent and have outpaced that for the OECD, including the USA, France, West Germany and Italy.

Rising GDP was also accompanied by a falling rate of inflation (12 per cent in 1982 to 3.3 per cent early in 1988) and, after 1986, falling unemployment. Rising tax revenues from economic growth were enhanced by the windfall gains from the 'privatization' of public sector industries (since 1979 these sales to the private sector have realized a total in excess of £11 billion) which allowed for successive cuts in tax rates and a budget surplus from 1988. However during 1988 the old constraints on growth of rising inflation and a large and growing external deficit were causing widespread concern as the Government raised interest rates. Nor was the fall in unemployment necessarily an achievement. It partly reflected changes in methods of enumeration† and the 1988 level was still almost four times that of 20 years earlier. The growth performance has also been from levels of output lower than many comparable OECD countries and, historically, less impressive than in the much-maligned era of Keynesian fine-tuning. In the years from 1953 to 1967 growth averaged 3 per cent per annum with minimal inflation *and* full employment.

For the economy's long-term prospects debate is focused upon the significance to be attached to the erosion of manufacturing capacity and the gradual exhaustion of the oil reserves. The UK's traditional surplus on trade in manufactures has long been in decline under the influence of export competition, the shrinking of traditional markets and import penetration. These processes were accelerated by a strong oil-pound in the early 1980s. In 1982, for the first time in 200 years, the dwindling surplus turned into a deficit and by 1987 exports of manufactures, by value, had fallen to 87 per cent of imports. In the car industry, that barometer of manufacturing,

---

* The comparative economic statistics cited here are published in a wide variety of official sources. They are conveniently summarized in the statistical appendix to the *National Institute Economic Review* which is cited in the references.

† In November 1982 the method of counting the unemployed was changed from those registering as unemployed to those on benefit. Additionally, there has been a sequence of changes in the official definition of unemployment which have excluded groups previously considered as unemployed – such as those on youth training programmes. These changes have consistently *reduced* the official, monthly unemployment figure and have attracted widespread political and academic controversy.

production for export in 1986 was 38 per cent of the 1978 level while the share of imported new cars into Britain grew from 49 per cent to 54 per cent over the same period. This growing trade deficit was shown in manufacturing's share of GDP which fell from 29 per cent in 1975 to 25 per cent ten years later to be replaced in output, if not in employment, by oil and gas extraction. At the same time, as in other developed countries, private sector services have maintained strong growth.

Two broad views have been taken of these developments. There are those who maintain that the impermanence of North Sea oil and gas reserves* and their dollar price volatility make them an inadequate substitute for lost manufacturing capacity and its reduced export contribution to the balance of payments. The other approach (which dominates Government policy) is to argue that the shift into services is already providing an alternative to manufacturing and that the eventual decline in oil and gas production will, through a falling exchange rate, make British manufacturing exports more competitive and thus arrest the decline in the manufacturing base and the after-oil threat to the balance of payments. Similar differences in outlook and prognosis are also evident with respect to manufacturing itself with decline seen either as 'deindustrialization' or as a painful, but necessary, movement away from the older, contracting, obsolete industries towards services and the new, expanding, high technology sectors.

These rival explanations do, however, share the same expectations as regards developments, ie that short of a radical change in policy (and perhaps even with it), the contribution of the goods-producing industries to GDP will continue to decline – largely through further falls in manufacturing – and that private sector services will continue to grow in importance. In addition, the movement from manufacturing towards services continues to be strongly uneven in its regional impact. The lost manufacturing jobs are mainly concentrated in the traditional manufacturing areas: Scotland, Wales, the Northern regions of England and now the West Midlands – the older centre of the British car industry. At the same time the growing service sector is essentially located, though not uniformly, in the already relatively more prosperous South and East of England. It is also clear that high technology employment is reinforcing the regional imbalance as the new industries increasingly locate in the same regions.

Employment

These strengthening economic pressures are having a major impact upon occupational structure. The expanding service sector favours the growth of jobs traditionally performed by females. On present trends women will

---

*At 1985 production levels related to proven reserves it has been estimated that UK oil will be exhausted by 1999.[4]

constitute half of total employment in the 1990s, dominating support and personal service occupations. But even within contracting manufacturing industries certain occupations are being influenced by new technology applications, notably in the movement away from single-skilling to multi-skilling and the rise of the technician.[5] Furthermore, influencing both expanding and contracting economic sectors is the growth of the 'flexible workforce' (part-time, temporary and self-employed) which was estimated in 1986 as one-third of all employment. It is also dominated by women (two-thirds of all flexible workers) with the largest concentrations in hotels and catering, distribution, repairs, and professional and business services.[6]

Flexible work is of course not new but it is currently being widely promoted among British management by agencies, consultants and some academic institutions through the familiar model of the 'flexible firm'* which distinguishes between core workers (multi-skilled, full-time, good pay, conditions and benefits); peripheral workers (short-term, temporary, part-time with less favourable pay, conditions and benefits); and external workers who are not employees of the firm (agency temporaries, workers in contracted-out services and the self-employed). The logic of the flexible firm is labour cost minimization by limiting core workers, relative to peripheral and external workers. It has potentially far-reaching implications for industrial relations and trade unions since the core is conventionally unionized and recognized in contrast to other workers.

In its comprehensive form the flexible firm has not been widely adopted although two specific kinds of flexibility have been very much in evidence. The first, multi-skilling, is common in collective agreements, even in industries such as shipbuilding and car manufacture where craft demarcations have been traditionally strong. The second, 'flexibility of time', has been long established in continuous process industries for *technical* reasons but is now being extended by employers for *market* reasons to industries subject to seasonal or cyclical variations in demand. In its most radical form (known as 'annualization') the employer concedes a cut in the average length of the working week without loss of pay. In return the union agrees for the employer to vary the actual length of the working week within upper and lower limits and subject to an annual total of hours worked. Recent surveys have shown that although all the forms of flexibility have normally been introduced through collective bargaining, the unions generally do not welcome them and see them as a product of weakened trade union organization and influence.[7] More recently, national negotiations in the engineering industry have failed, after two years, to deliver a shorter

---

* Interestingly this model's antecedents come from the pioneering academic work in labour segmentation first developed in the United States which analysed, but implicitly deplored, the institutionalization of primary and secondary labour markets. The model of the flexible firm has in contrast been developed by some academics to *encourage* its adoption by firms.

working week for the unions in return for management's wish for greater flexibility in labour utilization. Perhaps even more significantly, early in 1988 rank-and-file workers in the car industry (notably Ford) included opposition to flexibility among their reasons for striking.

Another employer initiative in the use of labour, associated with the decline of the manufacturing sector, is a reduction in the number of manufacturing plants and the average number of employees in each plant – usually following mergers, takeovers and management buyouts. Part of this is in response to market pressures, but also the now apparently stronger relationship of smaller scale to higher efficiency via new technology applications.

Labour utilization innovations are usually thought to be associated with foreign firms, notably Japanese and American. This is undoubtedly an exaggeration. The introduction of radical changes in working practices ('Japanization') in particular is not especially linked to Japanese companies.[8] American firms – which had total UK investments in 1985 ten times larger than Japanese in value terms – have had a much longer involvement in the UK economy without any marked tendency to innovation in labour utilization. For the Japanese the significance of their presence lies in their approach to collective bargaining. This will be returned to later in the chapter.

Government Intervention, 1979–88

The strong commitment of the new 1979 administration to a monetarist, free market alternative to Keynesian intervention was compatible with the British, traditional 'voluntarist' or 'abstentionist'[9] approach to industrial relations. However, the perspective which saw trade unions in themselves as powerful, labour market monopolies which generated inflation and reduced efficiency gradually came to supersede the simple reliance on monetary targets to control pay settlements. Monetary targets were in fact quietly dropped after 1983 and formally in 1986 at the same time as the free market, individualist perspective was being even more strongly promoted – complemented by the newer instruments of privatization and deregulation. The trade unions with their traditional role in wage bargaining and collectivist pursuit of their goals were seen as seriously impeding individualism and the working of free labour markets. The outcome was a strategy which sought to subordinate labour law and the trade unions to the Government's economic and ideological goals and which marked a sharp rejection of the old abstentionism. In implementing this strategy the Government has its power to legislate as well as its direct role in the public sector both as major employer and ultimate paymaster.

The legislative programme was put into effect 'step by step' in four Acts of Parliament: the Employment Acts of 1980 and 1982, the Trade Union

Act of 1984, and a further Employment Act in 1988 following its landslide election victory in 1987.* Supplementary legislation were the Wages Act and Sex Discrimination Act, both becoming law in 1986. The following is an outline of the main changes introduced by the legislation:

1. *Individual employment rights.* A range of statutory individual employment rights was introduced in the 1960s and 1970s by Labour (and to a lesser extent Conservative) governments. These statutory rights, under the jurisdiction of a system of tribunals established in 1964, made it possible to go to tribunal for compensation for redundancy, to claim equal pay and to seek redress on race and sex discrimination and on a limited number of health and safety matters. However, the work of the tribunals was, and is, dominated by unfair dismissal claims† which exceed 70 per cent of all cases.

Since 1979 unfair dismissal claims have been subjected to a two-stage increase in the qualifying employment period before a claim can be brought, ie from six months to two years. There was also a shift in the burden of proof: formerly the responsibility of the employer, it now rests equally with the dismissed employee. In the event there has been an overall fall in the number of unfair dismissal *applications*. From 1981 to 1986 they fell from 36,000 to 28,000, although of the cases actually proceeding to the tribunal itself (ie those not withdrawn or settled by agreement following ACAS's required conciliation) the employees' success rate has remained fairly constant at about one-third.[10] However, only about 1 per cent of the successful applicants get their jobs back, the normal award being financial compensation.

Women's rights have had a mixed experience. Although maternity payments and access to maternity leave have been made more difficult, time-off is now available for ante-natal care. In 1986, anti-discrimination provisions were introduced and there is now an important new right to claim equal pay for work of equal value. This specific right derives from the impact of European Community regulations to which the UK has been subject since its entry into the Community in 1973. Equal value claims have recently been underpinned by a number of significant legal decisions (see Chapter 16).

2. *Collective bargaining.* Recognition is a critical step in the extension of collective bargaining. Under the Labour Government's 1975 Employment Protection Act a unilateral *statutory* procedure to seek recognition

---

* See Chapter 13.
† Unfair dismissal claims were introduced under Edward Heath's Conservative Government in 1971 and retained by the succeeding Labour Government after 1974.

was given to independent trade unions. This statutory procedure* was abolished by the Conservative Government in 1980 although the *voluntary* procedure† was retained. Hence, since 1980 there has been a reversal to the pre-1975 position: British employers are not, in law, required to recognize or bargain with trade unions and can withdraw recognition previously granted. Since 1980 there has been a decline in the growth of recognition agreements although this decline has been in the context of more powerful pressures and even when the statutory procedure was in force it was rarely used.[11] At the same time European Community regulations have again worked in the opposite direction. Employment contracts, recognition and collective agreements are protected following takeovers or the restructuring of existing companies.‡ There is also a general pressure for UK employers to follow the more developed procedures for consultation and employee involvement which exist in other European countries.§

A further change influencing collective bargaining was the 1988 removal of the remaining statutory immunities protecting closed shop agreements. Now dismissal (or action short of dismissal) of an employee for not being a member of a trade union, or a particular trade union, is 'unfair' in all circumstances and industrial action to enforce union membership is now unlawful.

3. *Statutory pay regulation.* The UK (unlike the USA and other countries) has never provided for a statutory minimum wage covering all employees. However, it has long had a mix of statutory institutions and

* An independent trade union ('independence' is assessed by the Certification Officer – a public official under the 1975 Act – using the criteria of history, membership base, organization and structure, finance, employer-provided facilities, and collective bargaining record) had the right to pursue a recognition claim against a recalcitrant employer via the services of ACAS. ACAS's enquiries did not necessarily require evidence of majority support in the bargaining unit to make a positive recommendation. Such a recommendation could be supported by a legally-enforceable award against the employer from the Central Arbitration Committee (CAC).

† At the request of either a union or an employer, ACAS can be asked to conciliate in a dispute over recognition. The outcome can be the employer voluntarily agreeing to recognition, either full or partial (ie grievance representation only).

‡ This right became law in Britain under the Transfer of Undertakings (Protection of Employment) Regulations 1981. Such regulations cannot be amended by Parliament. The right may, however, be a hollow one. An industrial tribunal, in a case involving the formation of a new company from three existing ones, has ruled against the transfer of employment rights and recognition. The decision was upheld on appeal. *Banking, Insurance & Finance Union* v *Barclays Bank plc* 32146 (1986); *BIFU* v *Barclays Bank and others*, EAT 479 (1987).

§ Under the Single European Act of 1987 the European Community will move to a single market by 1992. This development should increase this pressure and provides trade unions with the possibility of extending collective bargaining across frontiers. One union (Manufacturing, Science and Finance) has already produced a report on the prospects for 1992 as well as the TUC.[12]

procedures providing defences against low pay and supporting claims based on comparisons between different groups of workers. The most notable institutions are the Wages Councils with a history going back to their Trade Board predecessors of 1909. The 'tripartite' (trade union, employer and 'independent' representatives) Wages Councils over time had their original statutory powers to set minimum wage rates extended to include piecework and overtime rates, holiday pay and holiday entitlements. In 1986 the Government reversed this trend restricting the Councils to the setting of a single minimum hourly and overtime rate and removed young people under 21 from their jurisdiction. It is now planning to abolish the Councils entirely. They currently number 26 covering some 2.5 million workers.

The use of pay comparisons with other workers was given statutory support under the 1975 Employment Protection Act (Schedule 11). Unions could apply for legally enforceable awards to the Central Arbitration Committee (CAC) based upon arguments that their members were being paid less than the generally prevailing rates in their particular trade or industry. Schedule 11 was abolished in 1980. A similar prop to pay comparability applied to workers employed by companies having contracts with government, both central and local. Successive Fair Wages Resolutions of the House of Commons (ie a simple majority of Members, the last in 1946) guaranteed, though without the force of law, that workers on public sector contracts would be paid no less than their counterparts in their trade or industry as a whole. These Resolutions were overturned by the House of Commons in 1982.

4. *Industrial action.* The 1984 Trade Union Act (Section 11) defined industrial action as 'any strike or other industrial action by persons employed under contracts of employment'. Its main expressions, apart from the strike, are the overtime ban, go-slow, or work-to-rule. Furthermore, since under British *common law* virtually all industrial action is illegal (ie in breach of contract) the 'right' to take industrial action needs to be guaranteed. The practice in Britain, which developed in the nineteenth century, has been to confer *statutory* immunities (against court actions by employers) upon workers involved in industrial disputes.* More precisely, immunity has been available 'in contemplation or furtherance of a trade dispute' since the Trade Disputes Act of 1906. However, in 1982 the statutory definition of a trade dispute was significantly restricted 'wholly or mainly' to terms and conditions of employment. This correspondingly widened the scope of prohibited 'political' as opposed to industrial action.†

* Thus, for example, there is no positive right to strike under British law, in contrast to other comparable countries. How this arose is a matter of historical debate.[13]
† For example, industrial action by a union against privatization because of its potential impact upon its members' jobs was prohibited. Mercury Communications Ltd v Scott Garner & POEU (1984) ICR 74.

In 1984 the immunities were further restricted to those unions securing majority support for industrial action in a secret ballot (although the balloting requirements do not apply to unofficial industrial action) held no more than four weeks before the planned action. Further constraints on the balloting process have also been introduced in the new Code of Practice of which perhaps the most significant provision is that unions should consider not acting on an affirmative ballot unless the turnout in the ballot is at least 70 per cent.* Failure to comply with the law on balloting leaves a union and its officials open to civil actions by employers (or union members since 1988) in the form of injunctions prohibiting the action and, if it still takes place, fines and sequestration with further sanctions in receivership or even imprisonment. The financial penalties can be onerous. In the case of the 1984–85 strike of the NUM the total of fines and costs was some £1 million or 5 per cent of the union's total available funds. In the case of the much smaller National Union of Seamen in 1988, fines and costs totalled £1.3 million. Employers, furthermore, at a later stage have the option of seeking damages from the union or unions involved.

The immunities are also at risk during the industrial action itself. Picketing (now limited in practice, by the police supported by the courts, to six persons) must be confined to the workers' own place of employment and 'secondary' (ie solidarity) actions by others can only be applied to the *direct* supplier or customer of the employer. Furthermore, under the 1988 Employment Act individual trade union members are now protected against disciplinary actions by their unions should they refuse to take part in a strike or other industrial action even if the action has majority support and is in accordance with all the statutory requirements.†

Finally, the circumstances under which workers involved in industrial action can be fairly dismissed were changed in 1982. Under the Employment Protection Act of 1975 workers taking industrial action (including action across a number of plants) could not be dismissed selectively or, following the action, re-engaged on a selective basis. Now selective dismissal is only unfair at the actual place of work ('establishment') of the workers claiming victimization. Hence employers can dismiss workers taking industrial action on a plant-by-plant basis.

---

* The 'Statutory Code of Practice on Trade Union Industrial Action Balloting' has been published by the Department of Employment as a draft (ie subject to representations and revision). The final Code (eg that on picketing) will have no legal standing but can, and probably will, influence legal decisions.

† Individual members taking their unions to law may also have the advice and assistance of a Commissioner for the Rights of Trade Union Members established under the 1988 Employment Act.

Secondly, selective re-engagement is within the law if it takes place three months after dismissal.

5. *Trade union organization and ballots*. The Government's enthusiasm for balloting extends beyond its application to industrial action. Thus all members of a union's national executive body, including its senior officers of President and General Secretary, must now be elected by the membership at least every five years by an independently scrutinized secret postal ballot.* Furthermore, unions which wish to pursue 'political objects' have, since 1913, been required to ballot their members to seek majority support to set up a political fund separate from their general funds. The fund is financed by special contributions, the 'political levy', from which individuals can 'contract-out' without penalty. Since 1984 affirmative ballots must be achieved at ten year intervals to retain a union's political fund.† Since 1988, as with ballots for national executives and senior officials, they are to be by post and independently scrutinized.

Since 1980 unions have been able to claim part of their balloting costs from the Government via the Certification Officer.‡ This subsidy is only available for secret postal ballots and for the following purposes: industrial action, union elections, rule changes, amalgamations, political funds and employers' offers on pay or its equivalent. For industrial action workplace ballots are still lawful but these do not qualify for financial support.

The potential impact of this surge of legislation is far-reaching but the new legal remedies available against strikes require *employers* to initiate action. Such initiatives seem to be growing in incidence but according to one study, still apply 'mainly at the margins'.[14] In major disputes the anti-strike laws have been limited to their use by newspaper publishers against the printing unions and by sea-going ferry operators against the National Union of Seamen (NUS). Actions against the National Union of Mineworkers (NUM) and its leaders in 1984–85 were taken by *members* and under common (not statutory) law for breach of union rules.

The balloting requirements of the 1984 Trade Union Act were designed as an important and direct constraint on industrial action. The number of ballots totalled 152 for 1985–86 rising to 280 in 1987. However, the 1987

* Voting and balloting is of course commonplace in British trade unions. However, the unions' debate with the Government has primarily been about the kind of ballot, ie at geographical branches, at workplaces or by post. The Government favours the postal form and supports it financially (see Chapter 14).
† Through affiliation fees and substantial special payments during general elections the political funds are the principal source of the Labour Party's finances.
‡ In 1987, 42 unions received refunds for 526 ballots costing a total of £1.16 million. In 1986 the comparable figures were 40 unions, 399 ballots and £0.74 million.

figure was little more than a quarter of the Department of Employment's recorded stoppages of work in that year (which includes unofficial strikes for which ballots are not required) and of the 280 ballots 90 per cent resulted in majorities for industrial action. However, votes in favour did not often result in actual industrial action and were sometimes presented, and used, as a means of strengthening unions' negotiating positions.[15] Thus, while it is probable that ballots are becoming an established feature of the negotiating process it is thought to be too early to assess their longer-term impact on behaviour. Even more uncertainty must be attached to the effect of the provision in the 1988 Employment Act which allows individual members to ignore a strike call, following a lawful ballot, without fear of disciplinary action. It also remains to be seen how the new Code of Practice on balloting influences trade union behaviour.

A much clearer outcome of the new balloting procedures was the complete endorsement of trade unions' political funds. It was feared by many in the unions that the balloting requirement would cut them off from 'political' campaigns (such as supporting the National Health Service) and undermine the financial base of the Labour Party to which most of the major unions are affiliated. In the event, following vigorous campaigns among their memberships, all trade unions with political funds (totalling 38) retained them mostly by very large majorities and 14 unions have so far set them up for the first time.[16] Yet the need to ballot every ten years remains and it is far from certain, given changing political circumstances, that such a positive reaction can always be guaranteed. However, the core issue is the role of the political funds in financing the Labour Party. Without the funds, or an alternative such as state subsidies and/or mass membership subscriptions, the Labour Party is quite unable to compete financially with the Conservative Party's business backing.

In addition to lawmaking, the Government has intervened directly, and vigorously, in public sector industrial relations through its role as employer. In 1984 it banned trade unions at the Government Communications Head Quarters (GCHQ) as incompatible with the national interest, replacing them with internal staff associations. The ban drew it into a bitter political controversy and a major confrontation with three civil service unions, which included the small but influential First Division Association (FDA), the union of senior civil service advisers to government. The unions eventually exhausted their legal action against the Government with the rejection of their case in 1986 by the European Commission on Human Rights. This inevitably soured relationships still further and two of the three unions (but not the FDA) later initiated a strike over pay during the 1987 General Election campaign. The most recent episode of this long and bitter dispute has been the dismissal at GCHQ of those who have retained their union membership.

But undoubtedly the most vivid case study in intervention was in the miners' strike of 1984–85. The Government in the summer of 1984 abandoned its initial non-interventionist stance in favour of the large scale national mobilization of its physical, financial and propagandist resources in direct support of a public sector employer, which in 1985 resulted in the defeat of, and division within, the National Union of Mineworkers.* This confrontationist stance emerged again in the long-running struggle with the teachers' unions. The Government at the end (1987) imposed a pay settlement and unilaterally suspended the teachers' negotiating rights.

Finally, the Government's overriding belief in the efficacy of market forces has pressed it to intervene in the processes and rationales of pay bargaining. It has consistently resisted comparability arguments in public sector pay negotiations as well as abolishing agencies charged with their propagation.† Instead it has championed ability-to-pay and regional pay flexibility. More recently there has been a strong attack on the role of national pay bargaining which has been charged with being inflationary and insensitive to local labour market conditions. It has consequently been abolished in the nationalized water industry which is soon to be privatized; has been reduced in importance in civil service pay negotiations; while decentralized pay determination has been strongly advocated in local government as well as in future arrangements for setting the pay of teachers. The private sector seems to be following the Government's example in moving away from national bargaining. The most significant examples are perhaps the large but declining engineering industry (a former bastion and 'model' of national bargaining) which failed to reach an agreement on flexible hours and a shorter working week in 1987 after protracted negotiations; the equally large, but growing banking sector which abandoned national bargaining in the same year; and British Rail which at the end of 1988 announced its intention to regionalize collective bargaining.

Assessing the Future

The overall strength and direction of those economic and political factors which influence industrial relations and the role and power of trade unions have not been interrupted by the General Election of 1987. On present economic policies unemployment is not likely to fall significantly below 2 millions especially given the re-entry of those old familiar constraints on growth – rising inflation and a balance of payments deficit.‡ At the same time the goods producing industries' contribution to GDP will continue to

---

* Between the end of 1985 and the end of 1987 the effect of pit closures, manpower cuts and the founding of the breakaway Union of Democratic Miners (UDM) was to reduce NUM membership from 248,000 to 91,000.[17]

† Notably the Standing Commission on Pay Comparability and the civil service's Pay Research Unit.

‡ Additionally, at the time of writing (November 1988) average earnings were on a rising trend, fuelling speculation over the re-emergence of a wage-price spiral.

decline in favour of private sector services, a process more than approved of and encouraged by the Government which seeks every opportunity to privatize all or part of individual public sector services.*

The Government's direct interventions in industrial relations still have a strong momentum. The 1988 Employment Act was primarily intended to enhance the power of individuals within trade unions at the expense of unions' collective objectives and it is clear that this Act does not mark the end of the programme begun in 1980. The trade unions' remarkable victory on the political funds ballot could eventually provoke further legislation to replace 'contracting-out' by 'contracting-in' of the political levy, ie the individual trade union member would be required to make a positive decision to contribute to his or her union's political fund – a return to the position of the 1926 Trade Disputes Act which followed the collapse of the General Strike. The Government has also signalled its intention to inhibit industrial action with the new Code. Nor is the Government, as an employer, showing any signs of relaxing its tough attitudes towards public sector unions and its moves against national negotiating machinery.

But not everything is working against the trade unions. Foreign-owned enterprises, especially those from the United States, often choose to work co-operatively with trade unions. Even Japanese employers, who have provided jobs in exchange for the very mixed blessing (ie to the unions) of the single union deal† would probably prefer no union at all or their workers organized in a company union. Unemployment, even allowing for re-definition, has also been falling since 1986 while for those in work average earnings have been consistently rising ahead of inflation. Some unions are also reporting small increases in membership with others a fall in the rate of decline.‡ There is also the generally positive effect of European Community legislation on workers' employment rights and the single market after 1992 gives opportunities for trade unions operating across the national frontiers of twelve countries as well as companies. Indeed, at the 1988 Trades Union Congress, Jacques Delors, the President of the EC Commission, unequivocally declared his support for the 'social market' as a necessary feature in the development of the single market.

Yet there is still a strong tide flowing against the trade unions' capacity to resist employers' demands. Nor are the union oars all pulling in the same direction as the damaging internal dispute over single union deals and the expulsion of the 330,000 electricians' union testifies. Tides do of course turn but, as yet, the water still seems to be rising.

* Such as the policies towards the National Health Service, state education, and the railways; there is also a scheme to transform civil service departments into semi-private 'agencies', a process already begun with the Department of Employment's Professional and Executive Register.
† This is discussed later on pp 26–27.
‡ See pp 16–17.

The Trade Union Crisis

From 1968 to 1979 membership of British trade unions grew by almost a third, standing at 13.3 million in 1979. The rate of increase of total membership outdistanced that of potential trade union membership (which itself grew steadily from 1972 to 1979) so that trade union density* rose from 44 per cent in 1968 to over 54 per cent in 1979. Even this high water mark, as an average, concealed wide variations. Although in agriculture, construction and private services densities were substantially below the average they were greatly exceeded in manufacturing at 70 per cent and were above 80 per cent in the public sector.

Since 1979 the engine of growth has gone into reverse. The total gains in membership from 1969 to 1979 have all been lost and density, which had declined to 43 per cent in 1985 is estimated at 42 per cent for the end of 1987. Losses of membership of this magnitude, *should they continue*, would take density to below 30 per cent by the year 2000, that is as low as it was in the period between the world wars.

A possible reaction to these dire predictions is that it has all been seen before. Density stood at 45 per cent in 1920, halved over the next 13 years and by 1952 was back to the 1920 level.[19] It should also be noted that in the 1950s and 1960s trade union growth virtually ceased and commentators were then predicting permanent stagnation under the twin influences of rising prosperity and consensus politics. These predictions were then of course followed by the eleven years of sustained growth described earlier.

While it is possible to exaggerate the scale of the crisis facing British trade unions – and this will be returned to later – it would nevertheless be wrong, not least in trade union circles, to deny that a crisis exists. We must now turn to describe in more detail, and assess, the scale of that crisis since 1979.

Membership and Density Since 1979

The steep decline in membership is shown in Table 1.1. Total losses between 1979 and 1987 were almost 2.9 million or 21.7 per cent. The fall in membership exceeded the fall in employment over the whole period largely because of the continuing contraction of the unions' traditional manufacturing and industrial areas of recruitment. Rising employment after 1983 has mainly been concentrated in the service sector where unions have greater organizational problems so that total membership and density continued to fall at much the same rate.

---

* This important and much used and abused statistic is *actual* trade union membership (as reported by unions themselves) as a percentage of *potential* trade union membership. For these figures the denominator is civilian employees in employment (which includes managers with contracts of employment) plus the unemployed.[18] The problems of measuring density are discussed on pp 20–21.

Table 1.1 *Trade union membership and density in the UK, 1979–87*[a]
(000s and %)

	Civilian employees in employment	Unemployed[b]	Potential trade union membership	Trade[c] union membership	Trade union density %
1979	23,244	1,261	24,505	13,289	54.2
1980	22,409	2,100	24,509	12,947	52.8
1981	21,602	2,764	24,366	12,106	49.7
1982	21,126	3,097	24,223	11,593	47.9
1983	21,170	3,079	24,249	11,236	46.3
1984	21,464	3,219	24,683	10,994	44.5
1985	21,633	3,273	24,906	10,821	43.4
1986	21,718	3,229	24,947	10,539	42.2
1987	22,051	2,696	24,747	10,402[d]	42.0[d]

Source: *Employment Gazette* (various issues), Department of Employment

[a] At end of each year.
[b] Subject to Department of Employment changes in methods of enumeration and coverage.
[c] This series is from two main sources (for Great Britain and Northern Ireland) to give the UK as a whole. For Great Britain they are for those unions holding a statutory Certificate of Independence issued by the Certification Officer (see footnote on p8). For Northern Ireland the figures are those of the Department of Economic Development.
[d] Author's estimates based on TUC membership decline 1986–87 (Table 1.2).

The fortunes, or misfortunes, of the 20 largest unions affiliated to the Trades Union Congress, are illustrated in Table 1.2. The overall loss of membership of TUC affiliates from 1979 to 1987 at over 3 million exceeds the losses using the broader definition of trade union used in Table 1.1. The proportionate fall was also greater – 25.0 per cent compared to 21.7 per cent. Some of the big affiliates (notably the two largest TGWU and AEU) lost members at a rate well above the average, reflecting the contraction of employment in their traditional manufacturing and industrial strongholds. Mergers slowed down membership losses or, in some cases, seemed to assist membership growth, such as the new MSF which, following its creation in 1987, gained 22,000 members. The GMB, however, still recorded a substantial loss over the whole period despite its absorption of the sizeable Amalgamated Society of Boilermakers (ASB) in the early 1980s. Yet in the expanding banking and insurance sectors BIFU showed strong growth gaining more than 34,000 members.

The most recent annual membership returns (see Table 1.2 for 1986 and 1987) show evidence of a 'bottoming-out'. A fall in the overall rate of decline for 1987 (substantially less than that for 1986) included the three largest affiliates, the electricians (EETPU), the printing union (SOGAT

82) and the biggest teachers' union, the NUT. Four of the top 20 unions converted decline into growth (NALGO, MSF, USDAW and the UCW) while the growing unions continued to do so (UCATT, BIFU and the NUCPS). However, two unions with substantial National Health Service memberships (NUPE and COHSE) continued to lose heavily in 1987. Unions important in British trade union history continued to contract. Both the steelworkers (ISTC) and the mineworkers (NUM) which have now much less than 100,000 members are well out of the top 20, a fate which looks likely to overtake the railwaymen (NUR) in the next few years*

Inevitably there are now fewer large unions. Twenty-six passed the 100,000 mark in 1979 (excluding the then ASB) compared to twenty in 1987. The TGWU was the only union to exceed one million in 1987 (two unions did so in 1979) but had fallen from more than two million eight years earlier.

Trade Union Finances

The main source of British trade union income derives from its membership. In 1979 84 per cent of all income came from subscriptions and it was still 81 per cent in 1986.[20] Substantial falls in numbers can therefore pose serious financial problems for British trade unions. However, contrary to what might be expected, financial problems are not widespread and are largely limited to those unions experiencing special difficulties for which solutions are available.[21] Solvency has been preserved by a substantial increase in subscription income which from 1979 to 1985 more than doubled to almost 64 pence per week. Furthermore, as membership falls income from other sources, such as investment, can be shared out among fewer members.[22] Even the TGWU which has lost over 700,000 members since 1979 had total assets and funds of £76 million and £73 million respectively at the end of 1986 compared to £40 million and £38 million seven years earlier.[23] There could also be more scope for increasing income from membership. Subscriptions as a proportion of average weekly earnings only increased from 0.33 per cent to 0.38 per cent from 1979 to 1985. This figure is very low in international terms† although increases are still subject

---

* To secure an automatic seat on the TUC's governing body (General Council) an affiliate must report a membership of 100,000. The wish to maintain influence in the trade union movement through a place on the General Council *can* lead to affiliation at inflated membership figures. This practice needs to be borne in mind when using the figures of membership in Table 1.2.

† In the USA a *1977* study[24] reported that a large majority of unions required an initiation fee for new members and this was generally less than $40. Current United Automobile Worker (UAW) dues (which *may* be typical) are on the basis of two hours pay per month, representing 1.15 per cent of regular monthly income.[25] In the UK 'admission' fees, once common the craft unions, have been phased out over the past three decades. UK dues (as a proportion of earnings) are about half of the West German level and two-thirds of the French and Italian.[26]

Table 1.2

Change in membership[a] of the 20 largest trade unions affiliated to the Trades Union Congress, 1979–1987

		Number of members				Increase or decrease	Increase or decrease %		
		1979	1985	1986	1987	1979–87	1979–87	1985–86	1986–87
1. Transport & General Workers' Union	TGWU	2,086,281	1,434,005	1,377,944	1,348,712	− 737,569	−35.4	− 3.9	− 2.1
2. Amalgamated engineering Union	AEU	1,298,580	974,904	857,559	815,072	− 483,508	−37.2	−12.0	− 5.0
3. General, Municipal, Boilermakers & Allied Trades Union	GMB	967,153	839,920	814,084	803,319	− 163,834	−16.9	− 3.1	− 1.3
4. National & Local Government Officers' Association	NALGO	753,226	752,131	750,430	758,780	+ 5,554	+ 0.7	− 0.2	+ 1.1
5. Manufacturing, Science, Finance	MSF[b]	691,954	641,254	631,000	653,000	− 38,954	− 5.6	− 1.6	+3.5
6. National Union of Public Employees	NUPE	691,770	663,776	657,633	650,930	− 40,840	− 5.9	− 0.9	−1.0
7. Union of Shop, Distributive & Allied Workers	USDAW	470,017	385,455	381,984	387,207	− 82,810	−17.6	− 0.9	+1.4
8. Electrical, Electronic, Telecommunication & Plumbing Union	EETPU	420,000	347,635	336,155	329,914	− 90,086	−21.4	− 3.3	−1.9
9. Union of Construction, Allied Trades & Technicians	UCATT	347,777	248,693	249,485	255,883	− 91,894	−26.4	+ 0.3	+2.6
10. Confederation of Health Service Employees	COHSE	212,930	212,980	212,312	207,841	− 5,089	− 2.4	− 0.3	−2.1
11. Union of Communication Workers	UCW[c]	203,452	194,244	191,959	197,758	− 5,694	− 2.8	− 1.2	+3.0

12. Society of Graphical & Allied Trades '82	SOGAT 82[d]	205,784	205,916	199,594	193,838	− 11,946	− 5.8	− 3.1	− 2.9
13. National Union of Teachers	NUT	248,896	207,651	184,455	178,294	− 70,602	− 28.4	− 11.2	− 3.3
14. Banking, Insurance & Finance Union	BIFU	131,774	157,468	158,746	165,839	+ 34,065	+ 25.9	+ 0.8	+ 4.5
15. National Communications Union	NCU[e]	125,723	161,315	155,643	151,407	+ 25,684	+ 20.4	− 3.5	− 2.7
16. Civil & Public Services Association	CPSA	223,884	146,537	150,514	149,484	− 74,400	− 33.2	+ 2.7	− 0.7
17. National Graphical Association (1982)	NGA[f]	111,541	126,074	125,587	124,638	+ 13,097	+ 11.7	− 0.4	− 0.8
18. National Association of Schoolmasters/Union of Women Teachers	NAS/UWT	122,058	127,612	123,945	120,544	− 1,514	− 1.2	− 2.9	− 2.7
19. National Union of Civil & Public Servants	NUCPS[g]	154,161	118,066	118,506	118,740	− 35,421	− 23.0	+ 0.4	+ 0.2
20. National Union of Railwaymen	NUR	180,000	130,261	125,000	117,594	− 62,406	− 34.7	− 4.0	− 5.9
Total TUC membership		12,172,508	9,585,729	9,243,297	9,126,911	− 3,045,597	− 25.0	− 3.6	− 1.3
Number of TUC affiliates		109	88	87	83				

Source: *Trades Union Congress*

[a] At year end.
[b] Formed from a merger of Association of Scientific, Technical & Managerial Staffs (ASTMS) and Technical, Administrative & Supervisory Section (TASS) in 1987.
[c] Formerly Union of Post Office Workers (UPW).
[d] SOGAT merged with the National Society of Operative Printers, Graphical and Media Personnel (NATSOPA) in 1982 to form SOGAT 82.
[e] Formerly Post Office Engineering Union (POEU).
[f] The NGA merged with the Society of Lithographic Artists, Designers, Engravers and Process Workers (SLADE) in 1982.
[g] Formed from a merger of the Society of Civil & Public Servants (SCPS) and the Civil Service Union (CSU) in 1987.

to the obvious constraints of competition between unions and resistance from members.[27]

The continuing financial viability of most British trade unions acts as a counterweight to membership decline. But the trade unions, relative to the company sector, are far from rich. For example, even the combined funds and assets of the largest union (TGWU) which were £148.9 million in 1986 were only about one-seventh of the annual *profits* of Imperial Chemical Industries (ICI) and represented only £100 per member. Clearly, continuing membership losses on the scale experienced overall since 1979 should they continue, must in the long run seriously weaken the bargaining power and financial viability of British unions.

Explaining Trade Union Decline

Although there is clear evidence for declining membership and density from the high point of 1979, the evidence does pose some measurement problems. For example, the key statistic of trade union density can be measured using three different statistical series for trade union membership and a further three for potential membership. Density, using these statistics can therefore be measured nine different ways. Applied to the 1985 figures the nine measures give a range *from* 51.4 per cent to 35.8 per cent.[28] The problem is further compounded by the unreliability of the membership figures reported by the unions and the uncertainty and controversy surrounding the official unemployment figures in those measures which include the unemployed in the denominator.

The inclusion or exclusion of the unemployed also raises an analytical issue. Bain and Price include the unemployed on the grounds that their links with unionized, employed workers are not immediately severed – if at all – when they fall out of work.[29] But for measuring the strength of trade union organization at the workplace, or *bargaining power*, excluding the unemployed and using employees in employment as potential membership, gives a more appropriate indicator.* The Bain and Price method can then be reserved for measuring trade union *influence* in the wider society.[31] There is also a possibility that the distinction is more than 'academic'. A 1986 workplace survey concluded that despite the negative effects of high unemployment and job losses:

'. . . union density remained high and the formal structures of workplace organization appeared generally to be intact.'[32]

Yet despite the usual cautionary caveats and the possibility that the TUC

---

* Reworking the data in Table 1.1 to exclude the unemployed reveals density declining from 57.2 per cent to 47.2 per cent rather than 54.2 per cent to 42.0 per cent.[30]

unions (from their 1987 figures) are now on a modest revival path* the extent of decline since 1979 is both undeniable and serious.

General explanations of decline *and* growth have attracted a good deal of attention in both Britain and the USA. One group stresses the effects of war and social unrest as primary influences either directly, or through intervention by government to maintain industrial peace by passing laws favourable to trade unions. Another sees underlying longer-term influences at work.[34] An influential British review in the context of earlier comparative studies combines the determinants of growth under six headings which seek to explain both variations in rates of unionization *over time* as well as differences *at any one time* between groups, occupations and industries.[35] The six are:

1. *Composition of potential union membership* which includes the impact of the growing numbers of women and white-collar workers in the labour force and the associated shift in the economy towards services.

2. *The business cycle*, in particular the influence of inflation, and changes in wages and unemployment upon trade union membership.

3. *Employer policies and government action*, ie the role of government, through its legislation and policies, in encouraging or discouraging employers to recognize trade unions.

4. *Personal and job-related characteristics* such as age, gender, incidence of part-time employment, labour turnover, as well as occupational status and its influence on unionization.

5. *Industrial structure*, by which is meant the extent to which industry is organized in large groups of employees.

6. *Union leadership* or their influence upon growth via their success in organizing new members.

The Bain and Price approach does have the merit of being comprehensive although the relative importance of each of their determinants in explaining British trade union decline since 1979 is not easy to assess. It is however clear, on the Bain and Price analysis, that membership loss from 1979 to 1987 is very largely attributable to unemployment (within the 'business cycle' determinant) and that this was most in evidence when its level was both high and increasing at a strong rate[36]† especially between 1979 and

---

* For example, Bain has recently observed that a density figure of 40 per cent could be the unions 'low water mark' and that it was just as reasonable to predict further growth as decline should unemployment continue its downward path.[33]

† But note that unemployment need not necessarily weaken trade union bargaining power following the distinction between influence and power discussed earlier (p 20).

1981 (see Table 1.1). However, the negative effect of unemployment upon unionization both assisted, and was assisted by, the sharp turnaround in government policy after 1979, including the shift against positive encouragement of trade union recognition. Bain and Price in discussing the influence of government upon employers' approaches to recognition after 1979 suggest a 'vicious circle' relationship as employers took advantage of declining union density to limit, or push back, recognition[37] although the effect has been perhaps more to inhibit recognition rather than towards actual derecognition.

Government is obviously a powerful influence upon unionization especially when employers are susceptible to official example-setting. But this influence is short term (and can eventually even be reversed) relative to the compositional and structural changes which have been exerting an inexorable and accelerating influence over a longer period. The shift in the balance of the economy towards services; the increasing numbers of women and white-collar workers; the growing incidence of temporary, part-time and peripheral employment and the decline in the number of workplaces employing large groups of people* have come together to diminish those environments and circumstances favouring trade union growth and enlarge those in which recruitment and recognition are an uphill trudge.

Trade Union Responses: Five Strategies

Up to 1983 it was realistic for British trade unions to work towards the return of a Labour government with the prospect of expansionist economic policies favouring the goods producing industries, which would have at least partially restored their membership strongholds, as well as a return to the industrial relations policies and legislation of the 1970s. The Labour Party's heavy electoral defeat of that year was followed by slowly accumulating evidence that changes in the economy and labour force were eroding the unions' traditional membership base. By 1985, a number of unions, and the TUC, were beginning to devise, fund and implement revival – or in some cases survival – strategies. They were encouraged by the success of their post 1985 campaigns to retain their political funds but once again lost their main political lifeline with a further defeat of the Labour Party in 1987 and the third in a row since 1979.† Out of the debates and reappraisals five strategies – some traditional, some new, from which unions are choosing – can be identified: work for a Labour government and supportive legislation; merge with other unions; recruit new members in

---

* According to the Workplace Industrial Relations Survey '. . . the greater loss of employment by large, highly unionised workplaces is a major factor behind the contraction of trade union membership since the end of the 1970s.'[38]

† The last time this fate betell the Labour Party was in the years 1951, 1955 and 1959.

the fastest growing industries and among previously neglected groups; improve services to members; and revise trade union purposes.

The strategy of working for the election of a Labour government – as old as the Labour Party which was itself the creature of the TUC* – served the unions well until 1979. The Labour Party was in power for 17 out of the 34 years from 1945 to 1979, enacting a whole raft of legislation favourable to the unions, especially after the defeat of the Heath Government in 1974. This policy has, however, never implied *not* trying to work with Conservative governments except following the Industrial Relations Act of 1971. For their part, Conservative governments have normally sought constructive relationships with the trade unions, mainly for *realpolitik* reasons. After 1979 this began to change. The Government progressively diminished the TUC's role in consultation and representation on tripartite bodies with employers and itself; stiffened its attitudes towards its own employees and unions in the public sector; and enacted its industrial relations and trade union legislation over TUC and union protests. These rebuffs left the trade union movement's only route to political influence through the Labour Party. The most notable initiatives were the founding of the campaigning, fund-raising body Trade Unions for a Labour Victory and its successor Trade Unions for Labour. The former organized the successful political funds campaign. The latter provided a major organizational contribution in the constituencies in preparation for the 1987 general election and contributed £3.8 million of the Labour Party's election fund of £4.6 million. More recently, a group of the largest unions have proposed increasing their per capita affiliation fees to the Party at the same time as supporting the Party's own proposals for a nationally-organized low subscription, mass membership base of trade union and constituency members.†

It is highly unlikely that the TUC and its affiliates – although some have reservations – will seek to abandon a strategy which was established even before the formation of the Labour Party as the other 'wing' of the labour movement. Nor is it in the interests of the Labour Party to alienate the major plank in its financial platform. In present political circumstances the Labour Party's ability to form a government would be seriously weakened in financial and organizational terms by the rupture or weakening of the trade union connection; and the trade unions' prospects of arresting the decline in membership could still be materially transformed by favourable government policies, especially those which would encourage recognition, advance collective bargaining and extend employment rights. The present Government's continuing hardline on legislation may indeed strengthen this strategy.

* The Labour Representation Committee, the precursor of the Labour Party, was created by the TUC in 1900. The Labour party was founded in 1906.
† Individual membership levels have been falling for a number of years. They are currently under 300,000 in contrast to socialist parties in mainland Europe where individual membership is commonly over a million.

Mergers and amalgamations have a long tradition as a means of survival and growth. Between 1949 and 1979 about 300 trade unions were absorbed in this process[39] and since 1979 the number of TUC affiliates has fallen from 109 to 83 – almost entirely from mergers. The most spectacular recent merger was that between the TUC's formerly sixth and tenth largest white-collar affiliates to form a new union of nearly 700,000 members – Manufacturing, Science, Finance. Other mergers under negotiation are between the present fourth and sixth largest unions (NALGO and NUPE) and the AEU and EETPU. The electricians have of course been recently expelled from the TUC and a merger with the AEU could bring their members back into the fold.

Merger or absorption are often sought as means of survival where finances are shaky. Sometimes, as in the formation of the MSF, the process is seen as a prelude to further 'natural growth'. Natural growth, with or without merger, through the recruitment of new members has been strongly promoted by the two big general workers' unions (TGWU and GMB) which have together lost over 900,000 members since 1979. Their organizing efforts have been especially concentrated in the service sector industries which combine growing employment with low union density, high levels of female employment, a large proportion of temporaries and part-timers, high employee turnover and low member retention. Thus the industries with the greatest opportunities for membership growth present the most difficult problems.

Both the TGWU and GMB have begun to use 'workplace audits' among part-timers to assess the levels of unionization and the TGWU is having some success through agreements with employers to extend permanent workers' wages and conditions to temporaries. It has also polled the attitudes of young workers towards unions as a prelude to special organizing drives geared directly to young people and often now inaugurated with rock concerts.

Women workers are an important target group for both unions. The TGWU now has a national women's officer with special responsibilities to organize more women members and raise their profile and influence within a union traditionally led and dominated by men. The GMB has reserved 10 out of 40 places on its National Executive Committee for women and in workplaces and branches is introducing women's discussion groups and equality officers.* It has also turned its attention to the self-employed (another expanding group) offering administrative help and services

---

* An interesting recent finding on women in British trade unions is that '. . . full-time women employees are as likely to be trade union members as full-time men employees, but that part-time women employees are half as likely to be members as full timers . . . part-time employment . . . rather than gender might well lie at the root of the difference.'[40]

without the need for membership. The building union UCATT has also ended its principled opposition to self-employed status for building workers and now targets them in organizing drives.

Other unions, notably the printing union (SOGAT 82) and the shopworkers (USDAW) have responded to membership loss with similar policies. SOGAT, following its defeat in its dispute with Rupert Murdoch's News International and with a membership vulnerable to new technology and the breakdown of occupational demarcation in printing, is running organizing campaigns to appeal to young people and women in its traditional strongholds of papermaking, books and magazines.

SOGAT, as other unions, has also been active in expanding its membership services. This has long been a feature of professional, managerial and white-collar unions. More recently blue-collar unions have set the pace with advisory and financial services in insurance, savings, investment and bond/equity purchase. The EETPU has, for a number of years, even succeeded in including private health insurance in some collective agreements and now provides new technology training for its members, an example which has been followed by the engineering union (AEU) using funds and equipment from the Manpower Services Commission (now within the Department of Employment as the Training Agency). The development of these services has been greatly assisted by the development of accurate, computerized, membership records. Paradoxically the Government has assisted this process by its strong preference for secret postal ballots in the conduct of union business which clearly requires accurate membership registers. These registers were made a legal requirement in the 1984 Trade Union Act.

The TUC, under General Secretary Norman Willis, has played an active role in support of these strategies. Willis himself even advocated (contrary to TUC traditional non-intervention in such matters) a merger of the two big teachers' unions (NUT and NAS/UWT) in the context of the failure of their industrial action in 1987. The two unions' deep rivalry, rather than Willis's intervention, prevented any progress. He has also firmly supported the unions' new emphasis on organizing new members, developing services* and attracting women workers – especially temporaries and part-timers. The TUC Women's Conference in 1987 (with a history going back to the 1930s) itself criticized the TUC's record on women and voted in favour of seeking to set up a Department for Women within the TUC.† The TUC is also considering its own computerized balloting service for affiliates. Another TUC enthusiasm is the video film – influenced by the

---

* The TUC is even introducing its own package through its own bank (Unity Trust) including personal pensions, financial advice and services, legal advice, banking and travel, and a credit card.

† This requires a decision of the TUC itself to bring into effect. It parallels the Labour Party's commitment, in the 1987 General Election, to set up a Ministry for Women in government.

experience of US trade unions – and their successful use in the British political funds campaign.

The video film is only one of the US innovations which has influenced the TUC. Others include its credit card which will be in circulation in 1989 (the GMB already has one) and, following the AFL–CIO's example, it is pressing for a 'designated organizing areas' scheme to give named unions freedom to organize in specified non-union areas.

The TUC's leadership role has been much less successful in the acrimonious and divisive debate over the purposes of trade unions. Two broad streams of opinion have emerged as responses to the decline in members and influence since 1979, the *new realist* and the *new traditionalist*.

The new realists are closely associated with the expelled electricians (EETPU) and, to a lesser extent, the engineers (AEU). They argue that the primary, even exclusive, purpose of trade unions is to improve the pay and conditions of individual members. This is seen as 'realistic' in that it is what most members want and that wider social, community and political goals are at best an irrelevance and at worst a threat to the primary purpose of trade unions – and even their existence – should the political climate become hostile. However, principle is assisted by practice. The craft skills of, for example, electricians tend to give them 'core' worker status (therefore bargaining strength) and the ability to upgrade their skills through new technology.

The new traditionalists are led by the big general worker unions, the TGWU and GMB. They largely represent the interests of the 'non-core' groups most threatened by changes in the economy and labour markets and are seeking to extend their membership into what the GMB calls the 'new servant class' in the growing service sector. This involves developing a wider, community-based approach to potential trade union members notably women, the young and the disadvantaged. Such an approach strengthens these unions' identification with the Labour Party at local and constituency levels.

The conflict between the two approaches has manifested itself in the competition for members and the bitter disputes over single union/strike free agreements which culminated in the expulsion of the EETPU. The first single union agreement was between the EETPU and the Japanese company Toshiba in 1981. The EETPU's then national engineering officer (Roy Sanderson) has said that this agreement arose from a *joint* identification, with management, of the causes of industrial conflict in Britain and the best method of reducing these causes.[41] Such agreements have been primarily sought by Japanese companies and typically, although not universally, have six principal ingredients: recognition of a single union; labour flexibility; single status (ie extension of white-collar conditions to blue-collar employees); an extension of worker participation (ie company councils for all employees, unionized or not); binding pendulum arbitration (ie the arbitrator has to choose either the employer's offer or the union's claim without a compromise); and no strike provision (ie arbitration mandatory).[42]

The inter-union conflict over single union agreements was partly about an issue of *principle*, ie the alleged willingness of the EETPU in particular to exchange its freedom to strike in return for recognition. In response the EETPU claimed that the 'right' to strike has remained since the agreements are not legally-binding and that its rivals (especially the GMB and TGWU) have negotiated identical agreements.* Principle has however been confused with *tactics*, ie competition for members which is traditionally regulated by the Bridlington Principles.† The case against the EETPU on these grounds was, firstly, that it had reached single union agreements with employers before work had begun (and before it even had workers in membership) on new ('greenfield') sites, using the strike free clauses as inducements. Secondly, that it had signed single union agreements with employers on existing ('brownfield') sites where other unions already had members. The first part of the case clearly allowed no scope for workers to choose their union by ballot. The second, when it occurred, constituted a clear breach of the Bridlington Principles. Protracted discussions within the TUC to draw up a Code of Practice on single union agreements acceptable to all parties failed to resolve the schism and the EETPU was suspended and expelled following its refusal to withdraw from two agreements ruled to be in breach of Bridlington.‡

Yet the dispute over single-union deals was not simply about competition for members but also ideology. It is of course possible to argue that while it is useful to distinguish between new realists and new traditionalists, one should not exaggerate the differences between them; nor is there homogeneity within them. The AEU, for example, is somewhat disenchanted with its famous agreement with Nissan, manufacturing cars in the North-East of England. It has recently been estimated by the AEU itself that union membership at the plant is currently only 7 per cent of the workforce.§ There are also sizeable dissident and organized groups within

* For example, in May 1988 for a new plant jointly owned by Jaguar Cars and Guest, Keen & Nettlefolds, the GMB and AEU competed for sole bargaining rights. A single union/strike free agreement – similar to those elsewhere with Japanese companies – was concluded with the GMB. This followed a similar GMB agreement with another company earlier in the same month.

† These provide, among other things, for reference to a TUC Disputes Committee which makes decisions binding on the unions concerned. Bridlington, a seaside town, was the venue for the 1939 Trades Union Congress where the rules were drawn up. Similar rules existed before that time.

‡ It should be noted here that the action against the EETPU was *not* because of its preference for single union/strike free agreements but its refusal to accept the rulings of the TUC.

§ The Nissan agreement, signed in 1985, did not include provision for a closed shop (union membership agreement). At that time a *new* closed shop required secret ballot support of 80 per cent of those entitled to vote in order to keep the legal immunities. After 1988 even a ballot is not enough.

both the AEU and EETPU opposing single-union deals and the group within the EETPU is now working towards a separate, re-affiliated union following the expulsion from the TUC.

But accepting the inconsistencies there is a real difference between the two camps (which is confirmed by the differences within them) which goes much further back than single-union agreements to the old controversy over trade unions' industrial and political purposes. The EETPU, its leadership and other unions which support it, is firmly identified with 'business union' objectives and openly derides the political goals and ambitions of its rivals, especially the use of the strike for 'political' purposes. Eric Hammond, the EETPU's general secretary, was vehemently opposed to the 1984–85 miners' strike and its leadership, a position which generated acute and bitter conflicts within the unions and the Labour Party but largely isolated the EETPU. The Union's principal opponent in the 'political union' camp is the TGWU with strong support from the GMB. The TGWU has had a long line of politically active and influential leaders within the Labour Party. However, the EETPU is still affiliated to the Labour Party (and hopes to retain this connection even outside the TUC) and its suspension and expulsion was opposed by the AEU which also takes a business union stance but has no wish to leave the TUC. Furthermore, even the 'political' unions are normally pragmatic and accommodating with regard to strikes and industrial action.

Nevertheless, although the differences between the two camps is frequently exaggerated they are more than a matter of degree. The simple pursuit of improvements in pay and conditions remains as an important goal of British trade unions but since the turn of the century and the rise of the Labour Party has been overshadowed by the movement's political complexion, both in means and ends. However, what was settled 82 years ago is now beginning to be questioned. It might have been different if the Labour Party had been in power at least once in the 1980s.

Conclusion: The Prospects for the Trade Unions

The Labour Party's defeat in the General Election was a major setback for the trade unions especially in the context of being the third in a row with the real prospect of a fourth defeat in 1991. If the direction of union growth is dependent upon a triangular and '. . . crucial inter-relationship between economic forces, employer policies and government action.'[43] then under a Labour government a programme would have been implemented within at least the second and third sides of this triangle which would have favoured trade union recovery. The Labour Party did not promise a simple return to the labour laws existing in 1979 and both it and the trade unions accepted the reality (even value) of the Conservatives' innovations on ballots. Yet on the critical issues – positive government backing for trade union recognition and the extension of collective bargaining as well as greater freedom to impose secondary industrial action – a 1987 Labour government would have been a welcome lifeboat for its brothers and sisters in the unions.

The defeat was also one of considerable scale. The unions virtually funded the campaign and deployed a substantial part of their own organizational and manpower resources. Yet the large Conservative majority was barely lower than in 1983 and the unions were even unable to guarantee that a majority of their own members would vote Labour. In the 1983 election 39 per cent of trade unionists voted Labour; by 1987 this had only increased to 43 per cent.* Nor has the Labour Party so far improved its potential electoral standing since 1987, that is according to opinion polls.

On the industrial front the Labour movement has fared little better. The success of the Ford workers' strike in February 1988† was swiftly followed by the 'Dundee debacle' in March in which Ford abandoned its plans to locate a new electronics plant, employing 1000 workers, in Scotland. The decision was widely interpreted as arising from the TGWU's objections to the AEU's single-union agreement with Ford although little media time was given to the TGWU's defence of the national agreement.‡ What was clearly demonstrated by both disputes was the bargaining power of a multinational company to secure favourable agreements where it had locational freedom as well as facing the minimal leverage of British trade unions.

Trade union weakness was again demonstrated in the summer of 1988 with the virtual collapse of the NUS strike as the employer (P & O) dismissed the strikers and withdrew recognition from the union while the courts were imposing fines and sequestration of the union's assets.

Meanwhile the closed shop agreements are faced with complete elimination and trade union members now have legal defences against discipline by their unions should they decide to defy a majority decision to take industrial action following a lawful ballot. Single-union and 'no-strike' agreements are now circulating, although not yet common currency, while derecognition, once virtually unknown, is showing some signs of spreading. Some British commentators, as American, are beginning to discuss the 'non-union option' available to employers encouraged by adverse changes in

---

* The percentages for earlier elections were 73 per cent (1964), 55 per cent (1974) and 51 per cent (1979).[44]

† Ford proposed a three-year pay agreement alongside labour flexibility and changes in working practices. Following an all-out eight-day strike of 32,000 workers in all Ford's assembly plants the Company's revised offer reduced the length of the agreement to two years and promised to seek labour flexibility and changes in working practices voluntarily. The unions involved in the agreement were the TGWU, AEU, EETPU, UCATT and MSF.

‡ The TGWU, supported by MSF, accepted the AEU single-union agreement (which received majority support on the TUC) but insisted that in pay and conditions it should not be outside (ie inferior to) the long-established national agreement with Ford to which the TGWU and the other unions were signatories. The strike in February 1988 was over the renegotiation of that agreement.

employment and labour markets and weaker trade unions competing for members. Roberts has recently commented that British trade unions have reached a 'watershed' faced with the growing availability of the non-union option and that there was a real prospect of membership falling to US and French levels.[45] A further contribution from his colleague at the London School of Economics[46] suggests that Japanese companies in Britain would prefer, if possible, to organize their industrial relations without trade unions.

Bain takes a view more comforting to the trade unions citing the positive effect of falling unemployment on membership* and it maybe that the post 1979 losses will be replaced by slow recovery. Indeed, in the public sector densities still remain at high levels† and while a single-union deal may be the private sector employer's preference over a multi-union agreement, this is not to say that non-unionism is a significant available option. It still remains possible to reach multi-union agreements involving major changes on 'brownfield' sites which can be negotiated by management who see them as '. . . an antidote to single unionism and non-unionism'.‡

The trade unions themselves also have some influence on their own destinies. They are now beginning to grasp the organizing nettle and targeting key groups of workers with new methods and attractive packages of services. They have also begun to address the need to adapt the career rewards for full-time officials away from success in negotiating towards success in organizing new members. In all of this the TUC has been active and it may even yet become a marriage-broker as witness Norman Willis's attempts to bring together the two big teachers' unions. One trade union leader even predicts a TUC dominated by four 'superunions' by the year 2000.§

The other nettle which has already been grasped is the single-union agreement via the new Code.‖ Unfortunately, this outcome was bought at a very high price – the departure of the EETPU with its 330,000 members and its £300,000 in affiliation fees. There is also the possibility, mentioned at the beginning of the chapter, of a rival grouping to the TUC which would

---

* See p 21.

† A 1987 study of trade union densities in the public and private sectors using membership of TUC and non-TUC unions as a proportion of the *employed* but excluding the armed forces and police shows: private sector 38 per cent; public sector 81 per cent; whole economy 51 per cent.[47]

‡ Management commenting on a four-year pay agreement between Metal Box Ltd and four unions involving single status, multi-skilling and major changes in shift patterns.[48]

§ The four unions would be the TGWU, GMB, MSF, and NALGO/NUPE each with one million members.[49]

‖ The Special Review body, in its first report to the 1988 Congress included a Code of Practice to regulate competition for single-union agreements. It, among other things, specifically excludes '. . . agreements which remove, or are designed to remove, the basic democratic lawful rights of a trade union to take industrial action in advance of the recruitment of members and without consulting them.'[50]

include the EETPU and a number of smaller unions with a principled objection to strikes as a tactic. But at the time of writing the latter is no more than a 'possibility' with the sympathetic AEU and the Royal College of Nursing (a large, non-affiliate opposed to strikes) already declaring against joining a rival to the TUC and the EETPU itself may not wish to tie itself to a new marriage immediately after leaving the old. But even without a rival to the TUC the likelihood of damaging competition for members remains strong and a consequent weakening of the trade unions' collective strength *vis-à-vis* employers.

Sober assessments of the prospects for British trade unions must try to take account of these uncertainties. It may be that trade unions and their members have run the painful gauntlet of Thatcherism remarkably well, bruised and shaken but still largely intact and considering their options. It may be, as Bain suggests, that they still need a 'breakthrough'[51] in the form of a Labour government. The Labour Party is still a significant force within the Labour movement and British politics. But whether it can form a government in 1991, or even later, is the greatest uncertainty of all. On present evidence and trends it looks unlikely but if, as Harold Wilson used to say, '. . . a week is a long time in politics . . .' then three years is approaching eternity.

References

1. *Annual Report 1986*, ACAS March 1987.
2. *Annual Report 1987*, ACAS March 1988.
3. For a contribution to the analysis of the historical forces shaping current industrial relations see Fox A (1985) *History and Heritage: the Social Origins of the British Industrial Relations System*, Allen & Unwin.
4. Ray G F 'Natural Resources' in 'The British Economy in the Long Term' *National Institute Economic Review* **4/86** No 118 November 1986, pp 53–58.
5. A study of occupational change in the UK is Rajan A and Pearson R (1986) *UK Occupation and Employment Trends to 1990*, Butterworth.
6. Hakim C 'Trends in the flexible workforce' *Employment Gazette*, **95** No 11 November 1987, pp 549–560.
7. 'Flexibility Examined' Labour Research Department *Bargaining Report*, No 56 November 1986, pp 5–12.
8. See, for example, Turnbull P 'The Japanisation of British industrial relations at Lucas' *Industrial Relations Journal*, **17** 3 Autumn 1986, pp 193–206; Oliver N and Wilkinson B (1988) *The Japanisation of British Industry*, Blackwell.
9. For a perceptive, socio-political analysis of the government's policies towards the trade unions as well as a comprehensive exposition of British labour law see Wedderburn Lord (1986) *The Worker and the Law*, Penguin.
10. 'Industrial Tribunals and the Employment Appeal Tribunal', *Employment Gazette*, **95** No 10 October 1987, pp 498–502.

11. For a recent discussion of recognition and derecognition see Towers B 'Trends and developments in industrial relations: derecognising trade unions – implications and consequences' *Industrial Relations Journal*, **19** No 3 Autumn 1988, pp 181–185.

12. *'Meeting the Challenge'* First Report of the Special Review Body, TUC 1988.

13. For a thorough discussion see Wedderburn, 1986 op cit

14. Evans S 'The use of injunctions in industrial disputes, May 1984–April 1987' *British Journal of Industrial Relations*, **XXV** No 3 November 1987, pp 419–435.

15. *ACAS Annual Report*, 1986 op cit p 11.

16. Leopold J 'Moving the status quo: the growth in trade union political funds' *Industrial Relations Journal*, **19** No 4 Winter 1988, pp 286–295.

17. For analysis of the wider issues of 1984–85 see Towers B, 'Posing larger questions: the British miners' strike of 1984–85' *Industrial Relations journal*, **16** No 2 Summer 1985, pp 8–25; Adeney M and Lloyd J (1986) *The Miners' Strike 1984–85, Loss without Limit*, RKP; Beynon H (ed) (1985) *Digging Deeper: Issues in the Miners' Strike*, Verso.

18. Bain G S and Price R 'Union Growth, Dimensions, Determinants and Destiny' in Bain G S (ed) (1983) *Industrial Relations in Britain*, Blackwell.

19. *Ibid* p 5.

20. *Annual Reports, 1980 and 1987* Certification Office for Trade Unions and Employers' Associations, Appendix 4.

21. Kelly J 'Trade Unions Through Recession 1980–1984' *British Journal of Industrial Relations*, **XXV** No 2 July 1987, pp 275–282.

22. Willman P and Morris T (1988) *The Finances of British Trade Unions*, Research Paper No 62, Department of Employment.

23. *Annual Reports* Certification Office, op cit.

24. Hickman C W 'Labor Organizations' Fees and Dues' *Monthly Labor Review*, **100** No 5 May 1977, pp 19–24.

25. *The UAW Makes Us Strong* United Automobile Workers' Education Department Publication, No 356 Detroit, 1987.

26. 'Europe's Unions – What do Members Pay?' *Labour Research*, **77** No 6 June 1988, pp 8–11.

27. Kelly J op cit pp 277–8.

28. Kelly J and Bailey R *British trade union membership and density in the 1980s* London School of Economics and Political Science, Department of Industrial Relations (Mimeo), pp 9–13.

29. Bain G S and Price R (1980) *Profiles of Union Growth: a Comparative Statistical Portrait of Eight Countries*, Blackwell, p 7.

30. See also Beaumont P B (1987) *The Decline of Trade Union Organisation*, Croom Helm.

31. Kelly J and Bailey R op cit pp 15–21.

32. Batstone E and Gourlay S (1986) *Unions Unemployment and Innovation*, Blackwell, p 264.

33. 'End of union decline foreseen' *Financial Times*, 2 October 1987.

34. For a US review of these explanations see Stepina L P and Fiorito J 'Towards a Comprehensive Theory of Union Growth and Decline' *Industrial Relations*, **25** No 3, Fall 1986.

35. Bain G S and Price R (1983) op cit pp 12–31.

36. *Ibid* p 18, pp 248–264.

37. *Ibid* pp 18–19.
38. Milward N and Stevens M (1986) *British Workplace Industrial Relations, 1980–84*, Gower, p 303.
39. Buchanan R T 'Mergers in British Trade Unions: 1949–79' in McCarthy W E J (ed) (1985) *Trade Unions*, Penguin.
40. Witherspoon S reported in Milward and Stevens op cit pp 61–2.
41. Basset P (1986) *Strike Free: New Industrial Relations in Britain*, Macmillan, p 122.
42. *Ibid*.
43. Bain G S and Price R (1983) op cit p 33.
44. Coates K S (1988) *Trade Unions in Britain*, Fontana, p 360.
45. Roberts B C 'Watershed for trade unionism' *Financial Times*, 9 October 1987.
46. Thurley K 'Changing the agenda: learning from Japanese industrial relations' *The Anglo-Japanese Economic Journal*, **2** No 2 July–September 1988, pp 15–17.
47. 'Public Sector Trade Unions' *Public Sector Digest*, Incomes Data Services, May 1988
48. 'Four year pay deal at Metal Box plant' *Financial Times*, 27 July 1988.
49. 'Four superunions forecast by year 2000' *Financial Times*, 8 June 1988.
50. 'Meeting the challenge' op cit p 19.
51. 'End of union decline foreseen' *Financial Times*, op cit.

Chapter 2

Industrial Relations in the Public Sector*

P B Beaumont

The analysis and recommendations of the Donovan Commission (1965–68) viewed the problems of British industrial relations as being very much problems of the private sector. This was because in the mid-to-late 1960s the public sector was an area of employment where authoritative, national level collective bargaining was subject to little challenge or threat from fractional bargaining or unofficial industrial action at the level of the individual workplace. And at the same time, formal, comprehensive incomes policies were in their relative infancy in Britain so that the wage outcomes of the public sector had not, as yet, been subject to any sustained and substantial 'attack from above'. The result was that the public sector hardly figured at all in discussions of the desired direction(s) of reform in British industrial relations in the 1960s.

Some 20 years after the report of the Donovan Commission, the position has changed to such an extent that many commentators now view any industrial relations problems in Britain as being overwhelmingly centred in the public sector. This view has been particularly stimulated and enhanced by the various instances of national level industrial action in, for example, the steel industry, the civil service, the NHS, the water industry, the coal industry, and by the two-year-long teachers' dispute since the coming to power of the Conservative government in 1979. Moreover, even as this chapter was being revised (September 1988) a two-week long national dispute in the Post Office (concerning, among other things, the use of temporary employees) was just coming to an end.

However, most commentators have taken a somewhat longer time perspective and viewed the whole of the 1970s as constituting a significant turning point or watershed in public sector industrial relations in Britain. Indeed, in the 70s one saw the traditional model of public sector industrial

* The author wishes to thank members of the Incomes Data Services (IDS) Public Sector Unit, particularly Geoff White, for the provision of a good deal of the information contained in this chapter.

relations challenged, undermined and at least partially replaced by a new model, the latter involving, among other things: the decline of the principle of comparability with the private sector; the pressure for decentralization of rule making; and the development of circumscribed collective bargaining.[1] The details of these various components which are elements of this new (still emerging) model of public sector industrial relations will, we hope, become clear as a result of our subsequent discussion.

Throughout the 1970s, academics began increasingly to compare and contrast public and private sector industrial relations arrangements in Britain, with the implicit assumption in such work being that the extent and nature of industrial relations differences between the two sectors far outweighed any differences that existed within each of the two sectors. It is certainly possible, and indeed desirable, to identify a number of *structural* features that differentiate public sector from private sector industrial relations arrangements in Britain. A list of the distinguishing features of public sector industrial relations arrangements would typically include the following:

The key role of the government as a direct (or indirect) employer of labour.

The relative remoteness of market (as opposed to political) forces.

The relatively high level of unionization.

The relative strength of national level bargaining arrangements.

The 'mixed' management side (ie immediate, local employers and relevant central government department) representation on a number of negotiating bodies in the public sector.

In pointing to these (and other possible) differences between the public and private sectors, it is important, however, not to lose sight of certain important industrial relations differences within the public sector itself. For example, in the case of the public corporations there is not the mixed management side representation on negotiating bodies that has existed in the case of education and the health service. Furthermore, in those parts of the public sector that have been taken relatively recently into public ownership from the private sector, there are likely to be important historical and traditional influences shaping contemporary structures and patterns of behaviour that differentiate them from the more long-standing parts of the public sector. Accordingly in the discussion that follows, any relevant differences within the public sector itself will be highlighted. This discussion is presented under four basic headings, namely: joint procedures; pay determination; the changing context of public sector industrial relations; strikes and the union response. It is to the first of these headings that we now turn.

Joint Procedures

The public sector has long been the most highly unionized part of the economy, a position that still pertains today; currently the Incomes Data Services Public Sector Unit estimate the level of union density in the public sector to be some 81 per cent, compared to 38 per cent in the private sector. This high level of union density is far from being overwhelmingly a manual worker phenomenon, as union organization in the public sector extends well up the white-collar employment hierarchy, reaching levels and positions that are relatively underorganized in the private sector. Closely related to this high union density is the relatively high level of collective bargaining coverage in the public sector. In 1978, for example, 90 per cent of male managers in the public sector had their pay determined by collective bargaining arrangements, whereas in the private sector the comparable figure was only 27 per cent. Moreover, the public sector has long been the part of the industrial relations system dominated by national- or industry-level collective bargaining.

The dominant position of national- or industry-level collective bargaining arrangements in the public sector has had a number of important implications for industrial relations there. First, because the public sector is characterized by a relatively small number of individually large-sized bargaining units, it has proved relatively susceptible to attempts at control via incomes policy. Second, this level of bargaining has limited, at least relative to the private sector, the extensive spread of well-developed shop steward arrangements and structures at individual employment establishments. Third, it has limited the development of the personnel management function in that, as Alan Fowler has noted: '. . . for personnel officers in local government, a significant feature of the whole national industrial relations system is that it provides no formal role for them . . . the whole system is heavily biased towards the establishment and maintenance of national agreements and procedures, and the role of the individual authority is consequently minimal.'[2] Finally, it has meant that when strike action does occur in the public sector, the result is a disproportionate contribution to the total number of working days lost through such activity in Britain in the particular period of time concerned.

There has been some notable movement away from the totally dominant position of national-level bargaining in different parts of the public sector in recent years. For example, the 1983 Water Act, which abolished the National Water Council, resulted in the five national negotiating bodies covering pay and conditions in the industry being wound up. The government was in favour of completely abolishing national pay bargaining in the newly reorganized industry. However, some national arrangements were retained, with four new national negotiating bodies (manuals, craft, staff, chief and senior officers) being created. Their constitutions limit them to deal with pay and main conditions of service, with some items (eg subsistence allowances) to be solely negotiated at the individual employer level; staff can also no longer take grading appeals to national level. Moreover, individual water authorities can withdraw from the national agreements after giving 12 months' notice of their intention to do so.

The Thames Water Authority (with some 9,000 employees) gave notice of withdrawal from the senior officers' JNC in 1985 (followed by four other authorities) and now sets pay separately for senior staff, while late in 1986 it announced its intention to withdraw from the other three national bodies, on the stated grounds that it does not have sufficient influence on the annual negotiations with the Water Authorities Association and would like greater independence to negotiate local incentive schemes, with more emphasis on customer service. The Northumberland Authority subsequently expressed a similar intention, while more recently (in anticipation of privatization of the industry) the water industry employers, as a group, have come out in favour of ending national level negotiations.

The present government's dislike of national-level bargaining arrangements in the public sector (and indeed, more generally) which was apparent in the case it put forward for the water industry, has been further emphasized in some remarks of the Chancellor of the Exchequer, the Environment Secretary and the Minister of Employment in late 1986 and early 1987. The latter, for instance, noted that: 'in the public sector . . . we will seek to gain acceptance of a wider geographical variation in pay rates.'[3]

A view or belief to the effect that there should be more decentralized collective bargaining in the public sector did not, of course, originate with the present government. The McCarthy Review of industrial relations in the NHS in 1976, for example, contained a recommendation in favour of more bargaining being conducted at the regional level, and a report by the Prices and Incomes Board in 1967 recommended that payment by results or bonus schemes be extensively adopted in the local government sector in order to improve productivity and ameliorate the low pay problem there.

The implementation of this recommendation, at least for male manual workers, has resulted in bonus schemes constituting the most important element of authority level bargaining in local government. The 1982 New Earnings Survey, for example, indicated that PBR schemes accounted for nearly 16 per cent of the pay of full-time manual men in local government (nearly twice the comparable figure for the workforce as a whole), while some 70 per cent of such employees in local authorities were covered by such arrangements (compared with a figure of 45 per cent for the workforce as a whole). Moreover, early in 1987 local authority employers were engaged in a major restructuring review exercise for manual workers in which the issues of regrading, equal pay for work of equal value and flexible working arrangements were all involved. Local authority employers currently do not appear to favour a move towards regional bargaining, although some recent consultative documents have argued that the number and scope of national agreements should be reduced; local authorities in the tight labour markets of South-East England have been particularly prominent in urging the need for more local level bargaining and hence variation in terms and conditions of employment. (The IDS Public Sector Unit recently reported that a third of some 33 direct labour organizations examined in the local authority sector were operating outside the scope of the national agreement.)

The anti national bargaining structure stance of the government has been criticized for, among other things, underestimating the current extent of more decentralized bargaining in the public sector. The contents of the New Earnings Survey for 1985, for example, listed 50 national agreements for male employees in the public sector with nearly one-third of these (16) involving more than a third of the relevant workforce being affected by supplementary bargaining. The most significant areas of supplementary bargaining were BSC (75 per cent affected by supplementary bargaining), gas (42 per cent), water (49 per cent), British Shipbuilders (53 per cent) and parts of the road passenger transport industry. The degree of supplementary bargaining activity is apparently considerably less in the case of women employees, as here only four of the 21 listed national agreements involved more than one-third of the relevant workforce being affected in this regard. The most recent proposed and/or actual moves towards decentralized bargaining in the public sector have been as follows:

1. Following the passage of the Transport Act 1985, national bargaining has been abolished in the National Bus Company, the municipal undertakings and Passenger Transport Executives; a national forum still exists for municipal buses, but pay bargaining is now conducted at the individual company level.

2. At BR, negotiations for the wholly owned subsidiary, British Rail Engineering Ltd, are conducted separately.

3. In the non-industrial civil service there has been the break-up of multi-union bargaining. (Only four unions negotiated together in 1987.)

In considering joint procedures it is relevant to note that another traditional distinction between the public and private sectors has been the greater presence of unilateral arbitration arrangements in the former area of employment. However, a government report in the early 1980s which examined 17 arbitration agreements in the public sector recommended that, in 11 of them, the employers withdraw from and renegotiate the existing arrangements. The essence of the recommended change was a move away from the right of unilateral reference to arbitration on the grounds that such existing arrangements: encouraged irresponsibility among the parties (in that they had no responsibility for the final agreement and thus tended to hold to their original bargaining positions); favoured the union side; and were potentially inflationary in that they tended to undermine the effective operation of incomes policy and cash limits. In 1981, for example, the Government removed the right of unilateral access to arbitration in the education sector (as noted later, these Burnham committee arrangements have since been abolished).

The present government's more general disquiet with the operation of arbitration arrangements was well-evidenced by their rejection of its usage in the civil service and NHS disputes of 1981 and 1982 respectively. In the latter dispute, for example, the government repeatedly refused to allow the claim to be referred to arbitration, arguing that it was solely the government's responsibility to decide how much it could afford to pay and that, having decided on a figure, it must then stick to it. Indeed, the Health Minister at the time stated quite explicitly that such a demand should not be placed in the hands of arbitrators who were ultimately not accountable to the public at large and who, he argued, tend so often to try to fashion compromise solutions by splitting the difference between the positions of the two parties.

Inevitably, a good deal of attention has been given to the decision of the government to ban or decertify trade unions at GCHQ at Cheltenham from March 1984. Following the House of Lords ruling in November 1984 in favour of the government, the employee ballot results (announced in January 1985) showed that 58 per cent of those employees who voted (the turnout figure was 66 per cent) were in favour of a staff association at GCHQ; the constitution of the resulting 'Government Communications Staff Federation' prohibits all forms of industrial action.

The reaction of the unions is well known. Their offer of a no-strike agreement as a substitute for decertification was not accepted by the government, protest stoppages occurred in the public sector (involving 120,000 working days lost in the quarter ending March 1984), the TUC temporarily withdrew from the NEDC, the TUC has threatened a one-day stoppage if any of the few remaining union members at GCHQ are dismissed,* the Council of Civil Service Unions took the case (unsuccessfully) to the European Court of Justice, and the unions have raised the question of whether this particular instance of union decertification will stimulate and encourage further moves along these lines in both the public and private sectors.

The latter possibility has not occurred to any major extent in either sector of employment at the present time; the labour editor of the *Financial Times* estimates that there have been some 40 known cases of union de-recognition in 1984–88 (these have been essentially in the private sector, although British Rail senior management staff no longer have a union recognized for collective bargaining purposes). There has, however, been considerable speculation over the question of whether public sector

---

* Local protest stoppages occurred in the civil service in October 1988 when four of the remaining 18 union members were dismissed.

management is breaking from traditional practice and taking an increasingly 'hard line' with the unions. For example, during the course of a dispute in the Post Office in 1985 (over the introduction of new technology, the extension of part-time work and the further development of local productivity schemes) management threatened, in the face of union opposition, to introduce the desired changes by unilateral action, but senior management were insistent at the time that this tactical threat did not indicate that they were becoming determinedly anti-union.

It is, however, abundantly clear that the government as an employer is trying to set an example for the private sector to follow in relation to the position of closed shop arrangements. In the hope of encouraging a generally tough, anti closed shop line from management, the public sector has been very much to the forefront in the decertification of closed shop arrangements: British Rail, British Gas, British Telecom, the water authorities and the Post Office have all withdrawn from agreements providing for such arrangements.

Pay Determination

To many commentators, public sector industrial relations is essentially about pay determination arrangements. This sort of view reflects the 1970s experience in which governments of both political persuasions came into open conflict with public sector unions as they struggled to reconcile their responsibility for macro economic management with that for the well-being of their own employees. Throughout that decade, public sector unions frequently claimed that the government of the day had dishonoured their traditional commitment to act as a good employer of labour by seeking to enforce the restrictions of incomes policy most vigorously on their own employees. The *intent* of governments to act in this way is open to little doubt, but in practice it would *not* appear to be the case that the public sector *as a whole* bore a disproportionate burden of the *actual* wage restraint achieved during *all* periods of incomes policy in the 1970s.

The lack of a clear cut, consistent pattern in this regard should occasion relatively little surprise when it is noted that the content and administration of these various episodes of incomes policy was far from homogeneous in nature, and that the extent and nature of union bargaining power is highly variable between the different parts of the public sector.

The present Conservative government has frequently stated its opposition to the introduction of any sort of formal, comprehensive incomes policy. Such statements need, however, to be viewed in the light of frequent critical calls by ministers for the exercise of 'responsible' wage behaviour and the government's use of the cash limits approach in the public sector. The essence of the latter has been: first, the Government's *prior* announcement of a pay provision figure for central government services (ie 4 per cent in 1981–82, 3.5 per cent in 1982–83, 3 per cent in 1983–84, 3 per cent in 1984–85 – this practice was discontinued from 1985–86); second, strict limits in the Rate Support Grant and rate-capping for any overspending authorities in local government; and third, the use of external financing limits to constrain the spending of public corporations and the setting of performance targets for each of these industries. (BR, for example, was instructed at the end of 1983 to reduce government support for the passenger railway by over 25 per cent by March 1987).

A general review of pay movements in the public sector since 1979 reveals first that the rate of earnings increase in the public sector generally exceeded that in the private sector in 1979–80 and 1980–81. The relative gain of the public sector in 1979–81 should be seen in the light of the relative wage movement against the public sector from the mid-1970s and the resulting 'catch-up' awards of the Clegg Comparability Commission (which was abolished in August 1980). In contrast, in the four years 1981–82 to 1984–85 relative wage movements were against the public sector (in some cases, very strongly so), whereas in 1985–86 and 1986–87 there appeared to be rather less difference in the rate of earnings increase in the two sectors. Secondly, in any one year, the vast majority of public sector wage settlements have exceeded the government's prior stated pay provisions, although the government could clearly claim some degree of success in helping to bring down settlement levels in consecutive years, from a range of, for example, 13 to 20 per cent in 1981–82 to 4.5 to 6.5 per cent in 1984–85. Thirdly, there was some notable variation in the size of wage settlements within the public sector itself. The size of settlements for the police (with their special indexation arrangements), for example, have consistently exceeded that of the public sector as a whole; a fact that has caused some considerable disquiet among local authority employers in recent years.

The IDS public sector unit have recently examined the result of the 1987 pay round in some detail, the full results of which are set out in Table 2.1.[4] As the public sector unit have stressed, it is important to distinguish between groups whose pay is determined by a pay review body or by reference to a pay formula and those where collective bargaining is still the determining factor. In the NHS at least 50 per cent of employees are currently covered by the recommendations of pay review bodies, while in local government both the police and fire services now have their pay linked (albeit in different ways) to average earnings movements. The majority of public sector wage settlements are now concentrated in the months of April and July (the April concentration has been particularly encouraged by the TUC public service committee) and in the 1987 pay round we find that:

The range of settlements fell broadly in line with the range in the private sector, between 4.5 and 7 per cent.

The review body groups received awards broadly in line with average earnings increases; 9.5 per cent for the nurses, 8.25 per cent for the doctors and 4.7 per cent for the armed forces.

The indexation arrangements for police and firemen yielded 7.75 and 7.3 per cent respectively.

Average earnings in the public sector were £197.3 per week in April 1987 compared with £199.7 per week in the private sector. (The average increase in 1986–87 was 6.9 per cent in the public sector, compared to 8.1 per cent in the private sector.)

Table 2.1: *Public sector pay 1987*

Negotiating group	Settlement %	Date
Central Government		
Armed Forces	4–7*	April
Civil Service Staff (other than IPCS)	4.25†	April
Civil Service (IPCS)	3.9 + restructuring (6–11)	April/Sept/April 1988
Top Civil Servants (TSRB)	4.6–5.2* (staged)	April/October
UK AEA Manuals	5 (+consolidation)	April
University Lecturers	(stage 2 of 1986 deal from March 1988)	
University Manuals	6.1–7.2	April
National Health Service		
Doctors and Dentists	8.25*	April
Nurses and Midwives	9.5*	April
Paramedics	9.5*	April
Clerical and Admin	5	April
Ancillaries	5 (on paybill)	April
Ambulance Personnel	5	April
Local Government		
Teachers (E&W)	16.4 (staged) (new structure)	Jan/Oct (15 months)
Teachers (Scot)	16.4 (staged) (new structure)	Jan/Oct (15 months)
FE Lecturers (E&W)	16.9 (staged)	April/Sept/July 1988
Police	7.75 (Indexation)	September
Fire	7.3 (Indexation)	November
Local Authority Manuals	10.6 (on paybill)	Sept (backdated to July)
Local Authority Staffs	7.1–8.8 (staged)	July/February 1988
Local Authority Builders	5.5 (7 month deal)	February
Nationalized Industries		
British Coal Miners	4.28 (stage 2 of 1986/87 deal)	November
British Steel	2 (2.5 consolidation)	April
Electricity Supply Manuals	5.6	April
Electricity Supply Technicians	5.6	February
London Buses Platform staff	4.5 (staged)	March/July
London Underground Ltd	4.5	April
Water Industry Manuals	5	April
British Rail	4.5	April
Post Office postmen	5 (on paybill)	April
BBC	4.5 (+3.2 for some grades)	July

Source: *Incomes Data Services*
* Review body
† Basic increase. Extra increases and supplements for particular groups.

Prior to 1985, major and even minor salary structure adjustments were relatively few and far between in the public sector. However, in response to the increased bunching of white-collar staff at the top of salary structures in a number of areas of the public sector, and the government's general desire to see pay related more closely to performance and market forces, 1985 witnessed the following developments:

Merit- or performance-related pay proposals. In the case of the Civil Aviation Authority, for example, management proposed that the incremental structures for the majority of staff be replaced with a unified system of merit-based increases.

Salary restructuring to alleviate pressure at the top. Such restructuring occurred in some eight public sector organizations in 1985. In the case of electricity supply, for example, management and higher executive salary scales were restructured by deleting an increment at the bottom of the scale and adding a new one at the top.

Market rates to help to fill hard-to-fill vacancies. This practice was most apparent in the case of the civil service where 1985 saw special pay additions for secretarial staff in Inner London, scientists at the Atomic Weapons Research Establishment at Aldermaston and the Royal Ordnance Factory at Burghfield, insolvency staff at the Department of Trade, discretionary payments for computer staffs and payments for GCHQ scientists.

Both the 1986 and 1987 pay rounds saw salary restructuring moves along these lines continuing in various parts of the public sector: the attempt here being to relate pay to 'merit and skills', and to local labour markets. In 1987, for example, a new salary structure for professional, scientific and technical civil servants involved a new pay spine of 37 pay points replacing 160 existing separate scales. Other major salary restructuring developments in 1987 involved teachers, the NHS, local government groups, staff at the Civil Aviation Authority, British Rail, Travellers Fare, London Transport and the United Kingdom Atomic Energy Authority. For example, the four scales for classroom teachers were replaced by a main professional scale (with certain special pay additions), a revised structure for local authority chief executives reduced the number of population bands from 35 to 16, the new salary structure for professional and technical grades at the Civil Aviation Authority broke the link with civil service agreements, and senior managers at British Rail were placed on a new 5-grade structure with individual contracts of employment. Obviously questions, not to say criticisms, continue to surround such proposals in a sector where objective, quantifiable measures of output and hence of performance, are so frequently lacking; such opposition has been most notable in the NHS.

Above it was noted that the present government is strongly in favour of public sector pay being more closely related to the movement of market forces and measures of individual and organizational performance. The other side of this coin is the desire significantly to reduce the role of comparability in the wage determination processes of the public sector; this is obviously related to the anti national bargaining stance of the government. Comparability has in fact been the major principle of pay determination in much of the public sector over a number of decades. The commitment to comparability has been explicitly institutionalized in the case of the non-industrial civil service where arrangements have come into frequent conflict with the operation of incomes policies and, subsequently, cash limits. The present government's preference for arguments based on ability to pay and recruitment and retention figures in the civil service, was an important part of the background to the termination of its agreement with the national staff side in 1981 and its willingness to accept a 21-week strike in order to keep down the size of the pay settlement in the civil service. The final settlement package included the establishment of the Megaw Committee of Enquiry into civil service pay, whose recommendations (in July 1982) downgraded, rather than eliminated, comparability as a factor in civil service pay determination.

The government's desire to 'de-prioritize' comparability as a factor in wage determination is not confined to the civil service. Two *tangible* expressions or indications of their more general desire in this direction are: their general reluctance to allow any further groups of public sector employees to achieve 'special case' status through coverage by review bodies* or indexation agreements; and the ending of a number of formal, intra public sector wage relationships, such as that between manual workers in local government and the NHS in 1980. (Since 1980 local authorities' manual workers' pay has increased by 64 per cent, compared to only a 47 per cent increase for NHS ancillary workers.)

It is important to emphasize here that the attack on the role and strength of the comparability principle in public sector wage determination did not originate with the present government. The National Board for Prices and Incomes which operated in the years 1965–70, for example, was a most outspoken critic of the strength of this particular influence in the public sector.[5]

Finally, one should note here the differing findings of two recent studies of the determinants of sectoral earnings movements in Britain. Some researchers at the National Institute of Economic and Social Research report that public corporations appear to lead other sectors, whereas work at the Centre for Labour Economics at the LSE finds that it is the private sector which always constitutes the lead sector in earnings movements;[6]

---

* The need for the Government to provide an extra £138.5 million in October 1988 to fund fully the 17.9 per cent pay award for nurses will undoubtedly have strengthened their resolve in this regard.

these differences indicate the sensitivity of estimation results to a particular model specification and the basic data source utilized.

The Changing Context of Public Sector Industrial Relations

The most obvious feature or facet of change here has been the decline in public sector employment since 1979. In mid-1987 an estimated 6.4 million members (25.7 per cent) of the total workforce were employed in the public sector, a figure comprising 1.0 million (4.0 per cent) in public corporations, 2.3 million (9.3 per cent) in central government and 3.1 million (12.3 per cent) in local authorities. Since 1981 public sector employment has fallen (to mid-1987) by 11 per cent on a headcount basis and by 15 per cent on a full-time equivalent basis. Excluding privatization of public corporations, the relevant reduction is of the order of 5 to 8 per cent. A more detailed set of figures is contained in Table 2.2. Public sector employment is now at its lowest level since 1970, a fact that has had some obvious implications for the overall level of union membership there. Some estimates produced by the Department of Employment, for example, indicate that union membership in national government fell by some 9 per cent in 1984–85, although in

Table 2.2: *Employment changes by sector 1981–87*

	000s	% change
Total employed labour force	+ 566	− 2.3
Private sector	+1380	+ 8.0
Public sector	− 815	−11.3
Public corporations	− 871	−46.7
General government	+ 56	+ 1.1
Central government	− 107	− 4.4
HM forces	− 15	− 4.5
NHS	+ 5	+ 0.4
Other	− 97	−11.0
Local authorities	+ 163	+ 5.6
Education	+ 32	+ 2.2
Social services	+ 48	+13.7
Police	+ 5	+ 2.7
Other	+ 78	+ 8.6

Source: M. Camley, 'Employment in the Public and Private Sectors 1981 to 1987' *Economic Trends*, No 410 (December 1987) p 98

1985–86 there was an increase of some 1.7 per cent.* Nevertheless, in line with a number of other countries, the proportion of public sector union membership in the union movement as a whole appears to be on the increase. (Currently the 39 unions with members in the public sector account for some 44 per cent of total TUC employee membership.)

The present government entered office with the explicit aim of reducing the size of the civil service from 732,000 to 630,000 posts by April 1984. In fact, the government more than achieved this target, with the civil service being reduced by nearly 15 per cent by mid-1984. In November 1983 the government announced its intention of seeking a further 6 per cent reduction of the civil service in the following four years (the manpower target for Apil 1988 was 590,400 with Civil Service staff numbering 597,800 in April 1987). It was estimated that only some 10 per cent of the reduction in the size of the civil service in 1979–84 had resulted from privatization (including contracting out), although it is generally felt that its proportionate contribution is likely to rise in the years 1984–88.†

The present government's commitment to privatization has taken a number of forms. Selling off, in whole or part, has been the main strategy for the trading part of the public sector, with some 16 major organizations having been privatized since 1979. In the service part of the public sector, the main policy approach has been to contract out services previously performed by direct labour to private companies. The particular services targeted here for privatization are primarily cleaning, catering, laundry and security services. In 1986 it was reported that some 16 per cent of local authorities had contracted out direct labour services to private contractors. In the case of the NHS some available figures indicated the following basic position: the vast majority of competitive tenders have been for domestic services, with 29 per cent of these going to outside contractors and with 5 per cent and 22 per cent of the smaller total number of tenders for catering and laundry services respectively going to outside contractors.[7] (Currently more than 85 per cent of contracts in the NHS have been awarded in-house.) The recent Local Government Act is designed to ensure that local authorities seek tenders for refuse collection, street cleansing, building maintenance, ground maintenance, vehicle maintenance and catering, while the Government plans to privatize both electricity supply and the water industry in the life of this Parliament. (British Steel and, most recently, the coal-mining industry have been added to this list.)

Public sector unions have expressed a number of worries and concerns about privatization, not least of which has been the fear that their

---

* Falling membership levels were an important factor in the merger of the CSU and SCPS to form the National Union of Civil and Public Servants. Currently the CPSA, the largest civil service union, is engaged in exploratory merger talks with the GMB.
† The Government's acceptance of the Ibbs Report which favoured the establishment of agencies to undertake some civil service work is potentially important here.

membership levels will plateau and then begin to decline. It is this particular fear that clearly influenced NALGO to pass a rule-change to its constitution in 1984 allowing it to recruit members in the private sector. (Currently some 5 per cent of NALGO's membership is in the private sector.) There have certainly been a number of well publicized instances of local-level strike action against proposed privatization moves in the public sector* (three particularly long strikes involving unions in the NHS occurred in Barking, Hammersmith and Cambridge), although information provided by some of the key union officials involved in the *early, large-scale* privatization moves did not suggest any uniform pattern of substantial costs and losses to the unions concerned. The results of this investigation are summarized in Table 2.3.

However, alongside these findings it is important to note the recent critical review by the unions of the first two years of privatization in British Telecom. Among the union complaints and allegations were the following: the fall in safety standards; the loss of more than 22,000 jobs since 1983, although BT engineers and technicians now work some 41 per cent more overtime than before privatization; the terms and conditions of remaining BT employees have worsened; and collective bargaining structures have been undermined by decentralization, withdrawal of union recognition for managers, and the use of short-term contract staff. Such criticisms, although denied in a speech by BT's chairman at the CBI conference in 1986, obviously form an important part of the background to the 17-day BT dispute in January/February 1987.

In the highly controversial area of competitive tendering, the IDS public sector unit has, in conjunction with the Institute of Personnel Management, recently produced a report which summarizes a good deal of information on the current position in the civil service, the NHS and local government, and provides a useful checklist of the factors that personnel managers should consider in relation to contracting out within their own organizations.[8] This particular report certainly did not mince words in making the following observation about one key effect or result of this process:

> There can certainly be no doubt that contracting out does lead to a decline in terms and conditions of employment. Pay rates do not necessarily suffer, the NHS has been particularly successful to date in obtaining basic Ancillary Staffs General Whitley Council hourly rates in the contract with the tendering organizations, but even here cost savings are made by a worsening of conditions of employment such as pensions, standard hours, sickness pay, holidays and through the eradication of bonus schemes.[9]

---

* In 1980–83 public sector employees were involved in nearly 50 per cent of all redundancy disputes compared to 15 per cent in 1976–79.

Table 2.3: *Results of privatization*

	Associated British Ports	Amersham International	British Aerospace	Britoil	Cable and Wireless	National Freight
Changes in bargaining system?	No	Yes, better	No	No	Yes, better	No
Tougher attitude to pay?	No	No, easier	No	No	No	In some respects
Acceleration in job loss?	Yes	More jobs	Yes	More jobs	Yes	No
Change in consultation?	No	Worse	Better	Better	Yes	No
Change in attitude to unions?	No	Worse	Better	Better	Better	No
Change in closed shop?	No	N/A	N/A	N/A	N/A	No
Impact of worker shareholders on unions?	None	None	None	None	None	None

Source: David Thomas, 'Privatisation and the Unions' *New Society* (21 June 1984) p 479

Competitive tendering is only one (albeit the most controversial in nature) of the measures that the present government has encouraged in its attempt to increase competitive pressures and efficiency in the public sector. Other well-known measures include the Rayner scrutinies and Financial Management Initiative in the civil service, the Griffiths Report recommendations and Resource Allocation Working Parties in the NHS, new systems of local government audit, more centralized control in the allocation of local authority funds and the setting of performance targets for the individual public corporations.

The whole thrust of the government's approach is towards more decentralized 'bottom line' oriented management in the public sector. Such moves may well be stimulated further by findings such as that of the companion volume to the 1984 workplace industrial relations survey, which reported that the rate of technical and organizational change in the public sector was below that of the private sector, while a recent civil service document was highly critical of the relative absence of flexible working arrangements there; the Council of Civil Service Unions have, however, produced a highly critical response to this particular report.

To the unions this trend has raised questions about the adequacy of local level union organization.* Equally, such decentralization tendencies within the management hierarchy raise questions about the respective roles and influence of line and staff management. In the civil service, for example, following the 1983 report of Cassells on personnel work, the emphasis has been on devolving the determination of personnel policies and procedures from the management and personnel office to individual departments so that policies and procedures could be tailored to meet individual organizational and staff needs.[10] Moreover, the Cassells report called for a redressing of the balance of authority between line and personnel management so that personnel work could be made more effective and, combined with other changes, make line management more fully accountable for overall performance. One study of the personnel management function, which revealed some interesting differences between the public and private sectors with regard to how personnel managers have allocated their time between different subjects and issues in recent years, indicated that discipline/dismissals, negotiations and disputes have clearly been the preoccupations of public sector personnel managers in these years.[11]

Strikes and the Union Response

Although individuals may disagree about the strength of the particular causes involved (eg reaction to incomes policy, changes in workforce composition, changes in the political complexion of union leadership), it was generally held that the changing nature of public sector industrial relations in the 1970s derived from, or was at least most clearly manifested in, important changes in the *character* of the unions concerned. In essence, it was argued that employee representation bodies, particularly in the civil service, the NHS and education sector, became increasingly less staff association-like and, conversely, more union-like in their attitudes and behaviour during the course of the decade. This was indicated by a variety of actions that departed from traditional practice, most notably the

* In mid-1983 only 2.4 per cent of the 12,741 shop stewards in the non-industrial civil service were full-time, with some 87 per cent spending less than 20 per cent of their time on union duties.

increased occurrence of strikes and other forms of industrial action.* The level of strike frequency in the public sector in the 1970s should certainly not be exaggerated, but there is no denying that it came increasingly to the forefront in discussions of the problems of British industrial relations.

There are arguably three major reasons for the disproportionate amount of attention given to public sector strikes in the 70s (and subsequently). First, a number of national disputes involved groups of public sector employees that had never previously been on strike (eg civil servants, firemen). Second, a considerable number of them were viewed as having constitutional overtones in that they were directed essentially against government policy of the day; certainly, virtually all episodes of incomes policy in Britain have been broken, at least formally, by public sector strikes, with groups of public sector employees spearheading the resulting 'pay explosions'. And finally, these strikes have been alleged to be particularly high cost ones, being especially harmful to the public at large and in some cases raising the possibility of threats to public health and safety.

Since the present government came to power in 1979, there have been instances of national strike action in the public sector in virtually every year. The predictable result has been that the public sector has tended to account for an increased proportion of working days lost through strike action in these years. In 1982, for example, there were some 3.4 million days lost in the public sector compared with 1.9 million in the private sector. (In 1980–86 strikes in the public sector have accounted for between 44 and 88 per cent of all working days lost in individual years.)

These national level actions have mainly concerned wage questions, although the miners' strike against pit closures in 1984–85 has been viewed as constituting the most direct challenge to overall government strategy in the public sector. This particular dispute involved over 26 million working days lost, the highest in any industry since 1926, and as a result, the total number of working days lost through strike activity in Britain was the second highest (after 1979) since the war.

There have been numerous discussions and analyses of the merits of the miners' case, the tactical errors made during the course of the dispute and the larger implications for unions and management in the public sector. There has also been much interest in the *post-strike position* in the industry where certain key individuals have moved on, further pit closures have occurred, the NCB has proposed major changes to the existing consultation and conciliation machinery (and attempted to improve workplace communications by introducing team briefing in certain areas of the country),

---

* Increased affiliation to the TUC was another relevant indicator in this regard. In 1977 the Association of First Division Civil Servants affiliated as a result of the operation of incomes policies and the belief that this was necessary in order to avoid becoming increasingly isolated in the civil service.

while disputes have continued to occur (for example, some 195 stoppages in the first six months of the 1986/87 financial year). Furthermore, the decision of the NUM in South Wales in September 1988 to reject the proposed framework of flexible six-day working at the planned Margam pit has led British Coal to consider altering its rules on union recognition to allow the break-away Union of Democratic Mineworkers to represent the workforce there.*

The long-running teachers' disputes, both north and south of the border, have also been viewed as constituting important challenges to the government's 'efficiency-flexibility' approach in the public sector, with the outcomes having significant public expenditure implications. The most obvious short-term outcome was the passage of the Teachers' Pay Act 1987 which dismantled the Burnham Committee negotiating machinery and allowed the Secretary of State to impose his own settlement of some 16.4 per cent over 21 months (with new contracts of employment). This Act, which runs to 1990 (but can be extended) has, needless to say, not been well received by the major teaching unions; half-day strike rallies in selected centres occurred as protest measures both prior to and during the election campaign of mid-1987. The Secretary of State for Education has, however, given an undertaking (in September 1988) to the National Union of Teachers to have a national pay negotiating body in place by April 1990.

Major public sector disputes in Britain have frequently been followed by calls from various organizations for the introduction of 'no-strike clauses' in 'essential services'. A report by the Centre for Policy Studies† in the mid-1980s, for example, called for such restrictions to be introduced for the health service, the fire service, gas, electricity, and water and local authority workers responsible for burials and cremations.[12] The present government was originally keen to proceed in this direction, although there has been little tangible outcome from discussions on this subject to date. This is presumably as a consequence of disagreements over the definition or scope of 'essential services' in the public sector and over the desirability of institutionalizing compulsory arbitration arrangements in return for re-moving the right to strike.

As a 'second best' alternative the government is likely to continue its present approach of encouraging the increased representation and status of 'non-militant' employee organizations in the public sector. The membership growth of the Royal College of Nursing in recent years (a 55 per

---

* In addition British Coal has begun negotiating a two-year productivity-linked pay agreement with the UDM, but has refused to negotiate with the NUM until the latter recognize the UDM.

† This 'think-tank' of the radical right was founded in 1974 by Sir Keith Joseph to propound monetarist and free market economic principles within official Conservative circles, and to develop policies somewhat independently of the mainstream party machinery.

cent increase in 1979–85) has certainly been well above that of its TUC rivals, COHSE and NUPE, while other 'alternative' non-TUC affiliated unions now exist in the coal industry, British Rail, education, the civil service and local government. The most important of these are undoubtedly the Union of Democratic Mineworkers in Nottinghamshire and South Derbyshire, the Professional Association of Teachers (with its no-strike clause), and the Federated Union of Professional and Managerial Officers in local government (which favours the break up of national bargaining there), all of which have been accorded national-level recognition status. In education the recent membership growth of the moderate Assistant Masters and Mistresses Association has been such as to lead them to claim to be the second largest teachers union in the country, after the National Union of Teachers. This claim has been hotly disputed by the National Association of Schoolmasters/Union of Women Teachers. The certification officer's figures seems to support the latter's case, although the difference between the two is now relatively small.

Although the media have stressed that any membership growth in the public sector in recent years is very much associated with the more moderate unions, other commentators have made reference to the increased 'politicization' of public sector unions in recent years.

This has been observed in relation, for example, to ballots for political funds under the Trade Union Act 1984. The Institution of Professional Civil Servants is the latest union to establish a political fund for the first time; some 15 unions have done this, with a high proportion of them being in the public sector (including four in the civil service). Furthermore, the Royal College of Nursing balloted its membership (for the second time in the 1980s) on the question of removing the non-industrial action clause from their constitution in early 1988, although the vote was in favour of retaining the status quo. (The Royal College of Midwives also balloted their members on this question in October 1988, with the vote being in favour of retaining the no-strike policy.)

In addition, the frequent rhetoric about public sector union coordination appears to have had some more tangible content in recent years. The Public Services Committee of the TUC (established in 1979) has sought to develop a common core approach to collective bargaining which, in 1984, for example, involved: the negotiation of targets in excess of the government's then current (ie 3 per cent) central government service guideline; reductions in hours and overtime; six weeks' annual holiday, and early retirement on adequate pensions; a minimum pay standard of two-thirds of average male earnings; and moves towards a common settlement date across the public services (essentially similar guidelines have been issued in subsequent rounds).

Conclusion

The present Conservative government, which entered its third term of 'office following the June 1987 election, enjoys a reputation second to none of being 'anti public sector'. This is because, first, it has moved well beyond the approach of previous governments of making *ad hoc* attempts to reduce wage and employment levels in the public sector to actually questioning and constraining the institutional role of public sector unions.* And second, because it is clearly trying to make the public sector more like the private sector in many of its industrial relations arrangements and practices, although a number of the specific reforms or changes sought here have not, as we have noted, been unique to the present government – but the particular reasons for, and priority attached to, these changes may differ from those of previous governments.

The present Government is committed to restraining public expenditure, further privatization moves, decentralizing collective bargaining and extensive salary restructuring developments in the public sector. These policies, when placed in the context of recent instances of industrial action, pressures for 'catch-ups' in public sector pay, the reported difficulty of attracting and retaining qualified staff in certain parts of the public sector (eg executive officer grades in the civil service) and widespread complaints of low employee morale, certainly suggest the aptness of a recent report which concluded that: 'public sector industrial relations are still in search of their identity, and the road to rediscovering it seems likely to be both long and rough.'[13]

---

* The latest edition of the Civil Service Staff Handbook no longer encourages employees to join unions, and the civil service national agreement on time off for trade union duties has been revised.

References
1. Hepple B 'Labour Law and Public Employees in Britain' in Wedderburn Lord and Murphy W T (eds) *Labour Law and the Community* (1982) Institute of Advanced Legal Studies, University of London, p 75–9
2. Fowler A *Personnel Management in Local Government* (1975) IPM, London, p 141
3. *The Times* 12 February 1987
4. IDS Public Sector Unit *Public Sector Pay: Review of 1986, Prospects for 1987* March 1987
5. National Board for Prices and Incomes Report No 122 *Fourth General Report* July 1969, Cmnd 4130, HMSO, 1969, p 30

6. Foster N, Henry S and Trinder C 'Public and Private Sector Pay: A Partly Disaggregated Study' *National Institue Economic Review* No 107, February 1984; and Zabalze A 'Comments on Public and Private Sector Pay: A Partly Disaggregated Study' London School of Economics, Centre for Labour Economics, Working Paper No 611, 1984

7. Institute of Personnel Management and IDS Public Sector Unit *Competitive Tendering in the Public Sector* October 1986, pp 17, 26

8. Institute of Personnel Management and IDS Public Sector Unit, *loc cit*

9. Institute of Personnel Management and IDS Public Sector Unit, *ibid* p 66

10. Cassells J S *Review of Personnel Work in the Civil Service* HMSO, London, 1983, p 38–9

11. Mackay L 'Personnel Management in the Public and Private Sectors' *Industrial Relations Journal* **17** 4, Winter 1986, p 312

12. *Essential Services – Whose Rights?* CPS, May 1984

13. Fogarty M with Brooks D *Trade Unions and British Industrial Development* (1986) PSI Research Report, p 151

Chapter 3

New Technology and Industrial Relations

Colin Gill

The new technology, or information technology, is a 'heartland' technology in the sense that it will effect radical transformations throughout society and in the world of work in particular. There is no doubt that this technology is destined to spread to a vast range of economic activities, even though we are not sure how fast this will happen. It will lead to the emergence of new products and to new forms of work organization. It will also lead to changes which will save capital, labour, materials and energy, and it will undoubtedly bring about an even greater use of these factors of production. Nearly every enterprise will be afffected in one way or another by the new technology, regardless of its activities. Its impact will spread across the entire structure of an enterprise from manufacturing to administration, and from planning to marketing. It is just a matter of time.

This chapter outlines the economic and political context within which new technology is being introduced into industry and commerce and then examines its impact, in the short and long term, on industrial relations from both a management and trade union viewpoint.

Economic Change, New Technology and Jobs

There has been a slowdown in economic growth throughout the Western economies from the early 1970s onwards. Enterprises have had to operate in a climate of general economic instability, frequent and unpredictable cyclical fluctuations, reduced productivity, rising costs of production and much stiffer competition. All this has led to increased pressures on profits and cashflows which has limited the scope for investment. In such a changed economic climate there is a strong incentive to embark on labour-saving techniques and to seek radical transformations in company organization. The adoption of new technology provides an attractive means of ensuring the survival of the enterprise. It can be incorporated into new or considerably modified products, such as digital electronic controls on various types of machinery, robots, computer-numerically controlled machines, word processors and new office technology, traffic system controls and so on. It will also have a considerable influence on the provision of various services; finally, microelectronics will be employed in the manufacture of traditional goods. Whichever of these three forms are considered, it becomes clear that there will be substantial changes in the way that enterprises operate.

Currently, Western European countries, together with other advanced industrialized societies, are experiencing an employment crisis. High rates of economic growth throughout the West slowed down dramatically during the early part of the 1970s and there has been a widespread increase in unemployment in all Western economies since 1975. The generally accepted opinion is that high levels of unemployment are likely to persist and might even worsen in the foreseeable future. Although this rise in unemployment started well before the widespread application of the new microelectronic-based technology, there is a real danger that the spectacular advances in information technology – particularly arising from the marriage of automated data processing (ADP) and telecommunications – will lead to even higher levels of unemployment.

Traditional manufacturing industry has declined substantially in the Western industrialized societies. Between 1970 and 1981 manufacturing industry in the European countries lost 5.5 million people (of which 2.5 million jobs were lost in the UK, 1.8 million in the Federal Republic of Germany and 0.7 million in France). This industrial exodus accelerated in the early 1980s, and is mainly affecting the heavy and material processing or manufacturing industries. This suggests that the European countries are gradually moving towards a kind of 'de-materialized' production system where 'light' products and processes will be the foundation of European economies for some time to come.[1]

In the short term at least, one of the major implications of such a transition is the great number and variety of process innovations (as opposed to product innovations) which are transforming the production system in the Western world, thus contributing to the reduction (saving) of the employed labour forces. According to Christopher Freeman,[2] in the present international context of strong competition, process innovations are likely to remain dominant over the next five to 10 years, although energy-based, microelectronics-based and telecommunications-based innovations may also lead to some important new products during this period.

Freeman bases his predictions on the work of the Russian economist Kondratiev, who in 1926 pointed out that economic activity moved in 'long waves' of around 50 years in duration, linked to major pervasive technological innovations. He suggests that the discoveries which will lead to major pervasive innovations may occur decades before their widespread adoption affects the economy. These pervasive technologies, spreading across a wide range of industries and infrastructures, such as steam power, electric power, the internal combustion engine etc, may produce an economic spurt for several decades, resulting in a massive demand for labour, and involve drastic changes in regional distribution of industry and patterns of investment in it. While governments are able to provide short-term encouragement by helping to build up the appropriate infra-structure and stimulating demand, the long-term potential is only realized when industries themselves have adapted accordingly. How does informa-tion technology fit into this perspective?

Freeman claims that information technology is of such a nature that the changes it produces will be the result of process innovation rather than product innovation. It is therefore less likely to generate automatically the extra demand needed to avoid rising unemployment. It is not only in manufacturing where job losses will arise, but there will also be poor prospects for employment growth in utilities, banking, insurance and distribution. Only in personal services are we likely to see much opportun-ity for employment growth.

It is significant that information technology is being adopted during a time of continuing depression by a whole range of large service industries, such as banking, insurance and the civil service. Here, unlike the mechanization of manufacturing production, where increased productivity can generate more profit and further investment, the office sector offers little opportunity for increased profit and further investment, so there is only a shake-out of labour, producing a further slowdown in the economy.

Gershuny[3] points out that information technology is not being used to develop the necessary infrastructure for a whole range of new activities which would provide the necessary stimulation for economic growth. As his research reveals, more and more people are buying capital goods, made by fewer and fewer people, to service themselves at home. The increased productive power of the household has increased our ability to replace the need for much service employment, thereby limiting the growth potential of this sector.

The increased proportion of those employed in the service sector in Britain rose from 59 to 65 per cent in the period from March 1980 to January 1986; during this period 1.66 million manufacturing jobs were lost and only a net 0.24 million service jobs were added. The increase in service employment could not even keep pace with the loss of a further 0.43 million jobs from basic utilities, such as agriculture, coal, gas, water, electricity and construction. At the same time, more and more people are entering the labour force. It has been estimated that if we wish to see registered unemployment return to one million in Britain, 3,000 jobs have to be created today, tomorrow, the next day, and every day for the next five years. In 1985 new jobs were only created at the rate of 752 per day, on a falling trend.[4]

The high level of unemployment is only one of the problems that face society as the pace of technological innovation accelerates. Even though jobs are being created there has been a massive shift towards part-time employment. Over the 30-year period from 1951 to 1981 in Britain, the proportion of part-time to full-time jobs rose from 1 in 23 to 1 in 5.[5] This period was characterized by a simple substitution process in which the British economy lost 2,375,000 full-time jobs (81 per cent of the loss being experienced by men), and gained 3,700,000 part-time jobs (82 per cent of the gain being experienced by women).[6] Seventy per cent of the women part-timers were employed in low-paid service jobs for fewer than 16 hours a week. In the three years up to March 1986 this process accelerated.[7]

The Management of New Technology

Although we are still in the embryonic phase of the so-called information revolution, a number of challenges present themselves to management of enterprises in the near future, as a result of the incorporation of microelectronics in products:

Technological developments are proceeding so rapidly that the life-cycle of products is becoming much shorter than previously. This means that a premium is placed on flexibility in production and marketing planning.

The need to locate industrial sites according to the most favourable labour and product market criteria will become less and less important as time goes on. Proximity to component supply centres and technological know-how will be more important.

There is likely to be a diversification of business organization towards complementary mechanical and electronic activities in order to absorb overmanning and improve profitability, by creating a network of small enterprises which are highly specialized in specific fields.

There is likely to be less emphasis on production itself, with a greater commitment to pre-production (research and development) and post-production areas of the business, such as marketing, technical assistance and applicative software. All this will have profound implications for management structure and functional responsibility in enterprises.

We can expect to see a continuous appraisal of 'make or buy' decisions in enterprises because enterprise management will be aware of the risk of finding that component parts are unavailable, thus jeopardizing the success of an entire range of its products.

The increasing importance of information in management decision-making is an inevitable consequence of advances in technological development. This will be true in the cases of incorporating microelectronics in products, the provision of services and in product manufacture.

The management function will also be affected in other ways as a result of the introduction of computer-based systems in organizations. For example, in a survey which was carried out for the Engineering Industry Training Board, most users of computer-aided design (CAD) found that they had to reorganize themselves to cope with a computer by making their procedures more explicit and to think (often for the first time in years) about their procedures and standards.

Skill factors are also crucial in the adoption of new technology. Management skills are needed in combination with engineering skills to assess not merely returns on investment at profit centres, but system costs and benefits.

When companies introduce computer-aided design/computer-aided manufacturing (CAD/CAM) and other forms of computer-automated manufacturing into the enterprise,[8] they may have to change their organizational structure to allow for a product-based form of organization rather than a functionally-based one. They may even need to adopt a 'matrix'* form of organization.

In summary, microelectronics is expected to have profound effects on enterprises in terms of being incorporated into products, in its use in manufacturing and in its application to the service sector. It will require a major restructuring of enterprises, not just at the manufacturing stage, but at all levels. In certain industries, particularly in the growing area of electronics, there is an increasing need for high investment in research and development, which is of fundamental strategic importance. The pressure of competition, with the short life-cycle of products, will mean that companies must be able to keep one step ahead of their rivals in order to survive. More particularly, only if a company is able to lead innovation in a particular product can it achieve the level of earnings needed for reinvestment in R and D. On the other hand, in order to be a leader in innovation, sufficient resources need to have been invested in R and D. This 'catch 22' situation increases competitiveness and the rate of innovation. This places a premium on the need for enterprises to forecast when the commercial production of the next product generation is likely to take place, then design their products to coincide with the availability of the new components.

One of the major effects of the new technology is to permeate the whole of the enterprise. It is not simply the case that the new technology substitutes human labour with a form of automation, important though that is. It is the role of information that is significant. Only if this information is appropriately used, can its flow enable enterprises to adjust to the

* Matrix organizations are those in which neither a product nor a functional division predominates, but where there is a product organization overlaying a functional organization. In such cases, individual specialists are dedicated to a clearly identified product group in which they have a product or project manager, while at the same time maintaining a formal relationship with their functional manager.

challenges of increased competitiveness; failure to so do could have catastrophic consequences. Information technology also serves to highlight any inherent weaknesses in an enterprise's structure, as well as its managerial capabilities and market position. This will be true whether the company is incorporating microelectronics in its products or whether it uses microelectronic-based equipment in its production, administration or service activities.

A new employment model is emerging where new technology is strongly linked to an increasing tendency for labour segmentation to emerge, where an increasing number of jobs become less secure, more flexible and increasingly isolated from the external labour market and the wider trade union movement. As Professor William Brown noted:

'. . . at one extreme it is becoming easier to play the labour market for some types of work, obtaining relatively cheap and easily disposable employees of the required competence, and allowing their anxiety about job loss to sustain acceptable effort levels. At the other extreme, it is also becoming easier to build up a package of employment, training and payment practices that elicit high labour efficiency through the very different route of cultivating commitment.'[9]

Coupled with these tendencies are changes in a whole range of employment practices which can all be described under the catchphrase of industrial relations in the 1980s – flexibility: flexibility in skills, payment, hours of work, training, working practices, occupations, security of employment, promotion, careers, and so on.

Large European businesses in the public and private sector are following US trends by developing a two-tier or segmented labour force. This trend involves the break up of the labour force into peripheral and flexible groups of workers clustered round a stable core. As the market expands the periphery grows to take up the slack; as growth slows, the periphery contracts. Those of the low-paid periphery are workers on short-term contracts, homeworkers, the self-employed, Manpower Services Commission sponsored trainees, part-time workers and those employed by sub-contractors. In 1983, 5.9 per cent of those in employment in Britain (1.5 million people) were in temporary, seasonal, casual or fixed-term contractual jobs, rising to 6.4 per cent by 1984.[10]

An Institute of Manpower Studies Report,[11] published in February 1987, predicts 650,000 job losses in British manufacturing between 1985 and 1990, with the creation of 500,000 jobs in the private services sector. The job creation projection does not hold out much hope for the long-term unemployed, still less for trade union membership. The predominant job creators are likely to be three main sectors: business services (215,000 jobs), hotels and catering (120,000 jobs), and wholesale distribution (70,000 jobs). The main beneficiaries are likely to be female (two-thirds of jobs), part-time (one-third) and young workers (up to a quarter).

If these trends continue (and there is every reason to suppose that they will) there is a danger that new technology will be associated with an increasingly divided society. Not only will there be a division between those with jobs and the unemployed, but also between those with 'pauperized' employment (in terms of pay, job design, content and security). The obvious consequence of this marginalization of employment is increased poverty. The US labour market has advanced this trend further than Britain. Nearly 35 million Americans (12 million children) live below the poverty line, the highest rate for nearly 20 years. Changes in disposable income in 1983 represented a transfer of $25 billion ($2,000 per family) from the poorest 20 per cent to the richest 20 per cent. In the UK, inequalities are about half those in the USA, but recent trends reflect what is happening in America.

A number of authors have noted the likelihood that organizations will become smaller as information technology is more widely adopted in work organizations. Indeed, the recent growth of part-time employment (an increase from 15 per cent of the working population in employment in 1971 to 25 per cent in 1985), self-employment (covering 10.8 per cent of the working population in 1985), subcontracting, together with homeworking and temporary employment has led to a decline in the average size of both establishments and enterprises in British manufacturing industry since 1978. As William Brown has observed:

> 'Having been growing in size [until about 1978], the proportion of the workforce in establishments of 500 or more employees fell from 35 per cent in 1978 to 48 per cent in 1982 . . . while the proportion in enterprises of 10,000 or more employees fell from 35 per cent to 30 per cent over the same period. This shrinkage is of particular significance in view of the sensitivity of so many industrial relations variables to the size of factory and firm.'[12]

There is every indication that these trends will continue. Francis has suggested that computer automated manufacturing (CAM) will lead to new organizational structures within the enterprise. He notes that a popular fashion in Sweden, promoted by the Swedish Employers' Federation (Svenska Arbetsgivareforeningen) is to set up 'companies within companies'.[13] This can involve reorganizing an area within the factory so that the design, planning and production facilities for one particular product are located under one roof, quite separate from other products:

> 'What is lost in economies of scale and from benefits of functional specialization is claimed to be more than recouped through the increased administrative efficiency, faster response times and quicker throughput. In addition, benefits in working attitudes, morale and commitment are sometimes claimed.'

The realization of the 'small is beautiful' notion is linked with the implementation of computer-automated manufacturing. The availability of relatively cheap forms of automation by reprogrammable CAM devices[10] will enable enterprise to batch-produce items that were previously produced with hard-wired automation, and to reduce the size of economic batches. Thus, smaller firms may be able to take on business that was previously carried out only by large companies. In the newspaper industry, for instance, new technology has obviated the imperative of mass circulation newspapers being bound to heavy advertising revenues; instead, they can now survive with a much smaller circulation and with more of their revenue coming from the cover price. The *Independent* and *Today* are both examples.

Information technology will enable rapid coordination to take place throughout different management functions in the enterprise. Hence, the need for the various stages of the production process to be situated under one roof, coordinated by a vertically integrated management hierarchy, is no longer a necessity once the new technology is fully implemented.

Much speculation has taken place about the potential that information technology offers for the development of homeworking or some form of self-employment. A quick scan through job advertisements (especially in the data processing field) will provide several examples of jobs which can now be largely carried out away from the employer's premises. Homeworking has been traditionally important in certain industries, such as clothing and textiles.

The main attraction of homeworking for employers is financial: there is no need to provide factory or office facilities. In most cases lower wages or salaries can be paid because of the reduced ability of homeworkers to take collective action through trade unions. In any case, it is much easier to lay off workers when they are not based on the employer's premises. Information technology considerably expands the number of occupations that can be suitable candidates for homeworking, particularly clerical work.

In the manufacturing area, a major constraint which has prevented factory workers from carrying out their work at home up to now has been the need to operate large and/or complex machinery which needs factory backup facilities or the availability of rapid access to information. CAM removes many of these impediments.

Similarly, a large amount of office work can easily be carried out at home by means of computer terminals which are linked to a central computer via the telecommunications system. Work can therefore be carried out at home, monitored and controlled in a central office. This obviates the necessity for exercising managerial control, which has always provided a major constraint for the expansion of homeworking. Many areas of female clerical work lend themselves readily to homeworking, and the consequent dangers of social isolation for women within the home are readily apparent.

Women are likely to be particularly affected as they become increasingly drawn into homeworking as time goes by. Up to now, the expansion of service industries and office employment has gone hand in hand with the expansion of paid employment, particularly in the post-war years. Since services were less vulnerable to recession than other sectors of employment, they have afforded women a certain protection from unemployment in times of recession. With the advent of new technology, the advantages that women offer to employers – ie cheap and relatively docile labour – become less and less relevant. Moreover, the type of work that many women do – often low-level, repetitive and monotonous – makes them particularly susceptible to rationalization, both in manufacturing and services.

Management itself will also be increasingly affected by homeworking; Rank Xerox has initiated networking arrangements with some of its specialists whereby they now work from their own homes on individualized contracts, and often have Xerox 820 microcomputers linked to the company's head office.

One of the features of economic development during the 1960s and 70s in the Western industrialized nations was a general trend towards larger organizations, as more and more mergers took place. The same period saw a growth in employment concentration, and the rise in the numbers of large, complex multi-plant companies which spread their activities across a wide range of industries. The problems of management structure in these organizations increased as companies grew in size and diversification, with the need to employ more specialist staff and to innovate in an increasingly competitive environment. Throughout this period, companies had to employ more and more managerial, technical and administrative staff, with the consequent elongation and complexity of management structure. All this meant that companies were forced to give considerable attention to ways of improving coordination, integration and control so as to ensure that these giant companies functioned efficiently.

However, new technology is spawning novel ways of dealing with the problems of managerial complexity; the small is beautiful philosophy and the move towards matrix forms of managerial organization are but two of the possibilities for the future. In fact, while the new technology creates greater choice for the structure of management organization and the exercise of its functions, there is a general expectation that it will also permit the contraction of management hierarchies and a radical simplification of management structures. Management in the future will not only have more 'generalist' rather than specialist skills but they will be expected to be much more educationally qualified than they are at present.

At the extreme, the core of an organization need contain no more than a design function, a costing and estimating function and a marketing function, as well as coordinating management. Within the public services sector there have recently been moves to privatize certain activities. The reason why such trends are emerging lies in the ability of small specialist groups in the service sector to run themselves more tightly. Unlike the manufacturing sector, economies of scale in services peter out very quickly because the bureaucratic burden becomes too great too soon:

> 'In production systems large is cheaper. In service systems small is efficient.'[14]

The phenomenal success of Japanese companies has been the envy of politicians, businessmen and the public in the West for a considerable time. Despite constraints on expansion in the form of uncertain energy supplies, labour shortages, fierce international competition and rising prices of most natural resources, the Japanese economy has demonstrated its resilience in the face of such obstacles. While Japanese success is in part due to the positive role that the Japanese banking system has played in fostering industrial development by being willing to invest on a long-term basis without demanding or expecting short-term returns, together with the cooperative relationship between government and industry which has been fostered by the Japanese Ministry of International Trade and Industry (MITI), many people have pointed to the cooperative relationships between management and employees at enterprise level as the key to Japanese success.

A number of commentators[15] have speculated that employment patterns in the West are moving towards the Japanese model, largely as a result of the effects of new technology and the recession.[16] The structure of British trade unionism in private manufacturing industry is particularly susceptible to a set of management strategies which tend to isolate workforces both from the labour movement outside the enterprise and from the external labour market itself. Those companies that pursue strategies of training their employees in the particular package of skills appropriate to their own technologies, rather than simply buying in a time-served craftsman or starting a conventional apprentice are effectively limiting trade union control and enhancing the employee's dependence on the employer:

> 'The more an employer can occupationally isolate his employees, the more it becomes worthwhile to offer them inducements to stay with the firm, accept periodic retraining, and work with flexible job descriptions.'[17]

There seems to be a consensus that the twin effects of the recession and new technology are considerably enhancing managerial control at the level of the enterprise, both in Britain and elsewhere in the West. As the *Financial Times* remarked:

> 'Flexibility is the name of the game in the 1980s labour market – in wages, skills and training. It is fashionable among British and other European

policy-makers to admire the relative flexibility of employment in the US, scme of which is ascribed to that country's large, relatively low-wage, labour-intensive service sector, and its enterpreneurial drive.'[18]

Effects on Trade Unions and Workers

The history of trade unionism is strongly linked to the way technology has progressed from the Industrial Revolution onwards. The first Industrial Revolution, concerned with the development of steam engines, was followed by a series of secondary revolutions – those of the introduction of railways, electricity and electronics. The evolution of technological progress has shaped the labour movement, and it is in the history of the labour movement that the discontinuous nature of technological change can be seen most clearly. The very essence of trade union history is one of alternating advance and retreat; of gains secured, eroded and restored; of organizations formed, degenerating and reformed.

It is a history which can, perhaps best be portrayed in a 'Darwinistic' pattern. Here, trade unions are seen as life-forms which continually have to adapt to threats posed by changes in the economic, political and technological environment. Each successive period of economic advance has presented contradictory faces to labour, undermining the old framework of economic security and, at the same time, creating opportunities for new and enhanced forms of labour influence.

At the risk of over simplification, each phase of technological development has been accompanied by a shift in the locus of industrial bargaining power; first from the home to the factory tool room, then from the tool room to the mass production line, and finally to more remote control and planning administration. Throughout these phases of technological development, new occupations have come into being and old occupations have either disappeared or the bargaining power associated with them has been eroded.

Trade unions have always been conscious of the impact of new technology on their jobs and skills, but their fears of widespread job displacement were never realized because new industries were created and fresh employment opportunities arose, particularly during the 1950s and 60s. During this period, rapid technological change in Britain was managed with a certain degree of success against a background of steady economic growth and low unemployment. In contrast to the USA, where at that time a debate was raging over whether automation led to unemployment, the unions in Europe generally took a positive view of technological change, provided that it was against a background of growth, and benefits could be obtained through higher wages. In many European countries, productivity agreements were signed which were specifically designed to promote technological change.

The British Trades Union Congress, following a survey of the effects of the early computers on employment levels during the 1960s,[19] felt that there was no intrinsic reason why technical change should cause large-scale unemployment. However, in the 1970s, trade union concern began to mount (particularly in the Western European countries) at some of the potentially negative effects of technological change. This was stimulated by two factors: first, the growth of unemployment and the decline in rates of economic growth, and second, the increasing concern about the effect of the new technology on the quality of working life and the potential effect on working conditions. Significantly, this was in marked contrast to the USA and Japan, where there was little concern shown about the employment implications of the new technology. In part this can be explained by the fact that the mid-1970s were periods of relatively rapid growth in both countries. Both Japan and the USA gained from some of the shifts in the pattern of world production and employment generation that were taking place, and against a background of relatively rapid growth, the traditional areas of highly unionized labour were less seriously affected by what job losses there were.

By the end of the 1970s, as the effects of unemployment and the recession were being felt through the Western industrialized countries, trade unions became increasingly concerned about the employment effects generated by new technology. In Britain the 1978–79 dispute at Times Newspapers lasted for almost a year and proved to be a foretaste of things to come in the British newspaper industry, with the 1986 Wapping strike. The 1978 dispute[20] brought to the surface many of the underlying contradictions in Fleet Street industrial relations: management's long-standing abdication of control over the production process to the unions; the shift of power from union leaders to in-house chapels; the internal political and institutional tensions within the print unions; as well as the wider issues such as the introduction of US-style labour relations tactics in British industry and the role of rich foreign proprietors. However, central to the dispute was the issue of control of the new technology by the print unions.

The trade union response to change is inevitably conditioned by the state of the labour market. During the 1970s, the labour market showed a steadily rising labour surplus, and it was to be expected that the trade union response to the new technology would be subsumed into the overriding aim of trade unions to better their position in relation to both employers and government by seeking to tighten up on the labour market – in other words, by seeking to reduce the length of time worked (reducing labour supply) and/or arguing for reflation (increasing labour demand).

Trade unions are at a distinct disadvantage with new technology. There are obvious reasons why this should be the case: the emergence of microelectronics in a period of economic depression; the dominance of multinational companies and national governments in controlling and exploiting the technology; the fact that the technology itself has a particular form and design before it is presented to the workforce as a *fait accompli*; and the rapid pace of technological development itself. In such circumstances the criteria of profitability, efficiency, and international competitiveness which underpin technological innovation have a momentum of their own. Moreover, new technology emerged as an industrial relations issue at a time when radical changes were taking place in labour markets with significant changes in work patterns.

By the beginning of the 1980s, two main strategies had evolved for responding to the implications of technological change. The US unions attempted to build outwards from the system of corporate (or company) bargaining by seeking to establish global collective bargaining with the large multinational companies such as Ford, Massey Ferguson, IBM and Philips by the setting up of international joint union councils under the auspices of the international trade centres. This strategy met with limited success, however, because such bodies achieved only very limited measures of recognition from the companies, and what little success they had was largely concerned with the synchronization of pay settlement dates. The Western European unions sought to persuade their national governments to reflate the European economies and to exercise state power as a means of regulating the large multinational companies; and sought to control the direction of the new technology by a combination of data agreements and new technology agreements with companies at plant and company level.

Data agreements were pioneered originally by the Scandinavian labour movement at the beginning of the 1970s, and they were later to become the model for many of their sister European trade union movements to follow. In Britain, the TUC began its response to the developments in microelectronics rather late. The 1978 Congress had requested the General Council, 'to carry out as a high priority a comprehensive study of the employment and social consequences of advances in the new microelectronic technology and similar advances in UK technology, together with the wider ramifications of its applications by our competitors'. Congress went on to call for the General Council to prepare a draft policy statement in consultation with affiliated unions for a conference on the subject; the matter would be further taken up at the 1979 Congress.

Following this, an interim report[21] was produced by the General Council as a basis for discussion at a special conference of affiliated unions on employment and technology held in May 1979, which was attended by 116 delegates from 61 unions, representing 90 per cent of all affiliated membership. Afterwards, another report, which was an amended version of the interim report, was produced for the September 1979 Congress. This second report[22] formed the basis for a lengthy composite motion moved by a number of the largest unions. The report and motion, which gained widespread support from affiliated unions, offered the most substantial and coherent statement from organized labour on new technology since the 1955 TUC debate on automation.

Some of the concerns expressed by the unions in 1955 resurfaced, and many of the arguments expressed remained fundamentally the same. There were, however, two major differences between the two debates. The first was that the context surrounding the two debates was radically different. The 1955 debate took place when trade union members had experienced no job losses which could be traced to computerization, and the future potential job loss that could be expected was largely based on guesswork. In contrast, the second debate took place when it was becoming clear that the capacity of automation to destroy large numbers of jobs was immense. The second difference was that in the 1979 debate there was an emphasis placed on the need for government planning and intervention, and on the explicit linking of new technology with industrial democracy and planning at company and national level.

The TUC report on 'Employment and Technology' stood at the peak of a serious and substantial attempt to introduce new technology and the concept of bargaining to a very large number of officials and ordinary members.[23] The report began by stating that: 'whether technology will prove to be a friend or foe will depend, not on the technology itself, but on the application and the policies adopted by governments, trade unions and employers'.[24] It then went on to argue that there was a correlation between high productivity growth and low unemployment rates and argued for an expansion of the service sector of the economy and of R and D effort. There then followed a brief explanation of the development of microelectronics and its applications before embarking on its main task which was to discuss the possible employment effects and to formulate a policy for the trade union movement to adhere to in order to cope with the challenge of the new technology.

Undoubtedly, the most important policy recommendation of the report was that 'new technology agreements' (NTAs) should be negotiated wherever possible. A framework for these agreements, which was set out as a 'checklist for negotiators' formed the last chapter of the report. The 10-point checklist is set out below:

1. Objective of 'change by agreement': no new technology to be introduced unilaterally; status quo provisions recommended.
2. Challenge to union organization: inter-union collaboration in negotiations; build up of technical expertise by unions; technology stewards.
3. Access to information: all relevant information to be provided to union representatives before decisions taken; linked to regular consultations on company plans.
4. Employment and output plans: preferably no redundancy agreements, or improved redundancy payments if impossible; planned approach to redeployment and relocation of workers; purpose commitment to expanding output.

5. Retraining: provision of retraining, priority for those directly affected by new technology; principle or maintained or improved earnings during retraining.

6. Working hours; scope for reducing working hours and systematic overtime.

7. Pay structures: avoid disruption to pay structures and polarization of workforce; ensure income levels maintained and improved; move towards single status and equal conditions.

8. Control over work: union influence over systems design and programming; no computer-gathered information to be used in work performance measurement.

9. Health and safety: stringent standards for new machinery and processes, including visual display units (VDUs).

10. Review procedure: joint union/management study teams to monitor developments and review progress.

Given the more hostile economic and political climate at the end of the 1970s, it was not surprising that the British trade union movement should adopt a response to the new technology which could be characterized as adaptive and retrospective, very much in line with past responses to earlier technological innovation. Thus, given the *raison d'être* of British trade unions as being primarily concerned with collective bargaining both as a means of maintaining and improving the terms and conditions of employment of their members and of limiting managerial prerogative, the approach was essentially defensive, concentrating on job losses, pay and working conditions. The fundamental questions about the wider societal impact of the new technology was largely subsumed under a broad acceptance of technological inevitability. This response can perhaps best be summarized by the introductory paragraphs of the report:

> 'Technological change and the microelectronic revolution are a challenge, but also an opportunity. There is the challenge that the rapid introduction of new processes and work organization will lead to the loss of many more jobs and growing social dislocation. Equally, however, there is the realization that new technologies also offer great opportunities – not just for increasing the competitiveness of British industry but for increasing the quality of working life and for providing new benefits to working people.'[25]

Significantly, the TUC failed in its attempts to secure an understanding with the employers' organization, the CBI. The decision to attempt to negotiate such an understanding was taken at the January 1980 meeting of the National Economic Development Council (NEDC). The meeting considered the TUC's 'Employment and Technology' document and the CBI's 'Jobs: Facing the Future', and it was felt that there was some common ground. The TUC had a lot more to gain from such an understanding than did the CBI. The recession was biting hard, and the employers had considerably more bargaining power as unemployment continued to rise. An umbrella code of practice, setting agreed standards and guaranteeing consultation, would clearly set a valuable precedent for company plant agreements. The TUC also hoped that after striking an accord with the CBI on new technology, it could then proceed to broader areas of agreement on matters such as trade and investment, pricing and even incomes. However, the CBI, after the discussions had reached an advanced stage, decided that it was not prepared to be used as a pawn in the TUC's anti-government stance. While both sides could agree on relatively modest measures such as the need for more effective manpower planning and training, the provision of information, extra payments for extra skills and consultations on health and safety, the bulk of the CBI membership felt that a national agreement on technology would be a nuisance, and not something necessary to concede.

The TUC philosophy also encountered criticism from several radical commentators. For example, Mike Cooley, an AUEW-TASS past-president and the main author of the Lucas Aerospace combine committee's alternative corporate plan, argued that the TUC had implicitly assumed that technology was neutral, whereas in fact it was not.[26] This criticism was also made by Manwaring, who argued that:

> 'The technology is not socially neutral, but embodies, and is developed within, antagonistic relations of production . . . the silicon dream is of increased leisure and higher material standards of living brought about by shop-floor bargaining over the introduction of new technology and sympathetic government action . . . however, the critique above suggests that the dream is more likely to become a nightmare.'[27]

Whatever one's view about the neutrality or otherwise of the new technology, there were a number of contradictions in the TUC approach. First, while the TUC (and nearly all its affiliated unions) saw the shorter working week as a universal palliative to cope with the impact of new technology, this belief has to be reconciled with the fact that employers have maintained a hostile stance to any major reduction in the length of the working week. Moreover, it is debatable (and doubtful) whether labour markets work in such a way to ensure that a reduction in the length of the standard working week necessarily saves jobs. As we will see later in this chapter, the British trade unions have singularly failed to achieve such reductions in the new technology agreements that have been negotiated so far.

Second, the 'social democratic' or 'Keynesian' philosophy which underlaid the commitment of the TUC to relying on future economic growth as a means of facilitating the introduction of the new technology must be set against the subsequent reality of the continuing recession, the long-term decline of the British economy, the demise of Keynesian demand management policies on the part of government, and the absence of any coherent planning mechanism to usher in the new technology with the minimum of economic and social disruption. In addition, while new technology certainly enables British industry to increase productivity, it should be remembered that it also gives similar opportunities to foreign competitors.

The organization of the British trade union movement itself, with its complex structure of overlapping and interlinking forms of organization cutting across occupations, skills and industrial boundaries does not lend itself readily to coping with microelectronic technology. The standard pattern of multi-unionism at plant level means that it is difficult to achieve a common approach to a technology which blurs occupational and skill boundaries at the workplace.

Given the enormous effort put in to formulating a coherent policy by the TUC for British trade unions, how do the new technology agreements that had been negotiated so far compare with the 'model' agreements suggested by the TUC? In an early survey of new technology agreements carried out by Manwaring[28] based on information reported in issues of *Industrial Relations Review and Report*, a number of agreements which had been negotiated by trade unions in 1979 and 1980 were analysed. According to Manwaring:

> 'The most striking feature of these agreements is that unions have not secured a reduction in working hours. In fact, none of those presented have seen hours cut . . . Similarly, though unions have often – though not always – secured agreements that there will be no reduction in earnings and no downgrading for those offered redeployment, they have seldom secured an increase in earnings for those operating new technology . . . In short, new technology does not guarantee increased earnings and there remains much which must be bargained for.'

While there was evidence in this study that the unions had been able to achieve agreements ensuring no compulsory redundancies, such guarantees merely protect the job security of the job holder but do not preserve the job position. There was some evidence that certain unions had secured agreement on the following: that computer systems would not be used to monitor work performance; that there would be no subcontracting of work; that there would be no unilateral introduction of shift work; that work would not be deskilled; that there would be training and attendance payments for training courses; that there would be a union membership agreement (closed shop). However, these achievements won by the unions tended to be the exception rather than the rule, and as Manwaring states:

> 'It would, therefore, not be an over-exaggeration to conclude that unions have been largely unsuccessful in securing a share of the benefits of new technology: the rhetoric of model agreements has not, in general, been translated into negotiated concessions in clauses of actual new technology agreements.'

A much more comprehensive analysis of 100 NTAs, many of which were signed in 1981, was carried out by Williams and Moseley of the Technology Policy Unit at the University of Aston.[29] The authors defined NTAs as: 'formal agreements which directly and explicitly attempt to exert trade union control and influence over the process of technological change and its effect on work and conditions of employment with new technology'.

An important finding from this study was that over 90 per cent of the agreements that were signed were exclusively concerned with white-collar workers. Moreover, 75 per cent of the agreements had only one union signatory to them, despite the fact that new production and administration systems frequently embrace a wide range of occupations in the workplace. This finding is particularly significant because trade union studies which were carried out in British Leyland (Cowley) by the Trade Union Research Unit at Ruskin College, Oxford and studies produced by the 'Coventry Workshop' of GEC Telecommunication and Alfred Herbert in Coventry, highlighted the detrimental effect that new technology had on trade union organization in the workplace.[30] In particular, the researchers in the Coventry studies concluded that collective bargaining was not an effective mechanism for negotiating technical change. Problems are found in union organization, the overloaded agenda of wage negotiations, and in the lack of information disclosure and trade union training.

In addition, the Coventry trade union study showed that the differences between groups of employees (skilled and unskilled, technicians, designers, foremen, computer specialists, clerical workers, management) were considerably sharpened. All of these groups perceived the threat of new technology differently, and since each group was represented by a different union, inter-union relations were soured as a result. It does seem, therefore, that even when trade unions in Britain do manage to persuade management to negotiate a new technology agreement, it is difficult for them to bury their inter-union and inter-occupational differences.

A later study of new technology agreements was carried out by Robin Williams and Fred Steward of the University of Aston.[31] This survey involved a review of 240 new technology agreements from 1977 to 1983 and produced as equally unfavourable an assessment as the earlier Williams/Moseley study of the progress of TUC-affiliated unions in meeting the objectives originally set out in 'Employment and Technology' in 1979.

One important feature of NTAs that is of considerable value to trade unions (if they are able to achieve it) is a provision which allows them to influence technological change by being involved in management's proposals from a very early stage. Trade unions have much more to gain from taking the initiative with new technology, and hence shaping it from the start, than in reacting at a late stage to plans presented to them which have already been formulated by management. The earlier Williams and Steward study examined the content of the agreements and classified them according to a range of procedures which employers undertook to follow with the unions if they wished to introduce such technological change. Overall, the authors found that 'mutuality' was an exceptional achievement, although a majority of agreements stipulated that consultations would take place before change occurred.

In terms of access to information on technological change, it was found that on a number of specific topics (type of equipment, proposed siting and timing, extension of equipment, work methods, work flow, manning, skills, training, remuneration, effects on careers, job satisfaction, health hazards, and costings), over one-third of all NTAs contained no clauses at all relating to the provision of information.

One of the objectives that the TUC were seeking to achieve in the checklist for negotiators which was published in its 'Employment and Technology' policy document was to encourage unions to ensure that income levels were maintained and improved, and that increases should be shared out among the whole workforce to avoid a polarization between a highly skilled, highly paid élite and an unskilled, low paid workforce. Only 13 of the agreements examined explicitly linked the introduction of new technology to shorter hours and higher pay. The researchers concluded that the TUC argument that 'the case for accepting technological changes rests largely on a fair distribution of the consequent benefits' was far from being achieved. In almost all the cases where pay was increased for accepting new technology, such increases were confined to new technology operators themselves rather than being distributed throughout the workforce as a whole. This may, of course, have been no more than a reflection of the drastic decrease in trade union bargaining power as a result of the recession.

Given the widespread predictions of technologically induced job loss, what did the agreements specify on questions of manning levels and grading? Only a small number of agreements included specific commitments to at least maintain the current levels of manning (4 per cent) and grading (10 per cent), and the most common approach was one of protecting existing job holders at the expense of people not employed in the establishments. Thus, 36 per cent of agreements dealt with manning reductions by natural wastage, with a further 14 per cent allowing for voluntary redundancies as well. Thirty-nine per cent of agreements stipulated that an individual's wages/grading would be maintained, even though the job might be downgraded (ie replacement labour would be at a lower grade). Twelve per cent of the agreements even set up mechanisms which allowed downgrading of individuals (typically after a fixed period of time had elapsed or following consultation on, for example, redeployment).

More ominously, Williams and Moseley had noticed a distinct tailing off of NTAs in the 12-month period of their study and there was much evidence to suggest that most technological change was being introduced unilaterally by management without any kind of agreement at all. Even where an NTA is in operation in an establishment, if it is not adequately monitored it can be used as a facilitative device by management, thus removing the need for any renegotiation when new technological systems are introduced.

The 1984 Workplace Industrial Relations Survey,[32] a major survey of over 2,000 establishments in Britain which was carried out by the Department of Employment/Economic and Social Research Council/ Policy Studies Institute and ACAS, adopted the introduction of change, and particularly change involving new technology, as the main substantive subject. Contrary to the conventional wisdom, the survey results showed that there was little worker or trade union resistance to the introduction of new technology into the workplace. As the survey emphasized:[33]

> 'From these reports it was clear that the general reaction was support for change, and often enthusiastic support. This was the case on the shop floor as well as in the office. Indeed, the picture we found suggested that commentators should replace their stock phrases with references to worker support for change and trade union support for change when talking about worker and union reactions to technical change.'

In contrast, where the introduction of new technology into the workplace involved major organizational changes there was a great deal of hostility and resistance by both trade unions and workers.

In sum, the new technology agreements that have been so far signed in Britain have been modest, and largely limited to the white-collar sector. There seems to have been a great deal of resistance by employers, both individually and collectively, to such agreements, and all the evidence points to redundancies being created in many instances where new systems are introduced. It appears that the recession, high unemployment and a government committed to reductions in public spending and set against any kind of planning for industrial and economic expansion have all combined to limit severely the ability of trade unions to influence the direction and form of the technology by means of new technology agreements. Indeed, NTAs are now less common than they once were in the immediate post-1979 period, and where they do exist some of them are seen by management as facilitative devices which give them a *carte blanche* to introduce whatever new technological systems they may wish in the future. Given the most recent results of the DE/ESRC/PSI/ACAS Workplace Industrial Relations Survey, it is arguable that we should turn our attention away from new technology agreements and concentrate instead on the new forms of work organization that accompany technological change.

Conclusion

It is clear that new technology will provide one of the biggest challenges to trade unions throughout the 1980s and beyond. It has been introduced at a time when union membership is falling rapidly and unemployment throughout the western economies remains at historically high levels. It is no longer possible to rely on high rates of economic growth in the economy as a means of providing alternative job opportunities in an expanding service sector. Information technology increasingly cuts across occupational boundaries and fundamentally alters skill patterns within the labour force. In such circumstances, the very heart of trade union organization at enterprise level is threatened.

So far, the early experience of workers in Britain and throughout Western Europe confronted with rapid technological change has been uneven. Some workers have only experienced a small amount of technological change, which has been absorbed in working practices with little dislocation. The heartlands of manufacturing industry have been most affected, with thousands of jobs disappearing in the latter part of the 1970s and early 1980s, due either to radical shifts in markets or from rationalization brought about by a much more hostile competitive environment, in which technological change has featured prominently. While the 'quality of working life' movement of the early 1970s offered the prospect of a move away from 'Taylorized' production lines, we now see fresh dangers that employers will seize upon their renewed bargaining power to introduce greater forms of degradation in skills and working life generally, not only on the factory floor but also in the office.

Information technology is still in its embryonic stages, but it does seem that it emphasizes the need for new approaches from the trade unions if they are to survive as a viable force. With traditional technology, the issues for negotiation focused upon the physical equipment, machinery and materials involved in the production process. In order to deal with such technology the unions were familiar with a range of standards, codes and regulations which could be used whether they were to be found in collective agreements or in legislation. With information technology, the effects upon working conditions, skills and work organization depend much more on systems design rather than on the physical hardware *per se*, and trade unions may well find that procedures and bargaining strategies which were adequate in the past are no longer as effective.

Whether the trade unions rely on the negotiation of new technology agreements or on the establishment of legislative standards, these can only be seen as the first steps in the process of seeking to regulate the new technology at company and workplace level. The crucial question is to what extent such 'codes of best practice' can be implemented in practice. Scandinavian research has suggested that the effectiveness of the new technology and the system of work organization that results from its introduction depends on a number of factors: their power base; their awareness of their potential for influencing changes; the development of workgroup knowledge of the effects of the technology; the access to outside expertise; and the commitment of the trade union organization to pursuing its objectives over a sustained period of time. In contrast, much union activity in the Scandinavian countries has been concerned with the representation of the trade union in company project groups, the creation of support groups within the union, with the necessary educational backup and the establishment of a procedure for transferring problems to a higher level.[34] Such methods would be particularly effective in dealing with the organizational changes in the workplace that can accompany the introduction of new technology, a major problem identified by the 1984 DE/ESRC/PSI/ACAS Workplace Industrial Relations Survey mentioned earlier.

Managerial employment policies are also likely to undergo fundamental change in the future. While it can be said that the new technology itself is not acting in a deterministic manner in shaping company employment strategies, the increasing importance of issues of 'flexibility' in the management of labour will be reflected in the personnel and industrial relations management function. For example, the personnel manager in the flexible firm will be expected to deal with the contradictions and ambiguities that will be inherent in his or her role, such as resolving the conflicting managerial needs for control and certainty with implications for centralization, employee redundancy, deskilling and alienation) with the organizational needs of employee commitment, understanding and initiative (with implications for participation, cooperation and decentralization).[35] As Sheila Rothwell pointed out:

'New technology may indicate these problems: it will not resolve them; but lack of attention may create intolerable levels of organizational stress and conflict and, ultimately, costs which may prove unacceptable to organizations, their employees and the wider society.'[36]

References
1. Lamborghini B in Friedrichs G and Schaff A (eds) *Microelectronics and Society: for better or for worse* (1982) A Report to the Club of Rome, Pergamon
2. Freeman C 'Keynes or Kondratiev? How can we get back to full employment?' in Marstrand P (ed) *New Technology and the Future of Work and Skills* (1983) Frances Pinter, London
3. Gershuny J and Miles I *The New Service Economy: the Transformation of Employment in Industrial Societies* (1983) Oxford University Press, Oxford
4. Sparrow P 'The erosion of employment in the UK; the need for a new response' *New Technology, Work and Employment* 1 2 (1986) pp 101–112
5. Robinson O and Wallace J 'Growth and utilisation of part-time labour in Great Britain' *Employment Gazette* (1984) pp 391–7
6. Meager N 'Temporary work in Great Britain' MSC Labour Market Quarterly Report (November 1985)
7. Sparrow P op cit
8. Francis A 'The social effects of CAE in Britain' *Electronics and Power* (January 1983)
9. Brown W A 'The changing role of trade unions in the management of labour' *British Journal of Industrial Relations* (July 1986)
10. Sparrow P op cit

11. Institute of Manpower Studies report *Services – The Second Industrial Revolution?* by Amin Rajan, a report by the IMS to the Occupational Services Group, Butterworths (February 1987)
12. Brown W, op cit
13. Francis A, op cit
14. Handy C *The Future of Work* (1984) Basil Blackwell, Oxford and New York, p 80
15. Brown W 'Britain's Unions: new pressures and shifting loyalties' *Personnel Management* (October 1983); for a useful outline of Japanese employment practices see Littler C R and Salaman G *Class at Work* (1984) Batsford, London; Littler C R *The Development of the Labour Process in Capitalist Societies* (1982) Heinemann Educational Books, London; Dore R P *British Factory – Japanese Factory* (1973) London, George Allen and Unwin
16. For a very readable account of the trend towards 'Japanization' in a major British company see Turnbull P 'The Japanisation of British industrial relations at Lucas' *Industrial Relations Journal* **17** 3 (Autumn 1986)
17. Brown W, *ibid*
18. Lloyd J 'Wages: The Battle for a Flexible Future' *Financial Times* (April 4 1984)
19. TUC *Automation and Technical Change* (1970) p 10
20. For a detailed analysis of the 1978 dispute at Times Newspapers see Routledge P 'The Dispute at Times Newspapers Ltd: a view from the inside' *Industrial Relations Journal* **10** 4, Winter 1979/80
21. *Employment and Technology* TUC Interim Report, April 1979
22. *Employment and Technology* (September 1979) Report by the TUC General Council to the 1979 Congress
23. Benson I and Lloyd J *New Technology and Industrial Change* (1983) Kogan Page, London, p 171
24. *Employment and Technology* op cit, p 9
25. *Employment and Technology* op cit, para 1
26. Cooley M *Architect or Bee?* (1980) Langley Technical Services
27. Manwaring T 'The Trade Union Response to New Technology' *Industrial Relations Journal* (1981)
28. Manwaring T, *ibid*
29. Williams R and Moseley R 'Technology Agreements: Consensus, Control and Technical Change in the Workplace' Paper presented to the EEC/FAST Conference on *The Transition to an Information Society* (1982) Selsdon Park
30. Reported in Changement Social et Technologie en Europe *Bulletin D'Information* No 8 (July–August 1982) Pool Européen d'Etudes, Brussels
31. Williams R and Steward F 'Technology agreements in Great Britain: a survey 1977–83' *Industrial Relations Journal* **16** 3 (Autumn 1985) pp 58–73
32. Daniel W W (ed) *Workplace Industrial Relations and Technical Change* (1987) Frances Pinter in association with the Policy Studies Institute, London
33. *Ibid* p 264
34. Gill C *Work, Unemployment and the New Technology* (1985) Polity, Oxford, ch 6
35. Basil D C and Cook C W *The Management of Change* (1974) McGraw Hill
36. Rothwell S 'Company Employment Policies and New Technology' *Industrial Relations Journal* **16** 3 (Autumn 1985)

Part Two
The Practice of
Industrial Relations

Chapter 4

Managing Industrial Relations

Chris Brewster

During the last decade it has come to be accepted as axiomatic that management plays a key role in industrial relations. It was hardly challenged in the 1960s and 70s that industrial relations was 'about' trade unions; in industry, managers saw their job as coping with the situation in which the unions put them. To caricature the position, most managers saw industrial relations as like the weather: something they could bemoan, but do little to influence. In the academic world the subject of management was simply disregarded as an area of study for industrial relations specialists.

Things have changed. Developments in industry and commerce have led to a manifest weakening in the influence of the unions. This has been paralleled by an upsurge of academic discussion of the role of management in industrial relations. The combination of these factors has led to a clarification of the fundamental importance of the process and policies of management, and an emphasis on the capacity which managements have to plan and influence industrial relations.

Managers, of course, are an extremely varied and heterogeneous group. The term covers individuals who may be very different in terms of function, status, age, income, philosophy – and capability. In industrial relations, too, managers perform very different roles. There are a few managers whose primary concern is with industrial relations, but many have industrial relations as only a small part of a complex of responsibilities. On the narrowest definitions of industrial relations, those involving managerial relationships with trade unions, only a very limited amount of managerial time and resources is committed to the subject. Even on wider definitions, which involve managerial relationships with employees, whether formal or informal, group or individual, there are few managers who devote more than a minority of their time to the issue.

It is arguable, of course, that on the widest definition almost anything that a manager does has some effect on the other, non-managerial, employees. Such an argument is valid in its own terms, but the danger of so comprehensive a definition is that it conglomerates industrial relations with many other subjects and makes it of little analytical value. The occasions on which managers deal consciously with issues concerning their employees are fewer than the pundits sometimes like to admit.

The importance of industrial relations in the managerial consciousness is both less and greater than is usually understood. Again, the issue is definitional. The obvious occasions – annual wage negotiations, disciplinary or grievance hearings, bargaining over rosters, meetings with shop stewards – are distinct and comparatively isolated incidents within a complicated managerial workload. In this respect the importance of the subject can be exaggerated.

Yet if it can be exaggerated, it is also easy to underestimate the importance of industrial relations to an organization's management. For most organizations, even those in high technology areas, the major operating costs are those associated with their human resources. Financial success or failure, even survival or non-survival, can be determined by such issues as half a per cent on wage costs, a lack of commitment on the part of employees, the need to spend extra money on recruitment, or the difference between a cost-effective shift roster and an expensive one. In times of economic crisis it is not surprising that the first area that management examine with the objective of cutting costs is the workforce – hence the wave of redundancies in the early 1980s (493,700 in 1980, 532,000 in 1981, 400,400 in 1982). This is a message that has not been lost on British managements. Employees are the largest operating cost, the most important resource, and the one that above all requires greater attention and increasingly cost-effective management.

This chapter reflects the growing power of management and increasing interest in management's role in industrial relations. It examines changing managerial styles and identifies elements of a new approach to industrial relations. Finally, it attempts to look into the future to determine the probability of a continuation of the trends identified.

Changing Styles

British managements are in a situation markedly different from that of a decade or so ago. From their point of view there are new pressures which impinge on their approach to industrial relations: increased competition (particularly internationally and with the prospect of the single European market in 1992 approaching); a free-market oriented government and increased pressure on employment costs. At the same time, other changes have increased opportunities for managements to organize industrial relations as they desire: a high level of unemployment; an increasing segmentation of the labour market; reduced trade union power and influence and reduced legal constraints. Inevitably these pressures and opportunities will operate differently in different sectors of the economy: increased international competition will be more central for sectors of manufacturing; government action will have a greater impact on teachers, and so on. Overall, however, most managers in Britain in most sectors of employment are faced with greater pressure for the cost-effective use of human resources and greater opportunities to achieve it.

In many organizations the US term 'human resources' is being taken up. Its connotations of dealing with employees as just another factor in the input-output equation, to be managed as efficiently and tightly as any other resource, captures the essence of a new managerial approach.

This new approach may not yet be widespread; it is perhaps the case that changes of this kind take many years to work through, and will develop at different speeds in different industries and in different companies within industries. There can be little doubt about the trend, however, and it does not seem inappropriate here to concentrate upon those organizations where managers have been among the earliest to accept the new approach.

The essence of this change lies in the objectives personnel and industrial relations specialists among managements are pursuing. Prior to 1980 these were concerned with *social awareness*: responsibility for the workforce and even responsibility to society at large. Forward-looking specialists in industrial relations judged themselves, and were judged by others, on their ability to maintain good relationships with their trade unions. They sought and achieved the increases in formality recommended by the Donovan Commission: written-down recognition arrangements, established procedures and formally-minuted substantive agreements. They aimed for an image in the community at large as a caring and concerned employer. Above all, they tried to avoid industrial disputes.

With such criteria, the personnel and industrial relations specialists adopted a role within the management team akin to that of a 'loyal opposition': ever ready to criticize, ever keen to put the point of view of trade unions or employees before those groups heard of anything threatening or worrying.

From the watershed of the turn of the decade more and more managements were first of all forced, and then chose, to define different objectives for themselves in their relationship to employees. They began to develop criteria of cost control, of flexibility and amenability from their employees and of the most productive use of the workforce. The touchstone became *cost-effectiveness*: the cost-effective use of the human resource.[1]

Many specialists found this a difficult change to make. The Institute of Personnel Management still attempts to develop a 'professional' approach, based largely on the old criteria, whereby a professional specialist can, like the older legal, accountancy or medical professions argue that they have different standards, above those of the organization for which they are currently working.

Other specialists have, however, embraced the cost-effective approach enthusiastically. They argue that their department must aim to contribute to the efficient and successful running of the organization in the same way as any other department. Indeed, because the workforce is in most cases the major operating cost, because it is where the major benefits of productivity, innovation and service are found, and because poor industrial relations can ruin all other policies while organizations with good industrial relations can often overcome deficiencies elsewhere – for all these reasons it is argued that cost-effective industrial relations can be the key to organizational survival and success.

The specialists who argue this way are not crudely discarding previous policies. The different objectives may lead to similar policies. Socially aware policies would include opposition to racial and sexual discrimination, since these are unlawful and socially repugnant; the provision of company training and development would give employees the chance to make a contribution and better themselves; providing good facilities for senior shop stewards would improve the relationship with the union.

Cost-effectiveness might involve the same policies, but with a different rationale. Thus, discrimination would be opposed because it limits managerial ability to obtain the maximum output from all employees equally; company training and development makes employees more efficient and makes their skills less transferable to other organizations; and good facilities for senior stewards make it easier to keep the full-time officials out of the workplace.

In some areas the rationale will run against old policies. Three of these in particular will be considered below. Here, a management pursuing cost-effective policies would be prepared to risk the relationship with the unions, operate increasingly through informal agreements, subordinate its image in the community and even face up to industrial action (and take steps to win it) in order to achieve the goals of control, flexibility and productivity.

To some extent, of course, this section on managerial objectives presents a caricature. The earlier objectives were never so dismissive of the overall corporate requirements, nor are current objectives so singularly hard-nosed and uncaring. Like most caricatures, however, it is based fundamentally on reality; and like most it pinpoints some important and perhaps less than universally welcomed features. While there are indeed many managers, especially perhaps among the personnel and industrial relations specialists, who find the cost-effective strategy distasteful, its elements are accepted by many managers and exist in many organizations now. Whether or not the future lies, as these managers would argue, with those who can take advantage of this new approach to industrial relations, it is clearly important to understand it.

Cost-effective Industrial Relations: the elements

The main elements of this approach are labour flexibility, individualism and localization, and the management of trade union relationships.

None of these elements is entirely new and it is probably true that nearly all organizations are making changes in at least some of these areas. What marks this out as a new approach by management is the way in which organizations at the forefront of this development have welded these elements into a conscious and coherent strategy for all aspects of their management of employees. Such a strategy inevitably overlaps with many of the issues covered in later chapters of this book, and with other subjects often defined as being outside industrial relations – manpower planning, recruitment, development and training, even into marketing, production technology or finance. Practising managers will not need this book to know that problems come to them as issues, with all these ramifications; not in neat academic packages where solutions have no implications in other areas. Those managements who are developing a strategic view of industrial relations are building on these overlaps, rather than ignoring them.

Labour flexibility

There is clear evidence from a number of surveys and case studies that there have been extensive and widespread changes in working practices in Britain in the 1980s. Much of this evidence is from the beleagured manufacturing sector. The sort of changes most frequently made have been concerned with such issues as the introduction of new technology or increased efficiency with existing equipment, more flexible working practices, and flexibility in working times. The overwhelming majority of these working practice changes have been introduced without the conclusion of new technology agreements or indeed any other agreement. Managements have, quite simply, just reorganized the work.[2]

The most common reason for introducing increased flexibility of working practices is greater cost-effectiveness. In particular, this increased flexibility gives a more effective use of existing equipment and constantly updated technology. In most cases the unions have accepted readily the need for increased task flexibility.

A clear example can be seen in the Hitachi experience. In March 1984, when Hitachi bought out the GEC share of their joint venture and formed Hitachi Consumer Products (UK), the personnel function was charged with introducing job flexibility and establishing an environment where industrial action was unlikely to be taken. The principle behind job flexibility was that employees should be contracted to perform any duties within their capability when instructed to do so. Hitachi introduced single-status conditions, believing that this would facilitate job flexibility and remove the tension caused by the differentials between blue- and white-collar workers. Reviewing the first two years of operation of the Hitachi/EETPU agreement, the company's personnel executive argued that several of the indicators of the level of success could be attributed to the increased flexibility of working practices: operator efficiencies increased by 30 per cent and factory utilization by 20 per cent; there was a marked improvement in productivity; overheads were reduced dramatically and financial performance improved.[3]

While the organization and performance of many areas of work have been subject to substantial changes, the concept of *work time* has remained remarkably unchanged until very recently. However, things have changed very rapidly and there is now an enormous variety of working time arrangements being developed. The following examples could be multiplied.

Part-time work in Great Britain has expanded considerably in the 1980s. By the middle of the decade one-fifth of all people in work, over five million people, were in part-time employment. Britain has a higher proportion of part-time workers in its workforce than most other European countries.* Of this part-time labour force the vast majority are women, who often combine work with domestic and family responsibilities. From the management point of view, the use of part-time workers enables specific peak demands to be met without incurring the costs of full-time staff whose services may not be required for a full week. It also has the added advantage for managers of committing them only to limited legal rights for the employee.

Shift working has been a common feature for many manual employees over many years. It is now spreading to non-manual employees and to service industries. Furthermore, companies are moving towards matching their hours of work to suit their productive needs. This is resulting in an ever increasing variety of shift arrangements; there is hardly any longer a normal or standard pattern. Shifts may be anything from four to 12 hours in length and almost any pattern of days may be used, from employees who change each day to those who work on a fortnightly pattern. Other variations include changes in the length of the working week: four-and-a-half-day weeks (dropping Friday afternoon) or four-day weeks (not using Friday at all but working longer days the rest of the week) are now far from rare.

Variable working patterns other than shift arrangements are also widespread. Flexitime arrangements, where employees can vary their daily hours of work, largely at their own discretion, provided that the long-term required hours are completed, is now common in many offices. Annual hours arrangements, where hours are varied by management to suit business needs subject to an overall yearly total, are novel and so far not common, although they are being considered by a wide range of companies.[4]

'Standard' working hours are still the norm for many employees but fewer than half of those in employment now work a straightforward nine-to-five day. Increasingly, managements are devising working patterns

* Brewster C J and Teague P *European Community Social Policy: It's Impact on the UK* (1989) Institute of Personnel Management, p 247.

which reflect the needs of the business, such as those of production or sales cycles, the longer opening hours of shops or pubs, the need to contact organizations in other countries and other time zones. Flexible working time arrangements will continue to increase.

The third key area of flexibility concerns contractual arrangements. Many companies are now moving away from an automatic assumption that all work will be done by full-time employees on indefinite contracts. Three types of labour force have been identified: a core group, a secondary labour market and a peripheral labour market.[5] Those employed in the core group perform essential tasks which are specific to that firm and they are likely to be assured of a full-time permanent career. Those in the secondary labour market include part-timers, job-sharers and those on short-term contracts employed subject to the fluctuations in the market demand experienced by the firm. They cannot rely upon the security of permanent jobs, have no career structure and limited training and development. At the periphery is a labour market consisting of self-employed workers, agency temporaries and others who can be called on to perform specific tasks for a specific time period and who have no commitment for any length of time to that one firm. It is argued that the central employment distinction is not now between manual and staff status but rather between core and non-core workers. By the mid-1980s almost half of all establishments employed non-core workers.[6]

Managements make use of temporary workers, job-sharers, youth trainees and semi-retired people. Other options are homeworking, net-working, minimum-maximum contracts and first-call contracts. Many organizations are subcontracting whole areas of work to other organizations or to self-employed workers. Some companies are making use of the many individuals operating in the black economy.

The many variations in these forms of 'casualized' employment have all grown rapidly in recent years. It remains to be seen how far the use of these contractual forms will be developed or maintained. From the managerial viewpoint peripheral employment contracts provide opportunities to develop a dynamic, flexible workforce structured in ways that management deems appropriate, and responsive to short-term restructuring. It is difficult to see much decline in their use in the next few years.

Individualism and localization

Prior to the 1980s it would have seemed idiosyncratic to write so much about managerial policies in industrial relations with so little mention of trade unions. That it is relevant to do so now reflects another key element of cost-effective strategies: managerial attempts to individualize and localize industrial relations. The rationale for such policies is to avoid the errors of the past. It is generally accepted, not least by union officials, that within a workplace it is managerial action that has the major impact in creating collective thinking, trade unionism and effective opposition to management. Many managers also believe that significant problems have arisen from the involvement in industrial relations of those outside the workplace or the organization. It is as a direct reaction to these two views that managements are seeking to individualize and localize industrial relations.

New technology aids this approach in two respects. First, most forms of new technology enable work to be carried out in a quiet environment, with smaller units and fewer people in the immediate vicinity, and in ways that challenge existing working arrangements and require greater flexibility. They thus provide the conditions for breaking down traditional collective approaches and the development of more individual ones. Second, some of the new technology enables more direct communication between manager and subordinate – messages on VDU screens, instant copying, video tapes, for example.

Apart from the new technology, managements are exercising deliberate choice to develop relationships with individuals rather than groups. For example, communications channels other than collective bargaining and formal, indirect consultation committees are proliferating. It is particularly the direct, face-to-face mechanisms that are becoming increasingly fashionable. One popular new approach has been dubbed MBWA (to distinguish it from the widely accepted, cold, scientific MBO, management by objectives). MBWA stands for management by wandering about (ie 'visible' management). This is, of course, what managers in small organizations have always done but it has now been rediscovered as a 'new' management fad. Alongside such simple prescriptions there has been a growth in other forms of direct communication (see Chapter 9).

The new working arrangements, varied working hours and more casualized forms of employment contract also act to fragment the workforce. Together with individually tailored training and development programmes, career planning and promotion policies, and new pay systems utilizing merit pay, share options and performance linkages (discussed in Chapter 11), they act to differentiate between employees. Increasingly, each individual has less in common with the other people employed at the same workplace. Each of these policies has an intrinsic logic of its own, but for managements the increased segmentation of the workforce that each provides is more than just a bonus: it is a calculated strategic benefit.

Besides individualization, a key objective for management is localization. It may be the establishment, the site or shop, or the company which is taken as the local unit. That decision will not be taken on industrial relations criteria. More important will be business decisions about the location of cost or profit centres or accountability arrangements. With labour such a substantial proportion of most organizations' costs, it makes little sense to leave the locus of decisions in that area somewhere else.

One consequence has been a series of moves to disentangle industrial relations from external links. Thus employers' associations, whose membership has held up longer than trade unions, have now begun to lose members and money at an alarming rate. Managers see less reason to link the terms and conditions of their workplace to some industry average, and little reason to look elsewhere for help in dealing with their employees. Again, this development should not be exaggerated since employers' associations continue to provide many useful services and are still important. Their industrial relations services, however, are now being dispensed with by many organizations and their role in this respect is under considerable pressure.

External links are also being reduced by concentrating on internal comparisons in pay and rewards. Managers seek to relate pay increases to the success or failure of the enterprise, rather than to comparisons with other companies, or even inflation rates. Moves to extend profit-related pay and to provide internal share ownership have been encouraged by the Conservative government and have had a considerable impact. Such schemes can only work, by definition, at the company level.

The wider forms of communication discussed earlier are also noticeably concentrated at the local company level. Managers in most organizations, certainly in the private sector, have shown a marked reluctance to get involved in consultation or involvement schemes which include discussion of national-level or corporate policy issues, investment and disinvestment decisions and the like. This stands in direct contrast to the upsurge in popularity of forums for discussing local-level, work-related issues.

Managing trade unions

There is a limit to the processes of individualization and localization. For the foreseeable future most managers will have to deal with trade unions. Analysing the management of trade union relationships is a difficult task. At the very least there are a number of potential strategies available, and no evidence that any one is more closely correlated with the overall efficiency and success of the enterprise than any other.

Managerial support for trade unions remains widespread in the UK. There is evidence, though, that in the 1980s managers choose to deal with a non-union workforce if they can. Most new businesses set up in new towns are non-union.[7] On greenfield sites managements have preferred not to recognize a union or to recognize a single union for all employees. Among other implications, such a policy aids flexibility, prevents intergroup rivalries from developing and focuses union attention on the success of the enterprise.

Commentators have identified two distinct managerial strategies in the non-union companies.[8] The first of these has been dubbed *traditionalist*: all-out forceful opposition to the unions, 'Grunwick-style'. The second has been given the title of *sophisticated paternalists*: non-union companies (mostly) who devote considerable resources to ensuring that their treatment of employees gives little ground for trade union complaint and spend considerable sums on promoting the company to its own employees. Marks and Spencer is the most famous British example, and the group includes US companies like IBM* and Kodak and some of the Japanese companies operating in the UK.

For most managers a non-union or single-union workplace is not feasible. They have little choice but to deal with a number of unions. Two distinct strategies have been identified here, too. The *sophisticated moderns* recognize trade unions but encourage extensive consultation procedures and practices. They, too, tend to have centralized arrangements and to encourage a commitment to the overall company. The *standard moderns* are decentralized and pragmatic, with different approaches adopted at different locations or at different times.

This analysis of strategy is helpful in distinguishing between such approaches. It was developed at a time when the trade unions were felt to be very strong. The distinctions may be becoming blurred. There are two key decisions to be made by managements in industrial relations: do we accept the trade unions and, if we do, how do we manage them? The two approaches to keeping the unions out are clear and are used by many successful organizations. Most managements however prefer to, or feel they have to, deal with unions, and with a multiplicity of them. In general, larger companies in the public and private sector are developing strategies which amount to an amalgam of the sophisticated and standard modern approaches. These involve an extensive and heavily resourced internal communications exercise, built around the concept of individualization, the encouragement of localization or decentralization on a pragmatic basis and the development of a planned, strategic approach to industrial relations.

Extensive communication is closely linked with the concentration on the individual but has several other important aspects. The main objectives of these approaches are to ensure the highest possible commitment from individual employees (by no means exclusively among core workers) and maximum utilization of employee skills.

Managements are not, in general, 'taking the unions on'. Rather, a more subtle process is taking place. Managements are changing the nature of their relationship with their unions. They are organizing complementary forms of communications channels alongside traditional collective bargaining arrangements. Many of these amount to a form of 'internal PR': public relations for the employees rather than the customers. Thus, many companies now regularly tell employees about new orders or contracts, new technological breakthroughs or current advertising campaigns. Some

---

* But note that trade unions, on an international level, are currently seeking to develop a coordinated strategy to organize IBM employees.

organizations have developed coherent 'mission statements' that they spend much time propounding to employees. In modern industry or commerce and in most areas of the public sector, it is employee commitment and enthusiasm that marks out the successful organization. Communications channels are being used as part of the attempt to generate such commitment.

At the same time managements are looking for genuine upward communication, as long as it is related to work and quality of production or service. Upward communication on policy issues is not encouraged. There is substantial evidence that employees can make a positive and valuable contribution in terms of ideas about efficiency and quality if they are encouraged to do so. Managers are increasingly looking at the variety of quality circles, stand-up groups,* work improvement schemes and other techniques to harness these ideas.

The effect of these developments is to downgrade the union functions. Straightforward head-on attacks on the unions generate employee commitment to their representative group and are often counter-productive. A more subtle process of providing far more channels and more opportunities for employees to make a contribution means that the union ceases to be the main channel and becomes one of many. The collective bargaining system is increasingly limited to straight 'pay and conditions' issues. Employees are encouraged to look elsewhere for means of dealing with management on all other issues.

Bargaining unit restrictions complement this approach. Managements have found that previous policies of divide and rule are outmoded. On pay and pay-related issues this succession of deals led either to a great waste of time, with each negotiation resulting in identical deals, or to a 'ratcheting' process, with each group winning a little bit more in specific areas. Not only did this put the various unions on their mettle to achieve the extra gain, it also encouraged distinctions and barriers between sections of the workforce and hence inhibited flexibility and any focus on the success of the enterprise.

Developments in the collective bargaining arena are covered in detail in Chapter 6. Here it suffices to note that as union strength, real or perceived, has decreased, and as managerial pressure for flexibility and adaptability has increased, so managers are developing policies built around the concept of single bargaining units. Managers are insisting that they will only meet with the unions as a single body; they are refusing to deal with each union in turn, and asking the unions to resolve any differences among themselves before any subject is brought to management. Such a strategy risks uniting the unions against management, but diminished union power has reduced

---

* A system of consultation developed in the USA – by companies such as Boeing – which operates on the principle that any employee, at any level, has the right to call on any other employee for a few minutes to discuss a problem. These encounters are held immediately and on site.

any threat here. The corresponding benefits for management are substantial.

First, the number of shop stewards or employee representatives can be, and is being, reduced: slowly and carefully, but surely. The single bargaining unit concept and the development of other forms of consultation at the immediate work level means, *prima facie*, a reduced need for shop stewards. At the same time managers are much more sanguine about the existence of full-time shop stewards operating across several union constituencies. This provides management with the second benefit: an opportunity to link all union activities, not with particular union policies but with the success of the enterprise. A third benefit arises from this: there is a much reduced role for the unions' full-time officials. With the unions represented by lay employee officials within the workplace acting together and working through a senior representative, the external influence of any one full-time official is minimized. The reduced power of the unions means that full-time officials' mediating role is required much less; their greater negotiating skill and their support for national-level union policies are seen as unwelcome or irrelevant by management. The senior shop steward will not want his own position undermined and may well be of a different union from the FTO and will want to exclude him or her. Hence the paradoxical position that managements feel they can influence the unions to a greater degree if they encourage a full-time shop steward.

A planned strategic approach to industrial relations is now being developed by ever larger numbers of organizations in the public and private sectors. This does not prevent them taking hard decisions or being rigorous about the cost-effective use of human resources. There is a realization that this has two necessary features: a low-cost, highly capable and well-deployed workforce on the one hand and a high degree of commitment and enthusiasm on the other.

Managerial strategies in industrial relations have as one objective ensuring that the right kind of people (not necessarily employees) are available only when needed and at the least possible cost. This may involve some contentious and tough-minded decisions. It may include redundancies, substantial pressure on employees and the forcing of unpleasant choices on trade unions. On their own, however, such tactics can only be successful over a short time for they breed resentment and create opposition.

Managers need more if they are to achieve their wider objectives. In the public sector they are under increasingly tight budget constraints and public scrutiny; in the private sector under ever more demanding competitive pressure. Technology is more complex, public contact and service requirements more widespread. Managerial success requires the commitment, enthusiasm and initiative of employees. Managers must, therefore, balance two facts: the pressure to manage human resources as efficiently as any other resources; and the fact that this particular resource is unique, it thinks and reacts. Hence the evidence, continually galling to a succession of government speakers in the 1980s, that managers, strong as they are in relation to the unions are still in general prepared to work with them and to negotiate wage increases well above inflation.

Perspectives

For the purpose of this chapter the cost-effective approach to industrial relations has been described in broad outline and with few caveats. It must be recognized, however, as an abstraction. While many managements have developed or adapted particular aspects of this approach, few have created a coherent, consistent and comprehensive set of policies. And, of course, there are many managements who pay very little attention to their employees.

Nevertheless, the elements identified here are significant. It is more likely that such approaches will be extended than that they will be reversed. The pressures that led to these developments and the opportunities that made them possible were identified at the beginning of this chapter and are, in the main, unlikely to change. There is much debate about whether Britain is developing a 'new industrial relations': less antagonistic, more consultative and cooperative. If there is a new industrial relations is it simply a temporary reaction to recession, or is it a major change? On one side the argument runs that nothing has changed the inherently conflictive nature of industrial relations, that union quiescence is determined by weakness, that major disputes among miners, teachers, telecommunications workers show that a change in the economy will re-establish old patterns.[9] On the other side it is argued that there are fewer strikes, declining union and employers' association memberships, increased consultation and cooperation: a new climate.[10]

The analysis proffered here suggests a third interpretation: that managements have learnt from the past and are developing new policies in industrial relations. These policies are being built carefully upon new working practices, new working patterns and new contractual arrangements. They recognize the antagonistic possibilities and the conflicts of interest which go alongside the conjunction of interest of management and employees. Rather than fight that battle head-on, however, they are utilizing a more subtle and complex strategy, using consultation and collective bargaining together with other channels and working carefully to reduce the importance of the trade union relationship.

The elements of this new approach, taken separately or together, raise many issues far beyond the scope of this book. However, it would be disingenuous not to note that this approach raises at least three wider questions. The first concerns the extent to which society at large can, through the medium of social security payments, employment support schemes and training schemes, support the costs of maintaining flexible workforces in employing organizations. The second question is about the overall effect on society and the economy of large numbers of people pressured to be, rather than choosing to be, in marginalized employment. The third area of debate is whether the analysis is accurate: is it cost-competitiveness that is the fundamental problem? How does this relate to the argument that it may be more important to develop the ability to switch product or service quickly in response to markets, ie 'flexible specialization'?

Whatever the answers to such questions, the fact remains that there are increasing numbers of managements devoting substantial attention to their human resources and developing planned strategies for dealing with their employees and the trade unions. Such policies and strategies have proven to be largely successful in helping managements to achieve predictability and control in industrial relations and, particularly in the manufacturing sector, to achieve remarkable increases in productivity. In the mid-1980s productivity grew faster in Britain than in almost any developed country competitor. Such facts stem from the policies identified in this chapter and are not forgotten easily. Changes of government or employment law will affect the speed of these developments but will not reverse them. Managements will remain the dominant players on the industrial relations stage over at least the next decade.

References
1. Brewster C J and Connock S L *Industrial Relations: Cost Effective Strategies* (1985) Hutchinson
2. Daniel W W *Workplace Industrial Relations and Technical Change* (1987) Frances Pinter
3. Pegge T 'Hitachi Two Years On' *Personnel Management* (October 1986) pp 42–7
4. Desmons G and Vidal-Hall T *Annual Hours* (1987) Industrial Society
5. Atkinson J 'Manpower Strategies for Flexible Organisations' *Personnel Management* (August 1984) pp 32–5. These analyses are not uncontroversial (see eg Pollert A) but the extension of casualization in employment is manifest.
6. Millward N and Stevens M *British Workplace Industrial Relations 1980–1984* (1986) Gower, p 208
7. Beaumont P B and Rennie I 'Organisational culture and non-union status of small businesses' *Industrial Relations Journal* 17 3 (1986) pp 214–224; see also Beaumont P B *The Decline of Trade Union Organisation* (1987) Croom Helm
8. Purcell J and Sisson K 'Strategies and Practice in the Management of Industrial Relations' in Bain (ed) *Industrial Relations in Britain* (1983) Blackwell; following Fox A *Beyond Contract Work Power and Trust Relations* (1974) Faber and Faber
9. MacInnes J 'Why Nothing Much has Changed: Recession, Economic Restructuring and Industrial Relations since 1979' *Employee Relations* 9 1 (1987) pp 3–9
10. See Hawkins K 'The "New Realism" in British Industrial Relations' *Employee Relations* 7 5 (1985) pp 2–7

Chapter 5

Negotiations

Ramsumair Singh

Negotiating plays a central role over a wide range of human activity. Dunlop has rightly observed that 'Negotiations is (sic) the process of changing positions and making concessions from initial positions in the course of moving towards an agreement.'[1] Negotiating is, of course, used to resolve disputes in fields other than industrial relations. These include disputes between husband and wife, between children, and between nation states. But negotiating is more than a possible method of settling differences; it is also a means of preventing them from arising.

There are two primary purposes to negotiating in the industrial relations context. First, to reconcile differences between managements and unions and second, to devise ways of advancing the common interest of the parties. The first of these purposes attracts the greater attention in practice, but the second is of no less importance. Indeed, most of the issues that come within the ambit of negotiations are usually a mixture of conflicting as well as common interests. Successful negotiations are therefore *not* conducted only to advance the sectional interest of one party.

This is not to deny that negotiating is conducted by persons who have distinctive purposes of their own. Union representatives are often aspirants for higher office, with supporters and opponents within their own union and sometimes rivals in other unions. Likewise, representatives of management may see negotiations as a way of fostering their own aspirations, and the interests of various parts of the company. Thus the two sides are not *monolithic*, and negotiations must therefore reconcile differences *within* groups as well as *between* groups.

Among managements and trade unions that deal with each other on an ongoing basis, negotiating may at the outset take the character of mutual problem-solving. The process involves the recognition of the common interests of the parties, the areas of agreement and disagreement and possible solutions, to the mutual advantage of both sides. The negotiator's task is not only to gain advantage for his own constituents, but also to develop long-term constructive relationships between the organizations involved in negotiations.

These introductory remarks have been intended to draw attention to the importance of negotiations in resolving disputes. Many disputes could be more efficiently resolved if the negotiators were more skilful and the negotiation process more widely understood. We will therefore explore the practical side of negotiating with some theoretical analysis, with the aim of helping managements and unions to negotiate with each other with greater understanding and insight. The main focus is on negotiations in industrial relations in real-world situations.

Perspectives on Negotiations

Many influential writers have argued that negotiating is an art. Dunlop states that, 'I am inclined to believe that the art of negotiation can only be learned by experience – often hard experience.'[2] Yet Dunlop concedes that a framework for analysis, and a statement of principles, of negotiations may reduce the learning time or, perhaps, the pain of experience.

Raiffa has argued that there is both an art and science of negotiations.[3] The science is concerned with a systematic analysis of problems, while the art includes interpersonal skills, the ability to convince and be convinced, the ability to use bargaining ploys and the wisdom to know when and how to use them. Raiffa has, moreover, observed that the art of negotiating has not been well documented; the science is not only in its rudimentary stages but also not very accessible to the practitioner. He concludes that both the art and science have a role to play in negotiating as they can act synergistically.* To a large extent, negotiating in industrial relations is unique and can be differentiated from other types by the following characteristics:

1. Employers and unions expect to have a long-term relationship. Agreement over terms and conditions of employment, and their administration in practice, are essential for the efficient functioning of the organization to which they both belong.

2. The negotiators from managements and unions represent organizations within which there are important differences, and thus the parties to negotiations are not monolithic. Aspirations of a wide range of groups and individuals have to be satisfied. Negotiating is the art of putting together a package that both sides could 'sell' to their constituents. It is therefore essential not to have a 'winner' and a 'loser' in negotiations as this not only makes the agreement hard to sell, but does not make for good industrial relations. It could also reflect on the credibility of the negotiators on the losing side, and affect their attitudes to future negotiations.

* ie work together to the better understanding and greater effectiveness of negotiating.[4]

3. In general, negotiating is concerned with more than a single issue, or with one issue that can be broken down into a number of component parts for analysis and solution.

Practitioners, of course, often act intuitively in negotiating situations, in ways that are far more sophisticated than they can conceptualize and articulate. Even experienced negotiators can, however, benefit by examining negotiations within a theoretical framework. In this way they gain a deeper understanding of what they are actually doing and can better communicate their insights to others.

Models for Analysing Negotiations

A wide variety of models has been used to explain the negotiating process. These models, although mathematically elegant, tend to make a variety of assumptions that are far removed from real-world situations and therefore of little use to practitioners. A basic assumption in most theoretical models is that trade unions and managements are made up of monolithic and homogeneous entities. In fact, as already noted, there are often wide differences of opinion within organizations or between members of negotiating teams. These differences are not static but vary over time. A consensus within each party to negotiations is often necessary before a negotiated settlement can be arrived at. Thus, when two organizations are party to negotiations, it takes, in effect, *three* agreements to achieve a negotiated settlement between the parties: an agreement *within* each party and *between* them.

One of the most influential models used in analysing negotiating was proposed by Walton and McKersie. They distinguished four systems of activity or subprocesses in labour negotiations, each having its own functions for the interacting parties. The following subprocesses were distinguished:

Distributive bargaining, the function of which is to resolve conflicts between the parties.

Integrative bargaining, the function of which is to find common or complementary interests.

Attitudinal structuring, the function of which is to influence the attitudes of the participants toward each other.

Intra-organizational bargaining, the function of which is to achieve consensus within each of the interacting groups.

While the subprocesses are related and can occur simultaneously, particularly the integrative and distributive subprocesses, conceptually they are quite different.[5]

In discussing the subprocesses in labour negotiations, Walton and McKersie identified distributive bargaining as the dominant activity and noted that:

> 'Distributive bargaining is central to labor negotiations and is usually regarded as the dominant activity in the union-management relationship. Unions represent employees in the determination of wages, hours, and working conditions. Since these matters involve the allocation of scarce resources, there is assumed to be some conflict of interest between management and unions. The joint-decision process for resolving conflicts of interest is distributive bargaining. The term itself refers to the activity of dividing limited resources. It occurs in situations in which one party wins what the other party loses.'[6]

We shall concentrate mainly on distributive bargaining, as it is central to negotiations.

The Dynamics of Negotiations

The purpose of negotiations is to achieve a settlement, often moving from positions that are initially far apart. One may conceptualize this process in the case of two parties bargaining over a wage increase, as shown in Figure 5.1.

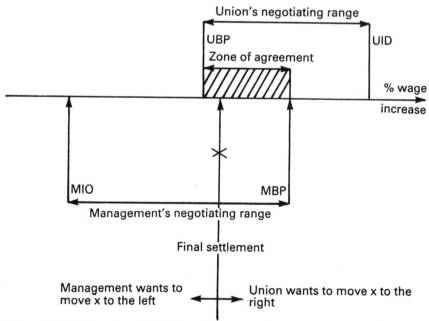

Note: if MBP is less than UBP there is no zone of agreement

Figure 5.1 *Dynamics of bargaining*

In negotiations, managements and unions tend to select the positions most favourable to their own interest. In the case of the union this would be its initial demand (UID) and of management its initial offer (MIO). In reality, one party is unlikely to persuade the other to accept its initial demand or offer, and thus would have to move towards the other party's position. There is, however, a limit to this process, sometimes referred to as the break-point or fall-back position. This is the critical point beyond which the parties would not go. In Figure 5.1 the union's break-point (UBP) overlaps with the management's break-point (MBP), thereby indicating a zone of agreement. The final settlement x is located within the zone of agreement, and the position of x depends on a number of factors including the relative bargaining power and negotiating skills of the parties.

If the management's break-point is less than the union's break-point, there is no zone of agreement and negotiations may become deadlocked. In this situation one or both parties may resort to sanctions to persuade the other party to adjust its limit and thus achieve a zone of agreement. Alternatively, the parties may resort to third party assistance, such as conciliation, mediation or arbitration, to break the impasse. These methods of intervention are discussed later in the chapter.

In wage negotiations it is usually possible to find a zone of agreement, and to achieve a final settlement within this zone. There are, however, a number of disputes where the parties may feel that fundamental principles are at stake, or for other reasons, such that they are unable to move from their initial positions. The grading of jobs and disciplinary issues often come within the ambit of this category. In this situation the parties may have little alternative but to seek third party assistance to the resolution of the dispute if overt conflict is to be avoided.

Frequently in practice, the parties have an imprecise perception of their own break-points, and make little or no attempt to locate the other party's break-point. Moreover, negotiations are a dynamic process and the break-points may change as negotiations progress. The astute negotiator not only influences the movement of his opponent's break-point in his favour, but also closely monitors this movement.

Preparation for Negotiations

Negotiations cannot be conducted fruitfully unless there is adequate preparation. For successful results the most intensive and detailed preparation is required. The extent of preparation will become readily evident at the negotiating table. A badly-prepared negotiator soon demonstrates that he has little knowledge of the issues under discussion and is not only a liability to his own team but loses the respect of his opponents. In sharp contrast, the well-prepared negotiator stands out and can lead events rather than reacting to them.

Preparing for negotiations is a year-round activity; every piece of information relative to one's negotiating position should be collected and collated, and its future use considered. Management and union, moreover, need to be making continuous studies of changes in wage rates, markets, the introduction of new technology and of industrial trends generally in order to obtain an informed view as to what changes are needed in the union-management agreement. From time to time, specialized studies are made of problems of particular interest to employers or unions and the results of such material could help the parties in negotiations. Moreover, with the use of computers it is now possible to analyse claims in terms of costs and benefits using different parameters.

There are many factors involved in the preparation for negotiations and it is not possible to consider them all. It is, however, helpful to examine a few strategic factors, especially bargaining objectives, bargaining power, and the role of the respective negotiating teams.

Objectives

Only the parties can decide what their objectives are for a particular negotiation. In different negotiations the objectives of the same party may be different. They may, however, be summed up as meeting one or more needs of the participants involved. This view of negotiations is often referred to as the 'need theory of negotiations'.[7] It is useful not only in preparing one's objectives, but also in analysing the strengths and weaknesses of the case of the other side. By defining their objectives the parties will be in a position to set up criteria for evaluation of their negotiating performance.

The formulation of objectives is a multi-disciplinary task, and should not be left entirely to personnel specialists. Persons with expertise in finance, production, sales and other functions have a vital role to play and their views should be sought before agreeing on a set of objectives.

All objectives do not carry the same weight, and exploration of priorities among issues is therefore an important pre-negotiation task. Objectives can conveniently be ranked under three subheadings: essential (E), desirable (D), and optimistic (O). The essential objectives are those which are fundamental to one's negotiating position; the desirable objectives are important but less so than those that are fundamental; the optimistic objectives would be a bonus if achieved, and may be a prelude to some subsequent negotiations. The objectives can be viewed along a *continuum* as shown in Figure 5.2, with essential at the lower end, optimistic at the

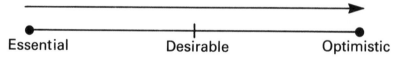

Figure 5.2 *Ranking of objectives*

higher, and desirable in between. Objectives are not static and expectations can change with the circumstances of the negotiations.

Having ranked one's objectives it would be necessary to determine the bargaining range for each issue in accordance with Figure 5.1. Likewise, it would be necessary to establish the linkages between issues and the effect that changes in the parameters of one issue would have on others.

Ranking involves judgement and is to some extent subjective. Objectives when ranked, however, provide a framework for negotiations.[8]

Bargaining power

Bargaining power has been defined as, 'the ability to induce the other side to make concessions that *it would not otherwise make*'.[9] Clearly, it means more than the mere fact of obtaining concessions. Hawkins has suggested that a crucial test of bargaining power is, 'whether the cost to one side in accepting a proposal from the other side is higher than the cost of not accepting it'.[10] Bargaining power is, moreover, not static but varies over time. To be of value, assessments of bargaining power would have to be related to a particular time in the negotiating process.[11]

Bargaining power is inherent in any situation where differences have to be reconciled. It is, however, not an end in itself, and negotiations must not rely solely on bargaining power. One side may have enormous bargaining power, but to use it to the point where the other side feels that it is impossible to deal with such a party is to defeat the purpose of negotiations.

The negotiating team

The number of people and specialisms that may compose a negotiating team will depend on many factors including the importance of the negotiations, the difficulty involved and the time available. In most instances, negotiating will be a team effort because a single negotiator may not have the scope and depth of expertise required. An evaluation of the skills and functions of team members is therefore of crucial importance.

There are three fundamental roles in negotiations: that of team leader or chief negotiator; that of the secretary or recorder; and that of the analyst. The chief negotiator will normally be the most senior member of the team and his role is to undertake most of the negotiating and to steer the negotiation towards a successful conclusion. The secretary, of course, is responsible for keeping minutes of the meetings but, in addition, should be alert to recognize verbal and non-verbal signals from the opposition. The analyst's role is to scrutinize what is being said; to ask for clarification of ambiguous points; and to summarize the issues, if and when this is appropriate.

Other technical specialists may also be members of the negotiating team, but it is important to define their roles. It may simply be to observe and listen carefully and report on what the opposition is saying. Before going into the negotiations it is essential that team members should understand their roles. The objective is to improve negotiating performance and to facilitate agreement on more favourable terms, or more rapidly, or both.

Role of a deadline

It is now common practice to have an expiry date in substantive agreements, and this allows both sides to plan for negotiations before the agreement expires. Thus, much of the planning can take place in a more relaxed atmosphere than would be the case if the agreement had already expired.

If the parties can agree on a deadline for the negotiating process this serves a useful function: it compels each side to establish priorities and make decisions within a time limit. With a deadline, the temptation to procrastinate is reduced. Conversely, without a deadline both parties can drag their feet and avoid confronting the issues under consideration. If union negotiators perceive management as behaving in this way they may well resort to industrial action to preserve their credibility in the eyes of their members and to focus management's attention on the importance of their claim. This is particularly true where the issue is a major one, such as a pay claim. There can be little doubt that a deadline encourages the parties to make decisions and to keep in focus the consequences of non-agreement.

Agenda

The primary purpose of the agenda is to bring order and structure to the negotiating process. To some extent the agenda reveals the positions of the parties in advance and thus permits each side to prepare a reaction to the issues that are to be discussed.

The issues might be listed so that the major ones are discussed first. Alternatively, minor issues regarded as relatively non-controversial might be listed just so that one side can begin the negotiations by making concessions, hoping that as the issues become more important they will receive concessions in return. Of course, the fact that one side makes concessions may be regarded by the other side as setting a precedent and a feeling may be established that concessions from the conceding side should continue. However, minor issues are sometimes easier to resolve, and their resolution creates an atmosphere of goodwill which can be of great value to both sides when the major and more contentious issues are being discussed.

It may not be possible to negotiate on an item-by-item basis. Items may be strongly linked as, for example, a union's claim for a wage increase which may be linked with management's proposals for increases in productivity. In such a situation it may be useful to combine the items in a package and to conduct negotiations on the package as a whole. If it is perceived by both parties that there are mutual benefits in negotiating on a package basis, the agenda can be planned accordingly and room for manoeuvre may be found which would otherwise be lacking. On the other hand, if a rigid issue-by-issue approach is adopted, both sides may lose room for manoeuvre and a failure to agree on one item may prevent progress from being made on the others. Thus, a valuable means of making progress in negotiations is through the linking of issues which have previously been treated separately.

Stages of Negotiations

Meetings of any negotiating team may well be said to pass through at least four stages. Initially, there are meetings to review formally the proposals submitted by each side, then comes the development of the cases, followed by the phase of seeking agreement. The final meetings will deal with the closure of negotiations.

Stage 1: the opening moves

There are no strict rules about conducting negotiations but there are some widely accepted negotiating conventions: negotiating should be fair and equitable; existing agreements should be honoured; each side should be prepared to move from its initial positions; sanctions should only be used as a last resort, and then only to assist negotiations and not in place of them. Most importantly, each side should so act as to encourage the development of respect for those on the opposite side of the negotiating table. Mutual respect facilitates understanding and is conducive to successful negotiations.

The introductory stage should set forth the importance of the negotiations and give an indication of the reasonableness of the proposer's case and the premise on which it rests. The benefits to be gained by the other side if it accepts the proposals should be clearly demonstrated. The need for both parties to gain something from the negotiations cannot be over-emphasized.

The position of 'take it or leave it' at the beginning of negotiations is a dangerous ploy for all but the strongest and most prescient. Movement from initial positions is the usual course of negotiations; this is the central aspect of distributive bargaining.

At the beginning of negotiations there is often ambiguity as to the status of various proposals and it is therefore important to clarify ambiguities at the earliest opportunity. Very often there are small issues that can be cleared up immediately, but there may be others that are out of the ordinary which should likewise be clarified. Otherwise, at a given stage in the negotiations it may be unclear as to what exactly is in dispute. In negotiating it is important to remember that there is no agreement until all items in dispute are resolved one way or the other, unless explicitly specified.

Stage II: developing the case

After the first review has been completed a break is necessary to allow each party to examine the proposals advanced by the other party. It is at this point that the negotiator has an opportunity to assess all the proposals together thoroughly.

Some conclusions can now be drawn as to whether a proposal can be accepted in principle, its negotiation range and possible settlement value. It is, moreover, important to note carefully the size of the gap between the two parties in a consideration of one's responses. The chief negotiator should now be in a position to brief team members on how individual items can be dealt with at the bargaining table. This will allow the negotiating team to direct their efforts to possible areas of settlement.

If a compromise is offered it should be drafted, since in drafting it additional features may come to mind and these can be discussed at the time that the proposal is put forward. Nothing is worse than to agree in principle to a proposal, only to find that one side wants to make so many exceptions or refinements to the proposal that the other party feels the need to utter charges of bad faith.

Stage III: seeking agreement

In entering the third stage of negotiation both parties should be in a position to advance specific proposals for settlement. It is, moreover, at this point that management can take the initiative and make the first offer. After all, it is usually the union that has probably made most of the demands, and it is difficult for union negotiators to begin with a reduction in the magnitude of their proposals before there is a definite offer from management.

Such an offer must, moreover, be sufficiently realistic to command the attention of the union side but, more importantly, if an impasse is reached and the offer is rejected by union negotiators or by the union membership, it must not prove an embarrassment to the union negotiators.

In the search for an agreement it is not unusual for requests for concessions from initial positions or previous offers to be accompanied by such phrases as 'this is our final offer' before some deadline or projected break-off in negotiations. There is a wide variety of gambits that negotiators use to encourage the other side to change their positions in distributive bargaining. Two important ones are summarized below.

The pattern of making concessions
The number of concessions made would depend on the context, but concessions should be made at the same pace and linked to those of your opponent. In the quest for movement from fixed positions the approach of the hypothetical linked concession is often used. The essence of this approach is that a proposal is made in a hypothetical form, as this allows

each side the opportunity of moving from fixed positions without commitment. The hypothetical proposal may call for the abandonment or reduction of some items in response to movement by the other party: 'If your side would reduce your claim from A to B, we would be prepared to reconsider our position on C.' The concession is hypothetical but it is likewise conditional, and it is an attempt to get real movement towards a compromise. Once the opposing side has accepted the hypothetical proposal in principle, this should form the basis of a negotiated settlement. Clearly, the linking of proposals should not be left to chance; they should have been considered during the preparations for negotiations.

Helping the opponent to change positions

It may be to one's advantage to let the other side change positions without loss of face. One could, for example, imply that the situation has changed, that new information has come to light, or that there has been a genuine misunderstanding. In these circumstances it is not unreasonable for the other party to change its position. Conversely, if a negotiator wishes to move from a position, one approach is to invite the other side to help. It is important to let either side retreat gracefully and with dignity, so that the credibility of negotiators is not undermined in the eyes of their constituents.

Stage IV: closing the negotiations

By the closing stage of negotiations the main features of an agreement should be readily apparent. The task now is to get a successful closure, the end product of which is a formal agreement ready for implementation.

It is not uncommon to find negotiators unable to terminate their negotiations. This is understandable, as they may not know when they have squeezed out every concession from their opponents. Unable to close, they keep negotiating and conceding what appear to be minor concessions but which, taken together, could be costly in financial terms and in setting precedents for future negotiations. The decision as to when to close negotiations is a matter of judgement, but there are some techniques used to get closure, and to a discussion of these we now turn.

The *concession closure*. This terminates the negotiations by offering a concession to secure agreement. If the opponent is near to making a final commitment he may be assisted by the offer of a minor inducement conditional on immediate acceptance. The concession should be made in such a way as not to be construed as an indication on the part of the conceding side that further concessions are to be had for the asking.

The *summary closure*. This terminates the bargaining procedure by summarizing everything that has been agreed up to that point, emphasizing the concessions made and the benefits to the other side if they accept what is on the table. The party using the summary closure should stress that this is their final offer and that there will be no further movement. If the opposing side accepts, then agreement is possible; if not another strategy may have to be resorted to.

The *all or nothing closure*. If the outstanding item is part of a total package, the rest of the package having been agreed to, then an indication is given that unless full agreement can be reached, the entire package is at risk. While this may be an extreme position to take, it can be justified if the negotiations have been on the basis of a package deal or one in which the issues were expressly linked from the outset.

Recording the Agreement

When agreement is finally reached, perhaps after long and protracted negotiations, there is often a high degree of euphoria on both sides as the tensions of the negotiations dissipate themselves in the natural relief of achieving an agreement. The euphoria can be soporific, and the negotiators may be tempted to call it a day. This temptation must be firmly resisted until both sides are absolutely clear about the terms of the agreement. A detailed summary must be written and agreed between the parties. The golden rule is: 'Summarize what has been agreed and get agreement that what has been summarized was agreed.'[12] The more complex the subject matter of the negotiations, the more room there is for misunderstanding and memory lapses. The negotiator's task is incomplete until all the items that have been agreed have been put in writing.

Implementing the Agreement

When the negotiating process has ended in agreement the terms will have to be interpreted and administered. Yet no agreement can provide for all contingencies and there may be minor gaps left in the agreement because full understanding cannot be achieved. It could be that certain administrative problems may have been overlooked during the negotiations. There should therefore be agreed procedures for resolving questions concerning the implementation of the agreement and in filling in such lacunae.

In the process of interpretation and administration of any agreement the parties should develop a set of questions and answers concerning the interpretation of particular clauses, and a complex body of common understandings. This is an ongoing process involving persons at various levels in the firm and in the union, reflecting the symbiotic ties between negotiation, interpretation and administration of an agreement. It is this process which puts flesh on the bare bones of the written agreement.

Adjournments

An essential feature of all negotiations is the timing of adjournments. The number, length and frequency of adjournments will depend on the negotiations and, in general, adjournments are readily conceded if either party requests them.

The primary purpose of an adjournment is to review and assess progress against the objectives you have set. An adjournment also facilitates the consideration of each party's response to the other side's proposals; it also allows each party time to reconsider both its own offer and also the alternatives of not reaching agreement. At this stage the negotiating situation is delicate: each side would prefer the other side to move to avoid a further concession itself, but such a move may create the impression of weakness and may be interpreted as a willingness to move all the way to the position of the other side. It is therefore important to bear in mind that whatever expectations an adjournment may create in the minds of the other side, one's own responses should be consistent with one's essential objectives.

We have been looking at adjournments to consider specific proposals from the opposition, but there are, of course, adjournments for natural breaks – meals, sleep, weekends, and so on. Such adjournments provide opportunities for informal discussions with the other side. They can relieve the tension of negotiating and can assist in reaching a settlement, especially when the issues are reasonably few, limited in scope and well defined. The distances between the parties should furthermore be relatively small. Thus, the final steps to agreement may be taken away from the negotiating table – although they must be ratified there.

Ronald Reagan, commenting on his experience on this aspect of negotiations as President of the Screen Actors' Guild said:

'I was surprised to discover the important part a urinal played in this high-altitude bargaining. When some point has been kicked around, until it swells up bigger than the whole contract, someone from one side or the other goes to the men's room. There is a kind of sensory perception that gives you the urge to follow . . . Then, standing side by side in that room that levels king and commoner, comes an honest question, "What do you guys really want?" . . . Back in the meeting, one or the other makes an offer based on this newly acquired knowledge . . . Then the other returnee from the men's room says, "Can our group have a caucus?" That is the magic word, like the huddle in football – it's where the signal is passed.'[13]

The use of sanctions

The primary purpose of sanctions in the context of negotiations is to alter the position of one side or the other. In the pursuit of their objective, workers resort to a wide variety of sanctions: go-slow, work to rule, overtime ban, strike, to name a few. Management can likewise resort to a lockout but this sanction is now rarely used.* Thus, negotiations may take place against a background of a strike, lockout, litigation, or with

* Of course, it is common, however, for the sides in a dispute to describe a stoppage of work as both 'strike' and 'lockout'.

campaigns to win public support for a case. Such overt conflict is, moreover, the most dramatic form of pressure directed to the bargaining table. Negotiations may be profoundly affected by it as the results of the conflict may alter the position of one side or the other, thus inducing agreement.

Good negotiations are, however, conducted by experienced individuals on both sides. Neither side is therefore likely to resort to sanctions without making a final offer or concession which represents a position on which the party is prepared to face the possibility of industrial action. Generally, the parties realistically appraise each other's position, and frequently a negotiated settlement is achieved before industrial action is resorted to. This does not mean that the parties might not reach an impasse at times, with a strike or other form of sanction being used. It does mean, however, that the parties are less likely to stumble into taking action without considering the consequences.

All this is not to deny that at times sanctions are used by workgroups without the approval of their union officials, as a spontaneous protest against something management has done or to indicate support for their union leadership in negotiations. Such unofficial action has continued to occur in spite of legal prohibitions and lack of official union support. Nor do workers lightly take industrial action. There are no easy solutions to unofficial spontaneous outbursts, but the answer probably lies in the particular tenor of management-union relationships, the types of procedure available to resolve disputes and how well these procedures fit the problems to be resolved.

The role of third parties

When the negotiating process has reached an impasse or deadlock, the parties may seek the assistance of a third party as a catalyst in the search for a solution. In Britain, such assistance in the form of conciliation, mediation and arbitration is provided free to the parties by the Advisory, Conciliation and Arbitration Service (ACAS).

The timing of third party intervention is, however, important. Where disputes have not been taken through all the stages of procedure, or where in the absence of formal procedure negotiations have been incomplete, the introduction of a third party may undermine the bargaining machinery by encouraging half-heartedness in the negotiations in the hope that a third party will save the situation. Not surprisingly, before considering requests for third party assistance, ACAS takes into account any dispute procedure agreed between the parties and whether it has been fully used for the dispute in question.

Conciliation, mediation and arbitration have in common the introduction of a third party into the negotiating process to assist the parties in the resolution of the dispute. The need for such involvement arises from a recognition by the parties that voluntary agreement is not likely to be reached without some outside assistance. Conciliation and mediation are a continuation of the negotiating process, whereas a recourse to arbitration is a recognition that further negotiation will be fruitless and that a settlement will have to be imposed from the outside. In essence, the role of the conciliator is to clarify the areas of agreement and disagreement between the parties; that of the mediator to make recommendations for a settlement or to reach a basis for a settlement; the arbitrator to hear the cases presented by both parties and make an award – that is, make a settlement of his own which the parties normally agree to accept beforehand.

The Trust Factor

Negotiations cannot be fruitfully conducted if there is distrust between the parties. In negotiations, management and unions may be forced to recognize that their survival is dependent on reaching an accommodation with each other. As Purcell succinctly puts it: 'We must find some way of reconciling our differences. We must learn to live together.'[14] Negotiations may not be possible unless there is a certain degree of trust between the parties.

The climate for negotiations is also profoundly important, as Walton and McKersie noted:

> 'A supportive and trusting climate facilitates joint problem-solving. Defensive and low-trust atmospheres inhibit the process. A supportive climate is marked by encouragement and freedom to behave spontaneously without fear of sanctions. A defensive atmosphere is one in which the parties perceive threat and risks associated with provisional behaviour . . . when support is lacking and a person anticipates threat, he behaves defensively, diverting energy from the problem-solving task.'[15]

The need for trust stems from the complex nature of negotiations, and trust provides the basis on which negotiators deal with each other as they seek to reach agreement. The quest for trust between the parties is a learning process, and opportunities should be given to each other for a high-trust relationship to develop and flourish between them.

The personal ingredient

Agreements are made not merely between organizations but also between individuals. It is, however, difficult to generalize about personality factors in negotiations, yet these factors are not inconsequential and some comments of practical importance may be made.

Some negotiators get on well with other members of their team, and with the opposing side; some do not. In many situations this does not make much difference, but in others it could be crucial. It is, for example, not unusual for the chief negotiators, sometimes with a colleague, to talk 'off the record' about a proposal for settlement. Clearly, in this situation personal relationships are important.

The astute negotiator will appraise the personal ingredient in negotiations, and take it into account in preparing and presenting his case. It may not be an analytically neat exercise but its practical importance cannot be over-emphasized.

Training for Negotiations

We have been concerned in this chapter to examine the general rules and guidelines that can be of use to negotiators involved in distribution bargaining. Knowledge about negotiating is, however, intimately associated with negotiating skills. Competence in both knowledge and skills can enhance the performance of the negotiator.[16] While opinions may differ as to what are the essential attributes for an effective negotiator, it is generally agreed that the art of negotiating can be developed by practice, and by a keen interest in the developments within the field of negotiating. There is an increasing number of specialized texts on negotiating, some of which have been discussed in this chapter, and courses designed to improve the skills of negotiators are now widely available. Negotiators should take full advantage of the opportunities available to improve both their knowledge and skills.

The Future of Negotiating

As means of resolving differences between employers and trade unions, negotiating towards the concluding of collective agreements has a number of advantages over other methods of regulating their relationships. For the significant feature of an agreement is that both parties are committed to live by it, and the likelihood of the parties enforcing their own agreement is far greater than that of accepting a decision adverse to one party from the outside. Furthermore, the two sides are in a better position to resolve their own differences, since they presumably know more about their problems than outsiders do.

The leadership qualities of the parties involved in negotiations are profoundly important in a rapidly changing economic and political environment. Improving their relationship and the process of negotiation should be a conscious goal of the parties. For negotiations not only play a vital role in conflict resolution today, but all the indications are that they are likely to be even more significant in the future.

References
1. Dunlop J T *Dispute Resolution* (1984) Auburn House, Dover, Mass, p 21
2. *Ibid* p 10
3. Raiffa H *The Art and Science of Negotiations* (1982) Harvard University Press, Cambridge, Mass, pp 7–8
4. *Ibid* p 8
5. Walton R E and McKersie R B *A Behavioural Theory of Labor Negotiations* (1965) McGraw Hill, New York, pp 1–7
6. *Ibid* p 11
7. Nierenberg G I *Fundamentals of Negotiating* (1968) Hawthorn Books, New York, ch 7
8. Kennedy G, Benson J and McMillan J *Managing Negotiations* (1980) Business Books, London, ch 3
9. Slichter S H, Healy J J and Livernash R E *The Impact of Collective Bargaining on Management* (1960) The Brookings Institution, Washington DC, p 918
10. Hawkins K *A Handbook of Industrial Relations Practice* (1979) Kogan Page, London, p 192
11. Atkinson G *The Effective Negotiator* (1983) Negotiating Systems Publications, London, ch 2
12. Kennedy G, Benson J and McMillan J, op cit, p 113
13. Reagan R and Hubler R G *Where's the rest of Me?* (1965) Dell Publishing Company, New York, p 225. Quoted by Dunlop J T, op cit, p 17
14. Purcell J *Good Industrial Relations, Theory and Practice* (1981) Macmillan, London, p 237
15. Walton R E and McKersie R B, op cit, p 141
16. Kniveton B and Towers B *Training for Negotiating: A Guide for Management and Employee Negotiators* (1978) Hutchinson, London

Chapter 6

Collective Agreements

Chris Brewster

Collective agreements set the basic terms and conditions of employment for most people in the UK. That, however, is one of the few generalizations that can be made with any certainty. As in other areas of industrial relations the formal outcomes of the system – the agreements – are complex, diverse and differentiated. The fact that substantial elements of pay and benefits are set by collective agreements for well over two-thirds of all people in employment means that at national level the overall economic impact of these agreements is considerable, if still much debated. The impact of the agreements at the organizational level is clear: pay is the major operating cost item for most public and private sector organizations. In the private sector particular collective agreements can mean the difference between profit and loss, even survival and non-survival. In the public sector the ever increasing pressure of labour costs puts a real strain on tightly controlled public expenditure. Even at the individual level, in the employees' pay packet, or in the way they work, the importance of collective agreements is hard to overestimate.

This chapter considers in turn: the complex and varied nature of collective agreements; the diverse content of these agreements; the levels at which the agreements are made; and, looking forward, the way in which the extent, coverage and format of the agreements is undergoing significant and important changes.

The Nature of Collective Agreements

There is a remarkable diversity of forms of collective agreement in the UK, some of them informal, some perhaps even unlawful, some hidden from senior management and union officials. Some of the agreements will have been reached with much satisfaction on both sides; others will have been made with much unhappiness under real pressure and difficulty. The majority, however, share a number of features in common and it is useful to note these first.

Trade union recognition

In broad terms all collective agreements are dependent upon union recognition. It takes two parties (at least) to reach an agreement. There can be no collective agreement until management has decided to deal with its employees, at least partly, through a trade union or a trade union-like body. There does not, in the British tradition, need to be a formal recognition agreement before there can be a collective agreement. But if management does not accept that the unions represent one channel through which it can deal with its workforce, then agreements cannot exist. In practice most collective agreements are made with independent unions formally recognized by the employing organization for collective bargaining purposes.

It is now understood that managerial attitudes are a key influence on the growth or decline of trade union membership. It should not be assumed that managers are opposed to trade unions in any automatic sense. Many managements are very positive towards the unions and actively encourage their recognition and participation in specific areas of organizational policy. They find that the unions provide a useful channel for communications with employees and that collective agreements are a simple and comprehensive way of altering employment contracts for many employees simultaneously. More importantly for these managements, the trade unions and collective agreements provide a means of generating commitment. Collective agreements have a strong moral force: the parties to them will not breach their terms except in case of real pressure. The unions want collective agreements because they formalize improvements to terms and conditions that the unions have negotiated and because they restrict managerial prerogative. The managements want collective agreements because they commit unions and the employees they represent to the terms of the agreement. Agreements are two-way processes: managers and unions both gain from them. Hence the readiness of managements to recognize the unions for negotiating purposes.

Once the union, or unions, is recognized the possibility is opened up for all forms of collective agreements. There are the formal, deliberate, planned negotiations leading to an annual wage increase. There are also local deals, developed more or less informally and with greater or lesser visibility. Many of these deals will not be conceived of as collective agreements, even by the parties concerned. The night duty manager agrees with the shop stewards that to prevent the problems caused by a new bus timetable the late shift will finish, and the night shift will start, 20 minutes earlier than indicated on the shift rosters. To create as little fuss as possible, the individuals concerned continue to log, and be paid, the same hours as on the roster. The legal position may be uncertain, there is nothing in writing, senior management does not want to know, but another collective agreement has been struck. Such deals would be difficult, perhaps even impossible, if the night duty manager had to convince each employee individually that this was an acceptable arrangement. Where a union is recognized, however, the manager is well placed to make such agreements.

Most collective agreements will be more open and more formal than this. They will still depend upon management being prepared to deal with or 'to recognize for negotiating purposes' (as the jargon puts it) a trade union representing the employees.

. . . not legally binding

Collective agreements have a unique status in the UK. They are, with a few exceptions, deemed not to be legally binding between the parties. If either management or union break the agreement the other party is debarred from going to court to enforce it. During 1971–74 the Conservative government changed the law so that the agreements were held to be legally enforceable unless the parties specifically stated otherwise. Almost every agreement during that period included a 'Tina Lea' clause: 'this is not a legally enforceable agreement'. Apart from that brief attempt, the presumption has always been that collective agreements cannot be enforced by the courts. The parties can make them legally enforceable if they so choose, and if they write them in a way that the courts find acceptable. Hardly anyone does.

The arguments for and against legally binding agreements have been well rehearsed.[1] Essentially, the culture of British industrial relations is such that both parties prefer to make their own deals without lawyers, and to retain flexibility. The case in favour of legally binding collective agreements is made most strongly, in general, by those not involved.

It is, however, over simplistic to state baldly that collective agreements are not legally enforceable. By the legal process of incorporation, clear terms made by parties with the authority to act as agents become part of individual employees' contracts of employment. Thus a wage increase, say, will become part of the individual legal contracts of the employees covered by that particular collective agreement. If the increase is not paid action can be taken by or on behalf of the individual; but not by or on behalf of the unions which were party to the agreement.

Format of collective agreements

The lack of intention to negotiate legal documents explains the format of most collective agreements. The non-practitioner, on first seeing a documented agreement, finds it hard to credit that events of such significance can be covered by such thin paperwork. The agreement that may determine living standards for dozens or hundreds of families, and have a critical effect on an organization's operating costs and competitiveness, will cover one or two sheets of foolscap, hastily typed and idiosyncratic. That these collective agreements are so thin and insubstantial reflects the negotiators' concept of their nature. They are not legally binding; rather they are reflections of an understanding, binding in honour upon those who drew them up. They are incremental; each agreement builds upon previous deals and arrangements. They reflect a present consensus, which is open to renegotiation; they are not intended to establish definitive or final positions.

Typically, in the UK, wage agreements last for one year. This is shorter than the norm in many other countries, which will have two- or three-year deals as typical, and it is a comparatively recent development in the UK, too. Agreements for different lengths of time are far from rare, even in the UK. This is dependent to some extent on subject matter: agreements on working practices may last only a few weeks; agreements on pay typically will last a year; agreements on hours may last several years; and in some areas – such as pensions, expenses and dirt money – agreements may well last for decades. There are now clear indications that from the mid-1980s onwards even wage agreements are tending to last longer. Deals lasting for two years or more are becoming the norm in the car and components industries and in petroleum and the docks. Employees in areas as diverse as the Greene King brewery, British Aerospace, Ford and the teaching professions have recently agreed long-term settlements.

It is important not to overgeneralize. Some companies have long-term, substantial, carefully worded agreements running to many pages and covering all sorts of subjects comprehensively. They are, though, very much in the minority. For most, the rather elemental few page agreement is typical. This typical format and the incremental and complex understandings that it represents are central to any analysis of collective agreements in the UK. The negotiating of agreements in myriad forms and myriad different places is a continuing and never-ending feature of the industrial relations scene.

The Content of Collective Agreements

The subject matter of these flimsy, temporary, incremental and legally uncertain agreements is perhaps more open to generalization. There is a simple distinction between procedural agreements, which are concerned with methods (see Chapter 7) and substantive agreements, which are concerned with the terms and conditions of employment.

The subject matter of collective agreements varies widely. Given the complexity of agreements, the different forms that they take and the varying levels at which they are made, it is not surprising that this is the one statement that can be made with confidence. The substantive agreements may be about one or more of a wide range of topics. What is or is not agreed will be determined by history and tradition, by the forms and levels at which the agreements are reached, by the strength and confidence of the parties to the agreement, and by the particular resources and issues of the moment. They are usually about pay, ie salary, remuneration, wages, incentive schemes, premium payments. They are often about working conditions or working arrangements. They are sometimes about other terms and conditions of employment; hours or pensions, training or holidays. Very occasionally they cover other topics. But agreements on such issues as recruitment, investment and product or service quality are rarities.

There are issues which are not covered. A recent, very comprehensive US agreement included sections on the company slimming plan, self-defence training and the allocation of tickets to the local football team. Few British agreements have a similar content. Agreements in Britain are more likely to include some or all of the following subjects:

Pay levels and structures. The basic collective agreement is about pay. Typically, this has been restricted to details of a general uplift of, perhaps, a certain percentage. Increasingly these agreements involve a more extensive re-examination of pay structures. These agreements, or separate ones, also cover many other elements of the cash equation, such as bonuses, shift and overtime premium, dirt money, uniform allowances, salary scale incremental points.

In the past, particularly when governments have been operating incomes policies to control the growth of wages, there has been much discussion of 'wage drift'. This term was used to refer to the way in which less structured, local agreements act to push actual earnings above those established in agreements. From the Donovan Commission onwards millions of words were written about this phenomenon, nearly all addressing it as a problem for which a solution was needed. This concern has abated, largely because the economic circumstances have forced managers to control labour costs more rigorously, but also because there is a greater understanding of the complexity of collective agreements, a wider acceptance of local responsibility for wage costs and the virtual abandonment of interest in formal incomes policies in government circles.

Other terms and conditions. Subjects such as hours of work, holiday entitlement, sick schemes, pensions and health and safety are, less frequently than pay (but still frequently), included in collective agreements.

Job evaluation. The majority of systematic job evaluation schemes rely on the involvement of employees. They are usually introduced and often administered by joint agreements between management and unions. All organizations of any size over a dozen or so employees will have schemes for comparing one job against another. In many cases this will be entirely informal and *ad hoc*, undertaken solely by the manager or owner of the business. Where formal and systematic means of assessing jobs against each other are adopted – in about one-fifth of all workplaces employing more than 25 people[2] the schemes are normally the subject of collective agreements.

Working arrangements. The phrase covers a multitude of different activities around the immediate work area. Depending upon the workplace, issues such as manning levels, allocation of work, the structure of workgroups and the manner in which the work is conducted may be determined unilaterally by management, in some few cases by the employees or their union representatives, or frequently by joint agreement.

New technology agreements. During the early 1980s, several unions and the TUC devoted considerable attention to agreements on the introduction of new technology. These agreements have retained some interest in the private manufacturing sector but have not become widespread: among establishments which recognize trade unions, negotiation over the introduction of technical change occurred in only 10 to 15 per cent of cases.[3] There are three reasons for this: it is often difficult to disentangle agreements on new technology from agreements on changing working practices or pay; new technology is a blanket term and in practice each situation is different, making general recommendations inappropriate or difficult to follow; and it quickly became clear that the economic circumstances and the managerial confidence which characterized the 1980s meant that managers were able to introduce new technology without having to reach agreements with unions.

Flexibility and productivity. The concept of productivity bargaining enjoyed a great vogue in the 1960s. A form of it is now back in favour, but it is a distinctly different form. The earlier productivity agreements involved payments over and above cost of living or incomes policy basic rises and were frequently concerned with limited changes to working arrangements such as reductions in overtime, shorter meal breaks and abolition of tea breaks. It was not uncommon for such agreements to be undermined, gradually, by a series of less formal agreements (or turning of blind eyes), so that the same practice might be brought out by management several times. In the 1980s agreements are more far-reaching, focused on flexibility among the workforce and linked explicitly to workforce reduction rather than to substantial extra payments.

Redundancy. There were large numbers of redundancies in the first half of the 1980s and there has been no absence of them since. In overall terms, more than 40 per cent of workplaces reported reductions in their workforce in the early 1980s.[4] Although many workplaces effect these redundancies by agreement, and not just management *diktat*, many of these 'agreements' will be grudging, unhappy and often forced on unwilling unions. In broad terms, the unions have concentrated on raising the compensation paid to redundant workers rather than attempting to retain the workforce at its original size.

Training. Traditionally the unions have limited their interest in training to apprenticeships. In some few industries, such as electrical contracting, the unions have developed a more comprehensive approach, but this has been rare. The virtual collapse of the apprenticeship system and the requirements for workers to train and retrain during a working lifetime have changed union attitudes. Unions are now much more prepared to bargain over training opportunities. Agreements on training are now common in many workplaces.

Levels of Collective Agreement

Collective bargaining is conducted at a wide variety of levels. The agreements made may have national coverage in a particular industry or organization, they may be regional or divisional, and they may apply to any level within a company. Furthermore, it is usual for any group of workers to be covered by more than one level of agreement. In a manufacturing company, for example, it is quite normal for an employee to have holidays set by a national industry agreement and pensions by an agreement with a conglomerate holding company. Other conditions will be agreed at the manufacturing company level, training is often determined by agreements reached at divisional level, wages at plant level and plus-payments and working arrangements determined by departmental or shift agreement.

Such complexity is extreme but it is certainly not rare. There will be few employees who have all their terms and conditions of employment agreed at one level. This complicated structure has to be borne in mind throughout any discussion of industrial relations – although it appears to be overlooked more frequently than it is remembered. At the end of December 1986 the Chancellor of the Exchequer launched a series of attacks by government speakers on national level agreements, arguing that local agreements would help to reduce unemployment. He was sharply rebuked by the TUC, which said that his argument revealed 'a deep ignorance of industry'.[5] It certainly failed to understand the complicated nature of collective agreements.

The level at which bargaining takes place is one of the areas of collective agreements about which most is known. It has been the subject of several surveys over the last decade. Unfortunately, the nature of such surveys is that simplistic questions have to be asked to cover a complex area. Questions about the most important pay bargaining level, for example, subsume all sorts of other questions such as: On what aspect of pay? Important for whom? Nevertheless, a generally accepted picture of the levels at which agreements are made in Britain is available. Four broad levels can be identified: national multi-employer industry level; company-wide or corporate level; site or establishment level; and agreements which cover only part of an establishment. Tables 6.1 and 6.2 give details of the level at which the last pay increase was awarded.

Table 6.1: *Basis for most recent pay increase (percentage of workplaces)*

| | Manual workers | | Non-manual workers | |
	1980	1984	1980	1984
Collective bargaining most important level:	**55**	**62**	**47**	**54**
national/regional	32	40	29	36
company/divisional	12	13	11	13
plant/establishment	9	7	4	4
other	1	1	2	1
Not result of collective bargaining	**44**	**38**	**53**	**46**

Table 6.2: *Basis for most recent pay increase, private manufacturing industry only (percentage of workplaces)*

| | Manual workers | | Non-manual workers | |
	1980	1984	1980	1984
Results of collective bargaining most important level:	**65**	**55**	**27**	**26**
national/regional	27	22	5	5
company/divisional	10	11	8	9
plant/establishment	26	21	13	11
other	1	1	–	1
Not result of collective bargaining	**35**	**45**	**73**	**74**

Source: *Millward and Stevens*, 1986, p 227

National industry-level agreements

In many industries multi-union, multi-employer agreements are reached at national level. They may or may not cover all organizations in the industry and they can take different forms. Some are followed very closely by the organizations who are represented on the bargaining body, for example, the electrical contracting agreement.* Some, such as the agreement in air transport† set, in effect, ceilings from which different companies can negotiate down. More typically the agreements set a national floor above which individual organizations are free to develop agreements at local level. There is a continuum of arrangements, from those where local agreements make only small differences, typical in the public sector, to those such as chemical and engineering where the floor-level national agreement is no more than a framework.

The degree of organization and cohesion within both the management side and union side of these arrangements reflects to some extent the influence of the national-level agreement. But the management side groupings – the employers' associations – often perform many functions beyond that of negotiating collective agreements, so that they may have greater cohesion than would otherwise be assumed.

The national arrangements exhibit considerable heterogeneity. Agreements are made in bodies which contain other parties. Thus, the legally constituted Wages Councils include an 'independent' group. The teachers' Burnham Committee, which was so prominent in the 1985–86 dispute, included a representative of the Secretary of State. Both of these bodies can make legally binding agreements.

In many, but not all, national-level bargaining arrangements separate agreements are reached for different categories of employee; manual, clerical, technical, maintenance, managerial.

The proportions of establishments and employees covered by agreements at national industry and at corporate level vary considerably with industrial sector. Given the unsatisfactory nature of surveys it is difficult to be precise, but it seems that in the mid-1980s national-level agreements were the major determinant of wages for 30 to 40 per cent of establishments with more than a few dozen employees. Smaller establishments are in general much less likely to be affected by national-level agreements. Paradoxically, larger establishments are also less likely to have basic pay determined at national industry level. Manual workers are more likely to

---

* Since its foundation in January 1968 the Electrical Contracting Joint Industry Board (JIB) has determined a wage agreement for the industry which sets actual (as opposed to minimum) pay rates. The JIB is governed by a national board composed of 14 representatives each from the EETPU and the Electrical Contractors' Association, together with an independent chairman. Its responsibilities extend far beyond the pay determination and monitoring function to training, welfare, disputes and employment. It has traditionally operated long-term pay deals.

† The National Joint Council for air transport was set up with the nationalization of the companies that now form British Airways, other major British carriers and some dozen unions comprise the Council. For many years the NJC has set rates which have been followed by BA (and in broad terms by the major foreign carriers operating in the UK). Other major affiliated British carriers have paid lower rates, either directly or by delaying increases, and small non-affiliated carriers have paid less.

have their major terms and conditions set by national industry agreements, and so are employees in the public sector.

Corporate-level agreements

Agreements are frequently made at national level by single employers. In cases such as the nationalized, or recently denationalized, industries, single employer, corporate-level agreements have much in common with the national industry-level agreement. More typically, however, many organizations make agreements with their unions at overall corporate level that cover only that organization and have a substantial impact on basic pay and conditions.

Corporate-level agreements were in broad terms the major determinant of pay and conditions in the mid-1980s in most nationalized industries and public services. In the private sector corporate- or divisional-level settlements were the most important determinant of pay for manual workers in about one-fifth of establishments, and rather more for non-manual workers.

Establishment-level agreements

Agreements made for a particular location, office, site or factory can be taken together as establishment-level agreements. They can be very varied. Pay levels are set at workplace level but much more important here are the non-wage issues: redundancies, manning levels, job evaluation schemes and various conditions of work, such as hours and holiday arrangements.

In most of the smallest companies terms and conditions are set unilaterally by management. Where these companies do negotiate agreements they are workplace-level agreements. Apart from these very small workplaces, however, the likelihood of establishment-level bargaining rather than bargaining at any other level increases with size. In the private sector, establishment-level agreements are more likely in certain manufacturing sectors, such as mechanical engineering, shipbuilding and vehicle building. They are more likely among manual employees. They are more common in foreign-owned firms. Overall, this level of agreement is most important for pay determination in about one-third of establishments in the private manufacturing sector and less than half that in the private service sector.

Agreements below establishment level

There is little information available about agreements made below workplace level. In many organizations, however, significant agreements are made at departmental or functional level. These agreements tend to concern working practices, shift patterns and plus-payments rather than basic pay. They have an importance for industrial relations that goes far beyond their financial implications because it is on these very local issues that employees can get most committed. Employee representatives are often elected to deal with these specific issues and justify themselves by their successes on these otherwise small matters.

Trends: A Strategic Approach to Industrial Relations

All the aspects of collective agreements covered so far are in flux. Agreements are becoming less important, are being made at different levels, and their form and content are being varied. The last section of this chapter examines a number of trends under each of these headings and suggests possible future developments.

Before going into detail, however, it is worth examining the overall situation. There is considerable debate as to whether the decline and change in collective bargaining is a temporary feature or represents a real watershed. Those who argue that it is temporary point out that many of the reasons underlying union weakness can be reversed: Conservative governments may fall, manufacturing industry can be revived, unemployment could be cut. In sharp contrast, it will be argued here that industrial relations in Britain has reached a watershed, that collective bargaining will continue to decline and that collective agreements, while they will remain influential across a wide range of employment, will continue to fall in importance. The Conservative Party's re-election in 1987 reinforces this view. However, even if a Labour government had been elected, manufacturing revives, and should there be a major fall in unemployment, there are other long-term reasons why we should expect collective agreements to diminish in importance. These, among others, are as follows:

The structural changes in employment are unlikely to be reversed. Technological change is blurring boundaries in employment, leading to retrenchment and retraining, even in successful organizations, and requiring greater employee flexibility. This creates difficulties for union recruitment and retention and for the collective bargaining process.

Workplaces are becoming smaller. There is a proven relationship between small workplaces and low levels of unionization.[6]

More workers have 'peripheral' contracts of employment. Part-timers, temporary workers, youth scheme workers and so on are very much less likely to join trade unions.

Groups that the unions have found more difficult to organize are becoming a bigger percentage of the workforce: the percentage of non-manual workers is increasing (even as the distinction between manual and non-manual becomes increasingly blurred) and there are more women and non-whites among the labour force.

The climate of opinion has changed. This is difficult to prove and capable of differing interpretations. There is at least some evidence that the basic legitimacy of the union role is now more frequently challenged, that union officials' confidence is less and that employees are not prepared to support their unions as totally as they did in previous decades.

The unions have problems. These are not insurmountable; the unions will remain and will recover some of their influence. But they are in general in financial difficulties, uncertain of their future, and not well-organized to meet the changing circumstances in which they find themselves and are now, for the first time in decades, fundamentally split by the expulsion of the EETPU from the TUC. They are struggling to adapt. By the mid-1980s the EETPU and the AEU were offering members and potential members very significant financial benefits in areas outside those which could be obtained through collective agreements – cheap car purchase, reduced holidays, medical cover, discounts and insurance, and so on. By 1987 the TGWU had launched a recruiting campaign for part-time workers and the GMB was aiming to recruit the self-employed. In the way of the British trade union movement, a wide range of different approaches to their problems was being developed.[7]

In contrast, managements now have a new confidence in their ability to deal with industrial relations. Managers do learn. Much of the debate about the future of collective bargaining and collective agreements seems to assume that managements have gained nothing from recent history. Managers have increasingly seen the advantages of different forms of employment structure, different ways of relating to staff and a more planned approach to industrial relations. It is not necessary to be too cynical or too jaundiced about management to argue that they are likely to want to continue those developments that left them as free as possible from the constraints of collective agreement.

It is against this background, of new opportunities for managements to develop and manipulate the employment situation and an increasing willingness by managements to do so in a subtle, planned and coherent manner, that a discussion of trends takes place. Collective agreements were the bedrock of industrial relations during most of the post-war period. They will not disappear, but they are changing in importance, form, content and level. Each is examined in turn.

The decreasing importance of collective agreements

Collective agreements will remain a major influence on employees' contracts of employment for many years to come. They are deeply entrenched as a method of determining pay and conditions in a very wide spread of British industry. They are, however, of declining importance in two respects. First, the number of employees whose main terms and conditions are set by collective agreements is decreasing. Second, the influence of those agreements in the employing establishment is also being reduced.

Fewer people are covered because:

Growth in employment is in new industries, new towns, new locations, small units, service industries. All are difficult for unions to organize and are much less unionized than the traditional industries and large sites where employment is declining.

In the private sector, companies are increasingly prepared to refuse union recognition, or withdraw it once granted, especially for higher-level employees.

In the public sector, areas of employment are being 'privatized' or subcontracted, often to non-union employers.

Overall, the considerable increase in the number and proportion of peripheral workers will not be reversed. By the nature of their employment many of these will have their terms and conditions determined individually.

The impact of these changes is likely to be longlasting. The effect has been to reduce the extent of collective negotiation between managements and unions and hence to reduce the coverage of collective agreements. The early evidence of this trend was already apparent in the first half of the 1980s; it is unlikely to have been reversed since then.

This has to be kept in proportion. For the foreseeable future collective agreements will remain the major influence on terms and conditions of employment for the majority of employees in Britain. There is no evidence of managers attempting wholesale rejection of this approach in those industries and companies which have traditionally operated this way. Furthermore, changing events, such as the election of a Labour government in 1991 or 1992, might give the system added although belated support. In general, however, it seems that whatever events may occur on a short-term basis, the high point of collective agreements has passed. Gradually Britain will come into line with many of its developed country competitors as the coverage of collective agreements is reduced.

Even where they exist the *influence* of agreements is being reduced. This is because:

Changes in the nature of the workforce, particularly the growth in peripheral employment, means that the proportion of workers in the establishment covered by each agreement is reduced.

Companies in the private sector are tending to refuse to accept or to withdraw recognition from groups within the workplace, especially managerial staff. The example of ICI was followed by both Cable and Wireless and British Telecom shortly after their privatization. These are the most widely known cases. For obvious reasons both management and unions are unwilling to publicize such cases, but they are by no means uncommon.*

Some issues are being dealt with more frequently by different forms of representation, such as briefing groups or consultative committees, which do not lead to collective agreements.

Other issues are simply not being put into the arena of collective bargaining by management. Managers continue to refuse to bargain over strategic issues like investment and the location of particular sites. The authors of the most authoritative workplace surveys struggled to come to terms with the fact that managers reported widespread joint regulation of many non-pay issues, but very little in other areas.[8] It may be quite straightforward: some things, such as pay and physical working conditions, are subject to collective agreement and some, such as the introduction of new technology, are not.

Again, these trends are likely to develop discontinuously and with variations, and they will be subject to a range of external factors. Here too, however, it seems that the overall trend will be towards the reduction of influence of collective agreements.

The changing form of collective agreements

Despite these trends, the importance of collective agreements remains substantial. The variety and heterogeneity of collective agreements also remains. A number of trends, pointing perhaps in rather different directions, can be discerned. A basic tension exists between the desire of some managers and some trade unionists to move towards more comprehensive, more legalistic and generally more substantial agreements, and those on both sides who want to move to simpler, less restrictive arrangements. There is evidence of both strategies in different organizations. Overall, though, three broad trends can be identified:

1. There is a move away from the increased formalization developed in the 1960s and 70s. In general terms, formalization benefits the weaker party to an agreement. The stronger party is in a position to make changes anyway; breaching a written agreement remains a constraint. In many areas, especially those outside the standard pay and conditions areas, managers are now preferring to work through informal and unwritten 'understandings'. Much new technology is introduced this way. Even in the pay areas managers are seeking enabling agreements that leave them an unwritten degree of flexibility. Thus, agreements may specify an overall increase of 5 per cent to

---

* The growing incidence, although still limited, of withdrawal of recognition is now being openly discussed at TUC level.

be distributed on the basis of a minimum 3 per cent for all; the rest to be allocated 'according to merit' (ie managerial judgement).

2. In recent years there have been signs of the development of more comprehensive agreements of longer duration. In that majority of cases where collective agreements remain important it is likely that this trend will continue. Agreements are becoming more comprehensive in so far as managements are consolidating numerous small agreements into one. Those managements who are consciously reviewing all aspects of industrial relations will not want to leave various elements of the employment package lost in the mists of an agreement reached many years ago. They will at least want to reaffirm it, and often want to amend it. This can be done alongside all the other agreements that come up for regular renewal. In this respect at least, agreements, usually not those on basic pay, will be of shorter duration. Agreements on the basic pay package, however, are being extended in duration because managers, in particular, see the benefit of having some predictability about wage and salary costs over as long a period as feasible. The steadying of the rate of inflation in the early 1980s made this process more acceptable to the unions. Longer-term agreements were typical in Britain prior to the 1960s and are still the norm in most competitor nations. British agreements in the 1990s may follow suit.

3. The growth of new forms of collective agreements.[9] These agreements are often, rather casually, described as *single-union/strike-free*. Such agreements vary, of course, but are built around a single union representing all staff, flexible working practices, well-understood salary systems, and extensive openness about management information with wide consultation. Some involve the use of pendulum arbitration: ie arbitrators must select either the last position of the union or that of management; they cannot 'split the difference' or select any other formula. These agreements are controversial (see Chapter 13); indeed, they led to the expulsion of the EETPU from the TUC. Many commentators and managers, taking a simplistic view of these agreements, see them as something of a panacea. Others, and some trade unionists, see them as a capitulation by the unions. The union officials concerned are dismissive of both attitudes. They point out that specific circumstances make such agreements possible and that their major problem is persuading managers to accept them. The degree of challenge to accepted ways of thinking and the extent of the openness required from management probably means that although these radical new agreements will spread (particularly on greenfield sites where both sides have the opportunity to start from scratch) it is likely that they will remain a small minority of all agreements for the foreseeable future.

Changing levels of bargaining

Chapter 4 identified a number of steps being taken by those managements who are consciously planning their approach to industrial relations. One key area was the focusing of collective bargaining at a level commensurate with business objectives. Thus organizations moving to a cost- or profit-centre approach would want to develop collective agreements, which are such a major determinant of cost or profit, at the level of the designated centre.

There is evidence that this is happening. All recent surveys show a move away from national-level, multi-employer agreements. The number of these agreements and membership of employers' associations declined sharply in the first half of the 1980s. The major agreements on pay were more often focused at company level.[10]

Company and establishment are frequently the same thing: the organization only exists on one site for about one-fifth of all companies.* For the others it is unclear whether the accountancy logic will continue to push the level of agreements down to establishment level.†

What is clearer is the desire of managers to consolidate agreements at the overall employing unit level, not just by pulling agreements down from national level, but also by pulling them up from workgroup level. This managerial strategy is likely to meet with greater shop steward or union representative opposition. The representatives are in general positive about such developments as profit-related bonus schemes, employee share ownership and similar features which require collective agreements at company level. They are less sanguine about specific workgroup issues on working conditions, manning levels and rosters being resolved under an establishment- or company-level joint union agreement.

Changes in content

Inevitably, changes in importance, format and levels of bargaining are correlated with changes in the content of collective agreements. There are three main aspects to this: changes in the scope of negotiations; the removal of subjects from collective agreements, to be determined unilaterally by management; and the inclusion of other subjects in collective agreements.

Changes in the scope of negotiations arise from the more planned approach to industrial relations that some managements are developing. Where strategic decisions are being taken against the criterion of the cost-effective use of manpower, management's options in negotiation are reduced. Traditionally, management negotiators have been given overall

* The Milward and Stevens survey reported 18 per cent. These were coded to establishment level in their tables on p 12 of their book. (Personal communication between author and Mark Stevens.)
† It has been argued that managements might want to keep collective bargaining at a different level from key managerial decisions as a matter of policy.[11]

cost targets and been charged with reaching a deal as far below them as possible. To do this negotiators have become skilled at packaging and repackaging elements of their offer in order to make it more acceptable.

Management negotiators can now find themselves in a much stronger position, given their greater strength – compared with the 1960s and 70s – to face down threatened industrial action or to win if it takes place. Management negotiators thus feel themselves to be in a better position to make realistic first offers, and to move only a little way from them in the course of the negotiations.

A strategic managerial approach to industrial relations both builds on this situation and feeds off it. As an example, consider a company that has decided to subcontract some services, reduce overtime, encourage a faster turnover of staff particularly among older employees who may find it difficult to adapt to new training requirements, extend flexible working practices and increase the flexibility of working hours. Such policies will have clear implications for collective agreements in the workplace. They will mean that management negotiators are restricted in what they can 'package' into an offer. So, if the management has decided to subcontract services, the negotiators may be unable to offer employment security guarantees. The objective of reducing overtime means that the negotiators have limited scope in overtime rates: any increase would tend to increase the attractiveness of overtime and employee resistance to its reduction. Equally, if the management wanted to encourage turnover, especially of older staff, it would be unlikely to offer pension improvements. Conversely, it may well want to make early retirement packages available. Policies of extending flexibility will lead managers towards reducing any element of the package which adds to distinctions between parts of the workforce. So there would, at a minimum, be no improvement of individual or group payments-by-results schemes; differential conditions or rosters would be reduced; and management would attempt to limit payments for shift or unsocial working hours. These give employees a stake in limiting the flexibility of working hours.

These are, of course, just examples, but they are far from uncommon. The implication of such policies is that managerial bargainers increasingly find that their room for manoeuvre in the negotiations is restricted and they cannot move very far before they come across another issue of principle which they must not jeopardize. It is still undoubtedly the case that managements are sticking close to first offers mainly because they feel themselves to be in the ascendancy. However, as the strategic approach to industrial relations becomes more widespread, so that in turn will also constrain managerial flexibility in what they can allow in collective agreements.

The removal of subjects from collective agreements is to a large extent a part of this process. A substantial number of non-wage items are the subject of collective agreements. The number of companies and establishments in which such issues formed the subject of collective agreements dropped markedly in the first half of the 1980s. This seemed to occur on all issues, in all sectors and for both manual and non-manual employees.

This trend looks set to continue. Issues such as recruitment, manning levels and work practices have not typically been subject to collective agreements and are now being taken out of agreements and held as part of the management prerogative in many organizations. Other issues, which have traditionally been the subject of collective agreements, are becoming less widespread. Thus, for example, the spread of formal job evaluation schemes which occurred in the 1970s has been halted: managements are finding that such schemes tend to restrict flexibility. By their nature these schemes 'freeze' jobs at a particular point in time and often involve additional payments if employees extend their activities beyond the written-down tasks. Hence these schemes are becoming less popular. Most formal schemes are subject to joint regulation. If job evaluation schemes are reduced, joint agreements about them will be reduced. It is unsurprising that by 1987 the government had put its weight behind opposition to job evaluation. Equally, various payment schemes, such as payments-by-results, which normally have a high degree of shop steward involvement, are also losing popularity. The fact that such pay schemes are built around joint agreements is probably a contributory factor in management's decision to replace them. The effect is again to remove an issue from the collective bargaining arena.

The addition of new items into collective agreements is a paradoxical approach. From a managerial viewpoint the rationale for such action lies in the greater commitment that can be achieved through an agreement. So some managements are beginning to include in their collective agreements a series of items that they want accepted by the employees. Agreements may include clauses on flexibility (of task or working time), on product or service quality, on confidentiality or security and on training and retraining.

The Future of Collective Agreements

This chapter has described the changing nature of collective agreements in Britain and made some, perhaps contentious, projections about how they will develop in future. To a considerable extent the pace of these developments will depend upon the complexion and policies of the government.

The Conservative administration has taken pains to reduce the role of government in industrial relations. Its policies have been concerned with establishing a scenario in which managerial power in industrial relations was strengthened and union power reduced – and then leaving the parties as free as possible to make their own collective agreements. This outcome was reinforced by the government's encouragement to the public service sector to contract out, or 'privatize', as much work as possible and by the objective of denationalizing as many State industries as possible. These approaches had the effect of removing many strongly unionized sectors from direct government responsibility, and again of allowing management and unions to come to collective agreements unfettered by any political or social factors.

In the area directly or indirectly under its control, the Thatcher government has tried as far as possible to reproduce the conditions under which collective agreements are negotiated in the private sector. Attempts have been made to reproduce 'market place' analogies (except in the notably exceptional cases of the groups covered by the Top Salaries Review Board, judges, senior civil servants, and the police). The aim was to move away from the comparability arguments of the 1970s and move closer to the 'ability to pay' criterion.

There seems little doubt that the present government will maintain these policies. Any future Labour government is likely to take steps to reintroduce, at least partially, 'good employer' criteria into state employment. It is also likely that such a government would extend the role of the State in collective agreements, perhaps introducing mechanisms for decisions on recognition claims and extending the roles for conciliation and arbitration, although the re-introduction of formal incomes policies seems increasingly a matter for discussion rather than practical politics.

What also may be practical politics is that even a future Labour government of the 1990s would find it not only very difficult to reverse present trends but might not wish to do so. The cautious development of performance or merit linked pay in the public sector, the increase in collective agreements below national level and the extension of collective agreements to such issues as flexibility, quality and training are likely to be supported by all political parties. Collective agreements in Britain are in a process of change and development, and of some decline. But they will remain the most important means of establishing employees' terms and conditions.

References

1. A particularly clear recent analysis is provided by Lewis R 'The Role of Law in Employment Relations' in Lewis R (ed) Labour Law in Britain (1986) Blackwell
2. Millward N and Stevens M British Workplace Industrial Relations 1980–1984: the DE/ESRC/PSI/ACAS Surveys (1986) Gower p 255
3. Daniel W W Workplace Industrial Relations and Technical Change (1987) Frances Pinter, pp 130, 149
4. See Employment Gazette various issues; Milward and Stevens, op cit
5. TUC Economic Committee paper for NEDC meeting December 1986, reported in IDS Report 487 (1986) p 29

6. Bain G S and Elias P 'Trade Union Membership in Great Britain: an Individual level Analysis' *British Journal of Industrial Relations* **xxiii** 1 (1985) pp 71–92; Millward and Stevens, op cit, p 58

7. Elements of this analysis are well covered in a symposium of articles 'Trade Unions and the Changing Labour Market: Moving Closer or Growing Apart?' *Manpower Policy and Practice* (Summer 1986) pp 30–52; and in response articles from Bill Jordan, Paul Rathkey and Liz Symons *Manpower Policy and Practice* (Autumn 1986) pp 22–5

8. Millward and Stevens, op cit, p 250

9. Bassett P *Strike Free: New Industrial Relations in Britain* (1986) Macmillan

10. See successive issues of the *Annual Report of the Certification Officer* for employers' association memberships; and Millward and Stevens, op cit, p 181 for details of their declining use.

11. Kinnie N 'Patterns of Industrial Relations Management' *Employee Relations* **8** 2 (1986) pp 17–21

Chapter 7

Industrial Relations Procedures*

P J White

This chapter explains the term 'industrial relations procedures', and considers why such procedures have become widespread in British industry. Some key procedural arrangements are then introduced and explained; problematic issues are highlighted; and some concluding reflections are made.

The Meaning and Extent of Procedures

Procedures which are entered into jointly by management and employee representatives are designed to ensure that certain standards of industrial behaviour and conduct are adhered to. Such procedures also encourage fair, consistent and prompt methods of dealing with alleged misbehaviour or misconduct on the part of employers or employees.

There are many types of procedure to be found in contemporary British industry. The principal ones (on which we shall concentrate) deal with negotiating (including disputes), grievance, disciplinary and dismissal, redundancy, and health and safety issues. Examples of other procedures include disclosure of financial information to employees, grading and job evaluation, and participation or employee involvement.

According to the recent investigation by Millward and Stevens,[1] the proportion of surveyed establishments possessing some sort of industrial relations procedure increased from 85 to 94 per cent between 1980 and 1984.

As a generalization, such procedures were more in evidence: in the public sector; in larger enterprises; where trade unions were recognized. Even in smaller firms, there was a tendency for procedures to be expressed in written form, and there seemed to have been increased provision for

* The author wishes to thank many individuals and organizations for their assistance in the use of examples given in this chapter, including the AA, ACAS, Bovis Construction Ltd, Tony Cormack, Kevin Hawkins, Alan McCreath, Seaforth Maritime Ltd, Society of Master Printers of Scotland, United Distillers Plc, and George Waterston and Sons Ltd. Thanks are also extended to Colin Duncan for very helpful comments on an earlier draft.

'outside' assistance (eg senior managers, or a body such as ACAS) when a dispute or issue could not be solved lower down.

One reason for the prevalence of procedures was the encouragement given to them by the Donovan Royal Commission Report of 1968,[2] which treated inadequate procedures 'as a major cause of industrial disputes'. The Commission therefore recommended the introduction of written, joint procedures.[3] Since the Commission's Report, other factors have also played a role, including various industrial relations statutes, codes of industrial relations practice, and government pronouncements. But the fundamental reason for the spread of procedures lies in the advantages which employers and trade unions have found in such an approach.

The Merits and Limitations of Procedures

Procedures can: lay down accepted standards of conduct and behaviour in the workplace; help management and employees to avoid conflict; provide early warning of potential problems; place emphasis upon fairness and rationality, and reduce the possibility of inconsistent or uncontrolled action; and influence the morale of the enterprise and the people who work within it.

Nevertheless, procedures are by no means a panacea, for they also have their drawbacks, and they highlight problematic issues. Procedures reduce the autonomy of both parties: each is bound to acknowledge the rights and interests of the other in any action that they take. However, it is extremely fanciful to suppose that procedures reduce each party's autonomy in equal measure. In some instances, the stronger party might successfully resort to procedures, but a weaker party might also be able to gain concessions by resorting to procedures as a delaying or frustrating tactic. Intra-party considerations might also be relevant, for a procedure might be seen by the employer as a means of curbing the power of workplace representatives and/or their constituents. Senior managers can exert control over individual managers in a similar fashion.

There is considerable debate in industry as to whether procedural arrangements should take a predominantly written or oral form. There are several advantages in having written procedures:

The mere act of writing joint procedures encourages discussion as to their purpose and scope.

An agreed text reduces the possibility of misunderstandings and ambiguities of meaning.

Written documents can be readily transmitted to, and retained by, those to whom the procedures relate.

Managers and trade union representatives leave and go elsewhere, taking with them their recollections of oral arrangements.

On the other hand:

Oral arrangements, or 'custom and practice', allow the opportunity for experiment, or for trying out novel arrangements without commitment on either side.

Written procedures can be restrictive: those managers who do not have written redundancy procedures, for example, might be able to cut their workforce more speedily, and some trade unionists would prefer not to sign a redundancy agreement for fear that they are seen to be admitting to the inevitability of redundancy.

Written procedures can introduce a 'legalistic' element into industrial relations, and can prejudice a relationship between management and unions which relies upon mutual trust, flexibility and a preparedness to compromise.

The written/oral distinction finds echoes in the formal/informal distinction in industrial relations. Formality can tend towards an over-rigid observance, while some degree of informality, or departure from the strict letter of a procedure, might be desirable when an extremely speedy decision is called for. Similarly, a dogged adherence to all stages in a procedure might prolong conflict, preventing concessions being made by those most directly involved in the issue.

Where it is decided to have written procedures, a further general problem might arise: they are expensive to produce and can create a daunting impression on a reader. In these circumstances, an enterprise might wish to produce a company handbook which summarizes the key features of each procedure, and which is handed to each new employee as part of the induction process. However:

The handbook must contain a comprehensive summary; a drastic summary can be meaningless and counter-productive.

Employees must be made aware of the locations of the full copies.

The full copies must be readily available for inspection at short notice.

Full copies should be given to all key personnel: eg trade union representatives, first-line supervisors.

Another general problem area concerns the question of whether various procedures (eg grievance, disputes) should be separate or combined. It seems usually to be preferable to have separate procedures for distinct eventualities:

Some procedures are 'triggered' by management (eg disciplinary) whereas others (eg grievance) are invoked by employees.

Some issues (eg grievance) might be felt to require less elaborate appeal mechanisms than might others (eg disciplinary).

Nevertheless, it is useful to conceive of procedures as possessing parallel paths, for example, where the same senior management are involved in hearing appeals. Similarly, some interrelationship should also be allowed for, such as where an individual grievance escalates into a matter of collective contention.

It must already be clear that procedural issues are complex. Accordingly, managers and trade unionists who are contemplating the introduction or modification of procedures might wish to seek advice from sources external to the establishment. In the case of managers, higher-level management (eg at head office) might be consulted, and management consultants might have a role to play; federated enterprises can call upon their employers' association. Workplace trade union representatives might seek guidance from full-time officials, local trade councils, shop steward combine committees and trade union research units. Where a joint management/ union approach is felt to be called for, then the advisory function of ACAS clearly has a role to play. Indeed, recent reports of the service demonstrate that ACAS is especially heavily involved in advising industry on its industrial relations procedures.[4]

Negotiating Procedures

A negotiating procedure lays down a framework in which the parties determine terms and conditions of employment.* Given the potential for conflict over such matters, some provision must also be made for the resolution of collective disputes. In some instances, 'disputes procedures' might be separate from, although connected to, those providing for negotiations, but our focus is upon negotiating procedures which incorporate measures to resolve disputes. It must also be borne in mind that some individual grievances, for example, grading claims, or a woman's claim for equal pay for work of equal value, can have collective attributes. There can be knock-on effects for an entire group or enterprise. Accordingly, the individual grievance/collective dispute distinction is often blurred in practice.

Elements in negotiating procedures

There are usually four elements in such procedures:

1. The definition of the area (in terms of geography, occupational group, or otherwise) in which the union's representative role is acknowledged, including the laying down of 'spheres of influence' where more than one union is involved.

---

* The distinction between 'framework' and 'terms and conditions of employment' is often referred to as a distinction between 'procedural' and 'substantive' matters.

Example: This agreement regulates the industrial relationship between XYZ Company Plc and those trade unions signatory to this Agreement and regulates the Conditions of Employment of hourly paid operatives (or, those holding positions up to Grade X) employed by the Company in Scotland.

2. Issues which are to be the subject of negotiation, ranging from wages and salaries to normal hours of work, from trade union membership to promotion.

3. The steps by which agreement is to be sought, including the determination of authority and seniority for both management and employees.

Example: Stage 1. In the first place the meeting will be between the divisional personnel director and the divisional officer of the trade union. Either person may be accompanied by colleagues who have a specific interest in the negotiations. The union side will consist of the divisional officer and no more than four accredited representatives with a maximum of two from each factory. If any matter cannot be agreed at this level the matter will be referred to Stage 2.

Stage 2. At this stage the committee will consist of the regional personnel director, the divisional chief executive, the divisional personnel director and one or more colleagues, together with the national officer of the union, the divisional officer and one or more representatives. If agreement still cannot be reached at this stage the matter will be referred to Stage 3.

Stage 3. At this stage the matter will be discussed by the company's regional chief executive and the appropriate union official.

4. The steps to be taken when there is a failure to agree.

Example: Should there be a failure to agree (at Stage 3) the matter may by mutual agreement be referred for conciliation and, if necessary, arbitration, either independently or through ACAS.

Some problems and issues

While negotiating procedures are designed to resolve disputes, they also acknowledge that disputes can and do arise. One of the functions of this sort of procedure, then, is to channel disputes and their resolution in a controlled manner. Otherwise, either party might be tempted to bypass procedure. For that reason, it is common to find a 'peace clause' built into procedures:

Example: The parties agree that at each stage of the procedure every attempt will be made to resolve issues raised, and that until all such stages have been carried through there shall be no disruption to normal working or other unconstitutional action by either party.

At the same time, agreements also acknowledge an important feature of

such collective agreements in Britain: unless the parties
contrary, such agreements are *not* legally enforceable con

> *Example*: It is the spirit and intention of the signatories t
> this Agreement shall be respected and implemented by b
> not the intention of the signatories that the terms of ~~this Agreement~~
> should in any way be binding in law.

As our earlier example made clear, provision can be made for conciliation
or arbitration by a person or agency external to the establishment. Our
example also made a distinction between the two principal methods of
collective dispute resolution.

Conciliation (undertaken by ACAS conciliation officers) takes the form
of attempts to persuade the parties to reach, by negotiation, a settlement of
their dispute. Arbitration is provided either by arbitrators(s)* nominated
by ACAS or by someone who is directly approached by the parties.
Arbitration takes the form of an award after the arbitrator has heard the
respective cases of the parties to a dispute. In general, arbitration is more
appropriate to *disputes of rights* (ie disputes over the interpretation or
application of an existing agreement) than it is to *disputes of interest*
(disputes over new terms and conditions of employment). In the former
case, an arbitrator would usually be expected merely to clarify existing
rules, but in the case of disputes of interest, the parties might be reluctant to
entrust the proposal of innovations, perhaps of a fundamental nature, to an
outsider.

There are several reasons why procedures have increasingly allowed for
third party involvement in negotiating and other procedures, reasons which
are underlined by the fact that the parties in Britain are not usually
compelled by law to seek outside involvement or to abide by the outcome of
such involvement.

A body such as ACAS can provide *bargaining assistance* to the parties,
where: there may be an impasse in negotiations, indicated by a breakdown
in the disputes procedure; one or both parties might be lacking in
experience of negotiations; or conciliation or arbitration can be viewed as
constructive alternatives to industrial disputes which are costly in economic
and psychological terms.

ACAS can also serve as an *outside authority* over a dispute, for
conciliators and arbitrators are not connected with or involved in the
dispute. This has several advantages: some disputes can be extremely
protracted, so that eventually the parties might not be able to 'see the wood
for the trees', or the factors which truly divide them; negotiating positions
can become so entrenched that suggestions or proposals by outsiders might
enable one or the other party to soften its negotiating position without loss
of face; emotions, or clashes of personality, can sometimes cloud reason,

* In some instances, a panel of up to three people might undertake arbitration.

whereas an outsider can encourage the parties to look at their situation more dispassionately.

Potential disadvantages with third party involvement include the possibility that management and unions come to treat resort to conciliation and arbitration as a 'soft option', along the lines of 'let ACAS sort it out'. In consequence, procedures might be undermined and rendered meaningless. However, before agreeing to intervene, ACAS satisfies itself that serious attempts have been made to follow a procedure through all of its stages. Third party involvement might also prolong the resolution of conflict by postponing rather than averting a trial of strength between the parties. In consequence, the conflict might be more embittered and deep-seated.

A criticism which is levelled at arbitration is that arbitrators 'split the difference' between the parties – they, too, take the soft option. It is partly for such a reason that 'flip-flop', 'pendulum' or 'last offer' arbitration has recently received some attention in British disputes procedures, often in conjunction with a no-strike clause.[5] Last offer arbitration requires an arbitrator to choose only between the latest claim of the union and the latest offer of the employer. Supporters of this practice maintain that:

> The incidence of stoppages would be cut – arbitration must be attempted first.

> Negotiators would be more cautious in their expectations, for when an arbitrator is forced to choose between positions, negotiators are more likely to compromise beforehand.

> Because the negotiators are being encouraged to narrow the distance between their respective positions, there is a greater likelihood of mutually agreed settlements being reached without recourse to arbitration.

> Arbitrators would no longer be able to avoid tricky issues by 'splitting the difference' or compromising between the two positions.

However, the claims in favour of a no-strike clause, combined with last offer arbitration, are somewhat exaggerated:

> Arbitrators do not always 'split the difference' – indeed, many disputes of right (for example, over dismissal or grading) can involve a straight choice between one position and another.

> Last offer arbitration might not readily lend itself to complex cases, where parts of both claim and offer might have considerable merit in the eyes of the arbitrator.

> The arbitration decision might itself be the source of some dispute between employer and union.

> Where arbitration is built in as an automatic stage, then the parties might be tempted not to negotiate in earnest, on the grounds that the arbitrator 'will solve our problem', but most managers and unions would

feel that this was an abdication of their responsibilities. It is partly for this reason that requests to ACAS for conciliation, leading to jointly negotiated agreements, far exceed requests for arbitration, where the parties could be said to forfeit some autonomy. (We consider the future role of arbitration in Britain in our concluding remarks.)

Grievance Procedures

Grievance procedures enable an individual employee to express a grievance or problem to immediate or, if need be, to higher management. There is much to be said for establishing a grievance procedure which is separate from negotiating procedures, for the former covers individual issues, in contrast to the collective focus of the latter. The distinction is not clearcut, however, as we have already observed. In consequence, there should be some provision for grievances eventually to be routed through the negotiating procedures, although it is generally advisable for all concerned that grievances be settled by the people who are directly involved.

Example: Both parties accept the principle that it is important to settle grievances as near to the point of origin as possible.

Elements in grievance procedures

These procedures should specify *how and to whom* employees can raise a grievance.

Example: Stage 1. Any employee who wishes to discuss the matter with management will, in the first instance, discuss the matter with his/her immediate superior.

It is customary for such procedures to spell out the *stages* through which a grievance should go. It is usually considered to be important to specify the *time limits* at each stage in order to ensure speedy resolution of the grievance. The *rights of representation* on behalf of the employee should also be spelt out; in non-union establishments, or among non-members, individuals should have the right to select as representative an employee of their choice.

If, therefore, at Stage 1 the supervisor has been unable to resolve the matter within 24 hours of its being raised:

Example: Stage 2. The employee may consult with his/her shop steward during the next break in working time. The shop steward, accompanied by the employee, should if necessary then discuss the matter with the employee's immediate superior.

Stage 3. Failing satisfaction, the shop steward should discuss the matter with the departmental manager, who should endeavour to resolve the matter within 48 hours of its being brought to his attention.

Stage 4. If there is no settlement at departmental management level, the senior shop steward should request a meeting with his general manager and may, if necessary, involve the local trade union official at the earliest opportunity. No time limit is put on this stage of procedure, but it is accepted that serious matters will be dealt with in a prompt manner.

Stage 5. If there is no settlement, a meeting will take place between senior management and the regional trade union official.

In common with other arrangements, grievance procedures tend to allow for external reference (eg to ACAS) where internal procedures have been exhausted.

Some problems and issues

The first stage of grievance procedures (the employee to the supervisor) could be said to be of especial importance:

A supervisor who through inaction regularly fails to resolve grievances may lose the respect of his employees, and suffer diminished authority.

Senior management must permit supervisors some delegated authority, at least on certain of the more routine problems, otherwise employees with grievances will be tempted automatically to bypass their supervisor.

On the other hand, senior managers tend to treat such procedures as controlling mechanisms, ensuring some consistency of behaviour among all supervisory staff, as well as reducing the supervisor's autonomy.

Some procedures at Stage 1 allow for the grievance to be presented either by the individual or by the individual in company with his representative. There are merits in permitting an immediate role for a shop steward where, for example, the individual lacks self-confidence and is reluctant to raise the issue in person. On the other hand, most workplace union representatives would prefer to withhold their intervention until they are truly needed: the notion of automatically involving the shop steward would not usually be helpful to that official, and it might also have the effect of alienating the supervisor and undermining his ability or willingness to resolve the difference directly with the individual.

The above-mentioned example of a grievance procedure included time limits at the various stages. However, there is an argument against including explicit timescales, on the grounds that an issue might sometimes prematurely force its way up the procedure, whereas a grievance stands a better chance of being effectively resolved by the parties who are directly involved. There might also be problems where trade union officials are difficult to contact within the prescribed time. For these reasons, the time

warning and without notice if an act of gross misconduct is committed. The following list, which is not exhaustive, gives some examples of offences which are treated as gross misconduct:

fighting, assault of another person on company premises;

being severely under the influence of drugs or drink while at work and thereby likely to endanger self or others;

theft from company premises of property belonging to the company, employees, suppliers or customers;

deliberate disregard of safety rules;

deliberate release of confidential company information to unauthorized persons.

Offences which might be felt to be less serious, calling for a series of verbal and written warnings before dismissal is contemplated, might also be spelt out.

Example: Other offences which have been repeated despite warnings will also lead to dismissal. Such offences include, but are not limited to, the following:

poor attendance and bad timekeeping;

poor workmanship and/or work performance;

unauthorized absence from the designated place of work;

repeated and/or sustained unauthorized absence from work.

A prime purpose of warnings is to rectify the behaviour or conduct of an employee. Clearly, then, it is important for management to monitor the individual's behaviour after warnings have been issued. But it is also advisable for the individual's shop steward to ensure that his member is given full opportunity to show improvement.

Generally, warnings are allowed to lapse after a specified period:

Example: Provided that there are no further breaches of discipline for a period of one year following the issue of the first formal warning, then it will be considered null and void and will be removed from the employee's record.

Where a serious offence has been committed, the warning might remain 'on the record' for more than one year, depending upon circumstances.

Even where an individual is felt to have committed gross misconduct, justifying summary dismissal rather than a warning, employers are nevertheless expected to allow an appeal against the decision, perhaps on a form specially devised for the purpose:

Example: Where an employee is dismissed summarily (eg for reasons connected with gross misconduct) the dismissal shall stand but it will be open to the employee or his trade union representative to contest the dismissal. An intention to appeal must be lodged in writing with the employer within 72 hours of the receipt of the disciplinary action. Unless the appeal is lodged within 72 hours, it will be assumed that the employee accepts the decision.

It is to be noted in the examples quoted that drunkenness can be treated as a serious offence, whereas absence is usually treated less seriously. But the question arises as to suggested company policy in the case of employees who are afflicted by alcoholism as distinct from excessive drinking on random occasions. One company (Seaforth Maritime Ltd) has attempted to tackle the issue in its procedures in an especially imaginative fashion.

First, the *background* is sketched in for all employees by quoting statistics to indicate that approximately 3 per cent of a company's workforce will suffer from alcoholism to some degree. The Health and Safety at Work etc Act 1974 is also cited as a reminder that employers have a duty to ensure the health, safety and welfare of all employees, while each employee has a duty 'to take reasonable care for the health and safety of himself and of other persons who may be affected by his acts or omissions at work'. (Health and safety procedures are discussed later in this chapter.)

Second, the company's procedure acknowledges that, although alcoholism as an illness is very difficult to recognize, nevertheless it might be *indicated* by any of the following: absenteeism, or uncertified sickness; decreased work performance – poor productivity, poor timekeeping; behaviour – moodiness, irritability, lethargy, uncooperativeness; drinking habits – suspicion of drinking at work, before work, or at lunchtime; hand tremor; facial flushing and bleary eyes; accident record – proneness to accidents.

Third, where management forms a suspicion that an employee suffers from alcoholism, managers are encouraged to *interview* him, with a representative if need be. Where the suspicion is confirmed, management will suggest that the employee consider making an approach to an independent alcoholism counselling agency. Should the employee be off work for this reason, then he would be covered by the company's sick pay scheme and would not suffer loss of pay.

Fourth, the company liaises closely with outside agencies (possibly including medical specialists) to draw up a *rehabilitation programme* for the individual.

Finally: 'following a return to work after or during treatment, should work performance again suffer as a result of alcoholism, each case will be considered on its merits and, if appropriate, a further opportunity to accept and cooperate with treatment will be provided'.*

---

* For further discussion of a policy on alcoholism, including the suggestion that consultation with trade unions is a prerequisite for success, see Mortimer B 'Alcohol and Work – An Explosive Cocktail' *Employment Gazette* **96** (February 1988).

In the various examples cited, opportunities for appeal have been mentioned. It is fairly commonplace for such appeals to be heard by a special committee or panel, and in some instances, trade union representatives might feel able to form part of such bodies. But in other cases, representatives seem to feel that they can provide better protection for their members where they argue the case to a body consisting solely of managerial personnel.

Where there is a failure to agree on a question of discipline, then an external stage (similar to that in other procedures) might be included, in the form of ACAS conciliation or arbitration. In any case, when an individual makes a formal complaint of unfair dismissal against his former employer, a copy of that complaint is automatically sent to ACAS for possible conciliation.

A conciliation officer from the service will then attempt to approach the employer and the individual, with a view to resolving the difference between them. Certain features of the role of ACAS can be stressed:

Conciliation is completely separate from the industrial tribunal system (conciliation officers are not members of tribunals).

Neither the employer nor the individual is compelled by law to discuss the matter with the officer.

Nevertheless, the officer provides an opportunity for a troublesome issue to be settled calmly and speedily.

The conciliation officer has no power to compel either party to settle their difference.

He will explore whether a disciplinary procedure has been fully used, and if it has not, he will encourage its full use.

He will explore with the *employer* whether he is prepared to consider the re-employment of the individual, failing which he will consider the scope for the voluntary payment of compensation to the individual.

He will explore with the *individual* whether he is determined to proceed with his complaint to an industrial tribunal or whether he would prefer an agreed settlement without a tribunal hearing; he will also explore the individual's preferred solution, eg re-employment or compensation.

Where an individual withdraws his complaint, or where an agreed settlement is reached under the auspices of ACAS, then the complaint to the tribunal automatically lapses, and the individual forfeits any entitlement to take his case to a tribunal, while the employer cannot renege on his decision (to re-employ or pay compensation) by then 'appealing' to a tribunal.

It is clear that a tribunal hearing is an alternative to settlement at ACAS, but it must be borne in mind that such hearings are held in public, with the attendant consequence of unwelcome press publicity. Compensation awards against employers tend to be higher than are those agreed at the ACAS stage, and tribunals have increasingly been attended by legal representatives, with the consequence that complex legal arguments tend now to be used in tribunal proceedings. Conciliation and tribunals do have certain features in common, however, for it is equally rare for a dismissed person to be re-employed by the former employer at either stage.

Redundancy Procedures

It might be argued that the negotiation of redundancy procedures is an admission of an inefficient business, and that the acknowledgement of the possibility of redundancy demotivates employees. However, redundancy procedures have a positive dimension, and (as recent British experience affirms) there are few enterprises which have avoided the need for redundancies.

Elements of redundancy procedures

A procedure might include a preamble along the following lines:

Example: Under normal operating circumstances, it is our intention to provide regular employment to all employees. However, reductions in manning may sometimes be felt to be inevitable, eg the demand for our product/service is unpredictable and might fluctuate.

The procedure might then itemize the steps which management would endeavour to take to reduce manning by means other than compulsory redundancies. Depending upon circumstrances, such steps might include: early retirement; natural wastage and/or the non-filling of vacancies; reducing or eliminating overtime working; slight reductions in basic weekly hours through negotiations; the redeployment or transfer of employees within the enterprise, with training where approriate; terminating the employment of temporary employees; the reduction or elimination of subcontracted work; voluntary redundancies.

Nevertheless, these steps might be insufficient to meet an employer's requirements. For instance, the measures as outlined might not bring about the desired reduction in numbers; that element of overtime working which is required to carry out essential repair or maintenance work places a lower limit on the extent to which overtime can be cut; early retirement can be extremely costly to an enterprise; and certain workers who are vital for continuing operations might leave first. In these circumstances, the issue arises of the selection of employees.

One frequently used method is last in first out (LIFO). This arrangement has advantages to employers, as it avoids their having to make invidious choices between individuals. It also appeals to trade unions, for it reduces the possibility that management might make selections on the basis of 'favouritism.'

But the application of LIFO is not without its problems. Should it, for example, apply by department or across the whole organization? Also, it might be inappropriate where operational requirements call for the retention of certain key occupational groups, such as computer personnel. Accordingly, employers might feel justified in considering other criteria, perhaps in the following sequence: operational and job requirements of the enterprise; skills and training levels; suitability for retraining; length of service; standard of performance, including past *verified* attendance record (*Example*: Misconduct (as defined in the disciplinary procedure) would not normally be treated as the sole reason for selection for redundancy but any current warnings issued (in accordance with the section on discipline) will be taken into account); personal circumstances.

As far as is possible, the selection criteria must be objective, in the sense that they are capable of some sort of independent assessment.

Some problems and issues

There are certain trade unionists in Britain who refuse as a matter of principle to negotiate redundancy procedures with employers, on the grounds that a joint procedure might render redundancies less easy to resist. Other trade unionists view the matter differently, on the grounds that a joint agreement enables them to influence the employer's manpower strategy, including the taking of measures short of redundancy (see above). There is also the risk that a union's outright refusal to negotiate over redundancies will leave inadequate scope for the negotiation of the most favourable terms of compensation on behalf of those who are made redundant.

It is now commonplace in British industry for redundant workers to receive payments in excess of the minimum laid down by Redundancy Payments legislation. When trade unionists perceive that some redundancies are inevitable, and when all alternatives to compulsory redundancies have been found wanting, then the best possible terms for affected members can be negotiated. In this connection, it is to be noted that the statutory scheme is linked to length of service, and that no one with less than two years' service with an employer would be legally entitled to any payment from him.

In some circumstances, the need for redundancies occurs with little warning by virtue of a major, unforeseen, external cause. In general, however, any changes in manpower can be anticipated and therefore planned. It seems to be a growing practice for employers to consult with trade unions and, in larger-scale cases, this is required by law.*

Extracts from a recent agreement between the Automobile Association

* For the current legal requirements on consulation over redundances see Chapter 13, p 281.

(AA) and APEX exemplify attempts at greater consultation over the issue:

Example: The AA agrees to disclose to APEX annual corporate and business plans. Twelve months' notice of proposals with job security implications will be given. Consultation takes place every six months on manpower forecasts and overall manning levels. This entails disclosure of all information concerning the proposals and allows reasonable time and opportunity for the trade union to examine and seek clarification on each proposal. Revised proposals will be given full consideration.

The criteria for the selection of redundant workers can be fraught with difficulty. Moreover, a worker who has been 'unfairly' selected for redundancy might be able to claim unfair dismissal where an employer has unreasonably departed from a procedure or customary arrangement. It is therefore advisable for management to consider the establishment of an appeals procedure, to which aggrieved employees can submit their cases.

Health and Safety Procedures

It would appear that formal health and safety procedures received encouragement in the post-Donovan climate through the publication of the Robens Report in 1972,[8] and the introduction of two statutory instruments: the Health and Safety at Work etc Act 1974, amplified by the Safety Representatives and Safety Committees Regulations 1977.

Elements in health and safety procedures

The basic philosophy of the legislation is that it is the responsibility of all people within an organization to seek to achieve safe and healthy working conditions. Alongside this universal obligation, the ultimate responsibility for health and safety policy in an enterprise rests with managers, in the following basic respects:

The provision and maintenance of plant, systems, and places of work that are safe.

The safe handling, storage and transport of articles and substances.

The provision of information, instruction, training and supervision to ensure the health and safety of employees.

The provision of a working environment that is safe and without risks to health.

The provision of adequate welfare facilities.

It is, then, the duty of every employer, usually at board level, to prepare a written statement of his policy concerning health and safety, and to bring this policy to the notice of employees. It is also incumbent on the employer to ensure that the system of recruitment, supervision and training within the enterprise reinforces the policy laid down.*

In the case of hazardous substances or operations, for example, it is clearly necessary to ensure that people who are *recruited* to work with these possess the requisite specialized knowledge. Or, to take another example, when the atmosphere is polluted, it is not enough for management to issue protective clothing to employees; *supervision* must also ensure that such clothing is worn. Nor does it suffice for policy and associated standards merely to be introduced; they must also be *monitored*, by such means as collating statistics, conducting investigations, and preparing reports on health and safety incidents.

The 1977 Regulations envisaged a prominent role for employees, notably through the employees' appointment of safety representatives and joint safety committees (JSCs). Several functions were conferred upon a safety representative, the most notable being:

To investigate potential hazards and dangerous occurrences at the workplace and to examine the causes of workplace accidents.

To investigate complaints made by any employee whom he represents, relating to that employee's health, safety or welfare at work.

To make representations to the employer on the foregoing matters.

To make representations to the employer on general health, safety or welfare matters within the workplace.

To carry out inspections of the workplace, or of documents in the employer's possession, or to obtain relevant information from the employer.

To attend meetings of JSCs in his capacity as safety representative.

It must be stressed that the powers that are outlined above apply to representatives, not to JSCs. It is also to be noted that the representatives must be members of a 'recognized trade union'; in other words, the statutory system of safety representation is trade union based.[9]

For the purpose of clarity, it is important for the employer to identify the relevant manager to whom the safety representative should report. The manager concerned should preferably have received training in health and safety matters, and should also have detailed knowledge of the matter and operations under discussion. It seems advisable, therefore, for the line manager or supervisor to be the first point of contact rather than, say, the

---

* For a dramatic instance of apparent corporate neglect, see the statement by Mr D Steel QC, for the Secretary of State for Transport, at the Inquiry into the sinking of the *Herald of Free Enterprise*. 'The disease of sloppy systems and sloppy instructions was not just on board ship, but extended well into the body corporate of Townsend Thoresen car ferries.' The *Guardian* 28 April 1987.

personnel or safety officer. Nevertheless, a representative's written report to his supervisor, perhaps on a specially prepared form, might be copied to other relevant people. The supervisor's reply to the representative could take a similar course. In other instances, the supervisor might initiate the completion of a special form, when, for example, an accident occurs.

Under the Regulations, an employer is obliged to establish a JSC with employees where at least two safety representatives request him in writing to do so. A JSC must then be established within three months of the employer's receipt of the request. Some JSCs operate under a constitution, containing the following elements:

Composition of the committee (the presence of a senior manager would affirm to employees the seriousness with which management regards the JSC).

Duration of office of the committee members.

Training provision for management and worker representatives.

Dates of meetings.

Determination of the agenda.

Functions and powers of the JSC.

Minutes of meetings: their writing and distribution.

The role and status of invitees (including safety officers) and subcommittees.

Attention has to be given to a hierarchy of safety committees, where more than one workplace is involved. The health and safety procedure at Lehrer/McGovern Bovis's Canary Wharf development has the following provision:

Example: An overall Project Safety Committee chaired by LMB will receive reports from individual Site Safety Committees and monitor overall safety and health on site.

Regard has to be paid to the relationship between JSCs and conventional Joint Consultative Committees (JCCs)*. Given the technical nature of health and safety considerations, there is much to be said for having separate committees, specifically for such matters.

The legislation is enforced by the Health and Safety Executive (HSE) through its inspectors. It is within an inspector's power to issue an employer with an 'improvement' or 'prohibition' notice in connection with an employer's infraction but, in reality, the inspector is more likely to attempt conciliation with the employer. It is extremely rare for the HSE to take enforcement action.[10] ACAS might also have an advisory or conciliatory role to play, but only after the relevant disputes/grievance procedure had been exhausted.

* See Chapter 8, pp 169–173 for a detailed discussion of JCCs.

Some problems and issues

The extent to which health and safety issues are truly a subject for dispute between employers and employees is debatable. The Robens Report best exemplified a 'unitary' perspective, contending that there is a high degree of common interest, given best effect through consultation between the two sides. The Regulations, in contrast, assigned an extremely prominent role to union representatives; a pluralistic perspective was stressed, and negotiations were seen as the best means of resolving conflicting interests.

Two interrelated matters for consideration can thus be seen to arise. First, are health and safety issues more rightfully appropriate for consultation than negotiation? Second, to what extent should safety representatives come from shop stewards' ranks, thereby emphasizing their links with the unions?

The process of consultation between employers and employees in Britain is often said to be characterized by shared interests: the parties jointly seek out all relevant information, they share it fully, they jointly work out solutions, they indulge in a positive-sum game (where both sides gain), and adversarial behaviour is eschewed. In general, managers tend to be more enthusiastic about consultation, for it allows them to retain their decision-making powers.

In the case of negotiations, on the other hand, the degree of information sharing is restricted, the parties engage in a zero-sum game (a win to one side entails an equivalent loss to the other) and the tactics of bluffs, threats and sanctions are used. Trade unionists are said to tend to favour this approach and to have a suspicion that an employer's fostering of consultation might serve to undermine the strength of workplace bargaining.*

In common with many such generalizations, the distinction between consultation and negotiation is, in reality, blurred: some consultative processes have elements of joint decision-making, whereas some negotiations occur in an environment of shared assumptions and constructive efforts.

In the case of health and safety, there is some doubt whether assumptions and interests are so fully shared that consultation is the solely appropriate mode. Thus, the creation of a safe environment carries a cost which the employer must bear and which he might seek to temper. In a study of safety in coalmining, the author concluded that the more money that was spent on roof supports, the safer was the mine.[11]† Yet, such automation could, in

---

* See Chapter 5 for a detailed analysis of negotiations.

† In the case of the *Herald of Free Enterprise* disaster, 1987, senior officers had apparently taken industrial action five years previously in order to press for safer closing of the bow doors. The company allegedly resisted the change on the grounds that safety had to be balanced against expense. The *Guardian* 29 April 1987.

principle, give rise to a further source of tension between employer and employees: the installation of labour-saving machinery might cause redundancies.

Evidence also suggests that when health and safety issues involve significant financial expenditure, safety representatives tend to process these through collective bargaining procedures rather than through consultation.[12] Trade unionists are unlikely to see JSCs as the principal vehicle for improvement, for several reasons: JSCs meet only occasionally, and are more suitable for long-run policy issues, whereas some problems call for immediate action; fully 'consultative' JSCs would have little or no power to authorize decisions; and representatives might receive more solid support from their constituents through collective bargaining.

The links of solidarity between representatives and their constituents is one reason why some trade unions prefer their shop stewards to serve as safety representatives too. The need to have people with considerable 'representing' experience is another reason. But other trade unions prefer a separation of roles. The danger of an overload of work is a prime factor (health and safety can involve many 'technical' issues, calling for specialist workplace knowledge), and it might often be more satisfactory for the workers' side to have one of their number catering for 'quasi-consultative' issues, leaving the shop steward to develop the more controversial ones in a negotiating framework.

There are several features of the safety representative structure which call for agreed procedural arrangements between management and workers:

The law places no restriction on the number of representatives that a union may appoint, but the significance of this issue would be reduced somewhat were the representatives to be drawn from the ranks of shop stewards.

The constituencies of the representatives require to be identified, bearing in mind that representatives have the right of inspection; different shifts or distinct occupational groups might have to be catered for.

In multi-union situations, each trade union would have the right to appoint a safety representative, but it might be decided that some representatives should cater for more than one union where the constituencies are small.

Attention has to be given to the position of non-union employees, who have no representative rights under the legislation.

Attention must also be given to the statutory requirements for representatives to have time off with pay, during normal working hours, in order to receive training: eg To what extent should the 'in-house' training be meshed with that provided by the unions outside the place of work? Should there be upper limits on the amount of time off that can be allowed in any one period? (There would appear to be some scope for trade-off – the larger the number of representatives, the less time off that they individually need.) How should lost overtime and bonus earnings be calculated in the assessment of pay?

These sorts of issue have the potential for dispute. Accordingly, some connection is called for between health and safety, grievance, and negotiating procedures. Potential links with disciplinary procedures also arise, for health and safety can form a basis for discipline and dismissal. Thus, there are those instances where the employer is allegedly not providing a safe environment – the safety clothing or equipment might be held to be inadequate, or the worker might feel that he is being recklessly exposed to disease or disability. In these instances, the worker might be able to claim unfair (constructive) dismissal when all other representations have failed to achieve relief. There are obligations on workers, too. A worker whose negligence or wantonness place the safety of others in jeopardy might be fairly dismissed.

In short, health and safety matters are the responsibility of all concerned; the procedures should recognize that fundamental proposition.

Procedural Checklist

When introducing and operating procedures, management and unions might be advised to keep the following points in mind. They should:

Be prepared to seek advice and learn from others who are knowledge-able about procedures; copies of procedures in other enterprises are well worth consulting.

Ensure that procedures are comprehensive yet not dauntingly complex.

Ensure that they are used and not locked away in drawers or filing cabinets.

Ensure that they are regularly updated to take account of experience gained with operating the procedures, developments in the law, industrial practice elsewhere, mergers or takeovers affecting the firm, technological change, or developments in the sphere of health, such as AIDS, the effects of VDUs, or measures to counter breast or cervical cancer .[13]

Bear in mind the contents of other procedures when changes to one of them are being contemplated.

Ensure that one manager (eg within the personnel function) and one union representative (eg a convener) are given the role of reviewing joint procedures every year or so, in the light of experience (a joint working party might sometimes have a role to play, perhaps under the auspices of the ACAS advisory function).

Acknowledge that good procedures, closely followed, are a sign of efficient managers and diligent workplace representatives.

Also acknowledge that sound procedures are no guarantee that all will be resolved peacefully and speedily, for they are only as perfect or imperfect as the people who negotiate and operate them.

Recognize that procedures are no substitute for sound policy making, but are merely the means through which jointly-agreed policies are jointly carried out.

Procedural Trends and Developments

Industrial relations procedures in Britain are rich in contrasts and paradoxes. Some aspects owe much to statutory encouragement, whereas elsewhere the law has had little influence; procedures give the impression of a decision-making process which is fully shared between managers and unions, but the reality is frequently different; formality and informality can both co-exist and be mutually incompatible; and there is an appearance of procedural innovation which probably changes little.

There is much to be said, in principle, for formal, written, comprehensive procedures, clearly spelt out for the guidance of all. Nevertheless, there are limits to the scope of such formality, for no procedure could possibly cover every contingency, and some degree of informality could be said to be both inevitable and desirable.

Nor should it be idealistically assumed that procedures find favour with, are enthusiastically supported by, and confer equivalent benefits upon, all concerned. Procedures can be viewed as control mechanisms, constraining to various degrees the behaviour of managers, trade union officials, and the mass of employees. It is partly for this reason that British industry is ambivalent towards procedures, so that a strict adherence to the letter of procedure is not always evident.

In April 1987, for instance, British Rail was reported as imposing a pay increase on employees, even though the claim was due to be arbitrated by the industry's tribunal. Moreover, BR made it clear that it would not regard the arbitrator's award as binding, even were he to award a higher increase.[14] Among employers in general it is clear that procedures that are jointly agreed with unions are but one route to the successful handling of industrial relations. 'Sophisticated moderns' assign a prominent place to such an approach, whereas the 'sophisticated paternalists' bypass the unions more or less completely.[15]

Trade unions, too, approach procedures with some scepticism. The fact that procedures are more common for terms and conditions than for, say, redundancy or discipline, partly reflects the unions' reluctance formally to concede specified rights to the employer. It might often be tactically and strategically preferable for trade union representatives to react to management decisions rather than attempt to share them.*

There seems to be little doubt that statutory forces have encouraged the development of certain procedures in Britain, notably in the spheres of discipline and health and safety.[17] The implementing of these procedures has also been overlaid by a legislative apparatus. In consequence, workers have a right of 'appeal' against management decisions to independent external bodies. Whether, in consequence, workers' interests are better protected is more debatable, however. Of course, the mere existence of the law might act as some constraint upon management, so that workers are disciplined, not dismissed, or working environments are rendered safer than they otherwise might have been. Nevertheless, the experience with unfair dismissal legislation does not seem to suggest substantial relief for workers,[18] and there is evidence that not even the minima as provided for in the health and safety legislation are always laid down.[19]

In the light of these realities, trade unions demonstrate scepticism towards the statutory reinforcement of procedural arrangements; law can have double-edged effects, serving to confirm management decisions, and adding a layer of extreme complexity and uncertainty to workplace industrial relations.

In marked contrast, the widespread incidence of negotiating and grievance procedures owes little to statutory encouragement, although such measures have been contemplated and attempted in connection with collective agreements as a whole. According to the Conservative government's Green Paper[20] two main advantages were likely to stem from the legal enforceability of collective agreements, which, as we noted earlier, British industry has shunned. First, enforceability would bring peace and stability to industrial relations; and second, it would encourage the development and use of disputes procedures. However, the Green Paper mentioned several drawbacks to such an approach, the most noteworthy for our purpose being that legal enforceability required clear agreements that were capable of interpretation in the courts, whereas the 'vast majority' of collective agreements in Britain were underpinned by *informal* understandings and arrangements.

That employers were at best apathetic to the attempt of the 1971

---

* For example, an ACAS survey[16] found widespread incidence of redundancy policies or practices as distinct from agreements. The survey concentrated on those employers who either had standing redundancy arrangements or had recently declared redundancies. Those employers who had no policies or practices, let alone agreements, were therefore excluded from the survey. On the lesser likelihood that disciplinary or dismissal procedures are jointly agreed, compared with negotiating procedures, see Millward and Stevens, op cit, p 189.

Industrial Relations Act to declare agreements legally enforceable suggests that managers also seem to regard the law as sitting uncomfortably with procedural matters. Indeed, employers' emphasis seems to be on autonomous developments, as exemplified by the recent extension of last offer arbitration in Britain.

It appears that such arrangements are especially to be found in the private sector, among multinationals, and in conjunction with single-union and no-strike agreements.[21] It also seems that the arrangements might have the effect of achieving the objectives of legally enforceable agreements – stability in industrial relations, a declining incidence of industrial disputes, more 'responsible' bargaining – with a flexibility which association with the law might impair.

For example, although the last offer agreement between Sanyo Industries (UK) Ltd and the EETPU does not formally provide for mediation, that device was successfully used in a recent dispute.[22] Moreover, there appear to be close similarities between the 'strike-free' clauses of last offer processes and the 'peace' clauses which have long been a characteristic of British procedures.

Nor could last offer arbitration be said to be innovatory in other respects, for disputes of right generally require the arbitrator to make a straight choice between one party and the other. Somewhat paradoxically, therefore, the development of last offer arbitration might render resort to arbitration even less frequent than has traditionally been the case in this country, in that it might encourage the parties to do their utmost to reach mutually acceptable agreements. Such a conclusion is supported by the fact that last offer provisions are rarely invoked.*

That the unions seem to have been prepared to enter into such arrangements says much about the contemporary situation. A few years ago, it perhaps would have been unheard of for a single union to reach an agreement with an employer to be given sole bargaining rights in return for promises purporting to offer 'strike-free' deals and 'automatic' arbitration. It is clear that mass unemployment and economic recession have fostered a mentality of survival of the fittest among the unions, and have encouraged the more entrepreneurial among them (eg the EETPU) to perceive these agreements as a lifeline to membership consolidation. But the recent experience with last offer arbitration also demonstrates that employers continue to play the dominant role in the introduction of procedures. The unions are unlikely to obtain much relief from any statutory framework that can presently be envisaged; the state of the economy, forces of competition and technological change will continue to compel employers to control manning levels and labour costs, exercise strong discipline and economize

---

* On the possibility that last offer arbitration might encourage adversarial behaviour, including the employment of lawyers, see IDS *Study* 409 'Pendulum Arbitration' May 1988.

on health and safety; and such control will probably be exercised more through the consultative mode than through the negotiating one. It would seem, therefore, that the unions will have to rely and draw heavily upon their own resources to utilize the large elements of informality which procedural arrangements continue to offer.

References
1. Millward N and Stevens M *British Workplace Industrial Relations 1980–1984, the DE/ESRC/PSI/ACAS Surveys* (1986) Gower, Aldershot, p 169
2. Royal Commission on Trade Unions and Employers' Associations *Report* Cmnd 3623, 1968
3. *Ibid* paras 68, 162–6
4. ACAS *Annual Report 1987* HMSO, 1988, p 73
5. See Leese J 'The Nissan Agreement – A Work Philosophy' *Employment Gazette* **93** (August 1985), p 327; and Singh R 'Final Offer Arbitration in Theory and Practice' *Industrial Relations Journal* **17** 4 (Winter 1986)
6. Hunter I 'Discipline at Work' *Employment Gazette* 96 (May 1988)
7. Op cit, p 176
8. Committee of Inquiry on Safety and Health at Work 1970–72 *Report* Cmnd 5034 (1972)
9. For details of representation in non-union situations, see Beaumont P *Safety at Work and the Unions* (1983) Croom Helm, Beckenham, p 186
10. Walters D 'Health and Safety and Trade Union Workplace Organisation – A Case Study in the Printing Industry' *Industrial Relations Journal* **18** 1 (Spring 1987)
11. Hopkins A and Palser J 'The Causes of Coal Mine Accidents' *ibid*; see also the Zeebrugge ferry disaster in 1987
12. Walters, op cit
13. On AIDS, see Department of Employment/Health and Safety Executive *AIDS and Employment* (1987) COI, London 1987; on workplace sources of ill-health among office workers, see *Employment Gazette* **95** (April 1987), p 217. Certain collective agreements are already providing for female employees to have time off for breast and cervical cancer screening. The British Printing Industries Federation has such an arrangement with SOGAT and NGA. Although there is no precise equivalent in the Scottish industry, the Society of Master Printers of Scotland reminds its members that on-site facilities could be provided where these are justified by the number of employees. It will probably be only a matter of time before such an arrangement is formally incorporated.
14. The *Guardian* (24 April 1987)
15. Purcell J and Sisson K 'Strategies and Practice in the Management of Industrial Relations' in Bain G S (ed) *Industrial Relations in Britain* (1983) Blackwell, Oxford, p 114
16. *Redundancy Arrangements: The 1986 Survey* Occasional Paper 37 (1987) ACAS, London, p 12
17. Millward N and Stevens M, op cit, p 170
18. See the author's 'Unfair Dismissal Legislation and Property Rights – Some Reflections' *Industrial Relations Journal* **16** 4 (Winter 1985)

19. Walters, op cit, p 48. It must also be observed that the author's study was in the printing industry, where trade union activity and vigilance would normally be expected to be relatively keen
20. *Trade Union Immunities* Cmnd 8128 (1981), p 55
21. Singh, op cit
22. *Ibid* p 333

Chapter 8

Employee Participation*

Mick Marchington

The idea of employees participating in some way in the administration of their working lives has long been a source of interest for practitioners and academics alike. Some would argue that such ideas are an unnecessary diversion from the primary job of management – that is, to supply a profitable and cost-effective service to the customers – and that employers should have the right to make decisions without being forced to consider employee interests. Others would suggest that an unbridled managerial prerogative is quite contrary to the democratic ideals upon which developed societies are based, and that employees ought to have a say in decisions which affect their working lives.

Indeed, the terminology itself serves to illustrate the quite different interpretations of employee participation: while employers talk of employee involvement, trade unionists talk of industrial democracy. That is, one starts from the assumption that managements might be willing to *allow* some degree of involvement by employees in the process of decision-making, while the other has its source in notions of democracy and the *right* of the governed to control those in positions of authority.

The period since the mid-1970s has seen practical illustrations of this conflict of interpretations, with initiatives ranging from worker directors through to team briefing and profit sharing, along with a resurgence of interest in joint consultation. In other words, while it might have become commonplace among progressive managers and trade unionists to argue that employee participation is a 'good' thing – for whatever reason – the practical expression of this concept has also led to significantly different forms of participation in different workplaces.

Notwithstanding the debate over terminology, a whole range of participation initiatives have been adopted by employing organizations within the UK. What matters to practitioners is whether these schemes actually provide advantages to those involved, either in terms of substantive

* The author would like to thank Barrie Dale, Philip Parker and Derek Torrington (all colleagues in the Manchester School of Management, UMIST) for their useful comments on the first draft of this chapter.

benefits or improved working relationships. Of course, the consequences of such schemes might not be those which their designers intended, and it is important to assess success (however measured) against practical examples rather than exhortations or rhetoric. In this chapter, the concern is to describe and analyse practice in a number of different forms of participation, chosen for their relevance to contemporary industrial relations activity.*

Forms of Employee Participation

A distinction can be made between these different forms of employee participation in the following way:

Direct participation is concerned with face-to-face contact between managers and their subordinates, and may primarily involve the passage of information from the former to the latter, communication between the two parties, or the exercise by subordinates of some kind of decision-making activity. The types of technique which can be included in this category would be team briefing and quality circles. The basic point about this form of participation, however, is that employees are involved on an individual level rather than through their representatives.

Indirect participation is concerned with the situation in which employees are involved in the process of management decision-making via their representatives, who have generally been elected from among their number to undertake such duties. Schemes may vary from worker representatives on the board of the company through to joint consultative committees which could operate at any level within the organization, and indeed may link together managers and shop stewards from a number of establishments in a large enterprise. Since individual employees delegate powers (explicitly or implicitly) to their representatives on such committees, these people have to achieve a balance between the potentially competing requirements of both parties to the employment contract. Understandably, this has led to some concern about the appropriate role for employee representatives on such bodies.

Financial participation is concerned with economic involvement by employees in the success (or failure) of the organization, and the link between a proportion of their pay and company or departmental performance. Typically, this would include profit sharing schemes, employee share ownership, and value-added payment systems. These

---

* The decision to focus upon team briefing, quality circles, consultation, worker directions and profit sharing was made on this basis. Inevitably, other practices could have been examined, the most important of these being autonomous work groups, information disclosure, pension fund trustees, and safety representatives, but there is insufficient space to do justice to all of these techniques.

may or may not be associated with mechanisms for involving employees in decision-making processes, and this in itself has led to criticism of such schemes.

The 1980s has seen developments within each of these different categories, although primarily in the first and the last. Direct employee involvement has become something of a growth industry, as managements have increasingly sought to inform their employees of the organization's position in the marketplace, in an attempt to win their cooperation (or at least acquiescence) in achieving the process of change. Indirect participation tends to be through joint consultative committees, which it was estimated by the mid-1980s existed in about one-third of all establishments in which 25 or more were employed. In the public sector, it was nearly half of all establishments.[1] Worker directors have become a rarity, even in the public sector, following the decade after the publication of the Bullock Committee of Inquiry. Financial participation has been stimulated by the Finance Acts of 1978, 1980 and 1984, to the extent that almost one-quarter of companies were estimated to have a scheme in operation by the middle of the decade, and in some sectors (notably finance) a majority of companies had adopted such techniques.[2]

Why should these trends towards greater employee participation, particularly of a 'soft' nature – that is, those initiated by managements, which do not challenge existing forms of decision-making – have taken place? Several general reasons can be put forward:

Employers have been seeking ways in which to elicit employee commitment to corporate rather than trade union goals (in particular, quality, productivity, and competitiveness) and it is felt that this is more likely to be forthcoming if employee participation is developed.

Managements may take the view that employees are more likely to cooperate in the process of change if they are aware of the circumstances confronting their company, the reason behind the need for change, and their knowledge of the alternatives.

A desire on the part of employers to avoid the consequences of industrial action by trade unions resentful of a failure to involve them in decision-making processes, and a preference to spend time and money in channelling conflict into peaceful and manageable procedures.

Increasing expectations on the part of working people who have learnt from a more democratic socialization that they ought to have some influence over their conditions of employment and the quality of their working lives.

The possibility of legislation influenced by Britain's membership of the EEC which compels employers to develop some form of employee participation.

Of course, following a late addition to the 1982 Employment Act, there has been a requirement for companies covered by the provisions of the Companies Act, and which employ more than 250 people, to report on action taken during the previous financial year to introduce, maintain or develop employee involvement. The focus on action, rather than policy, as in the case of employing the disabled, is meant to ensure that companies describe what is *actually* happening, rather than what ought to happen.

Four areas are specified: the provision of *information* on matters of concern to employees, which could be through a variety of mechanisms, such as employee reports, house magazines and briefing groups; *consulting* with employees or their representatives so that their views can be taken into account on decisions likely to affect them; *financial* involvement of employees through schemes like share ownership or group-wide productivity incentive systems; helping to achieve a *common economic and financial awareness* on the part of employees, which could be achieved via any of the other categories or mixtures of all three. The information is included in the annual report.

Welcome though legislative pressures are to analysts who consider that employers do little or nothing realistically to involve their employees in the affairs of the company, the requirement of this particular provision was not seen to be one which would force employers to do anything more. Moreover, if they feel so inclined, there is no sanction against employers who choose to file a 'nil' return, since there is no obligation actually to involve employees, only to report on what is being done on the participation front. Indeed, scrutiny of early returns indicated that almost 10 per cent of employers included no report on employee involvement. Conversely, about 20 per cent provided reports which illustrated positive encouragement for all four aspects of employee involvement.

There is little doubt that some organizations, especially the large multi-establishment conglomerates with interests in a wide range of industries, might experience problems in summarizing more than a small sample of activities. More fundamentally, among certain employers there is a feeling that the reporting requirement creates unnecessary work, encourages pious expressions of intent, and focuses attention on structures rather than the processes of employee participation. As we shall see in subsequent sections, the mere existence of a particular form of participation can tell us little or nothing about the *nature* of involvement, and the commitment of the parties towards it. Designing appropriate systems is no more than the first stage of any participation initiative, and the whole process requires the investment of considerable effort, time and motivation on behalf of all participants.

The major part of the chapter focuses on a series of employee participation activities that are, or might be, practised by employers and employees within the UK. With the exception of worker directors, the remainder are all management initiatives. This reflects not only prevailing structures of power and authority within employing organizations, but also the current economic, social, legal and political context within which industrial relations take place. In the concluding section there will be a brief discussion of future possibilities which depend, to some extent, on the ability of the British government to thwart European initiatives.

Team Briefing

Team briefing is a system of communication operated by line management, based upon the principle of cascading information down the line. Its objective is to make sure that all employees know and understand what they and others in the company are doing and why. It hinges around the principle of leaders getting together with their teams on a regular basis in a small group, in order to put across information relevant to their work. Although there is provision for information from the top, the major priority is local or departmental matters, and it is the leader's job to ensure that this occupies most of the meeting. Team briefing would usually last for half an hour or less.

As a technique, team briefing is increasingly gaining ground within British industry. There is nothing especially new in the idea of informing employees about company or departmental affairs, but the major proponents of team briefing – the Industrial Society – insist that the current schemes are different, in that the emphasis is on local matters and supervisory explanations (and therefore, to some extent, interpretations) of a central brief. Experience with team briefing is now extending beyond manufacturing industry, and there are examples of the scheme in practice within public corporations and the National Health Service.

According to the Industrial Society booklet '*Team Briefing*'[3] the system has a number of crucial benefits. In addition to the general objectives – of improving efficiency and satisfaction – there are a variety of highly practical benefits, such as:

> It reinforces the role of line managers and supervisors as leaders of their teams, by virtue of their being seen as different from their subordinates. In addition, it also enhances their reputation as the providers of information to team members, and reminds supervisors that they are accountable for the performance of their unit.

> It increases workforce and supervisory commitment to the primary task, and also to the organization as a whole. While team briefing will not succeed in making a boring job interesting, it will provide employees with a greater sense of purpose and direction in their activity. Also, while individuals may not agree with a particular course of action, they can accept it if they understand the reason for it.

> It reduces misunderstandings if information is communicated to

employees, and prevents a considerable amount of wasted time and rumours over potential decisions. There is often an assumption that people know what is happening, but it might be better to rely on the old saying that 'it is better to re-inform the informed than to leave the uninformed uninformed'!

It helps people to accept changes at work because the early provision of information can assist understanding about the change and the reasons for them.

It helps to control the grapevine, not by preventing it, but by ensuring that employees receive the 'official' version of any decision from their manager. Because individual supervisors have to provide the information themselves, there is also pressure upon them to understand any communications, and on the company to ensure that they are regularly briefed about activities.

It improves upward communication, since people will begin to feel after their initial exposure to team briefing that they now know some of the facts, and can therefore contribute to the organization in a more meaningful way.

In practical terms, team briefing has several key principles which have emerged over years of experience. These are:

The central message should be based upon ideas following a senior management or board meeting.

At each level, the central message should contribute no more than 30 per cent of the total message.

Teams should be based around a common production or service area, rather than an occupation.

The team should comprise between four and 15 people.

Meetings should be held at least monthly and on a regular, pre-arranged basis.

The aim should be to brief all employees within 48 hours.

The meeting should not last for more than 30 minutes.

There should be no more than four levels in the cascade system from senior management to the office or shop floor.

General discussion should be discouraged.

Time should be left for questions about the brief at the end of the input from the leader.

The leader should be the manager or supervisor of the section concerned.

Leaders must be trained in the principles and skills of how to brief.

As with any set of prescriptive points about a management technique, there are commonly two sets of objections. On a practical level, experience has shown that companies can run into problems when trying to tailor the principles of team briefing to their own organizational requirements. This is particularly the case for organizations with a pattern of work organization which makes it difficult to operate the system effectively. For example, extensive shift working means that more sessions have to be arranged than would otherwise be the case; there may be difficulties in getting information across to people who are not at work for several days – in organizations like the NHS, where substantial numbers of people are employed in the community, it is rare for all individuals to be at the main office for more than a few minutes each day; on continuous production or process operations, it may be impossible to brief all staff since a skeleton service has to be provided at all times. Of course, given the commitment on the part of management, it is always possible to minimize the problems, and perhaps allow for rotation or in exceptional circumstances longer periods of time in which to push out the information.

Team briefing is heavily reliant upon the skills of the leader as the imparter of information, the controller of the meeting, the fielder of questions, and the achiever of objectives. Not surprisingly, such a range of skills is not found in all that many managers – especially first-line supervisors – and it is crucial that training is provided for briefers. But the training itself may not be of the right nature, nor may the practical benefits be sustained by individual briefers beyond the first few sessions. Training requires not just the development of an appropriate set of skills, but also the continuous monitoring of those skills, and regular reviews of progress against objectives. In addition, if briefing is to be more than a flash in the pan and actually to bring about a change in attitudes and style of management, the system has to be sustained by the provision of relevant and comprehensible pieces of information. This may be somewhat easier in certain organizations than others, especially those in which financial, production and order statistics are compiled on a monthly basis. A lack of meaningful information, or repetition of historical material, can easily lead to disillusionment on the part of briefers and their teams, and to the degeneration of meetings into moaning sessions.

There are also more fundamental objections to any briefing system. The whole language of team briefing is managerial in tone, and is concerned with reinforcement of managerial prerogatives. Notions of teams – as groups or organizations as a whole – flow from a unitarist perspective,* as does the view that the interpretation of management decisions should not be undertaken by shop stewards. Not surprisingly, for this reason

---

* Unitarists are keen to view organizations as football teams, in which all participants are aiming for the same goal, have similar objectives, and are not in conflict with one another.

workplace trade union representatives may be suspicious of management motives when introducing such a scheme, and see it as little more than an attempt to weaken union organization by the back door.

Indeed, this was the line taken by the TGWU when the West Yorkshire Passenger Transport Executive attempted to introduce team briefing into their organization. The union was strongly opposed to any proposal that management should communicate directly and systematically with the workforce, feeling it to be a part of a deliberate attempt to undermine the trade union, and bypass normal consultative and negotiating procedures. Union opposition continued and actually became more entrenched once team briefing had been implemented, with the result that there were low attendances at meetings among certain groups of employees.

It would appear that team briefing has the greatest likelihood of implementation in two quite different sets of circumstances: on the one hand, where there is little or no union organization, and management's interpretations of events are those which are more likely to secure acceptance from the workforce; on the other, where unions are well organized, have good channels of communication with their members, and are supported by a progressive management philosophy. Conversely, where there is a history of distrust and overt conflict between management and the unions, there is more likely to be suspicion of any new initiative directed at individual members and workers. Paradoxically, a system such as briefing probably has the greatest chance of success when it is least needed, and the least chance of success when it is most needed.

In addition, some of the potential benefits of team briefing also appear to rest upon highly questionable and unestablished assumptions. For example, the notion that people may accept decisions they do not agree with because they understand the reasoning behind such decisions, can only really be sustained in the context of a power imbalance in the employment contract. There must also be doubts that the management chain can be reinforced via briefing, when one considers the essentially problematic role of first-line supervisors, especially those who have been promoted from the shop floor, and do not share the same value systems as managers.

Nevertheless, team briefing has been introduced into a great many organizations during the 1980s, and it must therefore be providing participants with something they value. If team briefing is used in conjunction with other forms of participation – notably those in which workers and/or their representatives have the opportunity to interact with senior management – the information provided by the system may prove to be of benefit to different interest groups within the employing organization. Similarly, if managements are seen not to use team briefing to subvert other regulatory processes, unions are less likely to challenge its existence.

Quality Circles

While definitions and features obviously vary between organizations, quality circles consist of small groups of employees who meet voluntarily on a regular basis to identify, analyse and solve quality and work-related problems. The membership of the circle would normally comprise between four and a dozen volunteers from the same work area, or those doing similar work, who meet under the guidance of the group leader. Usually, supervisors act as leaders of quality circles, and it is their task to encourage volunteers to set up the group, and then help to develop it into a cohesive team. Training of circle members is done by facilitators, who are available as a source of information and encouragement, and who act as a liaison between individual circles and the rest of the organization. Usually, in addition, the whole concept will have been initiated and will continue to be monitored by a steering committee, comprising representatives from various departments within the organization.

A leading writer on the subject[4] has identified three distinctive features of quality circles: the principle of *voluntary* membership; the encouragement to *solve* job-related problems, rather than merely to spot them; and the provision of *training* to enable people to solve problems in an organized and effective manner.

Quality circles were first practised on any significant scale in Japan, although the original ideas behind such systems stemmed from the USA. There are now estimated to be over one million quality circles in Japan and over 10 million workers are involved in them. They have also taken off more recently in the USA, Germany, France, Italy and the UK.

Here in the UK, it is estimated that circles exist in about 500 workplaces, both in manufacturing and service environments, and many more companies have either tried to implement them or been forced to suspend them for one reason or another. Some of the best-known experiments in the UK have been in companies such as British Telecom, May and Baker, Blackwell's, Wedgwood, Mullard and Jaguar cars.

In other companies, similar principles and practices are undertaken but under a different name, for example, the implementation of EI at Ford. Some companies have gone even further, and implemented total quality management (TQM) systems, which are also based on participative principles, and are geared up to tenets of customer service, error-free work, and the measurement of success through the cost of quality. The primary aim is to build quality into the product, rather than check quality standards by inspection. UK examples of TQM can be found in Armco, Ciba-Corning, IBM and Rank Xerox.

Some of the benefits claimed for these quality programmes are similar to those seen for team briefing, namely the likelihood of a greater commitment to work and interest in the job, but quality circles go further in that they actively encourage employee involvement in decision-making, albeit at task level and within specified boundaries. The aim is to improve decision-making and to iron out problems at the earliest possible opportunity. It is also felt that quality circles can have a positive effect on the atmosphere within an organization, and can assist in the development of individual abilities gained through training and participation in meetings, as well as improving the viability of the company in terms of cost and quality.

Key components of quality circles are that: meetings should be held weekly or fortnightly, in working time; the place and time for meetings should be arranged in advance; meetings should last for about one hour; members should be trained in a variety of techniques and interpersonal skills; leaders keep groups to the central task of dealing with work-related problems; the group endeavours to enlist support from top management. Indeed, the final component is seen as a primary condition for the successful introduction and operation of quality circles.

Based upon extensive research over a long period of time, the following factors have been identified by Collard and Dale[5] as necessary for success:

Secure the commitment of the board and senior management to the principle of quality circles, and ensure that they understand this means providing time and resources if they are to work properly.

Involve middle management and supervision, since this group will be central to any initiatives emanating from circle discussions, and can provide invaluable specialist assistance on particular issues.

Seek the support of the trade unions in a unionized environment in order to involve representatives in the process, and allay any fears that this will undermine the role of the union.

Delegate decision-making so that once circles have reached a satisfactory conclusion on a particular aspect of the job, they will either have the authority to implement the decision, or the right (in the case of a higher-level matter) to present proposals to senior management.

Provide adequate structured training both to circle leaders and members in order to assist them in fulfilling their roles.

Use a pilot study approach which will allow for a thorough evaluation of the benefits and drawbacks without a high profile, company-wide introduction.

Monitor events on an ongoing basis, and assist in reinforcing the work of circle members and assist them in propagating their ideas to fellow employees.

As mentioned above, however, many quality circles fail at the introduction stage, or after a short period of operation; the first three years appear to be critical for establishing long-term viability. While lack of top management support is often given as a reason for failure, trade unions can also have significant objections to the quality circle concept. As with briefing groups, there is a legitimate concern that quality circles – or for that matter any direct employee involvement technique – will be used as a mechanism to bypass or compete with the trade unions. This is more likely to be the case in circumstances where managements fail to convince union representatives of the value of quality circles – which happened with the initial attempts by Ford – or when circles are imposed unilaterally in a climate of hostility or tension. More specifically, trade unions will be particularly concerned about any implications for the quantity or quality of work, and the fact that modifications may be made to working practices without proper consultation and negotiation, and without any improvement in associated terms and conditions. They may be seen as an altogether more dubious form of participation, in that the *feeling* of involvement is greater, although the actual control and influence over strategic decisions is likely to be minimal. As with any other aspect of industrial relations, quality circles have significant implications – in this case, implicit and unwritten – for the balance of power in the workplace, and for conflict and cooperation.

Joint Consultation

Traditionally, joint consultation has had a somewhat tarnished image. It has been described variously as a waste of time, the three Ts (tea, toilets and trivia), irrelevant to the main needs of the business, or conversely as a challenge to trade union organization and collective bargaining. Even though some form of joint consultative committees (JCCs) has existed in a number of organizations throughout the whole of this century, interest has definitely waxed and waned within industry overall.

Following the introduction of Joint Production and Advisory Committees during and just after the Second World War, the extent of consultation declined during the 1950s and 60s. The conventional wisdom then became that joint consultation could not survive the development of effective shop floor organization; JCCs would have to change their character and become in effect negotiating bodies, or they would be boycotted by stewards and eventually fall into disuse. Two assumptions lie behind this statement. First, that stewards view consultation as in direct competition with negotiation, and a choice has to be made between one or the other. In fact, stewards in well-organized workplaces may value *both* processes, and find that they can cope with the different problems imposed by them. Second, that managements actually wish to use consultation in this way, viewing it as a mechanism for undermining union organization within workplaces. Although some may well use JCCs for this purpose, the evidence would suggest that many employers are also keen to maintain both consultation and negotiation, and provide facilities for workplace representatives on both sorts of committee. Certainly, the survey data for the 1970s indicates a period of revitalization in the extent of joint consultation, which has largely been sustained into the 1980s, despite the changed economic, social and political context within which companies now operate.

Joint consultation, then, is a process by which management seeks the views of employees, usually via their elected representatives, before final decisions are taken. To work effectively, it involves the provision of considerable amounts of information and time, and a willingness on the part of management actually to listen to alternative views, discuss implications and, if appropriate, explain and justify why a certain line of action is proposed. It requires a degree of openness and trust on the part of both managers and shop stewards, which will allow for meaningful discussion of problems and solutions. It is usually the case that JCCs do not have decision-making powers formally allocated to them, but it is always difficult to establish firmly where, how and when decisions are made in practice, and JCCs may actually influence the eventual outcome of any discussion.

The precise structure and design of a consultative system depends crucially upon the shape and character of the organization in which it is operating, but there are a number of key questions which need to be posed if JCCs are to be seen as successful both by managers and workplace representatives. Success can be measured in terms of the quality of decision-making, worker commitment, management awareness and sensitivity, as well as job satisfaction and company efficiency. Drawing upon examples of organizations which have had a long history of joint consultation, and where both stewards and managements express satisfaction with the outcomes, the following factors seem to be important:

There is a clearly defined statement that the JCC will not be allowed to discuss issues which are subject to negotiation, and this clarification will probably be equally desired by both managers and stewards, either of whom may act as the custodians of any collective agreements in a unionized concern. In a sense, consultation serves to fill in the gaps left by collective bargaining, and as such, can be relatively fluid in its exact area of coverage; indeed, it is this fluidity which causes greatest anxiety among analysts who argue that a clear distinction cannot be maintained between the two bodies, and consequently this must prove advantageous to management. Once again, though, this rests upon the dual assumptions that managers *wish* to gain such an advantage through JCCs, and that stewards possess neither the resources nor the ability to prevent this from happening or from appreciating management tactics.

Management needs to demonstrate its commitment to meaningful consultation by producing evidence that JCCs are to be taken seriously. This means that attendance at committees needs to be obligatory for managers who are of sufficient status to be the appropriate decision-makers at whatever level the committees operate. Consequently, at a departmental committee, it could be the plant manager; at an establishment committee, the works director; at divisional level, the divisional chairman; and, at group level, the company chairman. Employee representatives will soon question the value to management of a committee which purports to allow for influence over decision-making within the company, when attendance is by managers who are seen to lack status themselves, who fail to progress issues, or who regularly fail to turn up at meetings.

To be effective, worker representatives need to command the support of their constituents, and in a unionized company, shop stewards are usually likely to be the people who attend JCCs. While the task of drawing up the constituencies and preparing the groundwork for effective representation may be relatively easy in a single-union establishment, it can be rather more complex in a multi-site, multi-union organization. In addition, any attempt by management to ask for representation which may be based upon a non-union or non-steward presence is also likely to be viewed with some consternation by the appropriate unions, and reduce the commitment of the latter not only to the JCC, but also to other industrial relations institutions.

If management is committed to joint consultation, other details of the JCC which need proper consideration would be:

The committee should meet at regular, pre-arranged and adhered to times.

Meetings should be monthly, bi-monthly or less frequent depending upon the business.

The chair should rotate between managers and employee representatives on an annual basis.

Meetings should be held at a convenient time and in an appropriate location.

Management representatives should come from a cross-section of functions and levels.

Employee representatives should also be able to cover the whole range of their constituents.

The agenda should be published in advance, and be the result of informal discussion between the secretary to the committee and a senior employee representative.

There should be the opportunity for employee representatives to hold a pre-meeting.

Sub-committees can prove a useful mechanism for achieving detailed consideration of specific sets of items, especially on a large JCC.

The subject matter should be appropriate to the level of committee, and should be referred elsewhere if it is inappropriate.

Minutes should be issued promptly, and as a rule should not be too long.

Individuals should be identified to take action on specific issues.

Reporting back arrangements should be made, either via noticeboards, newsletters or briefing.

Individuals other than representatives should be invited to each meeting.

Any information which requires prior reading should be distributed in advance.

Any information given at the meeting should be clear and concise.

If reports from subcommittees are to be presented, this should be done by different individuals, and preferably a mix of managers and worker representatives.

There should be a planned turnover of committee members.

Training in the interpretation of information (eg financial or production) should be given to all members of a JCC.

There should be a regular monitoring of JCC effectiveness by committee members as well as an independent assessment of success.

It is probably indicative of the reputation of JCCs that considerably more has been written about failure than success.[6] Of course, it may well be that the parties to a consultative structure (and management in particular) are not keen on making it work in the way outlined above, and are more interested in using the JCC for some other purpose. Some employers have used consultation as a mechanism to resist collective bargaining and union recognition, especially in sectors in which there is little tradition of unionism or independent representation. Since consultation requires time and commitment on the part of management, this approach is rather more likely in establishments where a sophisticated paternalistic policy is used. In such cases, the process of consultation will primarily be one way and educative in its objectives; that is, a process designed to make employees aware of the economic circumstances of the company, and the effort which senior managers are expending for the good of the corporate whole.

The notion of consultation in direct competition with an already established system of collective bargaining has been briefly discussed above, and it is one that has gained in popularity during the current decade, perhaps explaining the renaissance of consultation. By providing employee representatives with a considerable amount of information, and involving them in the process of decision-making within companies, management's intention is to 'incorporate' stewards and convince them of the logic and inescapability of company policies and proposals. Thus, trade unionism can be weakened – if the policy is successful – by the back door rather than head on.

Finally, consultation can also achieve little or nothing for either party, being marginal to any activity in the workplace, and in the process of stagnation, leading perhaps to ultimate collapse. This is the kind of environment in which neither party shows any great commitment to the JCC, and both are likely to make use of opportunistic tactics to undermine the other. Of course, any attempt to revive consultation in such circumstances will require a fundamental change in attitudes, way beyond the effects which tinkering with the detailed questions may have on the system.

Worker Directors

For some analysts, none of the schemes which have been discussed so far offers an acceptable version of employee participation, in that they get nowhere near challenging existing systems of control and authority within employing organizations. The idea of workers on the board, while not actually producing workers' control, is somewhat more promising in that at least employee representatives get closer to the point at which strategic decisions are made. Not surprisingly, given this scenario, the concept of worker directors has attracted a considerable degree of hostility from employers. Given the political and economic circumstances which characterize Britain in the late-1980s, there are very few examples of this aspect of employee participation, despite the possibility of EEC legislation (see below) sometime in the future.

It is now well over a decade since the British debate on worker directors was at its most extensive. The Labour government of the time and the TUC (especially via the General Secretary of the TGWU, Jack Jones) initiated the Bullock Committee of Inquiry.* Its terms of reference related to *how*, rather than whether, representation on the boards of directors of private sector companies could be achieved, while taking into account the essential role of trade unions, and having regard to the interests of the national economy, employees, investors, consumers, and company efficiency. There were problems from the outset, not only in securing an appropriate membership for the Committee, but also with the eventual reports. In addition to the majority report, to which there was a note of dissent, a minority report was also published, containing the views of the industrialists. Even so, the latter report probably went much further than many employers would have wanted, especially those antagonistic to the principle itself. The reaction to Bullock was vitriolic and, despite a much

---

* The Committee of Inquiry on Industrial Democracy was chaired by Lord Bullock, and its members were drawn from both sides of industry and a group of independents. It was set up in December 1975 and it reported in January 1977.

diluted attempt in a subsequent White Paper (May 1978), the proposals on worker directors were never enacted.

Experience with the concept of worker directors is extremely rare in the private sector, and research based upon seven of the companies which operated such a scheme has demonstrated the substantial influence of managements over its implementation and operation.[7] It has been argued that each of the schemes was used in order to strengthen or reassert management control rather than to redistribute that control. The worker directors themselves experienced great difficulty in handling the information received at the board, partly because they were not party to the informal discussions which took place among senior management, but also because they lacked the resources to interpret or make effective use of the information. Consequently, the schemes tended to be regarded in a relatively poor light by the workforce, and the unions were either indifferent to them or ensured that they did not interfere with independent representation.

There is greater experience of board membership in the public sector, and two schemes – at British Steel and at the Post Office – have been the subject of detailed analyses.[8] Worker directors were appointed to the group boards of the newly established British Steel Corporation in 1965, and for the initial period these nominees were required to give up their formal union positions. Although there was some hostility at the outset among the other directors to the principle of board membership, their stance softened over the course of the next year and they, like shop stewards and ordinary employees, actually favoured the idea of worker directors. A majority of middle managers, however, remained opposed to the scheme. The 12 worker directors themselves were enthusiastic and strongly committed to their new role, seeing themselves as central to communication, cooperation and the exchange of ideas, and the other board members defined them as experts on the shop floor view. Nevertheless, there were also problems for the worker directors in moving into the new world of the boardroom, and in understanding the rules, language, customs and symbolism which operated therein. Also, the worker directors found themselves lacking in institutional support, given their enforced separation from union duties, and they came to realize that there were a variety of forums for discussion and decision-making outside the board. A number of modifications were made to the scheme in 1973 in order to overcome some of these difficulties. Primarily, the unions became involved in the process of selecting the worker directors, and the latter were allowed to continue in union office. One interesting incidental effect of the scheme was that works managers began to liaise with the worker directors in order to establish a direct link to the board. Overall, though, the independent assessment of the worker director experiment in the corporation was that the representatives operated as directors first and workers second, finding it hard to resist the logic of efficiency, markets and institutions.

In 1978, worker directors were introduced on to the main board of the Post Office for an experimental two-year period. The scheme was discontinued in 1980 because management opposed its extension. The worker directors were nominated or elected by the appropriate unions, and representation on the board was in line with the $2x + y$ proposals of Bullock, that is, management and unions had an equal number of seats (x) with a smaller number (y) going to the independent members. The union nominees contributed most to discussions concerning industrial relations affairs, and they were often critical of stances taken with regard to these; on other issues, they were less likely to become actively involved, but if they did, their contributions were basically consensual. The management members of the board saw the nominees' interventions as sectional and obstructive, and a delay to decision-making. However, the independent assessment concluded that their impact was barely detectable, principally because senior management were generally hostile to the experiment, and had the resources to nullify or soften its impact. In addition, the board also changed its character, and the management representatives tended to conduct much of their business – and any sensitive or confidential arguments between them – away from the board, leaving the latter as a much blander body. The union nominees also found themselves in the difficult position of attempting to defend member interests yet contributing to management decisions which may have negative implications for the workforce. Overall, the general conclusion to this study was that although industrial democracy brought few gains to the unions or management, it brought few losses either. It certainly could not be seen as a severe threat to management authority, or as a mechanism for achieving workers' control.

For this reason, it is difficult to appreciate why employers have been so hostile to the concept of worker directors, beyond seeing them as an extra burden rather than an aid to efficiency, since their effect on the processes of control is so clearly limited. However, throughout the 1980s, a campaign has been waged by UK industrialists and the government against EEC legislation in the shape of the Fifth and the Vredeling Directives.

The former legislation has been under consideration since the early 1970s, having been diluted somewhat from its original. Now, if passed, the directive would allow member states to choose from one of a number of options* for the installation of formal systems to involve employee representatives in company decision-making structures. It would also allow for the possibility of participation through collective agreements, rather than board membership, provided that employees acquired the same rights

---

* These options allow for unitary or supervisory boards, and for a process of election or co-option on to one or other of these bodies. In addition, there is provision for an alternative to workers on the board, in the form of a joint arrangement concluded by collective agreement so long as this applies the same principles of participation as would be achieved by board membership. This is the one which would cause least disruption to current UK arrangements.

and information as they would through representation on the board. Given the generally antagonistic stance of employers and most unions in this country to the principles and practice of board membership, it is probable that this option will be chosen.

The Vredeling Directive applies to multinationals with a head office elsewhere in the world, which have large undertakings within Europe. The requirement, if enacted, would be for information disclosure and consultation with employee representatives about decisions liable to have serious implications for employees' interests. Many of the issues covered by Vredeling are already the subject of information and consultation within more progressive UK companies, although these are provided on a voluntary not a statutory basis.

Arguably, much of the opposition to these directives in the UK stems from a distrust of legal intervention which *requires* employers to consult with employees, rather than allowing them to choose whether or not to do so.

In summary, previous UK experience, both in the public and private sectors, suggests the following conclusions about worker directors:

Managements are generally opposed to the principle of worker representation, especially through trade unions, on the board.

The trade union movement is ambivalent about worker directors, although certain unions are hostile to the concept due to fears of incorporation, role conflict, and a reduced ability to resist management actions.

Workers themselves express no great desire for board representation on their behalf.

Worker directors experience difficulty in coming to terms with boardroom norms and customs.

There will be little change to the outcome of board discussions.

Profit Sharing and Employee Share Ownership

While profit sharing and employee share ownership schemes are by no means a recent development, with examples of the former going back into the 19th century, it is only within the last decade that there has been a resurgence of interest in them, largely due to legislative encouragement via the Finance Acts of 1978, 1980 and 1984. Since such schemes are also part of the total pay and benefits package, they will be dealt with in more detail in Chapter 11, but by its very nature, economic and financial involvement is also a form of employee participation. Some would argue that to provide the opportunity for employees to share in the financial success (or otherwise) of their employer is an essential part of employee participation.

Others, however, would see such schemes as dubious both on philosophical and practical grounds, because of their effect on independence, trade unionism and financial security.

Profit sharing by itself represents a very diluted form of employee participation, and it is only when financial involvement is associated with mechanisms for creating industrial democracy, that it can represent anything more than an additional form of payment to employees. Government initiatives, via profit-related pay come into the former category (again, see Chapter 11), while value-added systems which allow for employee representation via works councils do at least formalize the relationship between participation, organizational productivity and individual reward. By so doing, calculative orientations held by employees can be recognized and placed within a participative context.[9]

In broad terms, the arguments in favour of profit sharing and employee share ownership are that they:

Help to increase individual identification with and commitment to corporate success.

Increase cooperation within the company.

Make employees more conscious of business needs and the value of profit to the organization.

Ensure employees benefit from company profitability.

Help to attract and retain key staff due to extra financial inducements.

The critics of such schemes, however, produce a number of equally convincing counter-arguments. First of all, it is argued that profit sharing fails to conform to one of the most basic rules of payment systems, namely that there should be a clear and identifiable link between effort and reward. Individual employees find that no matter how hard they have worked during the previous financial year, this is not reflected in the amount of profits which comes their way, nor in the value of shares quoted on the Stock Exchange. Equally, share prices may rise in order to produce high bonuses in a year when individual employees have worked less hard. Not surprisingly, therefore, profit sharing may consequently be seen as nothing more than a windfall bonus, and shares may be sold as soon as employees get the opportunity or need the money.

Second, it is felt that profit sharing and share ownership merely doubles the insecurity of individual employees. Not only do they risk losing their job if the company runs into financial difficulties, but they also face the prospect of losing any capital which may have accrued through such schemes. Employees may not always be fully aware of this possibility when they enter into such schemes, because they only conceive of a successful outcome.

There is also an objection to stand-alone profit sharing schemes, that is, those without any associated mechanism for participation, in that employees have no means by which to contribute to or challenge management decisions. Strategic decisions may be made by senior management which have significant implications for profits – for example, a decision to invest in new technology, or market a new product line overseas – whereas employee representatives, given the interests which their members have, might take an altogether different line. While senior managers may see value in implementing profit sharing schemes on current terms, this would soon turn to hostility if it were linked to realistic employee participation in and control over strategic decisions. Nonetheless, it indicates in the 1980s that share ownership is on the increase, fuelled to a large extent by the government's privatization programme, a part of which aims to extend financial involvement of employees in their company's success (or failure).

Conclusion

Employee participation is an area where much depends upon the nature of the political and legal environment within which industrial relations takes place. As we have already mentioned, EEC legislation is waiting in the wings, but it is highly unlikely that the current Conservative government would want to push for its implementation. Indeed, backed by virtually all sections of senior management within Britain, it is more likely to delay and minimize its impact in the UK. Whether the prospect of greater harmonization across Europe after 1992 will have any effect on participation remains an open question but, given the stance of Mrs Thatcher, this seems little more than a remote possibility.

Within Britain, the official opposition and the other political parties represented within Westminster are keen to develop current arrangements, albeit in different ways. The Labour Party and the TUC would like to extend workers' rights, especially to information, consultation and representation, in order to ensure that they have greater control over the decisions made by corporate managements. Others are attracted to profit sharing and also greater disclosure of information, although not to the same extent as the Labour Party and the TUC. However, given the prospect of a free-market and deregulatory Conservative government into the 1990s, there is little chance that these views will form part of any legislative programme in the near future.

The most likely developments in the next decade will be extensions to the voluntary measures established during the 1980s. Consequently, direct communication techniques such as team briefing can be expected to gain in popularity, as too can quality packages which tie together employee involvement and customer care concerns. At the same time, plant-wide bonus systems and possibly profit sharing schemes will also continue to increase in attractiveness and coverage. The former are now more regularly integrated with mechanisms for informing employees of company activity and securing their commitment to corporate goals. Although more competitive product market circumstances may have led to some well-publicized aggressive management approaches to employee relations, they have also heightened employer awareness of workers' contributions to the final product. In short, when confronted by a hostile product market and a tightening labour market, employers may no longer be able to ignore the tacit skills possessed by employees.[10]

Whatever systems emerge on a political level in pure structural terms, however, there will always be examples of organizations which are more successful than others in making employee participation work in practice. Much depends upon the commercial environment in which companies find themselves, and upon the kinds of issue which confront them, so facilitating or hindering the achievement of organizational objectives. Joint publications by the Industrial Participation Association and the Institute of Personnel Management provide a range of examples, as well as statements of principles and practice, and a guide to effective action. Rather than prescribe how participation should operate, the Action Guide poses a series of questions which need to be considered by organizations which are reviewing their position.[11]

Beyond this, the major point at issue concerns attitudes to participation, and the total *process* of conducting industrial relations in the workplace, office, plant or company as a whole. Participation packages can be bought off-the-shelf, but whether or not they work depends upon the quality of management-employee relations within the undertaking, upon the history of previous dealings, the level of trust, and above all on the commitment of management to making the system effective. Participation is not easy, but is a difficult and time-consuming process, which needs to develop over time and cannot be discarded once its initial objectives have been met. Since it *ought* to involve employees taking part in management decisions in one way or another, it is also beset with tensions and potential contradictions. But the fact that organizations continue to experiment with employee participation surely demonstrates that it offers some hope for the development of more constructive and permanent relationships at work.

References
1. Millward N and Stevens M *British Workplace Industrial Relations 1980–84* (1986) Gower, Farnborough
2. Smith G 'Profit Sharing and Employee Share Ownership in Britain' *Employment Gazette* August 1986
3. Grummitt J *Team Briefing* Industrial Society, 1983
4. Robson M *Quality Circles in Action* (1984) Gower, Farnborough
5. Collard R and Dale B 'Quality Circles – why they break down and why they hold up' *Personnel Management* February 1985
6. Nicholson N 'Can Consultation Work?' *Personnel Management* November 1978

7. Towers B, Chell E and Cox D 'Do Worker-Directors Work?' *Employment Gazette* September 1981; and 'Worker-directors in private manufacturing industry in Great Britain' Dept of Employment *Research Paper No 29* 1987

8. For a useful summary of both these experiments, see Brannen P *Authority and Participation in Industry* (1983) Batsford, London

9. Marchington M 'Worker Participation and Plant-wide Incentive Systems' *Personnel Review* Summer 1977

10. For a more complete exposition of these ideas see Marchington M and Parker P *Changing Patterns of Employee Relations in Britain* (1989) Wheatsheaf, Hemel Hempstead

11. Industrial Participation Association/Institute of Personnel Management *Employee Involvement and Participation, Action Guide* IPA/IPM, 1983

Chapter 9

Managing Professional and Managerial Staff*

Ed Snape and Greg Bamber

Professional and managerial staff are often treated rather differently from other employees, particularly manual workers. In this chapter, after defining the professional and managerial category, we consider such issues as recruitment, selection, mobility, education, human resource management, economic rewards and the unionism of managers.

Who Are Professional and Managerial Employees?

In defining managerial employees broadly, we include all those employees in the hierarchy above first-line supervisor but below the level of executives who report directly to the board. In addition, we include professional and technical staff of comparable status. For convenience, we use 'manager' to cover the whole group, thus including people such as personnel and marketing specialists, professional engineers and administrators, as well as line managers. Since all these occupational groups tend to have a similar relationship with the employer, this definition makes sense in personnel management and industrial relations terms.

There is some ambiguity about whether managers are *employers* or *employees*. Even if they do not have direct line authority, such staff often have a relatively high level of discretion in their jobs. Subordinate grades generally see managers as bosses, while the directors may see managers as agents of the employer, and expect them to act accordingly.

There was a dramatic increase in the absolute and relative numbers of managers in the decades after the Second World War. The increase has prompted employers to pay increasing attention to the management of this category of employee.

* The authors acknowledge that this chapter draws on research funded by the Economic and Social Research Council (reference F/00/23/00 98). Although focused on Britain, this research is linked with parallel studies undertaken in the USA, Australia, New Zealand, Japan and several other European countries. The broader international study has been published as: Romkin M (ed) *The Changing Character of Managerial Employment: A Comparative View* Oxford University Press, New York and Oxford, 1989.

Recruitment, Selection and Mobility

Appointing managers by internal promotion is an explicit policy of many large employers; they use internal advertising and/or succession planning. Many large organizations aim to recruit externally only if they lack suitable internal candidates, when they require specialist skills, or when wishing to bring in 'new blood'. Smaller organizations are more likely to recruit externally, as they may not employ enough people with potential for promotion.

Thus many managers have been promoted from within, especially in the longer-established industries. In recent years, however, most employers have recruited young people as management trainees, or have recruited people externally to particular managerial positions. It has become less usual for people to be promoted from a shop-floor job into management unless their shop floor role was part of a management traineeship.

We can distinguish between four typical recruitment patterns for managers. In the first pattern, external recruitment is restricted to junior levels of the organizational hierarchy, and managerial jobs are filled by promotion from within. This is typical of the finance sector, particularly the larger banks, who have traditionally recruited most of their staff at junior clerical level and thereafter promoted from within.

This may, however, lead to an organization becoming too inward looking, and fail to yield sufficient staff with the necessary potential for promotion to the senior positions. Hence, in many organizations there is an increasing use of 'tiered' recruitment patterns. This second pattern involves external recruitment at junior managerial levels (often new or recent graduates), along with some promotion from among manual or clerical workers, usually via technical or first-line supervisory positions. Higher level managerial positions are then filled mainly by internal promotion.

A third pattern involves external recruitment into junior managerial posts, with subsequent internal promotion to fill higher level jobs. In this case, however, there is no significant promotion into managerial jobs from among manual or clerical workers, who rarely progress beyond the first-line supervisory level. This situation often arises where managerial jobs are more technical, requiring specific qualifications, for example retail chemists, where managers must be professionally qualified.

The fourth, an 'open' recruitment pattern includes the possibilities of external recruitment and internal promotion at all levels. This pattern often develops where labour markets are tight and highly competitive, or where organizations are growing rapidly, so that they may be faced with shortages of managers and use any available means to recruit. Some retail chains pursue such a policy, as do some companies in the expanding, high technology industries.[1]

Our research in a bank revealed systematic differences between those managers promoted from within ('natives'), and those recruited from other banks ('migrants'). The migrants were more career-oriented, in that they were better qualified, were more willingly mobile, had greater expectations of mobility, and were less likely to be content with the bank's provision for training and career development. Most of the migrants had moved to this bank in search of better career opportunities, they often brought new ideas, and they tended to become a career 'élite' within the organization. An employer's pattern of recruitment has an impact on such personnel practices as training and development. Moreover, where there is less reliance on internal talent, there is greater competition for promotion.

Apart from press advertisements, how are managers recruited? The now privatized Professional and Executive Recruitment agency mails advertisements to eligible job-seekers. This service is generally seen as most appropriate for junior management positions. Several private consultants and professional institutions run recruitment registers, but these are used less frequently and mainly for specialist jobs such as finance, scientific or technical posts.

Rather than relying on their own expertise, an increasing number of employing organizations use recruitment agencies to design and implement an appropriate advertising programme. Particularly for recruitment at senior levels, there is also an increasing number of employers using executive search consultants ('headhunters').

Selection

When selecting managers and potential managers, many employers are less concerned with technical qualifications than with how well they would 'fit in', with their leadership qualities, and with other personality factors.

How do organizations select managers from among the available candidates? While some large organizations are using increasingly sophisticated procedures for selecting managers, more than 90 per cent of companies still rely almost exclusively on formal and/or informal interviewing. Many larger companies use panel selection boards. Relatively few use tests, and then mainly for graduate recruitment.[2]

Many employers recruit graduates by interviewing extensively at universities and colleges, before inviting some of the more promising candidates to intensive second interviews. This process, the 'milk round', is a useful way of dealing with mass applications from what initially appears as a fairly undifferentiated group. Such employers usually have a management induction scheme. The exact form of scheme varies considerably, but 'management trainees' may complete off-the-job training courses and projects before taking up a junior managerial position. Such schemes often involve a series of short placements in various departments. These schemes may extend from six weeks to over two years. More and more employers have introduced such schemes, as a growing number of organizations aim to recruit graduates.

Many graduates are, however, soon disillusioned with their first job. Many induction schemes are inadequate, and there is a mismatch between what graduates and employers expect of each other. Hence, graduate turnover from first jobs approaches 50 per cent after five years.[3] Ambitious individuals in their twenties often move between employers, in an attempt to win more experience and more rapid promotion than they would get with one employer.

It is likely that the recruitment and retention of graduates will become increasingly difficult in the next few years as demographic trends point to a marked contraction of the 18–24 year old age group. Inter-firm competition in the graduate labour market is likely to intensify, and employers may need to look to other groups, such as married women and older workers, to make up any shortfall in graduate recruitment.[4] One implication of this is that the number of women managers will probably increase, particularly if, as seems likely, employers attempt to accommodate women by extending career-break schemes.

Mobility

As more employers recruit managers externally, there has been an increasing tendency for managers to change jobs.[5] For the individuals concerned, a change of job can bring new stimulation and/or problems of adjustment. The main problems for managers in locational moves are: the disruption of their children's education, the disruption to friendships and social life, and the quality of health, educational and social facilities within the new area.[6] Managers seem less concerned about the problems of house-moving, leaving members of the family, the effect on their spouse's job, and uncertainty about the new job itself. Individuals are often reluctant to move to certain regions or cities: for example, southerners often will not move north and vice versa. Relocation has become an expensive issue. Many employers pay substantial sums as disturbance allowances. Some employers pay an incentive to encourage managers to move. To advise on such matters, in 1986 the Confederation of British Industry (CBI) established an Employee Relocation Council.

In spite of some cross-functional mobility, British managers are less likely than Americans to move beyond their own specialism. Many British organizations have a rigid 'functional' structure. Nevertheless, an increasing number of organizations are trying to introduce more flexible structures which foster more cross-fertilization between functions, especially in their promotion policies for potential high-flyers.

Management Education

A traditional view has been that 'leaders are born and not made'. This was reflected in the relative lack of management education in Britain, at least until the 1960s. British managers still tend to be less well qualified than those in many other countries.

In spite of some rhetoric from managerial interest groups, management is not a 'profession'; particular qualifications are usually required only where the job involves specialist, technical work. Most firms do not systematically train their managers for the jobs they hold.

A few universities have been teaching management since before the Second World War and several colleges have run short courses for managers for much of the post-war period. However, universities did not initiate specific graduate business schools until 1963, following the Robbins and the Franks Reports.[7]

By 1983, more than half of Britain's universities had management departments or business schools, offering postgraduate Master of Business Administration (MBA) degrees. In that year, however, less than 1,350 MBAs were awarded in Britain. To match the USA proportionately, Britain would have to produce about 15,000 business graduates per year.[8] Several institutions have recently developed novel forms of MBA programme. These include part-time study, distance learning and in-house schemes for particular employers or groups of employers. Nevertheless, MBAs are still accepted much less readily by most British employers than by their North American counterparts.

Besides MBA courses, many institutions offer shorter executive courses; these may either be broad or concentrate on particular fields such as finance, marketing or industrial relations. Partly arising from an apparent dissatisfaction with open courses, which are allegedly 'too general', many large employing organizations commission specially designed courses for their own managers. As management education is increasingly competitive, more business schools are willing to 'tailor-make' courses to suit particular employers.

Most polytechnics and some universities also offer full degree courses in business studies at undergraduate level. Polytechnics also offer part-time diploma courses, mainly to those already working in management. Study for professional qualifications is mainly by day-release, evening, or correspondence course, while doing a relevant full-time job. Relatively few employers seem willing to allow managers to have a substantial period of paid study leave, although many will provide financial assistance for evening-class fees.

The British Institute of Management (BIM) was set up in 1947 to help promote managerial effectiveness. The BIM publishes a journal (*Management Today*) and a newspaper (*Management News*), along with various books and reports on management topics. It maintains a library, publishes research, and organizes conferences. While the BIM does not seek to represent managers *vis-à-vis* their employers, it does represent its members' views to the government on such issues as pensions, fiscal policy and employee participation. BIM membership is open to individuals educated at least up to a diploma or degree level, who have several years' management experience.

Although there has been an expansion of management education and training, the provision is still varied and somewhat *ad hoc*. Too many British employers seem to regard such provision as being *costs* to be cut, rather than as carefully-planned *investments* in their human resources. Most British employers seem to give too low a priority to education and training, compared to their foreign competitors.

The growing concern about Britain's relatively poor management education, training and development was highlighted in two major reports published in 1987.[9] They recommended increased provision of management education and training, with greater flexibility to improve access, and more cooperation between employers and educational institutions. In addition, they called on employers to give greater emphasis to careful recruitment, training and development, and on large corporations to set a good example in these areas. In response to these debates the BIM, with the support of the Government and the CBI, has discussed the development of an accredited 'Chartered Manager' qualification, designed to raise the level of professional competence among British managers.

Human Resource Management

Before training managers, it is important for employers to evaluate their training needs, not least by appraising their current strengths and weaknesses, and their career development potential. Appraisal should also form the basis of a firm's promotion practices. Most employers have an appraisal system for their non-manual workers, particularly managerial staff. Appraisal may have several other objectives including:

Facilitating the planning of an individual's career development and setting future goals.

Providing a basis for annual salary reviews where pay is related to individual merit.

Motivating individuals, even in the absence of merit pay, by providing feedback on job performance.

Improving communications by encouraging managers to gather information on the views and concerns of their subordinates.

Assisting the process of personnel planning by helping to identify those staff with promotion potential.

Properly conducted, appraisal is a useful technique in relation to managerial staff, whose motivation and performance is crucial to most organizations, yet who have much more discretion in the performance of their jobs than most other employees. Appraisal became even more widely used during the 1980s, partly because of the increased use of merit pay (see later).

A problem with some appraisal systems is that they lack a clear set of objectives. Furthermore, linking pay to appraisal may encourage the individual being appraised to conceal job difficulties in order to safeguard a pay increase. This may conflict with the use of appraisal for career development and training purposes. Where merit pay is to be used it is worth trying to separate merit awards and appraisal interviews in the minds of employees, perhaps by keeping them several months apart and by emphasizing non-pay issues in the appraisal interview.

An appraisal may raise expectations, as it questions staff about their career ambitions and training needs. Where these expectations are not then realized, there may be a loss of morale. Hence, appraisal schemes should match the organizational realities, as well as the needs of the staff concerned. Schemes aimed at 'career' staff should emphasize their professional development, while those for non-career employees should focus more on immediate job issues.

Another problem often arises with appraisal schemes which are designed and initiated by a central personnel department, but left to line managers to implement. If the latter have not been involved in designing the scheme, nor fully trained in its operation, it rarely works as well as originally hoped, since most line managers have many other more immediate priorities than operating what they may see as personnel's 'airy-fairy schemes'. For appraisal schemes to operate effectively, it is important for the implementers to feel some degree of ownership of the scheme. This can be achieved if they are involved in designing and reviewing the scheme.

Most large organizations have specialists responsible for appraisal and management development; often they are also responsible for managerial succession planning. In practice, only a small minority of companies seem to have a systematic approach to such aspects of personnel management. Ideally, however, all of those aspects should be part of an integrated strategy for developing human resources.

Career blockages

Many organizations have found it increasingly difficult to meet the career aspirations of their younger managerial staff, who are confronted by a 'career blockage' of older managers. Such problems are exacerbated in organizations which have retrenched or grown more slowly than hitherto. Low morale and poor performance may result, as staff become frustrated, especially if their career aspirations remain high, given the more favourable experience of their predecessors.

The lack of career opportunities is a problem for many organizations in the public sector, in manufacturing, and for larger banks and financial institutions. There are some exceptions to this, however, in expanding sectors such as finance, retailing and electronics, and in certain occupations, such as computing and marketing.

There are many remedies to the career blockage problem. These include changing organizational structures and introducing 'intrapreneurial'* ventures, which may provide new opportunities for managerial staff. Redesigning career paths, with lateral transfers and even downward moves towards the end of a career, can make better use of managerial resources. Other remedies include job rotation, job sharing, part-time working and outward secondments. Some large employing organizations have seconded managers to work for periods of up to two years in educational institutions, government agencies and community projects. Such secondments may be a way of enriching the experience of younger managers or of easing out managers near the end of their careers.

Many organizations have encouraged staff to opt for early retirement to ease career blockages for their younger colleagues. But this may fail to provide a long-term solution to the career blockage problem, as it allows for only a once and for all displacement, unless their successors can also be retired early. Such early retirement is generally preferable for individuals than the harsher alternative: redundancy.

Redundancy

Managerial employment used to be seen as secure, but the view that managers have a 'job for life' has changed. In recent years, many organizations have reduced the size of their workforce, including their cadre of managers, and many companies have specifically aimed to 'flatten' their managerial hierarchies.

The broad occupational category of managers suffered a greater proportionate increase in unemployment in the early 1980s than most other categories. The expertise of managers is more likely to be organizationally specific than is the case for other categories of worker. Hence, redundant managers may find it more difficult to find another job in comparison, say, with craft workers whose skills are more easily transferable to other employers. Also, as some managers put it, 'the higher you rise, the harder you fall'.

Management vacancies generally remain unfilled for longer than other categories. Good managers are relatively scarce and employers also take longer to fill such vacancies, because managers have to give longer periods of notice than other staff and the selection methods are more elaborate than those used for subordinate grades.

* An intrapreneur is an employee who runs a quasi-autonomous business within a larger organization.

A Durham University survey of 91 large manufacturing companies found than 63 per cent of them had reduced their number of managers between 1979 and 1984. Of these, 20 per cent had an in-house resettlement unit to help those managers being made redundant. In some cases this involved helping them to start their own business. Several independent agencies provide outplacement counselling for redundant managers, although only a few companies hire such external help for their managers.[10]

Managers may receive a full pension and a substantial cash payment on being made redundant, particularly in the case of those over 55 years old, and those working in the public sector and for the larger firms. The cost of such redundancy payments can reach £75,000 per head. Compensation for unfair dismissal can be much higher. One recent out-of-tribunal settlement (via ACAS) was almost £1 million.

Equal opportunities

There has long been talk (and more recently legislation) about equal opportunities for women. By the mid-1980s, however, there were still disproportionately few women managers, although the proportion was increasing.[11] There is a significantly lower percentage of women employees in managerial jobs in Britain than in West Germany, France, the USA, Canada and Australia. Women managers tend to be concentrated at the lower levels; in particular functions, such as personnel, purchasing/ contracting and sales/marketing; and in industries such as paper, printing and publishing, retailing and other services.

Why are there relatively few women managers? One explanation for the lack of women's career progression is that they are less mobile than men. Many employers in banking, finance and retailing have mobility clauses in their contracts of employment for managers, which may deter women from seeking promotion. More generally, management may be seen as requiring certain 'male' characteristics, such as aggression and drive. The stereotypical female is assumed to lack those qualities, and so is presumed unsuitable for a managerial career. Women are socialized into 'female' attitudes and behaviour, which discourage them and others from seeing them as ideal managers. This is compounded by personnel policies which have thoughtlessly discriminated against women, by assuming an uninterrupted and typically 'male' career pattern. Also, women have not usually been sufficiently encouraged to study for professional qualifications.

The proportion of women managers will continue to rise, and there is increasing pressure to change personnel practices, by introducing provision for child care and extended periods of paternity, as well as maternity leave. Social stereotypes are changing, albeit slowly; there is a growing proportion of women in higher education, and an increasing tendency for women graduates to enter industrial and commercial employment. Further, men's opposition to women managers seems to be declining.[12]

Women are not the only people who are under-represented in management. There are disproportionately few managers from a working-class background and from the ethnic minorities. There has been increasing concern by some politicians and practitioners that 'something should be done' about the lack of managerial recruitment from women and ethnic minorities. Part of the concern is that managerial talent is scarce, and that discriminatory recruitment practices increase the scarcity. The contraction in the number of 18–24 year olds is likely to increase the pressure for equal opportunities (see above).

Several public policies have attempted to prevent such discrimination. Both the Equal Opportunities Commission (EOC) and the Commission for Racial Equality (CRE) have launched 'codes of practice', encouraging employers to promote equal opportunities and to develop their own 'monitoring systems'. Some large employers have responded; in some cases by appointing an equal opportunities officer to monitor recruitment and promotion. Unlike some of their US counterparts, however, few British employers have yet begun to discriminate positively in favour of women and ethnic minorities. Some unions have also appointed equal opportunities officers, to promote the interests of women and ethnic minorities.

Economic Rewards

In the 1970s, there was a compression of pay differentials between managers and their subordinates, but this trend was reversed in the 1980s. This reverse reflects the end of formal incomes policies, the increased tax efficiency of pay relative to other benefits, and employers increasingly aiming to reward individual performance, particularly among the more senior staff.

Those who design salary structures have to meet several objectives, which may conflict with each other. The patterns of rewards in an organization are shaped internally, by considerations of motivation, incentives, status, differentials and relativities;* and externally, by such considerations as the capacity to recruit and retain the appropriate people.

The pay of a particular manager may be related to two factors internal to the organization. First, the job level, and second, the manager's performance within the job. Organizations place differing degrees of emphasis on these two factors, according to labour-market conditions and their own corporate culture. Compare the individualistic ethos and merit pay systems of an electronics company, for instance, with the rigid salary scales and service-based pay increments of the civil service (although the latter is changing; see later).

* *Relativities* refer to the differences in the levels of pay (and/or other benefits) between comparable jobs in different employing organizations or negotiating units, whereas *differentials* refer to the pay difference between different jobs within one employing organization or a single negotiating unit.

Job evaluation* and salary structures

Most large organizations evaluate managerial jobs, in particular, into an approximate hierarchy and relate salaries to the level of the job within the hierarchy. There are various techniques of job evaluation, but most of them fall into one of two categories:

1. *Non-analytical approaches* involve either ranking jobs, or allocating them to predetermined grades on the basis of simple subjective comparisons.
2. *Analytical approaches* analyse jobs in terms of several factors, such as 'responsibility' and 'knowledge'. Each job is allocated a number of points per factor, the sum of points then determines the evaluation of the job.

A job may be allocated to a grade which carries a specified salary range. Alternatively, the points score from the analytical approach may be converted directly into a salary level, using a conversion formula.

How is an individual's salary determined within a given job? Most jobs have a salary scale, or a range based on specified percentages of the evaluated job value (say 90 to 110 per cent). Progression through the scale may be on the basis of annual increments, perhaps denied only to poor performers; or on the basis of a regular assessment of the individual's performance. Some salary systems involve a mix of automatic increments and merit payments; for example, progression up to a certain point in the scale may be automatic, with movement beyond this depending on merit, perhaps with several ceilings for different standards of performance. In addition, some organizations also pay cost-of-living increases independently of any incremental or merit award. This practice was particularly widespread during the inflationary period of the 1970s.

In designing salary structures for managers, there are several pitfalls to avoid. If salary scales overlap by too much, this may create problems in getting staff to accept job mobility and even promotion, since this may involve only a limited financial gain for an individual. Those who try to implement one salary system to cater for all of an organization's managers often experience problems in accommodating specialist groups. For example, some employers attempt to pay their professional computer staff on the same scales as middle managers. While this satisfies the desire for equity, it may compromise the organization's ability to recruit and retain computer staff, who command a premium in a competitive labour market. Separate salary grades or pay supplements for such staff may be necessary in order to recruit and retain them, but this may upset other staff and so reduce morale. Other solutions include having computer staff as self-employed contractors, or subcontracting all the computer operations to an

---

* Job evaluation techniques in general are described in more detail in Chapter 11.

agency. In either case, the effect is to distance the computer staff from the larger organization's pay structure.

Certain managers may be treated as 'special cases' for purposes of salary determination. Individuals may have their salaries 'red-circled'* following a new job evaluation exercise, a move to a less demanding job shortly before retirement, or a one-off project or posting. In such cases, the requirement for standardized treatment under a salary system may be relaxed to cope with special circumstances. A salary system is a personnel management tool; it should not become a straightjacket. As long as the exceptions do not become the rule, and do not provoke widespread resentment from staff, flexibility can be a virtue when dealing with managers, whose contributions to the organization may differ greatly.

An additional problem may arise when individuals reach the maximum salary level for their particular job, and when promotion is not possible, perhaps because of a general lack of promotion opportunities. Individuals may then become demoralized, in the absence of further salary increases. One way to avoid this is to offer occasional incentive payments or good performance bonuses to such staff. Again, the emphasis is on flexibility to cope with particular circumstances.

In the 1980s, some organizations have introduced merit pay for the first time, while others have reintroduced it, having abandoned it during the 1970s. Many of those organizations which already had merit pay schemes have extended them to account for a higher proportion of an individual's salary, sometimes abandoning general cost-of-living increases and automatic salary increments altogether.

The use of merit pay has increased for at least three reasons. First, it provides a mechanism for increasing pay differentials. Second, the reduction in the level of inflation has reduced the need for general cost-of-living increases. Third, it reflects a perceived need by corporate policy-makers to link rewards more closely with performance, as competition has intensified. Such links received political support from the post-1979 Conservative government. Furthermore, some organizations try to link earnings to company or divisional performance, for example, by paying incentive bonuses. This became more common in the 1980s, particularly at senior levels, where an individual's performance can have a significant impact on that of the company as a whole.

Many large corporations are organized into profit centres or subsidiary businesses. There is a trend towards greater autonomy for such units. In some organizations this extends to differentiating between the types and levels of reward in these units, depending on their profitability, local labour markets, product markets, or business policies. Increasingly, those responsible for profit centres and subsidiary businesses find that they can

---

* Although higher than the currently applicable salary grade, if 'red-circled' a salary is plateaued until the grade has caught up with this salary level.

choose to implement their own policies and practices, without being fully tied to a monolithic corporate arrangement. One disadvantage of introducing such differentiation is that it can then become more difficult to give managers a wide experience by moving them around. Therefore, unlike many other innovations in personnel management, such differentiation of terms and conditions for managers happens less readily than for subordinate categories, who are less likely to be mobile.

The remuneration package

Although most perks are now taxable, pay has long been more liable to tax than non-pay rewards, particularly for the more highly paid staff. This has contributed towards a proliferation of fringe benefits for managers.

In 1988, 70 per cent of managers were provided with company cars.[13] Other typical fringe benefits include health insurance, a telephone, assistance with children's education costs, housing loans or subsidies, allowances for clothing or consumer durables, and expense accounts. Since 1978, tax concessions have been granted to encourage profit sharing and employee share ownership generally, but most share option schemes have been registered under the post-1979 Conservative government's legislation, which allows schemes restricted to directors and managers. By 1988, 59 per cent of such staff worked for a company which had some form of employee share ownership scheme.

After 1979, the reduction in marginal income tax rates meant that cash payments became relatively more tax efficient. Many employers and staff increasingly preferred cash rather than other benefits. This preference was reflected by the increased use of merit pay and bonuses in the 1980s. Nevertheless, fringe benefits will not disappear; cars have been awarded to a growing range of staff since the 1970s.

An increasing number of employing organizations are introducing 'cafeteria-style' benefits programmes. Such programmes allow individual managers to choose from a range of alternative benefits, up to a maximum annual cost to the employer. Depending on individuals' personal circumstances, they may select particular perks, or choose to maximize their level of salary.

The rationale of these programmes is that if an employer provides the individual's preferred remuneration package, this should maximize value for money in terms of recruitment, motivation and retention.[14] Some employers are considering such flexibility for a broader category of employees. However, in view of the larger numbers of people involved, the salary administration becomes more complicated.

The public sector and privatization

The public sector has traditionally had salary scales through which managers progress on the basis of automatic annual increments. The emphasis has been on standard rates of pay, with individual performance being recognized through seniority and promotion. After privatization, former public sector corporations have aimed to move away from such standard rates, towards greater flexibility. There have been similar moves, even in those parts of the public sector not subject to privatization. There has been much subcontracting of services like cleaning, catering, transport and maintenance, as well as computing.

The public sector has also been seeking to pay bonuses related to individual merit. These schemes reflect: first, the decline in promotion opportunities, which threatens to demoralize staff; second, the government's desire to introduce private sector type management styles, and third, a need to raise pay in key areas to deal with recruitment and retention difficulties. In 1985, the government introduced a performance bonus system for senior civil servants. The scheme met with considerable union opposition, mainly because of the differences in implementation between departments, which the unions saw as arbitrary and divisive. However, merit pay seems set to become increasingly important in the public sector, not least in the hived-off executive agencies.

Unionization of Managers

Traditionally, most employers have determined managers' conditions of employment on an individual basis. Unions have often been seen as irrelevant for managers. Nevertheless, slightly more than 40 per cent of professional engineers and about 25 per cent of managers are unionized. There was some growth of private sector managers' unionism in the political and economic context of the 1970s, but there is still a significant difference in union membership among managers between the private (9 per cent) and public sectors (60 per cent).[15] This difference mainly reflects contrasting employer policies. Most public sector employers are legally obliged to engage in collective bargaining for all categories of employee, including managerial employees. By contrast, most private sector employers resist unionization of their managers.

Why do managers join unions? We distinguish between three broad categories of motive in order of importance. First, group motives include a preference for collective representation, especially in a large bureaucratic organization. Second, many managers cite such specific instrumental motives as job security and pay. Third, there are several external motives, including pressure from unions, colleagues, and the employer's policies.[16]

There is a greater likelihood of unionization among those managers promoted from within. Such people may have already experienced union membership in their earlier jobs. Furthermore, they may feel that further promotion is unlikely, so that collective organization is more useful as a way of safeguarding their interests than individual action. This contrasts with the direct management recruits, who tend to be younger, more ambitious and individualistic in attitude, and so may be less prone to join a union.

The bureaucratization of large employing organizations fosters the growth of managers' unions. Employers may fear that a union, once established, will reinforce bureaucratic procedures in the employment relationship, by pressing for standardization in the treatment of managers. However, unions do not necessarily oppose the individual treatment of managers, but they do oppose arbitrary treatment, and will try to establish structured procedures where possible. For instance, if an individual is accused of misconduct, they aim to ensure the right to a fair hearing, to be represented, and to appeal.

For unions, a moderate image is usually necessary in order to persuade managers to join; managers have often been reluctant to join unions where there is a risk that they may be drawn into militant action by non-managers. Like other unions, those which represent managers may be suspicious of some employer initiatives. Nonetheless, if approached constructively, managers' unions are inclined to adopt a cooperative relationship with employers. Managers' unions can usually be persuaded to accept perform-ance appraisal and job evaluation schemes, for example. They may want a say in the design and operation of such schemes, however, so that there is provision for union involvement and monitoring, and an established appeals procedure.

Unions generally oppose links between pay and a superior's assessment of individual performance. Unions have traditionally sought to establish a 'standard rate' for the job. However, some managers' unions have adopted a more pragmatic view, not least because many managers themselves have welcomed merit pay as a way of increasing their salary differentials over other groups, albeit on an individualized basis. In some cases, collective bargaining determines the basic salary scales, while the employer retains some discretion in relating pay to the individuals' performance.

In spite of the growth of managers' unionism, its impact is still negligible outside the public and cooperative sectors and some large, private sector companies. In the 1980s, the political and economic climate moved against managers' unionism. Unions in general were on the retreat, as unemploy-ment reduced their membership and weakened their bargaining power. ACAS no longer had a statutory role in relation to union recognition, which had been particularly significant for managers' unions. Some large com-panies were trying to diminish union influence over the managerial employment relationship, thus attempting to reverse the trends of the previous decade.[17]

Conclusion

Managers are an especially important category of employee. They play a vital role in implementing the objectives of most organizations, so that the management of such employees is crucial. Moreover, employers' innova-tions in managing managers are often subsequently applied to other categories of employee. Examples of such wider applications include: more sophisticated methods of selection, induction and development; pay systems based on job evaluation, which include performance-related elements; and other schemes ranging from appraisal to early retirement.

References

1. For further details of these four types see Snape E J and Bamber G J *Managerial and Professional Employees in Britain, Employee Relations Monograph* **9** 3, MCB University Press, Bradford, 1987, p 16
2. Institute of Personnel Management/British Institute of Management *Selecting Managers: How British Industry Recruits* IPM/BIM, London, 1980
3. Mabey C 'Managing Graduate Entry' *Journal of General Management* **10** 2, Winter 1984, pp 67–79
4. National Economic Development Office/Training Commission *Young People and the Labour Market: A Challenge for the 1990s*, NEDO/TC, London, 1988
5. Alban-Metcalf B and Nicholson N *The Career Development of British Managers* British Institute of Management, London, 1984
6. Guerrier Y and Philpot N *The British Manager: Careers and Mobility* British Institute of Management, London, 1978
7. Robbins Lord *Report of the Committee on Higher Education* Cmnd 2154, HMSO, London, 1963; Franks Lord *British Business Schools* British Institute of Management, London, 1983
8. Griffiths B and Murray H *Whose Business? – A Radical Proposal To Privatise British Business Schools* Institute of Economic Affairs, London, 1985
9. Constable J and McCormick R *The Making of British Managers* BIM, London, 1987; Handy C *The Making of Managers: A Report on Management Education, Training and Development in the United States, West Germany, France, Japan and the UK* NEDO, London, 1987
10. *The Economist* 6 April 1985, p 69
11. *Employment Gazette* **93** 1985, p 178; **94** 1986, p 138, using the major occupational groups I and V from Department of Employment *Classification of Occupations and Directory of Occupational Titles* HMSO, London, 1972
12. Rothwell S 'Women's Management Careers' *Business Graduate* April 1985, pp 34–9; McIntosh A 'Women at Work: A Survey of Employers' *Employment Gazette* Department of Employment, November 1980, pp 1142–49
13. Remuneration Economics *National Management Salary Survey, 1988* Remuneration Economics/British Institute of Management, Kingston upon Thames, 1988
14. Kochan T A and Barocci T A *Human Resource Management and Industrial Relations* (1985) Little, Brown, Boston, ch 7; Arnold H J and Feldman D C *Organisational Behavior* (1986) McGraw Hill, New York, p 354ff
15. Engineering Council *1985 Survey of Chartered and Technician Engineers* Engineering Council, London, 1985, p 16; Poole M, Mansfield R, Blyton P and Frost P 'Why Managers Join Unions: Evidence from Britain' *Industrial Relations* **22** 3, Fall 1983, pp 426–44
16. Bamber G J *Militant Managers? Managerial Unionism and Industrial Relations* (1986) Gower, Aldershot, p 50
17. Holbrook D 'Can Collective Bargaining Ever Change? The ICI Experience' *Personnel Management* January 1985

Chapter 10

Employee Relations in Small and Medium-sized Enterprises*

Ian Roberts, Derek Sawbridge and Greg Bamber

After defining a small firm, this chapter elaborates a systematic approach to managing key aspects of employee relations in such firms. We use the term *employee*, rather than *industrial* relations, as it is increasingly seen as more appropriate in the context of small and medium-sized enterprises, which are usually managed informally and rarely unionized. We consider the formulation of a human resources plan which includes the processes of recruitment, induction and training. We explore the issues of pay, communications, workplace regulations, dismissals and trade unionism.

Since the influential Bolton Report (1971), there has been an enormous growth of research on and publications about small firms in general. However, there has been a relative neglect of *employee relations* in small firms. Owner/managers generally accord a lower priority to employee relations than to such other aspects of their business as their output (a product or a service), selling it and accounting for it. Hence, one writer describes those who work in the small business sector as 'the invisible labour force'.[1] This neglect reflects a belief that small firms have 'good' (ie harmonious) employee relations. The belief is fuelled by the indicator that strikes are rare in small firms.

Nonetheless, in recent years, there has been a growing body of research on alternative indicators. When such issues as labour turnover, health and safety records, pay and the number of unfair dismissal cases are examined, the typical pattern of employee relations in small firms may appear to be worse than that in many of their larger counterparts.[2] Analysing such alternative indicators has given rise to another view of small firms, which has more to do with notions of the 'sweat shop' and exploitation than with notions of harmony.

* The authors acknowledge that much of this chapter draws on a research project 'Management and Industrial Relations in Small Firms', which was funded at Durham University Business School by the Department of Employment. However, the views expressed here are personal ones, rather than those of the Department. The authors gratefully acknowledge the helpful comments of Jim Kitay and Mike Scott.

Although there are examples which approximate to either one of these good or bad characterizations, most small firms fit somewhere between those two poles. In short, there are many different styles of employment relationship. The small-firm sector is diverse. There is a difference both in the external constraints and typical management styles, for instance, in a software house on the one hand, and an owner-managed transport firm on the other.

Being 'small' in terms of numbers of employees is not the only determinant of the pattern of employee relations. The industrial subculture is also important. The traditions of specific industries may exert a greater influence on the expectations of owner/managers and workers than the number of employees in a firm. For example, in view of the strong traditions of trade unionism in the printing industry, there is a high level of union membership in many small printing firms; but unionism is invariably absent in small firms in most other industries (as discussed later). Moreover, the style of employee relations varies considerably, even within the same industry. Among other variables, the style reflects the personalities involved, especially those of the owner/managers.

What is a Small Firm?

While an engineering firm employing 15 people could be described as small, a hairdressers employing the same number could be seen as rather large. There is no one accepted definition of a small firm. As shown in Table 10.1,

Table 10.1: *International definitions of small and medium-sized firms*

Country	Definition of small and medium firms
Australia	1 to 100 employees
Belgium	1 to 50 employees
Denmark	6 to 50 employees
Federal Republic of Germany	1 to 499 employees
France	6 to 500 employees
Eire	1 to 50 employees
Italy	1 to 500 employees
Netherlands	1 to 100 employees
United Kingdom	1 to 200 employees

Source: *Industrial Democracy and Employee Participation: A Policy Discussion Paper* Working Environment Branch, Department of Employment and Industrial Relations, Australian Government Publishing Service, Canberra, 1986:70; *Report on the Future of Small and Medium-Sized Business in Europe* Document No 4555 presented to the Parliamentary Assembly Committee on Economic Affairs and Development, Brussels, 1980

the definition in terms of size also varies greatly from one country to another.

The international range of definitions illustrates that any cutoff point in terms of numbers employed is arbitrary. The Bolton Committee, recognizing this problem, identified three qualitative criteria for defining small and medium-sized firms:

1. A small market share and therefore only limited power to influence trading conditions.
2. Personalized management, with the owners themselves actively participating in all aspects of management.
3. Financial independence, with the owners having effective control of the business.*

These qualitative criteria are important, because they set the context in which styles of employee relations are developed. Despite the diversity of the small-firm sector, when these three qualitative criteria are emphasized, there are many similarities between small firms across different industrial sectors. The most important feature is the personalized form of management, especially where the owner(s) actively participate in all aspects of management.

Most big firms have a personnel department, which includes specialists in the various aspects of employee relations, including recruitment, training, pay, and so on. In most small firms, however, an all too often harassed owner/manager has to handle all such aspects in any 'spare time' left over from the other functions of business management. Hence, personnel and employee relations issues are often accorded a low priority.

The prime indicator of success for the owner/managers of most small firms is the market performance of their output. In addition, most of them are intensely committed to the success of 'their' firm. With some owners this commitment becomes an obsession. Success at any price may be an admirable quality in an individual, but can lead to problems if this principle is transferred to the management of people, particularly as owners/managers tend to view employee relations issues in a unitary framework.†
Most owner/managers assume that their firm's goals are rational; therefore, as long as employees do what is good for the firm, they are also doing what is

---

* The financial independence and effective control criterion is problematic, given that many small and medium-sized firms are financially *dependent* on larger ones, for example, for contracts, franchise arrangements, bank loans, and so on.

† Such a framework is defined by the emphasis placed upon the common objectives and values, which are seen to bind all members of the organization together; so the only employee behaviour seen as rational is that which supports the goals of the company, as defined by management. See Gunnigle P and Brady T 'The Management of Industrial Relations in the Small Firm' paper presented to the Eighth National Small Firms Policy and Research Conference, 1985. On the distinction between unitary and pluralist frameworks, see Fox A *Man Mismanagement*, 2nd edition (1986) Hutchinson, London.

best for themselves. Managing employee relations is seen as a matter of 'common sense'. Hence, in the absence of a strike or other overt problem, such elements of management can be left to look after themselves.

Many writers on small firms have concluded that such informal management, based on the close relations between the owner and employees, is 'better' than the impersonal bureaucratic management which characterizes most larger firms. However, later research has questioned this conclusion:

> 'Small firms do offer more varied work roles and greater opportunities for close face-to-face relations in a flexible social setting with less of the bureaucracy of the larger enterprise. But, these conditions also offer greater opportunities for interpersonal conflict.'[3]

This, then, is the key to understanding the reality of employee relations in small firms. Relations are not of the impersonal 'structured' type, characteristic of many larger firms. But neither are they merely a collection of individual interpersonal relationships, involving a loosely structured distribution of power, as in ties of friendship. Rather, the characteristic feature of small firms is the overlap between personal and employee relations.[4]

We advocate an approach which aims to maximize the potential benefits of the close personal relationships in most small firms, while recognizing that these relationships are also structured by an employment relationship. A systematic management approach is needed to settle the conflicts which may arise if and when the more personal ties 'turn sour'. The rest of this chapter is devoted to such a systematic approach to managing employee relations in small firms.

Employing People

Given that most small-business owner/managers are output-oriented, they often see employing people as a nuisance or a 'necessary evil', that the labour law is too complicated and that one mistake can often mean the end of their business. This view is reinforced by some 'experts'. One book which purports to explain the law to small business, devotes two pages (out of 40) to employing people, and begins this advice with a warning, which typifies the whole section: 'One of the many minefields that any expanding small business has to negotiate is the hiring of employees. Hiring has deep perils.'[5]

Such a view has become the conventional wisdom among small-business owners. An ACAS analysis of enquiries from small businesses in the northern region during 1985 revealed that many owner/managers believed (mistakenly) that their business was governed by regulations on hours, pay, conditions etc. Of course employing people is not easy, but it is wrong to exaggerate the stringency of the law and the possible penalties for transgressing it.

To be a successful employer, a degree of planning and a systematic approach is generally necessary. There is an inevitable indeterminancy about the effort expended by employees in exchange for pay (the effort-reward bargain). Unless the pay system is completely based on performance, employees sell merely their *capacity* to labour. It is much harder for an owner/manager to plan precisely what the input from employees will be, than to estimate the rate at which a piece of machinery can work.

The managerial problem, then, is to maximize the potential input from employees. Should managers attempt to specify and closely control the rate at which employees work, as in the scientific-management style (sometimes called Theory X), or to harness the commitment and enthusiasm of the employees in order to maximize the 'variable' input of labour (Theory Y)?[6] Most styles involve some degree of both the X and Y approaches, but the latter is often more suitable in a small firm, which can usually exercise control less formally than a large firm. Most employees work closely with the owner/manager, so their performance is easily visible. Yet, in spite of this small-firm context, many owner/managers are inclined to start by being autocratic and unthinkingly to adopt a Theory X style of management.

A human resource plan

The first step in establishing a small firm should be to formulate a business plan. This should include plans for the output, selling, finance, and so on. If the business is to employ people, it should also include a human resource plan. Such a plan should specify the dimensions of the workforce, both in terms of quantity and quality. Furthermore, the plan should have a time dimension; employment needs should be projected as far into the future as practicable. Such projections should be revised periodically, in the light of changing circumstances and new information. Attention must be paid to the structure of demand for the particular product or service. The owner/manager should consider whether demand is stable over a given period (a year, for example), or whether there are peaks and troughs to plan for. In the shorter term, does demand fluctuate? If so, is this best accommodated through the employment of casual or part-time workers, or by subcontracting?

Once developed, the plan will enable the owner/manager to integrate the costs of employment with the available capital resources. This should ensure the most efficient use of all factors of production and avoid the pitfalls of increasing labour costs, which may arise, for instance, from overstaffing and skill shortages. In the initial stages, the production of such a plan will probably be the sole responsibility of the owner/manager. However, as the firm develops, it will be necessary to review progress and update the projections. At these later stages owner/managers should remember that planning the size and quality of the workforce affects the interests of existing employees, so it is 'important that they and their representatives should be involved in each stage of the process'.[7]

Owner/managers who see the firm as their own creation and as private property may be reluctant to involve employees in planning 'their' firm. But such involvement can benefit the owner/manager by inducing the commitment and enthusiasm of the firm's employees. For an owner/manager, involving employees in such planning has at least two more advantages: assimilating the workers' knowledge of the production process; and informing them in a direct way of the external constraints within which the firm has to operate.

Recruiting

Having formulated a human resource plan and decided to recruit (given that no internal solution to a labour shortage can be found), an owner/ manager should evaluate the precise requirements of each job vacancy. A task analysis of a job should specify its duties and responsibilities and the ways in which the job is to be done. Such an analysis should also specify the desired relationships between the job holder and the superiors, any subordinates and colleagues. Then a job description should be drafted, listing the job's main elements and its general purpose. Next, a job specification should be produced. This defines the qualifications, experience and personal qualities needed to do the job.

Where do applicants come from? *Employing people: The ACAS handbook for small firms* provides a guide to the main sources:

Jobcentres provide a free nationwide recruitment and advisory service.

Employment agencies can assist with the recruitment and selection process and provide other services.

Local Education Authority Careers Services can give employers information on suitable school leavers and other young people who are less than 18 years old, based on regular contacts with local schools.

Advertisements in local newspapers or specialist journals often attract good applicants at relatively low cost.

Word of mouth can be a useful method if the employer is able to judge the reliability of an employee's opinion.[8]

When recruiting, small firms tend to rely to a considerable extent on non-formal agencies of recruitment, entailing word-of-mouth recommendations from friends, relatives or existing employees. Owners often prefer to employ someone by personal recommendation, because such a relationship can provide a way of exerting pressure on the new recruit to perform satisfactorily. There is nothing intrinsically wrong with personal recommendations as a source of candidates; however, it may be unwise for a growing firm to rely entirely upon such sources, which:

'may lead to discrimination claims if it reduces the opportunity for all races and both sexes to apply. It is therefore recommended that this recruitment method should not be used where the workforce is wholly or predominantly white or black and the labour market is multi-racial.'[9]

Perhaps of more importance than possible legal sanctions, is the limitation that over-reliance upon this method of recruitment builds into the firm. Recent research at Durham revealed several examples of the collapse of such recruitment strategies. Well-established small firms encountered difficulties when the 'personal network' dried up. Not only were there no established systematic procedures for recruiting, but also, when 'outsiders' were recruited, they found it difficult to fit into workplaces mostly staffed by established friends and relatives. As a result, labour turnover increased and, where several 'outsiders' were recruited, they tended to form a clique, often leading to a degree of conflict between them and the more established workers.

Nevertheless, the advantages of recruiting personally-recommended candidates can be considerable and lead to a more integrated workforce than might otherwise be the case, as long as those candidates are suitable. It is absurd for owners to employ a friend or relative of either themselves or an existing employee if that person does not fit the job specification.

With the aim of employing the best person, employers should make a short-list of candidates from more than one source from which they can choose their new employee. Because individuals have different strengths and weaknesses the criteria to be considered in the interview should be standardized as far as possible. To this end, the job specification should be divided into simplified headings to be used at the interview. Two of the most popular methods are the seven-point plan developed by Alec Rodger and the five-point grading system produced by Munro Fraser.[10] The former includes:

1. Physical make-up – health, physique, appearance, bearing and speech.
2. Attainments – education, qualifications, experience.
3. General intelligence – intellectual capacity.
4. Special aptitude – mechanical ability, manual dexterity, facility in the use of words or numbers.
5. Interests – intellectual, practical, constructional, physically active, social, artistic.

6. Disposition – acceptability, influence over others, steadiness, dependability, self-reliance.
7. Circumstances – domestic circumstances, occupations of family.

The Munro Fraser system includes similar points, but listed under five headings:

1. Impact on others.
2. Acquired qualifications.
3. Innate abilities.
4. Motivation.
5. Adjustment.

The use of such systems should help to prevent engaging someone who is very good at performing at interviews, but less good at doing the job. Employers should be clear about the relative priority of individual attributes – whether they are essential or merely desirable. Furthermore, these systems should not be seen as exhaustive; extra items can be added. For example, if it is important to the owner that a candidate has some connection with a person already at the firm, this can be included.

In some circumstances, it may be possible to administer a selection test to measure individual ability. While this is relatively easy with potential typists, it is more difficult, say, for potential supervisors, whose job is less easily defined. Nevertheless, it can be useful to seek advice from a specialist recruitment consultant, who can administer a validated aptitude test. (Many owner/managers are too shy of using such external resources, which can provide valuable help.)

References can also provide an important stage in the recruitment process: first, to check the factual information given by candidates about previous jobs, pay, reasons for leaving etc; and second, to gain opinions about the character of candidates and their suitability for the specified post.

Choosing the correct candidate is inevitably a compromise; it is rare to find one who can achieve a maximum rating on all criteria. It is important, therefore, to standardize comparisons, not be swayed by outstanding ability in only one or a few areas.

Recruitment is influenced by the external labour market conditions. It is generally believed that when there is a slack rather than a tight labour market, employers have a larger available pool of labour to choose from and there is less upward pressure on pay levels. However, small firms can experience greater difficulty in finding the right employeee under such conditions. First, because such an employer may be overwhelmed by the number of applicants, so that selection can be difficult and time-consuming. Second, and more importantly, people may apply for work with which they will be less than happy. This factor rather than lack of technical skill, often underlies the complaint from small-business owners that they cannot get the right quality of staff. So, even in such favourable conditions, it is necessary to take a systematic approach to recruitment.

Induction

Once employees have been engaged, few small firms pay enough attention to induction. Typically, they are shown to their workstation, then expected to get on with the job immediately. Perhaps such expectation follows because the firm is small or because new employees were recommended personally or have already had experience in the industry. Sometimes new recruits are introduced to a worker doing the same type of work, who is expected to provide an example to follow. (This approach may be called 'sitting by Nellie'.) Such an approach can be a useful element of the induction process, but is insufficient. Much labour turnover occurs shortly after people join a firm; this is often known as the *induction crisis*. Furthermore, the level of such labour turnover is often under-reported in smaller firms as, when asked about labour turnover, owner/managers often do not include workers who left within a few days or even weeks.

A properly planned induction programme can speed up the process of integrating a new worker into the firm. This has benefits both for the individual concerned and for the firm. An induction programme should involve two aspects:

1. *A technical aspect.* How to do the job, including where tools and materials are located and, for a worker with experience of similar work, any methods specific to the individual firm.
2. *A personnel aspect.* Introductions to all members of the firm and a description of their function (supervisory staff are not always easily identified in the small firm). Factual information such as the location of eating, toilet, safety and health facilities etc should also be detailed.

These two aspects should not be considered in isolation. The explanation of how the firm works is best undertaken on a tour of the establishment, where appropriate introductions can also be made. This gives new recruits an idea not only of where their job fits in, but also where they will fit in the social system of the workplace. Recruits should be encouraged to ask questions; the information flow should be in both directions and it is important for the manager to get to know recruits, as well as for them to know the work environment.

Explaining the functioning of one small print shop is simpler than explaining how a large multinational enterprise functions. However, the goal is the same: employers should aim to integrate new employees into their organizations as smoothly and quickly as possible.

Training

An induction programme is not the only form of training that a small firm needs to offer. The need for the subsequent training and development of staff is probably even greater than in larger establishments, for at least three reasons. First, in most small firms, there is less division of labour, so it is more important for small firms to develop a flexible and adaptable workforce. This is one function of a good training scheme. Second, in view of their small size, the potential for promotion is relatively limited. Therefore, unless there is scope for other forms of development, such as more variation in work or increased responsibility, workers may look elsewhere for career progress. (This has been the experience of many small firms employing professional workers in the high-tech sectors.) Third, investment in the human resources of small firms is important because, compared with larger firms, they tend to be more dependent on the input from labour; most small firms are less capital-intensive than their larger counterparts.

Having established the need for training, of what should it consist? The requirements vary between types of business. However, the firm must initially specify the need and then ensure that the training suits both the employee and the firm. It makes no sense to train someone for non-existent jobs; the trained employee will be frustrated and may leave, so the firm gets no return on the investment.

Even in the smallest of firms it may be possible to initiate a self-development scheme for highly motivated employees and, as long as the training goals have been clearly identified, the practice can be relatively informal. Owner/managers often suspect external training; they criticize it as irrelevant to the specialized needs of their firm. This used to be a reasonable criticism, but recently many external providers of training have specifically aimed to satisfy the requirements of smaller firms. Information on training schemes is available from many sources including:

The Training Agency

Employers' and trade associations.

Local chambers of commerce and small business clubs.

Industry training boards and other specialist training organizations.

The Department of Employment's Small Firms Service.

Business schools, small business centres and/or industrial liaison officers in educational institutions.

Any form of training must be seen in its social context. Training to some degree will be relevant to all members of the firm. It is shortsighted to concentrate solely on one or two high-flyers. Such training may become a source of jealousy and envy, leading towards interpersonal conflict, which is usually counter-productive to the firm's goals.

Pay

In general, pay levels are lower in small firms than in larger ones, for broadly equivalent grades of labour,[11] but there are considerable variations by sector and industry. For example, some of the small high-tech computer firms pay higher salaries than IBM and other multinationals in the same sector. Nonetheless, most large firms offer more in the way of job security and opportunities for promotion.

The general pattern of lower pay in small firms may be linked with a specific orientation to work among small-firm employees. One researcher argued that such workers seem to be less motivated by money, but have more of an expressive orientation to work (ie they like working 'with people' and 'for companionship'). Small-firm workers may not always aim to maximize their economic rewards; instead they may be seeking other benefits, for example, a distinctive working environment which may be typical of small firms.[12] However, subsequent researchers challenged this finding; they concluded that the difference in attitudes between small- and large-firm employees had been exaggerated.[13]

Owner/managers usually claim that their firm pays 'what it can afford'. Nevertheless, such claims should be treated warily; if they were true, pay levels would fluctuate much more than they do in practice. How, then, do small firms determine pay levels? There are at least four external influences over pay levels:

1. Statutory regulation is conducted by wages councils. These used to set minimum pay and conditions in the lowest-paying sectors, which tend to consist mainly of small businesses. At their peak, in the late 1940s, wages councils covered some 15 per cent of all workers.[14] Since then, however, successive governments have abolished some of them. In the 1980s, the government has restricted the remaining wages councils to determining one minimum rate of pay and overtime, and has removed young people under the age of 21 from the scope of wages councils.

2. There are many national and/or local pay agreements with trade unions. For example, there are agreements between the printing unions, and firms which belong to the relevant employers' associations. Many small firms follow these agreements informally, irrespective of whether their workers are unionized, or whether the firm formally belongs to an employers' association. These agreed rates often serve as an approximate guide, around which in-house discussions may take place about other elements of pay, including overtime and bonuses.

3. Most localities have small-business clubs, which may circulate details of the local 'going rate' for key jobs. There may be a tacit acceptance

that such rates in small firms in the area are usually lower than those in the larger ones.

4. Wider market forces are also important. Pay in small firms appears to decline more in a slack labour market than in larger firms.[15]

While such external factors are real constraints, owner/managers do have considerable scope for determining precise levels of pay. It is important for owner/managers carefully to consider their own special requirements in terms of attracting, motivating and retaining particular individuals and groups. Also, in some contexts, bargaining can be important.

Bargaining

Formal company-level collective bargaining is rare in small firms, except in some unionized firms in the traditional manufacturing sector. In the services sector, employers usually determine pay more or less unilaterally, subject to the external factors mentioned above. However, there may be some individual bargaining in the face of labour shortages, especially in relation to highly skilled workers, for instance, professionals in high-tech companies.

Many large employing organizations have been trying to link pay more closely to performance than hitherto. This can be very difficult for large employers, given the complex interrelationships between different parts of their organizations. Making such a link can be easier in a small firm. Rather than making much attempt to evaluate different levels of performance or contribution to the firm, however, in practice owner/managers often determine an individual's pay subjectively, according to their own prejudices. They tend to reward those individuals who appear to be 'good workers' and to penalize those assumed to be 'troublemakers'.

Owner/managers should attempt to overcome such prejudices. Job evaluation is one useful way of establishing a more rational pay structure which can cover all employees. An optional element of performance-related pay can then be added on to the basic pay structure. Such an element can be in the form of bonuses related to objective indicators of group (or individual) performance. Incidentally, the structure must accord with the legal requirement for equal pay for men and women doing work of equal value.

Fairness is a key factor to be observed when determining pay, as employees usually have an accurate view of who are the good workers. An appropriate pay structure will reinforce the collaborative working patterns which are particularly necessary in a smaller firm; an inappropriate structure may destroy them. Whether a firm chooses a time-rated pay system or an incentive system based upon performance will depend upon the type of work and style of management. However, in general, most small firms prefer time-rated systems, as they are simpler to operate and cheaper to administer.

Communications

Many people assume that communications in small firms are automatically good. The frequency of contact is thought to guarantee ease of communication, rendering formalized channels of communication obsolete: 'In a small firm, the manager can know, and be known by, all the employees. Communication is easy because the workers can see the boss virtually every working day.'[16] This view can be challenged, however; the Commission on Industrial Relations Report:

'. . . called into question both the ease of communications . . . and the effectiveness of such communications as did actually take place. Communications tend to be one-way, because, as the report said of small businessmen, "it is not in their nature to consult".'[17]

Ordinary day-to-day personal contacts do not automatically lead to a satisfactory pattern of communication and consultation. Many owners put great faith in an 'open door' policy, but too often no news is seen as good news. Such an approach is too passive; to ensure effective two-way communications, a more active approach is required.

In most firms, it is a good practice to set up systematic channels of communication. For instance, regular consultative meetings can be arranged. The pattern and content of these meetings depends on the type of work, the location of employees and so on. For a group of employees in one location where the market is changing rapidly, it might be appropriate to have short daily or weekly briefing meetings. In a more stable market situation, where it is necessary to bring people together from several locations, it may be more practical to have monthly or even quarterly meetings. Meetings should not be so frequent that there is nothing new to say, nor so infrequent that there is no continuity between them.

Such meetings should not be too formal, but it will help to have an agenda. This is important as it helps to differentiate the content of the meeting from the less structured everyday interactions. Owner/managers could have much to gain from having a dialogue with employees, who usually have a great deal to contribute if encouraged to do so. Therefore, owner/managers should beware of turning these meetings into an opportunity to 'preach a sermon'. They should also ensure that such occasions do not turn into regular 'moaning sessions'. Besides confronting problems, meetings should also focus on more positive issues, such as the firm's progresss and development.

To complement collective meetings, personal discussions are also important, particularly so that individuals can be informed about how their job is contributing to the enterprise and how their own performance is evaluated. In such discussions the emphasis should also be upon dialogue, rather than monologue. Where dialogue is not seen as important, other communication channels can be used. A company newsletter, handbook or folder can contain general information. For other types of information, the use of noticeboards or enclosures in pay packets can be effective. Such communication practices themselves should be subject to joint discussion. Above all, information must be exchanged and messages must get through, for in the absence of effective communication the unsettling power of rumour can be a potent force.

A good communication system need not be gauged merely against the potential problems that would occur in its absence; such a system is intrinsically valuable. One lesson to be learned from the best Japanese managers is that, although time-consuming, a consultative management style is likely to pay dividends. In order to build high-trust working relationships, and improve employee commitment to the firm's goals, communication channels and consultation both need to be given a high priority.

Rules and Regulations

With the informality which is a hallmark of most small firms, rules and regulations are often seen as an anathema. Where there are written rules, they are often a mock bureaucracy, oriented to meeting external legal criteria, rather than to regulating the day-to-day functioning of the firm. This view is shortsighted. The purpose of rules is to provide standard procedures for all employees of the firm. This is especially important in the areas of discipline and grievances; the personalized relationships in a small firm can become a disadvantage when there is a breakdown of such relationships between employer and employee. In such a situation the availability of an impersonal, objective set of rules can be particularly useful.

Rules can also be useful in relation to other aspects of behaviour. Therefore, it is useful to make a concise company rule-book, so that the important information can be found in one place. Rules should be systematic and in writing, but this does not mean that they should be complicated. It is necessary to review the rules periodically, in the face of changing circumstances in the firm and outside it. Once formulated, the rules should be given to all employees (including part-time workers).

No set of rules is exhaustive and application should depend on the merits of each case. For example, where an employee has infringed a rule, were there any mitigating circumstances? It is helpful for the rules to illustrate the distinction between two types of unacceptable conduct: misconduct (which may lead to a warning) and gross misconduct (which could lead to summary dismissal). Examples of these two types of behaviour may vary between different types of business. One example of misconduct may be repeated lateness; however, working dangerously or stealing could be seen as gross misconduct. Other areas that company rules should cover include:

Absence procedures; who to notify and when.

Health and safety practices.

Standards of work performance.

Advice on special clothing requirements.

The use of company facilities, eg telephones.

Timekeeping.

Holiday entitlements.

These rules should be framed in a way that suits the needs of each firm; the stress should be upon simplicity and fairness. Punishment for infringement of the rules should not be overstated, while the aim of improvement should be emphasized. While the rules should be applied with sensitivity, the element of impersonal regulation that such rules imply is necessary, particularly in the small-firm setting. This can be illustrated in relation to dismissal, an issue that is often problematic.

Dismissal

The Conservative government has highlighted the issue of discipline and the small firm. Thus the government rejected the 1986 ACAS draft code of practice on disciplinary procedures. In January 1987, the Minister of Employment stated that the 1986 draft code seemed, 'to be aimed primarily at lawyers and personnel managers in large firms'. As well as its 'excessive legalism' he also criticized it as too long and complex. When revising this draft, ACAS was obliged to ensure that it could be understood in small firms.

As noted earlier, owner/managers often have an exaggerated view of the extent to which their business is subject to legal regulation, especially by the labour law. The British law on unfair dismissal is relatively mild, compared with some other European countries, yet there is a myth among owner/managers 'that it is now impossible to sack people'. During the first 10 years of these laws (1972–81), we estimate that less than 1 per cent of all employment terminations led to a complaint to a tribunal. However, small firms accounted for a disproportionately large number of these complaints.

This over-representation does not reflect the speed with which small-firm owner/managers may sack an employee whom they suspect is damaging their business. On the contrary, our evidence is that when there is a problem with an employee breaking a rule, owner/managers often do nothing and let the situation drift. The problem is allowed to continue until the employer can ignore it no longer, a confrontation ensues, both parties lose their tempers, and the employee is summarily dismissed. Problems, which initially would have responded to *corrective* discipline, end with the application of *punitive* discipline and dismissal. The intense relationships within small firms can have a negative effect. Thus, discipline and dismissal need to be handled impersonally and in a 'cool' manner.

There should be several stages to a disciplinary procedure, for example, as follows:

A formal oral warning issued for minor offences.

A written warning issued for a more serious offence or a repeat of a minor offence.

A final written warning issued for further misconduct. It should be made clear that dismissal will follow if there is no improvement.

Dismissal; the appropriate length of notice should be given.

If an employer uses this code in all disciplinary cases, the chance of an employee being able to bring a successful claim for unfair dismissal will be minimal. Although, to reiterate, the probability of an employee making such a claim is less than imagined by most owner/managers.

There is a similar need for an impersonal set of rules in relation to handling grievances. If there are only one or two tiers of management, it may be hard to convince employees that grievances will receive a fair hearing. Thus, such procedures should be in writing and known by all employees. A minimum of two stages will be necessary in order to provide the right of appeal; a short delay between stages will be helpful for the parties to cool down, although this delay should not exceed a few days and most firms should be able to complete all stages within seven working days. In this way, the procedure should be seen as a fair process, through which redress of grievances can be sought. The alternative is a situation where no one complains (which should not be confused with harmony), but frustrations are bottled up.

Trade Unions

In general, individual membership and recognition of trade unions are both much less usual in small firms than in larger ones. Most owner/managers and small-firm advisers see unions as irrelevant in small firms. A large majority of owner/managers think that union recognition in their companies is unlikely in the immediate future.[18] However, the manufacturing sector is more likely to be unionized than the service sector.

Small-firm employees may have a less sympathetic view of unions than their larger-firm counterparts. But the low level of union membership in small firms can also be explained in terms of the objective problems for unions of organizing many small establishments, the resistance of most owner/managers and the lack of union policies tailored specifically to the problems of workers in small firms.

Although most owner/managers dislike unions, few have much knowledge of how unions actually operate. Even in a small firm, unions can, if the right atmosphere is created, play a positive role. They can provide an effective channel of communication in the workplace. Moreover, full-time union officials have in some cases proved to be effective and almost 'independent' arbitrators in cases of discipline and grievance.

In industries where unionization is relatively high, it may be in the interest of the employer to anticipate any move towards unionization by the workforce, by inviting an appropriate union into the firm. In this way employers can choose a time that is suitable for themselves to arrange a good deal with the union. Thus, they may wish to seek a single-union agreement, to avoid the complications that can accompany multi-union representation.

When employees approach a firm asking for union recognition, the owner/manager has several options. There is no statutory obligation to recognize a trade union, although if a majority of the workforce support the union, the consequences of an outright refusal might precipitate some form of industrial action. If owner/managers think there is insufficient workforce support to justify full collective recognition, they may concede individual representation rights. In this case the union will have the right to represent individuals, for instance, in disciplinary cases or where an employee has a grievance. Alternatively, owner/managers may concede full negotiating rights and enter into a collective bargaining arrangement, whereby rules and procedures are jointly agreed with the union. This provides a method of jointly regulating employees' terms and conditions of employment.

In the foreseeable future, there is not likely to be much growth of unionization across the small-firm sector as a whole. There are fewer economies of scale for unions recruiting and representing people employed in small firms than in large organizations. However, the collapse of many heavy induustries and other shifts in the industrial structure imply a continued decline in the traditional strongholds of union membership, while many small firms have a long-term future.

Therefore, several unions have begun to pay more attention to recruiting in small firms. For example, in early 1987 the two large general unions – the TGWU and GMB – launched initiatives aimed at recruiting new members among temporary and part-time workers, particularly within the small-firm sector. Certain groups were chosen for special attention, such as contract cleaning workers (in the case of the TGWU). More recently there has been emerging evidence that unions are taking the issue of membership within the realms of small firms and the self-employed more seriously. The GMB, for example, have initiated the development of regional self-employed units providing a 'one stop shop' of advice and services for the self-employed. In this way they hope to initiate a union presence in enterprises at the initial level, in the form of the membership of the owner himself. It is believed that as growth occurs in some of these enterprises it will be easier to extend union membership to employees than in firms where owner/managers have never had a contact with trade unions. While union officials report some success in these endeavours, this kind of approach inevitably makes heavy demands upon union resources. It remains to be seen whether, in the long term, such approaches will succeed, or whether recruiting and retaining small firm members will continue to present intractable difficulties for unions.

Conclusion

Many owner/managers do not seek to maximize the growth of their firm, but view it as a supplier of income for themselves and their families. Hence it has been argued that:

> 'Small firms in Britain run out of steam as generators of new jobs when their workforce reaches 20, even though firms employing up to 20 people are the only net creators of jobs among the different sizes of businesses.'[19]

Why is the cut-off figure about 20, rather than five, 15 or 30? We can answer this question in terms of employee relations issues. When the number employed in a firm approaches 20, the limits of informality become apparent. At these staffing levels, problems arise in at least three areas:

1. Informal networks for recruitment are likely to be less satisfactory. Perhaps the limit of potential employees known to the owner/ manager is exhausted, or a social gulf has emerged between the owner/manager and potential shop-floor employees. In the absence of systematic recruitment policies, owner/managers can experience great difficulty in finding employees of the right quality.
2. When there are more than about 20 employees, informal styles of management are no longer appropriate. Communication becomes more difficult, as there are fewer occasions when the whole workforce is conveniently gathered together.
3. As enterprises grow, they tend to find that *ad hoc* responses to personnel issues are less satisfactory; conflict is more likely among workers and between employees and management. Thus, as the number of employees increases, a distinct personnel function begins to be viable and necessary.

An over-reliance upon the informal or non-formal regulation of employee relations in small firms may yield only a precarious harmony. Therefore a means of managing discord is necessary. Owner/managers should realize their potential for constructing high-trust employment relationships, but they should avoid the pitfalls of the non-formal approach. They must avoid being duped by an illusion of harmony. The first step, then, is to realize that a personnel management function is necessary. This function cannot simply look after itself; if so, tensions are likely to grow which, if left undetected, can undermine the efficiency of the firm as much as the under-utilization of capital resources.

In developing a small-firm personnel management function, owner/managers should realize that relations with 'their' workers are primarily based upon an *employment* relationship. Hence a systematic approach is necessary. Such an approach does not imply the formalization of day-to-day relationships between the 'boss' and the workers. This personal element of small-firm employment should be fostered. However, it is possible to develop personnel practices which are not arbitrary, nor too bureaucratic. These practices should be applied creatively. We advocate a blend of informality and systematic procedures. The precise mixture will depend upon the context of each small firm and the choices made by the owner/manager and the workers.

Given a systematic approach to personnel management, most employment legislation and external regulations will have little effect upon the firm:

'. . . independent research has consistently failed to find that employment legislation inhibited small employers from taking on employees or that the legislation played other than a marginal influence in day-to-day employer-employee relations.'[20]

In view of this finding, policy makers should perhaps aim to improve the management of employee relations in small firms, rather than focusing so much effort on the issue of legal regulation. Nevertheless, it seems likely that the current Conservative government will continue with its policies of seeking to deregulate the small-firm sector in particular.

References
1. Curran J 'Bolton Fifteen Years On: A Review and Analysis of Small Business Research in Britain 1971–1986' The Small Business Research Trust, 1986; also see Committee of Inquiry on Small Firms, chairman J E Bolton *Report* Cmnd 4811, HMSO, London, 1971
2. See Daniel W W 'Who Didn't Get a Pay Increase Last Year' *Policy Studies* **5** Part 1, July 1984; Daniel W W 'The First Jobs Taken by the Unemployed Compared with those they Lost' *Policy Studies* **6** Part 1, July 1985; Craig C, Garnsey E and Rubery J *Payment Structures and Smaller Firms: Women's Employment in Segmented Labour Markets* Department of Employment, Research Paper No 48, London, 1984
3. Curran J 'The Width and the Depth: Small Enterprise Research In Britain 1971–1986' paper presented to the Ninth National Small Firms Policy and Research Conference, 1986

4. For an elaboration of this view, see Roberts I P 'Industrial Relations in Small Firms: In Search of a Framework' paper presented to the Ninth National Small Firms Policy and Research Conference, 1986

5. Fazey I H 'The How To Of . . . Small Business' *Financial Times* London, 1985

6. On Theory X and Theory Y, see McGregor D *The Human Side of Enterprise* (1960) McGraw Hill, New York

7. *Employment Policies* Advisory Booklet No 10, ACAS, London, 1984

8. *Employing People: The ACAS Handbook for Small Firms* ACAS, London, 1985

9. *Employing People: The ACAS Handbook for Small Firms* ACAS, London, 1985

10. Rodger A *The Seven Point Plan* National Institute of Industrial Psychology, London, 1952; and Fraser J M *Employment Interviewing* 4th edition (1966) Macdonald & Evans, London

11. Daniel W W 1984, op cit

12. Ingham G K *Size of Industrial Organisation and Worker Behaviour* (1970) Cambridge University Press, London

13. Curran J and Stanworth J 'A New Look at Job Satisfaction in the Small Firm' *Human Relations* **34** 5, May 1981

14. Bamber G J and Snape E J 'British Industrial Relations' in Bamber G J and Lansbury R D (eds) *International and Comparative Industrial Relations: A Study of Developed Market Economies* (1987) Allen and Unwin, London, Sydney and Boston

15. Daniel W W, 1985, op cit

16. Wood G 'The Owner Manager and Other Small Firm Phenomena' *Personnel Management* **6** 11, November 1974

17. Rainnie A and Scott M G 'Industrial Relations in the Small Firm' in Curran J *et al The Survival of the Small Firm* vol 2 (1986) Gower, Aldershot; also see Commission on Industrial Relations *Small Firms and the Code of Industrial Relations Practice* Report No 69, HMSO, London

18. Beaumont P and Rennie I 'Organisational Culture and Non-union Status of Small Businesses' *Industrial Relations Journal* **17** 3, Autumn 1986

19. *Guardian* 13 October 1986

20. Curran J *et al* 1986, op cit

Chapter 11

Pay and Payment Systems

Colin Duncan

For employers, pay represents not only a cost but an important management tool for achieving all sorts of aims. Similarly, for employees and their representatives, pay is the basic determinant of living conditions, but is also the chief medium through which is pursued an equally broad range of individual, workgroup and trade union objectives. The problem of reconciling different goals via organizational payment systems has been a recurrent theme in industrial relations literature over many years, and disappointing results in this respect have contributed to Britain's relatively poor post-war economic performance. Long-standing symptoms of these difficulties persist: a low wage economy; high overtime working combined with poor manpower utilization; and rising unit costs relative to our main overseas competitors.

Developments in the 1980s have added new pressures – recession, rapid changes in the composition and structure of employment and the microelectronics 'revolution' – which would seem to warrant new thinking and approaches to pay and the organization of work. The problems facing an organization in formulating an appropriate remuneration policy in this volatile environment are compounded by the vast array of systems and methods of payment on offer. This chapter considers the process of selecting and implementing a suitable system of payment, discusses the main systems and methods available and reviews some recent trends in remuneration policy.

Classification of Payment Systems

Payment systems are simply methods of relating pay to the work done by employees, although the term is sometimes also used when referring to an organization's wage or salary structure. They can broadly be classified into two categories: *payment by time* and *payment by results*. The former represents the simplest method of payment, where a fixed sum is received per hour, week or month. However, Table 11.1 shows that an increasing proportion of employees receive some element of pay in the form of payment by results (PBR), that is payments arising from a wide range of

Table 11.1: *Growth in coverage of PBR*

| | % of employees on PBR | |
	1977	1987
Full-time men		
manual	36.8	40.7
non-manual	7.2	16.3
Full-time women		
manual	29.7	31.4
non-manual	3.5	11.6

Source: *New Earnings Survey*

schemes which seek to relate pay to aspects of performance other than time spent at work. The growth of PBR is especially marked among non-manual employees and seems to be part of a continuing trend; a CBI survey of employers operating incentive schemes in 1984 found that only 9 per cent expected to reduce the coverage of their schemes over the next five years, while nearly a quarter expected coverage to expand.[1]

Time rate or incentive

Despite the growth of PBR, simple time-rate systems remain the most popular method of payment in Britain and there are few situations to which they are wholly unsuited. While subsequent discussion focuses chiefly upon different forms of PBR, the relative merits of time-rate systems should be borne in mind:

They are simple and cheap to operate.

Forecasting of labour costs is easy.

They produce stability and predictability of earnings for employees.

Pay anomalies are less likely to arise.

They are generally associated with fewer industrial relations disputes.

Indeed, figures from the CBI Databank* show that the incidence of industrial action in recent years has been some 50 per cent greater in the case of settlements involving the introduction or extension of incentive schemes.

* The CBI Databank, established in 1979, is widely recognized as one of the major public indicators of trends in wage settlements. The Databank Survey gathers information on expected percentage increases in pay settlements. The returns are collated into monthly Pay Reports, the results of which are sent to the participants, with overall trends issued for publication. In addition to its monitoring role, the Databank provides a wealth of pay information in new formats which overcome some of the limitations of standard statistical sources.

The chief drawback of time rates, of course, is that little incentive exists to maintain or improve performance.

Terminology

In the literature on payment systems, and in common usage, terms are used so inconsistently that popular names have become almost meaningless. The term 'PBR' is a particular source of confusion. In government statistics, and in the sense used above, the term embraces virtually any payment system with a variable pay element including, for example, profit-sharing schemes, but elsewhere it is commonly applied only to those systems which systematically relate wages to the measured output of individuals or groups. To avoid this confusion the latter systems are referred to in subsequent discussion as *output-related systems*.

Introducing a Payment System

Objectives and expectations

There is often confusion about what the objectives of payment systems are. This reflects two factors. First, managers tend to rely on pay in pursuing *multiple* objectives which can include:

Ensuring that firms can recruit the appropriate quantity and quality of staff.

Reducing labour disputes.

Motivating high performance.

Achieving equitable pay differentials.

Reducing labour turnover.

Controlling costs.

Encouraging labour flexibility.

Inducing company loyalty.

Compensating for adverse working conditions.

Indeed, some commentators have argued that too many objectives are pursued via pay:

> 'In our view using money in all these different ways defeats its own purpose because the aim for achieving any one of the above objectives is to pay those employees to whom that particular objective applies more money relative to other employees. But by paying more money to groups of employees to whom each of the above objectives apply, the employer ends up cancelling out the impact of one differential by superimposing on it another which may go in a different direction.'[2]

A second source of confusion is that there are invariably differences in what people expect from the payment system, not only as between managers and employees but also within management hierarchies and among employees and their representatives.

The first point has implications for payment system choice; the second for the process of implementation.

Payment system choice

Three questions need to be considered:

What are the chief objectives to which the payment system is intended to contribute? This should be decided from an analysis of the most important aspects of performance from the company's point of view, and will involve the setting of priorities as between conflicting objectives.

What payment systems are available? The main options are discussed shortly.

Which payment system(s) is most likely to contribute to the intended objectives in the particular circumstances of the firm? This involves more than a simple matching process, as the system will require tailoring to particular characteristics of the firm and its environment.

Considerable progress has been made in developing systematic techniques to assist in choosing the 'best fit' system to satisfy given objectives. The procedure, labelled the 'contingency approach', is fully described elsewhere.[3]

The process of implementation

A central finding of the work of Bowey and her colleagues was that the extent of consultation and negotiation in designing and implementing the system can be more influential in determining its success than even the type of system chosen:

'Matching the payment system to the social and economic system of the organization, with its attitudes, motivations, inter-relationships, past history, expectations and interpretations, is more important than matching the type of payment system to non-social characteristics of the organization and its environment . . .'[4]

In other words, good results can be obtained with several different types of payment system in any organization, provided a number of ground rules are followed at the design and implementation stage:

Consult early. Early consultation with employees and their representatives has several advantages: local knowledge can be of much value in determining the operational requirements of a successful scheme; gauging employee opinion early on can avoid wasting time, money and effort on an unacceptable system; and the system will be better understood and accepted if employees have been fully involved in its design.

Communicate the system. The role and purpose of the scheme should be spelt out to all concerned. This will involve briefing employees and supervisors, including information on procedures to be followed in the event of disputes; training supervisors and employee representatives on the workings of the scheme; and ensuring that support functions (eg purchasing, sales, maintenance, stores) are made aware of the demands of the new system.

Monitor and review. A joint approach is best and machinery should be set up to deal with problems occurring during the 'debugging' phase and for the regular review of the system in the light of changing circumstances.

Allow adequate time. Many systems fail because the programme is crashed through too quickly, say, over six months. Four or five years later companies can still be trying to debug the system and overcome trade union hostility. Two years is considered to be a good guideline for the time required to design, implement and debug a payment system.

When contemplating changing a payment system it is important to bear in mind that the existing system may well serve purposes and reflect expectations other than those for which it is ostensibly designed. For example, the chief rationale underlying many productivity incentive schemes introduced in the latter part of the 1970s was simply to circumvent incomes policy and increase earnings for employees. The 'hidden agenda' of the existing system therefore requires careful investigation if meaningful negotiations are to take place and unanticipated consequences of change avoided.

Output-related Systems

For manual workers in Britain output-related systems are still the most common class of incentive scheme. *Piecework* is the oldest and simplest form, where a money 'price' is paid for each physical unit of output, while under *standard time systems* (sometimes also referred to as *premium bonus systems*) earnings are made to depend on the difference between the time taken to complete a job and an allowed time. Where a physical output is difficult to identify or measure this may be preferred to piecework. Most output-related systems, even simple piecework systems, now embody some element of time rates, for example in the form of fall-back rates where the bonus rides on top of the time rate, or waiting time.

Setting standards

The methods of fixing standard prices or times vary from casual judgement on the part of a rate-fixer to the more refined techniques of *work study*. The latter is now the more common approach and is more reliable. Work study combines a number of techniques but the two most important elements are *method study* and *work measurement*. The former is concerned with establishing the most efficient method of working, including properly planned layouts and defined methods of operation, and ideally should precede work measurement. Work measurement, on the other hand, is a three-stage process: the time taken to perform a given task is first measured; then the effort of the worker or workgroup is *rated*, that is an assessment is made of work performance relative to what is considered to be a standard pace; a standard allowable time or price is then set on the basis of the first two stages, with due allowances for personal needs, relaxation and varying contingencies. The most subjective element of the process is effort rating and even experienced work study officers can recommend rates which are too loose (lucrative) or too tight.

Sources of variation

There is an enormous variety of output-related systems which differ with respect to a number of subsidiary features in order to meet varying requirements. For example, some link payment to individual output while others relate bonus to group performance. The period to which bonus is related can also vary, being daily, weekly, monthly or even longer. Perhaps the most fundamental distinction is the way in which earnings are made to vary with changes in performance. There are several variations, as illustrated in Figure 11.1, each with a distinctive objective – to encourage learners, to encourage workers to beat a certain standard, or to discourage excessive performance, for example.

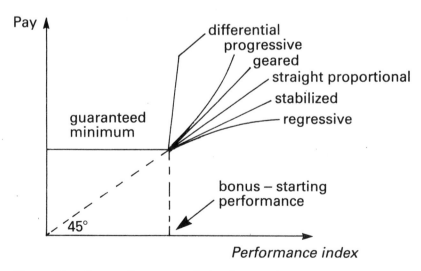

Figure 11.1 *Pay-performance relationships under various schemes*

If earnings and performance vary in the same proportion then the scheme is described as *straight proportional*. In *geared* schemes the rate of change of earnings, although constant, is greater than the rate of change in performance. If the change of earnings is less than the change of performance the scheme is known as *stabilized*. These relationships are linear in that the bonus *rate* does not vary with performance. In non-linear relationships on the other hand, the bonus rate varies with performance levels. When the rate of change in earnings gradually increases with performance, the scheme is termed *progressive* and when it gradually falls, it is called *regressive*. *Differential* schemes are a combination of two or more schemes, changing from one to another at specified levels of performance.

Pre-conditions

The following have been suggested as the conditions most suited to output-related systems:

The work should be measurable and directly attributable to an individual or group. In practice, this generally means that the work should be almost entirely manual, repetitive, and consist of fairly short-cycle operations.

The pace of work should be controlled to a significant degree by the worker, rather than by the machine or process he is tending.

Management should be capable of maintaining a steady flow of work, and of absorbing at least short-term fluctuations in demand and output.

The tasks involved should remain fairly constant through time, that is they should not be subject to very frequent changes in methods, materials or equipment.[5]

The process of decay

Output-related systems have attracted harsh criticism over the years on account of their proneness to 'erosion' or 'decay'. This tendency is exacerbated by poor system choice, hasty implementation and inadequate monitoring and control of the system. The more common manifestations include the following:

Rate drift. Times allowed for jobs become slack over time when changes in product or method require frequent renegotiation of rates, especially in circumstances of strong workplace representation. Minor improvements in technology or methods which are too small to warrant retiming of jobs can, over time, produce the same phenomenon, as can the 'learning curve' effect.

Worker fiddles. A particularly common fiddle is that of 'cross-booking' of time between tasks. This can have several objectives for workers: to hide loose rates arising from poor work study (thereby encouraging restriction of output), ironing out fluctuations in pay arising from factors outside the workers' control, or simply to maximize bonus earnings, for example. For the firm such practices can restrict output, inflate earnings relative to effort and can also distort the picture of labour costs for particular products, thereby inhibiting efficient production planning and control and distorting pricing policies.

Shortcuts. Shortcuts towards achieving high bonus can reduce quality, damage machinery and endanger safety.

Labour inflexibility. Cumulative errors in work study manifested in loose and tight rates can breed inflexibility. The perceived benefits of the scheme might also cause employees to resist change.

Pay anomalies. These can arise from a number of factors including poor work study or the varying bargaining capacities of individuals or groups. The situation can arise where semi-skilled workers on PBR earn more than skilled PBR workers or craft workers outside the scheme (eg maintenance) and this can create problems of morale, leapfrogging pay claims and spiralling wage costs.

The limitations of control

Careful preparation and control can do much to slow down the process of decay but some erosion of the scheme is more or less inevitable over time and five years is regarded in much of the literature as the standard life-cycle of such systems. Moreover, excessive adherence to formal rules may prove counter-productive: evidence suggests that some degree of informality and flexibility is required in operating a successful scheme. For example, a study of the Coal Board's scheme following the re-introduction of incentives into coalmining in 1977–78 found that the system's success owed much to the informal actions of colliery managers in relaxing incentive scheme rules and compromising on costs for other benefits, such as cooperative union relationships, sustained worker motivation and reduction of industrial disputes.[6]

Measured Daywork

This system is sometimes introduced as a substitute for a decayed output-related system of PBR, or as a means of providing some incentive in circumstances where an output-related system is considered inappropriate. Sometimes referred to as a 'halfway house' between an incentive scheme and payment by time, measured daywork (MDW) offers employees a fixed sum for maintaining performance at or above a predetermined level. There are three main types:

1. Payment on a time basis with a requirement that employees maintain a standard performance. By virtue of its simplicity this is the most common form.

2. Payment on a time basis with a fixed bonus for maintaining a standard performance.

3. As in either of the above but each individual can choose to maintain one of a series of performance levels to which different rates of pay are attached (eg stepped measured daywork, premium pay plan).

Under MDW, workers are therefore geared to an incentive level of performance, which distinguishes it clearly from time-rate systems, but pay does not vary in the short term with actual performance. Rather, the incentive payment is guaranteed in advance, putting the employee under an obligation to achieve the standard. Sanctions against those who consistently fail to meet performance targets, even after further training, vary according to the details of the scheme and can include job transfers, loss of bonus, demotion under stepped schemes, disciplinary action and ultimately, although rarely, dismissal.

MDW seeks to achieve an effort-reward bargain where management gain from a sustained improvement in performance, more effective control and predictability of output and costs and improved labour flexibility, while workers benefit from improved pay and greater stability of earnings and pay relativities. It is therefore most suited to situations where teamwork and labour flexibility are required, where predictability of output and costs are more important than very high levels of production and where stability of earnings is an attractive proposition to employees.

As pay does not vary directly with output, the system avoids some of the features of decay associated with conventional incentive schemes, although a fall in output or productivity is sometimes experienced when changing from piecework or standard time systems to MDW because of the reduced incentive effect. For time-rated workers a switch to MDW may be appropriate where overtime has become a regular part of the working week; low effort and long hours are replaced by sustained effort within the regular working week. The system may be especially suited to indirect workers, such as maintenance staff, particularly if excessive overtime reflects a desire to maintain pay relationships with production workers on incentives. A 'package deal' approach may be appropriate for such workers where MDW is sold not only in return for reduced hours but possibly a plant maintenance programme based on work study, craft flexibility and shiftworking.

Industrial relations implications

The industrial relations implications of a MDW agreement are similar to, and can be as far-reaching as, those of an elaborate productivity deal. Both seek a trade-off between pay and existing working practices and imply important changes in management organization, collective bargaining arrangements and workplace representation. The costs of the system are high, both in terms of 'buying out' the existing system and in planning and monitoring soundly-based manning levels, output standards and control systems. Effective work measurement is essential and job evaluation is often required to resolve pay anomalies prior to introducing the new system. The obligation to pay employees for waiting time and the importance of ensuring steady workflow put new pressures on production management. The role of shop-floor supervisors is particularly vital because the onus of maintaining employee performance shifts to their shoulders. The system is therefore generally unsuited to smaller firms lacking the technical resources and commitment required for a radical overhaul of management processes and work organization.

As it usually entails some formalization and rationalization of collective bargaining arrangements, the introduction of MDW has also several important implications for trade union organization. It can lead to increased trade union influence and the role of the shop steward may be transformed. When MDW takes over from a time-rated system the responsibilities of the shop steward are normally enhanced, while a shift from incentives transforms the role from shop-floor bargaining over pay and performance to concern over standards, manning, sanctions and flexibility. Responsibilities become more formalized and there may be less scope for individual initiatives than before, especially with regard to sanctions where action can become restricted by agreement. Shop steward training may be required in such areas as job grading, work study and job evaluation.

One further consequence of MDW is that in taking pay out of day-to-day bargaining it can have the effect of transferring conflict to a higher level, leading to greater pressures for comparability-based annual pay increases. Moreover, disappointing results with MDW systems in coalmining, the docks and car manufacturing in the 1970s demonstrated that the system can be just as prone to erosion as conventional incentives when there is inadequate consultation, planning and monitoring of the scheme. Effort drift simply replaces rate drift as the grounds for dispute change from output prices and times to manning levels and the speed of the line.

Plant or Enterprise-wide Systems

Under plant or enterprise-wide systems a collective bonus is paid on the basis of the overall labour performance of the plant or firm. The simplest systems link bonus to volume of output or to sales value over a set period. In practice many systems in the UK are derived from the *Scanlon Plan* or *Rucker Plan*.

Scanlon schemes are based on the ratio of total payroll costs to sales value of production. The ratio is estimated over a representative period and the figure derived gives a norm against which future performance is assessed. Bonus becomes payable when the ratio decreases over an agreed period.

The Rucker Plan is similar except that the ratio is payroll costs to *added value*. Added value is essentially a measure of the income generated by the application of employees' skill and company investment to bought-in materials and, under the Rucker system, is calculated as the difference between sales revenue of production minus the costs of bought-in materials and services. This meets the objection that under Scanlon schemes bonus is payable if prices increase to cover increased costs of raw materials and services.

Bonus calculations under each system are illustrated in Table 11.2 by means of an example. Assume that 25 per cent of savings go into reserve to provide a bonus in those months when no bonus would otherwise be payable; the remainder is divided equally between the company and employees. Thus under Scanlon the employees' share is:

$$\frac{£(2,000-500)}{2} = £750 \text{ or } 7.5\% \text{ of the wage bill.}$$

Under Rucker the figures are:

$$\frac{£(1,667-417)}{2} = £625 \text{ or } 6.25\% \text{ of the wage bill.}$$

Advantages and limitations

Points in favour of these schemes and their variants are:

They are economical to install and operate: it is not essential to have work measurement and excessive clerical costs are avoided.

A wider section of the workforce can be brought under the same scheme.

They reward cooperative effort not only with respect to output but in economy of materials, maintenance and general labour costs. Teamwork is thereby encouraged and further fostered through production or suggestion committees that are established for improvements in efficiency.

They may be conducive to union/management cooperation in that close consultation with union members is required and more information is disclosed to trade unions about the operation of the firm.

However, they have several limitations:

There is potential for inter-group/departmental rivalry if workers feel they are carrying others who are not pulling their weight.

Table 11.2: *Example of bonus calculations under the Scanlon and Rucker Plans*

Base period calculations

		£
Net sales over 3-year reference period	=	1,000,000
Less bought-in materials, supplies and services	=	400,000
Added value over 3 years	=	600,000
Payroll costs over 3 years	=	200,000

Percentage ratio of payroll costs to net sales (Scanlon) $= \dfrac{200,000}{1,000,000} \times 100 = 20\%$

Percentage ratio of payroll costs to added value (Rucker) $= \dfrac{200,000}{600,000} \times 100 = 33.3\%$

Bonus calculations

		£
Net sales over 1 month	=	60,000
Less bought-in materials etc	=	25,000
Added value	=	35,000
20% of net sales	=	12,000
Less actual wage bill	=	10,000
Savings available for distribution under Scanlon	=	2,000
33.3% of added value	=	11,667
Less actual wage bill	=	10,000
Savings available for distribution under Rucker	=	£ 1,667

They may have little incentive value because of the tenuous link between effort and reward. Incentive is reduced the greater the number of workers covered and bonus may become regarded simply as part of basic pay.

Production or suggestion committees can be a poor substitute for work measurement in identifying inefficiencies.

The bonus can be influenced by external conditions such as reduced selling prices or loss of markets, and while adjustments to the norm are possible, frequent refinements can lead to undue system complexity and reduced understanding and interest on the part of employees.

The schemes are much more than simple accounting ratios and require just as much preplanning, consultation and control as apparently more complex systems. They imply an open, participative management style which is not always favoured by trade union representatives, especially if suggestion committees and other facets of the scheme are perceived as designed to weaken trade union influence or bypass formal channels of representation. They are best suited where there is plant-wide acceptance of efficiency as a major objective and where the market and technological environment is relatively stable. The existence of adequate records (output, sales, wages etc) over a representative period is a further precondition. It is sometimes suggested that the limit of effective coverage is about 1,000 workers, although some firms have claimed success with company-wide schemes covering many thousands of employees.

Profit Sharing

There has been a sharp trend in recent years towards profit-based systems which accounted for 66 per cent of all new systems introduced between 1979 and 1984.[7] Profit-sharing schemes can be roughly grouped into cash-based systems where a bonus in cash is paid from profits, and share-based systems where profit bonus is in the form of shares allocated to employees. Each type has several forms. Under cash systems, for example, the bonus can be related to a fixed proportion of pre- or post-tax profits; to a proportion of profits above a stated threshold; to the dividends paid on share capital; or the amount may be determined on a purely discretionary or arbitrary basis. Sources of variation in share-based schemes include the rights attached to the shares issued, their marketability and various inducements offered to discourage early conversion to cash.

Nearly all the advantages and limitations of plant/enterprise-wide systems apply also to profit sharing, but share-based systems have some unique features, in that: They give employees a stake in the *ownership* of the enterprise; payment of bonus does not affect cashflow; certain forms attract tax advantages.

The main tax encouragement to 'all-employee' share schemes was introduced in the Finance Acts 1978 and 1980. Until then most all-employee schemes were cash-based, and share-based systems tended to be restricted to executive employees.

Tax-approved schemes

There are four main types of scheme which attract tax advantages:

1. Approved all-employee profit-sharing schemes (APS), first introduced in the Finance Act 1978. These are profit-sharing schemes where employees receive shares which are held in trust for a certain period. Under Inland Revenue approved schemes the employee is not liable to income tax on the value of shares (provided he does not sell them for at least five years) and the company can offset the costs of the scheme against corporation tax.

2. Save As You Earn (SAYE) schemes introduced in the Finance Act 1980. These are savings-related share option schemes where employees save a regular amount under a standard SAYE contract for either five or seven years, and then choose whether to take the money saved or buy shares at a pre-established price when the contract expires. Under approved schemes the employee is not liable to income tax on any gains made in exercising the option.

3. Discretionary share option schemes set up under the 1984 Finance Act. As with SAYE schemes these involve the granting of options over shares, any gain realized when the option is exercised normally being free of income tax. Unlike APS and SAYE schemes, however, there is no obligation on the company to include all employees and the vast majority in operation are in fact executive share option schemes.

4. Tax relief for employees receiving profit related pay (PRP) as introduced in the Finance Act 1987. Under PRP, a set proportion of pay is made to vary with profits. This idea is rather different from other forms of profit sharing where the benefits are usually distinct from, and additional to, normal wage and salary payments. Instead, an integral part of pay is determined directly by reference to profits and 'normal' pay will therefore vary with profitability. The Act provides that half of PRP will be free from income tax, up to the point where it is 20 per cent of PAYE pay or £3,000 a year, whichever is lower. Part-timers may be excluded and new recruits need not be included for up to three years, but at least 80 per cent of the other employees in the employment unit must be covered as a condition of registration for tax relief.

There has been a steady growth in approved share schemes recently, but mainly among top executives. By June 1987 the Inland Revenue had registered 2,080 executive share option schemes which, despite their later introduction, is roughly twice the total registrations of APS (666) and SAYE (647) schemes combined. The objectives of the executive schemes would seem to be rather different from the all-employee schemes. Survey evidence suggests that the most common reason for adopting the latter is to make employees feel more involved and interested in the company, while the aim of discretionary schemes, according to Nigel Lawson, is: 'to attract top calibre company management and to increase the incentives and motivation of existing executives and key personnel by linking their rewards to performance'.[8] With regard to PRP on the other hand, the Chancellor in his Budget speech, envisaged two main benefits: 'First, the workforce would have a more direct personal interest in the profits earned by the firm or unit in which they work: and second, there would be a greater degree of pay flexibility in the face of changing market conditions. Such flexibility is vital if, as a nation, we are to defeat the scourge of unemployment.'

Setting up a tax-approved scheme will typically involve wide consultation with interested parties, including the board of directors, shareholders, company solicitors and possibly registrars, consultants, stockbrokers, auditors and building societies. However, many companies have adopted the position that such schemes, and indeed profit sharing in general, are non-negotiable with trade unions. The experience of companies operating APS or SAYE suggests a period of about ten months to prepare the scheme and obtain Inland Revenue approval.

Assessment
The weight of evidence suggests a generally favourable evaluation of share-based tax-approved schemes although the rating of schemes in terms of very general objectives, such as to make employees feel more involved, tends to be higher than for more measurable objectives, such as incentive to improve productivity. Nevertheless, one recent study[9] found that firms that operated profit sharing had, on average, a faster subsequent appreciation of share prices, although the sample was not confined to tax-approved schemes. Some evidence of the relative merits of different schemes as perceived by companies was gathered in a recent survey commissioned by the Department of Employment.[10] Some companies had experience of both APS and SAYE and the chief findings were that:

Overall APS schemes consistently received a higher rating than SAYE arrangements.

APS schemes generally attract participation from a higher proportion of the company's employees than under SAYE.

SAYE schemes, on the other hand, require greater personal commitment from individual employees and are therefore more likely to result in a higher level of commitment to the company than APS.

SAYE schemes are regarded as administratively cheaper to operate.

Tax-approved schemes are rarer and considered less appropriate in smaller, privately owned firms. They are complicated and expensive to administer and share-based arrangements are often unsuited to their way of operating. The preference was for simplicity and the direct relationship to profit of cash-based profit sharing.

On the other hand, the government's consultative document on the PRP proposal, published in July 1986,[11] attracted a decidedly cool response from a wide cross-section of industry. Objections were raised both towards the whole concept of PRP and specific details of the government's proposals. The Engineering Employers' Federation (EEF) and Institute of Personnel Management (IPM) were particularly critical and doubts were also aired by the British Institute of Management, CBI, and TUC. The following were among the more specific reservations expressed in employers' responses to the Green Paper:

> It is hard to imagine why employees should feel 'involved' merely through the existence of a scheme which may or may not provide a bonus, especially as employees are not compensated for risk-taking by decision sharing.

> Difficulties in determining profit centres, measuring profit, allocating overheads and allowing for transfer pricing within a company could lead to arbitrary decisions on the level of profit attributable to particular employees and therefore produce a demotivational effect.

> External factors adversely affecting profits and hence pay could again be demotivational and, indeed, under conditions of falling profitability, less pay may be accompanied by increased workload.

> Profit cannot be assessed nor audited quickly enough to secure early reductions in pay when market conditions deteriorate rapidly.

> To maximize the PRP element of pay, employees could be motivated to resist recruitment, reduce numbers employed and favour short-term profit maximizing at the expense of investment.

> Managers could find themselves bargaining over two different parts of the pay packet at different times of the year, and making one part of the pay packet insecure could make bargaining harder for that part which is secure.

These limitations, together with several technical deficiencies which have been identified in the design of the tax relief, are likely to militate against widespread adoption.[12] By June 1988, the Inland Revenue had registered 694 PRP schemes, but mostly covering smaller companies with better paid employees which did not engage in collective bargaining.[13]

From the trade union point of view there would seem to be little distinction between attitudes to tax-approved schemes and more traditional forms of profit sharing, towards which unions have been lukewarm, if not hostile. The bases of union criticism typically include some of the following considerations:

> Many schemes are non-negotiable.

> They do not extend industrial democracy nor provide any real control over managerial decisions.

There is no trade union control over items which may be incorporated into the profit and loss account.

The actual amounts payable are small and paid at long intervals.

Profit sharing can be used as a fringe benefit to maintain an unorganized workforce and avoid collective bargaining.

Accordingly, as with plant/enterprise-wide systems, profit-sharing schemes, tax approved or otherwise, are most likely to succeed where there is a general management philosophy of employee involvement and, indeed, there is some evidence that the take-up of tax-approved schemes is highest among companies such as ICI which have practised profit sharing over many years. Despite the thinking behind tax concessions, the schemes are unlikely in themselves to change organizational culture but may usefully reinforce a participative culture which already exists.

Pay Structures and Job Evaluation

No less important than deciding the appropriate system of payment in an organization is achieving an appropriate internal structure of pay, and the two processes should ideally be considered in tandem as each has implications for the other. Symptoms of a malfunctioning pay structure include: problems of recruitment and retention; an increasing frequency of claims and disputes relating to restoration of pay differentials; disputes about the matching of jobs to grades; lower grades becoming empty as many jobs drift to the top of the structure; and manipulation of the existing structure by both management and unions.

The most common method of dealing with distortions in the pay structure is job evaluation. Job evaluation is concerned with establishing the relative position of jobs in a hierarchy by looking at the content and demands of the work. Its purpose is to enable organizations to develop a rational and defensible basis for their pay structures. Job evaluation differs from a payment system in that it evaluates the demands of jobs rather than the performance of job-holders. Moreover, although it is concerned with establishing acceptable pay relationships, it does not in itself establish the pay of different jobs. This is a separate process normally determined through negotiation. Nor is job evaluation a science: the aim is to be systematic and the process involves a degree of subjectivity, not least in the choice and weighting of assessment criteria. Because it is not a scientific nor 'objective' procedure a degree of employee participation in the design and implementation of the system is usually considered essential. Without this, the scheme will be built on management perceptions of what is fair and employees may remain unconvinced.

Methods of job evaluation

The four basic techniques of job evaluation are *ranking*, *grading* (or *classification*), *points rating* and *factor comparison*. The first two are usually described as non-analytical; the second two as analytical or quantitative. Non-analytical techniques assess jobs as a whole and produce simple rankings whereas analytical techniques break down jobs into a number of component factors or characteristics so that rankings and rank distances can be expressed numerically. Each method can be applied to both manual and non-manual employees, although they vary in their suitability for different situations. Many companies have more than one scheme in operation because of the different nature of the jobs concerned and, despite pressures towards integrated systems, the same scheme is rarely applied, without modification, to manual, staff and managerial employees alike.

Job Ranking
Job ranking is the simplest form of job evaluation. A job description is prepared for each job to allow its duties, responsibilities and qualifications to be identified. Each job is considered as a whole and is given a ranking. A ranking table is then drawn up and the ranked jobs grouped into grades to which pay levels or ranges are allocated. As the evaluation team requires an all-round knowledge of every job the method is more appropriate for small organizations with no more than 30 to 40 jobs. More can be handled if 'benchmark' jobs are used as yardsticks against which other jobs can be assessed without having to complete a full evaluation of every job.

The chief advantage of ranking is its simplicity: it is easily understood, installation costs are low and it does not make heavy demands on time or on administration. However, the results of the exercise can be difficult to defend as they are based on impressionistic judgements rather than clearly defined ranking criteria. A further drawback is its failure to measure the difference between jobs; it can show job A to be more difficult than job B but not how much more difficult.

Paired comparisons
Paired comparisons is a refinement of job ranking which is sometimes considered less subjective and which introduces an element of scoring to indicate the degree of importance between two jobs. Again, each job is considered as a whole but is then ranked against every other job in turn (this is unnecessary with basic job ranking) and points are awarded according to whether its overall importance is judged to be less than, equal to, or more than the other job. The points allocated in each case are usually zero, one and two respectively. By totalling up the scores a rank order is produced, as illustrated in Table 11.3.

One difficulty with this approach is that as the number of jobs increases the number of paired comparisons rises rapidly. If X jobs are to be ranked then the number of comparisons required is:

$$\frac{X(X-1)}{2}$$

Table 11.3: *Paired comparisons*

Job	A	B	C	D	E	Total Score	Rank Order
A	–	0	2	0	2	4	2
B	2	–	2	2	2	8	1
C	0	0	–	2	0	2	5
D	2	0	0	–	1	3	3
E	0	0	2	1	–	3	3

Hence if X=10, 45 comparisons are needed, while if X=20 the number of comparisons rises to 190. The number of calculations will therefore be impractical for a large number of jobs unless computer facilities are available.

Job grading (or classification)
Job grading is similar to ranking but starts from the opposite end: grades and grade characteristics are established first and the jobs are then fitted into them at the most appropriate level. The grade definitions are normally based on broad differences in skill, responsibility or qualifications. Jobs considered typical of each grade are selected as benchmarks and the other jobs are compared with these benchmarks and the grade description and slotted in.

The method is easily understood, quick and inexpensive as there is no need to compare individual jobs against each other. It is somewhat less subjective or arbitrary than ranking because although whole jobs are still compared, the method does identify the qualities and experience necessary for different jobs. Moreover, the decisions reached can be justified by reference to the grade definitions and, as the grades are determined first, the problem of quantifying differences between jobs is avoided. The method is best applied to a fairly homogeneous family of jobs, differentiated in terms of the qualifications or skills needed to handle extra responsibility (eg as in clerical or administrative functions). Because of the inflexibility of grade definitions, job tasks should also be reasonably stable over time. The method has been widely used in the public sector and for clerical staff by many private sector companies.

The main weakness of job grading is that complex jobs are often difficult to fit into the system as they may straddle grade boundaries and it can be difficult to decide whether to upgrade them on the basis of some facets or downgrade on the basis of others. Accordingly, there is a tendency over time for the original grades to become subdivided, rendering the scheme more complex and unwieldy. This difficulty may be eased if separate classification structures are used for different jobs classes. Nor is the

Table 11.4: *Staff job evaluation scheme, Imperial Tobacco Ltd, Table of Points Values*

Factors	Degrees and points										Maximum % of highest possible score (331)
	A	B	C	D	E	F	G	H	J	K	
Job knowledge and skills	10	20	30	40	50	60	70	80	90	100	30.2%
Problem solving	10	20	30	40	50	60	70	80	–	–	24.2
Scope (ie discretion)	8	16	24	32	40	48	–	–	–	–	14.5
Commercial significance	8	16	24	32	–	–	–	–	–	–	9.7
Supervision	5	10	15	20	25	–	–	–	–	–	7.6
Clerical operations	3	6	9	12	15	18	–	–	–	–	5.4
Manipulative tasks	2	4	6	8	–	–	–	–	–	–	2.4
Contacts:											
difficulty	2	4	6	8	10	12	–	–	–	–	3.6
relevance	2	4	6	8	–	–	–	–	–	–	2.4

Source: Imperial Tobacco Limited *Staff Job Evaluation Scheme Manual* p 42

technique as objective as it might first appear: evaluation may in reality be occurring prior to objective examination of job specifications as arbitrary impressions of job worth might prejudice the definition of job grades. Indeed, without employee involvement in grade definitions or, ideally, their preparation by an independent body, there is scope for conscious or unconscious sex bias or for an employer to seek to depress pay by defining grades in such a way that most jobs fall into lower categories.

Points rating

Points rating is the most widely used technique in Britain. It is an analytical method which, instead of comparing whole jobs, breaks down jobs into a number of selected factors. Each factor or sub-factor is further broken down into degrees, to which points are attached. The number or range of points allocated determines the *weighting* or relative importance of different factors. Once the factors are defined and weightings established, benchmark jobs are again identified and evaluated as reference points and the remaining jobs are examined against the factor definitions and benchmark job scores. The summation of the points for each factor, duly weighted, produces a total points score which determines the position of each job in the hierarchy.

Manual schemes normally include as factors skill, responsibility, effort and working conditions, but the factors chosen will vary with organizational requirements and the types of jobs covered. Table 11.4 illustrates the factors and weightings used by Imperial Tobacco Ltd in a scheme which covers the majority of its salaried employees in secretarial, clerical, technical, scientific and professional occupations. The scheme contains nine factors, each of which is rigorously defined in the job evaluation manual, as are the degrees or discrete levels of demand under each factor. Evaluating a job involves deciding which degree under each factor most closely corresponds with the level of demand in the job. The firm operates two other schemes – for factory operatives and factory supervisors – which are similar in design but have different factors more relevant to the occupations covered.

Points rating has several advantages over other schemes:

It is more objective and consistent in that common standards provide a structured discipline for evaluators; by focusing attention towards specific factors or characteristics it helps to break down traditional views of job worth and avoids the tendency under other schemes to assess the individual rather than the job.

It allows differences between jobs to be quantified and the evaluated structure is easier to explain and justify.

It is the most adaptable of all methods and can be applied across a very wide range of diverse jobs.

New jobs or regrading appeals can be easily measured against existing factors or weightings without upsetting the placings of other jobs. The method therefore tends to be stable and durable over time.

The method can help reduce traditional job demarcations. For example, an ambitious national points rating exercise was carried out in local government in 1986 covering one million manual workers in some 40 occupations, with a view to reducing the number of grades and promoting local job flexibility, hitherto constrained by the existence of rigid, nationally-defined job descriptions.

The disadvantages of points rating are:

It is costly and time-consuming to set up and maintain; the large variety of job characteristics to be covered by a limited number of factors or degrees require a long and costly series of discussions.

The choice of factors and weightings relies on human judgement and can be hard to justify; quite small differences in factor weightings can alter the positions of jobs.

The use of numerical measures can convey a spurious impression of precision which may breed rigidity.

The greater the number of factors the higher the possibility of the same aspect of a job being assessed from different angles. This results in over-weighting of that factor.

The method is prone to grade drift, as minor changes in jobs can provide grounds for regrading appeals.

Factor comparison

Factor comparison is an extension of the points rating method which attempts to rank jobs and attach monetary values concurrently. Jobs are again examined in terms of selected factors of which they are thought to be composed. Benchmark jobs are then examined factor by factor to produce a rank order of the benchmark jobs for each factor. This shows the relative importance of each factor within each job. For example, if A, B and C represent the benchmark jobs and X, Y and Z the factors, then the ranking produced under each factor could be as shown in Table 11.5.

Table 11.5: *Factor comparison – jobs*

	Factors					
	X	r	Y	r	Z	r
	A	1	A	1	C	1
Jobs	C	2	B	2	A	2
	B	3	C	3	B	3

r = rank order

Table 11.6: *Factor comparison – wage rates*

Jobs		X	r	Y	r	Z	r	Total
	A	£75	1	£75	1	£50	2	£200
	B	£65	3	£70	2	£45	3	£180
	C	£70	2	£35	3	£55	1	£160

An attempt is then made to establish how much of the current wage rate for each job is being paid for each of the factors. For example, suppose the weekly wage rates for jobs A, B and C are £200, £180 and £160 respectively, then the results of this stage might be as shown in Table 11.6. If the two rankings agree in their positioning of the jobs under each factor, as in the simplified example in Table 11.5 and 11.6, the benchmark jobs are accepted. If not, the money values of the anomalous jobs are adjusted, or they may be rejected from the calculations. The procedure results in a scale or range of money values for each factor, which is representative of the benchmark jobs in respect of that factor. The remaining jobs are then evaluated factor by factor against these scales, giving a total rate for each job.

In practice, however, this technique is highly complex, time-consuming and costly. It relies heavily upon choosing good benchmark jobs which must display a sufficient range of variation under each factor, and rather more such jobs are typically required (about 15 to 20) than under points rating schemes. A further requirement which can be difficult to meet is that the pay rates for these jobs must not be in dispute. The method is not easily understood on account of the number of hierarchies involved and there is a clearly arbitrary element in the way existing wage rates are ascribed to different factors. It can also result in reduced pay flexibility in that once differentials have been established, future pay increases need to be on a percentage basis if the integrity of the scheme is to be maintained.

Perhaps the major advantage of the factor comparison method is that in requiring custom-built installation, it can be more closely adapted to any special needs of an organization or unusual features of its jobs. For example, a modified form of the technique was successfully applied by the BBC to professional, technical and administrative posts, as other methods were felt to be unsuited to the unusual content of these jobs and particular organizational needs.

Other methods
The methods described are those most commonly in use but their limitations have encouraged attempts to find other ways of evaluating jobs. One approach which departs from traditional methods is to rank jobs on the basis of the types of decision made by the job occupants. The best-known

examples are Jaques' time-span of discretion method and Paterson's decision-band method. The former ranks jobs on the basis of the longest period which may elapse before the use of marginally substandard discretion in a job would be detected. Paterson's method on the other hand uses a scale of six different kinds of decision (or bands) whereby a job is ascribed to the highest band in which any of its tasks fall. Such schemes are still relatively uncommon and are not easily applied to manual occupations. Moreover, they come close to evaluating the individual rather than the job.[14]

There has also been a proliferation of consultants' proprietary schemes in recent years, which are either refinements of the basic schemes described or are 'hybrid' or composite schemes which combine the principles of two or more techniques. For example, the 'Direct Consensus Method' developed by Imbucon is an off-the-peg form of paired comparisons. The Price Waterhouse Urwick 'Profile Method' is a streamlined version of points rating while the consultants, Arthur Young, offer a refinement of Paterson's decision-band method. A composite scheme has been devised by PA consultants which is a form of points rating with factor weightings determined by paired comparisons. Perhaps the most widely adopted proprietary scheme is the 'Hay Guide Chart Profile Method' of Hay-MSL Ltd which is a variation of the points rating method, except that the factors used are aspects of the decisions taken in jobs.[15]

'Equal value' implications

The Equal Value (Amendment) Regulations 1983 that came into force in January 1984 have several implications for job evaluation. Prior to the Amendment a woman could claim equal pay under the 1970 Equal Pay Act only if she was paid less than her chosen comparator for 'like work' or work rated as equivalent under a job evaluation exercise. Under the Amendment, however, she (or he) may claim equal pay even though her work has not been rated as equivalent by job evaluation, on the ground that the work done, although different, is of *equal value* in terms of the demands that it makes. Moreover, there is scope in the legislation for challenging a firm's existing job evaluation scheme as discriminatory.

The legislation is widely perceived as necessitating some reconsideration of current methods of determining relative pay, including job evaluation, if firms are to reduce their vulnerability to claims. For example, in *Bromley & ors.* v *H & J Quick Ltd* (30.3.88) the Court of Appeal held that a valid job evaluation scheme under the Regulations must be 'analytical' and evaluate jobs under various demand headings, criteria which the company's paired comparisons method on a 'whole jobs' basis did not meet. An integrated, analytical job evaluation scheme (eg points rating covering both blue- and white-collar workers) is therefore generally considered as the best form in reducing employer vulnerability to claims. If such a system is negotiated with the union(s) and accepted by both parties it will be difficult to convince a tribunal of sex bias in the scheme and the claim could be blocked at the pre-hearing stage. However, such a system can be difficult to apply in a consistent fashion as factors appropriate to blue-collar jobs (eg difficult working conditions) might be irrelevant to white-collar jobs, and vice versa. Nor do such systems constitute an insurmountable barrier to a claim under the Amendment. For instance, the scheme may be considered sex-biased if factors such as effort, physical strength and working conditions are over-represented or over-weighted relative to factors such as manual dexterity or mental concentration.

There are indications that the effects of the equal value provisions on wage costs and pay structures might be less dramatic than was initially supposed, partly due to the extreme complexity of the law and the time-consuming process of making a claim. However, two recent House of Lords' decisions are likely to act as catalysts for more claims: in *Hayward* v *Cammell Shipbuilders Ltd* (5.5.88) it was held that a woman doing work of equal value to that of a man is entitled to the same basic pay as him even if her overall 'pay package' might be more favourable than his; and in *Pickstone & ors.* v *Freemans Plc* (30.6.88) the House of Lords ruled that the existence of a man doing the same work as a woman for the same pay, cannot prevent her from making an equal value claim, citing another man as the comparator.

The Equal Opportunities Commission has published a number of booklets on how to avoid discriminatory job evaluation schemes and will also advise directly on the implementation of schemes free from sex bias.

Limitations of job evaluation

Job evaluation may not be an appropriate technique within an organization which is attempting to cope with changing markets, technologies or other pressures which have implications for relative wages. It can impose a straightjacket upon management and maintaining the scheme can come to assume higher priority than organizational needs.

It may be difficult to operate some types of bonus scheme in conjunction with job evaluation. Where earnings vary with output, for example, pay relationships established by job evaluation are easily undermined.

Job evaluation is inappropriate to certain forms of group working, such as job rotation.

Job evaluation may represent no more than a temporary solution to distortions arising from a variety of pressures which will continue to exist and eventually will undermine the new structure.

An alternative to job evaluation would be to identify the causes of pay distortions and then design a pay structure as resistant as possible to those distortions in the given circumstances of the firm. How this approach might be tackled systematically, while avoiding the inflexibilities of job evaluation, is described by Lupton and Bowey.[16]

Harmonization

Harmonization refers to the trend towards introducing the same conditions of employment among all employees. 'Single status' and 'staff status' are terms which are sometimes used synonymously with harmonization when describing this process, although each term implies a slightly different approach. The IPM distinguishes the three terms as follows:

1. *Single status* is the removal of differences in basic conditions of employment to give all employees equal status. Some organizations take this further by putting all employees into the same pay and grading structure.
2. *Staff status* is a process whereby manual and craft employees gradually receive staff terms and conditions of employment, usually upon reaching some qualifying standard, for example length of service.
3. *Harmonization* means the reduction of differences in the pay structure and other employment conditions between categories of employee, usually manual and staff employees. The essence of harmonization is the adoption of a common approach and criteria to pay and conditions for all employees. It differs from staff status in that in the process of harmonization some staff employees may have to accept some of the conditions of employment of manual employees.[17]

Pressures towards harmonization

Harmonization has proceeded at a slow but steady pace at least since the Second World War. Some quickening in the pace of change was noticed from the early 1970s and again in the 1980s. The process is often justified by management on the view that traditional distinctions in employment conditions are irrelevant, anachronistic and unjust. However, there have been several recent pressures towards harmonization of which, in the view of the IPM, questions of morality are probably of least importance:

New technology. Status differentials can obstruct efficient labour utilization and the ability of firms to react quickly and flexibly to new technology. Indeed, concessions on harmonized conditions are invariably exchanged as part of an explicit agreement for more efficient work practices, such as reducing overtime or eliminating demarcation lines. Moreover, technology, by de-skilling many white-collar jobs, has made differential treatment more difficult to defend. It has also contributed to a declining manual worker base so that the cost of harmonization for many firms is also declining.

Legislation. Legislation concerning equal pay, sex and racial discrimination, and employment protection, has narrowed differences and extended rights to manual workers in areas previously the preserve of staff (eg maternity pay, time off for public duties). The directives and recommendations of the European Commission have also encouraged harmonized conditions. Moreover, pay restraint imposed by incomes policies led to bargaining by manual workers over non-pay issues, setting precedents for widening the scope of collective bargaining. A number of legislative initiatives have also provided opportunities for administrative savings through harmonization. Statutory sick pay and the removal of restrictions on cashless pay are examples.

Recession. Recession and intensification of competitive pressures have enhanced the perceived importance of cooperative attitudes and commitment from employees, qualities which tend to be undermined by traditional divisions.

Benefits and costs

More specifically, where companies have pursued harmonized conditions, it has usually been to achieve one or more of three objectives: improving labour productivity; simplifying personnel administration and thus reducing costs; changing employee attitudes, thereby improving cooperation, motivation and morale.

Harmonization will, of course, incur costs, the extent of which will be determined by the scope of the exercise and the nature of existing differences. Even where the aim is directly to reduce costs through rationalization of administrative procedures, there can be unanticipated problems. For instance, manual workers might not view cashless pay as a benefit and some cash inducement may be required to effect the change. Moreover, staff employees or unions might demand compensation, monetary or otherwise, for erosion of status differentials resulting from improved manual conditions. In general, there is likely to be a net increase in costs in the short term as many of the perceived benefits of harmonization, such as improved attitudes, are unlikely to produce immediate financial gains. For this reason most companies adopt a gradualist, cautious approach towards the exercise.

Occasionally, however, companies may opt for the 'complete package' or 'grand design' approach towards harmonizing a whole range of conditions including integration of pay structures and systems, the working week, sick pay arrangements, pensions, canteen facilities and many other items. This is really in the nature of an elaborate productivity deal and has all the same resource implications – a long consultative process and heavy demands upon management time and skills in negotiating, costing, administering and monitoring the change. However, elaborate programmes of this sort are more commonly associated with companies setting up on greenfield sites, especially Japanese or American multinationals, where costs may be reduced by avoiding entrenched attitudes and working practices. Costs are nevertheless incurred in the careful recruitment and induction programmes required and in the generous pay and benefits packages invariably offered in exchange for restrictions on normal trade union activity, such as single-union agreements, pendular arbitration and no-strike clauses.

Harmonization and pay

Harmonization has proceeded furthest in respect of conditions of service, such as holidays, sick pay or pensions, but more recently there has been progress in the more sensitive area of pay and payment systems. For example, some firms (eg Plessey Control) have moved in the direction of reducing the variability of manual pay relative to non-manual by consolidating bonus schemes into fixed salaries in exchange for concessions on working practices. There have also been moves toward aligning overtime base rates and calculators as between manual and white-collar staff. The repeal of the Truck Acts by the Wages Act 1986 removes the right of manual workers to insist on being paid in cash (unless there is a contractual obligation to this effect) and should hasten the trend towards integrated, non-cash methods of wage payment. Some companies have also made more elaborate moves towards integrated, single-grading payment structures based upon a common job evaluation scheme, such as Alcan Sheet, Continental Can, Courage Central at its Berkshire Brewery and Unigate at its new Westway Dairy in West London.

Questions for organizations

Harmonization should aim towards removing illogical and indefensible differences, but where their removal is not clearly to the mutual benefit of employer and employees the process should be viewed as akin to productivity bargaining. In deciding whether to embark upon a programme of harmonization, ACAS advises that organizations should first seek answers to the following questions:

What differences in the treatment of groups of employees are a rational result of differences in the work or the job requirements?

Is it possible to estimate the direct costs of removing these differences?

What differences in status are explicitly recognized as part of the 'reward package' for different groups in the labour force? What would be the possible repercussive effects of harmonization?

How do the existing differences affect industrial relations in the organization?[18]

Trends and Possibilities

There has been a significant growth in the coverage of PBR over the last decade, especially among non-manual employees. Much of this reflects the growing popularity of schemes operating at plant, division and company level, especially cash- and share-based profit sharing and added-value schemes (CBI 1985). These systems have also made significant inroads into manual areas of employment, where a gradual shift has been observed away from schemes rewarding individual performance to 'collective' schemes of various sorts based upon the performance of the workgroup, plant or company as a whole. The pace of technological change, conditions of recession and recent tax inducements are among the more important factors accounting for these developments.

Looking to the future, it is likely that current influences upon payment systems will persist, with greater emphasis placed upon schemes which seek to promote commonality of interests and reward work flexibility and cooperative effort. The relevance of output-related systems, for example, may increasingly be questioned with the more widespread introduction of robotics, computer-controlled machine tools and flexible manufacturing systems which weaken the link between individual effort and output. On the other hand, it has been suggested that a stimulus may be given to measured daywork because the system is a good fit with possible future trends, for example towards job flexibility.[19]

In responding to the government's proposals on profit-related pay, several employers' organizations (CBI, EEF, IPM) were especially enthusiastic about expanding added-value schemes which were considered a better measure of employee performance than profit and more worthy of tax encouragement. In the current political climate, however, the continuation of tax relief on profit sharing seems assured and share-based systems are likely to continue to expand over the next few years. Despite tax relief, however, the future of profit related pay is less certain because of the difficulties envisaged by many employers with respect to this system, and there is evidence that the rate of growth of registrations has recently slackened.[20]

The pace of change is likely to enhance the difficulties of maintaining acceptable and defensible payment structures, so that the well-established trend towards greater use of job evaluation is likely to continue, especially in larger organizations where complex organizational and occupational variety make some means of managing the pay structure almost essential.

At the same time, current methods of job evaluation might require modification to allow management to respond flexibly to change through, for example, job restructuring or the introduction of new forms of working such as multi-skilling, as the new jobs are likely to cut across the boundaries of present schemes. Developments in harmonization and equal pay legislation point to integrated analytical schemes, with factors currently viewed as appropriate for managerial schemes increasingly being applied to a wider range of occupations. A further possibility is towards appraisal or merit-rating schemes with greater emphasis placed upon evaluating the individual rather than the job in order to accommodate more easily flexible work demands.

Perhaps the central paradox of current developments is that fashionable emphasis upon harmonization, 'popular capitalism', 'Japanization' and other means of reducing traditional animosities has coincided with a marked (and largely unprecedented) *widening* in the dispersion of pay over the last few years, as shown in Table 11.7.

Table 11.7: *Dispersion of earnings of full-time adults – lowest and highest deciles expressed as a percentage of the corresponding medians*

	Men		Women	
	Lowest 10%	Highest 10%	Lowest 10%	Highest 10%
1979	66.0	156.9	69.4	158.6
1987	59.4	176.2	64.2	171.7

Source: *New Earnings Survey*

The figures in Table 11.7 reflect several factors, including the greater impact of the recession on the low paying small-firm sector, changes in employment structure from manufacturing to low-paying service industries and changing manpower policies of companies, in responding to current pressures, towards retaining the commitment and motivation of 'core' employees while increasingly contracting out work to smaller firms offering inferior pay and conditions. A 'secondary labour market' seems also to be developing *within* some larger companies where temporary or part-time workers are taken on who do not get the tenure or benefits of the regular workforce.

Deregulation and other government policies have also served to widen pay disparities. For example, the imposition of tight cash limits in the low-paying public services, the rescinding of Schedule 11* and the Fair

* Schedule 11 of the Employment Protection Act 1975 entitled workers to claim that the provisions of relevant industry or district collective agreements should be applied to them even though their employer was not a party to the agreements; and that where there were no recognized terms and conditions, to claim the 'general level of terms and conditions' applied by companies in the same industry or district and in similar circumstances. The provision was repealed by the Employment Act 1980.

Wages Resolution* and the greater exposure of private sector firms to market forces through monetary control, have all served to downgrade the role of comparability in pay determination, while the Wages Act 1986 has significantly reduced statutory protection for low-paid workers. One further influence has been the recent proliferation of merit payments confined to those in senior positions, and executive 'super bonuses' of the sort agreed at Burton's. For the most part, however, the trend towards greater inequality lies outside the influence of employers and will compound the difficulties facing genuine attempts toward enhancing cooperation and reducing 'them and us' thinking in the pay field.

* The House of Commons Fair Wages Resolution which was passed in 1946, but which dates back to 1891, obliged government contractors to observe terms and conditions of employment not less favourable than those laid down in collective agreements for that trade or district. It was rescinded in 1982.

References
1. Confederation of British Industry *Incentive Payments* CBI, London, 1985
2. Bowey A M and Thorpe R *Payment Systems and Productivity* (1986) MacMillan, London, p 33
3. Lupton T and Gowler D *Selecting a wage payment system* Engineering Employers' Federation, Research Paper No 111, London, 1969; for a useful summary of the techniques, see Lupton T and Bowey A M *Wages and Salaries* 2nd edition, (1983) Gower, Aldershot, ch 3
4. Bowey A M and Thorpe R op cit, p 150
5. National Board for Prices and Incomes *Payment by Results Systems* Report No 65, Cmnd 3627, HMSO, London, 1968
6. Edwards C and Heery E 'Formality and Informality in the Working of the National Coal Board's Incentive Scheme' *British Journal of Industrial Relations* **23** 1, March 1985
7. CBI, op cit
8. Quoted in IDS *Study* 357 'Profit Sharing & Share Options' March 1986
9. Richardson R and Nejad A 'Employee Share Ownership Schemes in the UK – an Evaluation' *British Journal of Industrial Relations* **24** 2, July 1986
10. Smith G R 'Profit sharing and employee share ownership in Britain' *Department of Employment Gazette* September 1986
11. *Profit Related Pay* Cmnd 9835, HMSO, London, July 1986
12. For further discussion, see Duncan C 'Why profit related pay will fail' *Industrial Relations Journal* **19** 3, Autumn 1988
13. See IDS *Report* 524 July 1988
14. For a critique of the Jaques and Paterson techniques, see Lupton T and Bowey A M, op cit, pp 20–28
15. For further description and assessment of the main proprietary techniques on offer, see IDS *Study* 348 'Blue-Collar Job Evaluation' October 1985
16. Lupton T and Bowey A M, op cit, ch 7
17. Roberts C (ed) *Harmonisation – Whys and Wherefores* Institute of Personnel Management, London, 1985
18. *Developments in Harmonisation* Discussion Paper No 1, ACAS, March 1982
19. Grayson D *Progressive payment systems* Occasional Paper 28, Department of Employment, Work Research Unit, February 1984
20. IDS (July 1988), op cit

Chapter 12

Motives for and Incidence of Seeking Single-union Agreements

John Gennard

Interest by both unions and employers in single-union agreements is not new. Contemporary trade union motives for and the incidence of seeking single-union agreements are diverse. One important factor however, is that although single-union agreements are not confined to new and expanding areas of the economy, some unions do see such arrangements as a means of gaining recognition in areas from which they have traditionally been absent. In doing this they hope to offset the decline of union membership in sectors of the economy (eg manufacturing) in which they have previously had a strong presence.

However, this strategy, on the part of a number of trade unions, has caused controversy in the trade union movement in that some single-union arrangements have been made without consideration for the interests of other unions and on terms which are restrictive (eg a commitment to no industrial action) and limit the subsequent role of the union. As a result, in 1987 the TUC set up a special review body to look at ways of reversing the serious decline in trade union membership and organization since 1980. At the top of the review body's priorities has been the devising of methods for resolving the growing controversy within the trade union movement over the terms upon which some affiliated unions are prepared to sign single-union agreements.[1]

Employer interest in single-union agreements, especially when opening new sites, has been stimulated because they see that such arrangements improve their competitiveness in domestic and international markets by providing a greater opportunity for them to secure a more flexible, cooperative and less conflict-prone workforce. A number of companies (eg Nissan) regard single-unionism as a necessary pre-condition for the development of a management philosophy embodying teamwork, quality consciousness and flexibility.

The Extent of Single-unionism

Single-union agreements offer employers the advantage of a single representative channel for all employees and the simplification of communications, consultative and bargaining structures. For unions, the potential benefits are to be seen in terms of security and stability of membership and bargaining rights. Although interest in single-union agreements has increased in the second half of the 1980s, they have always existed in the UK industrial relations system. The 1984 Workplace Industrial Relations Survey[2] showed that 65 per cent of all establishments recognizing unions for manual workers recognized only one manual union and that 82 per cent had only one manual bargaining unit. Of establishments which recognized unions for non-manual workers, 39 per cent recognized a single non-manual union and 61 per cent had only one non-manual bargaining unit.

Single-union agreements rarely embrace the whole range of manual, white-collar and managerial workers. Most commonly they cover manual workers although some take in more junior grades of white-collar workers. In some sectors, single-union bargaining has always been the norm (eg retail distribution) and is often based on clear spheres of influence which have long been established between the unions involved (eg white-collar civil service employees). However, in other sectors (eg engineering), such arrangements are more recent.

In the latter part of the 1980s interest in single-union arrangements has centred on them being a component of so-called 'new style agreements'. These have been identified with the EETPU and a number of Japanese companies which have come to the UK in recent years. In practice such agreements, which take a variety of forms, have arisen more widely than this. By 1988 they were to be found not only in a number of other foreign-owned subsidiaries (eg companies from USA, Sweden and Norway), but also in an increasing range of indigenous organizations which have set up new plants and offices. They also involve a growing number of unions (eg the AEU, TGWU, GMB, Iron and Steel Trades Confederation and the MATSA section of the GMB). Although the number of these 'new style' agreements is growing they are as yet extremely small in relation to the overall number of employers with conventional agreements with unions. It is estimated that in 1986 some 25,000 employees were covered by so-called 'new style agreements'.[3]

These agreements are novel not in their individual components, all of which have long been used from time to time, but because they form an integrated package of measures which, taken together, are designed to reinforce pressures for consensus. These agreements typically comprise a number of inter-related elements:

Single-union recognition.

Single status for staff and manual employees in such areas as holidays, sickness, pension schemes, car-parking and restaurant facilities.

Flexibility in working practices.

Strong emphasis on training and re-training.

Highly participative management styles offering levels of information disclosure and employee involvement through company advisory boards, company bulletins, etc.

Reliance on arbitration procedures (frequently involving pendulum arbitration) to preclude industrial action.

In practice, however, there are considerable variations on these basic themes of 'new style' agreements.

Union Recognition Problems

The fall in union membership in the 1980s and a hardening attitude to trade union recognition on the part of employers in the fastest growing parts of the economy has aroused a union interest in single-union agreements as a means of gaining recognition from employers. In December 1979 the TUC-affiliated membership peaked at 12.2 million. By December 1987 it had fallen to just over 9.1 million.[4] This decline has to be viewed against the background of growing total employment since 1982.

The majority of TUC-affiliated unions have experienced few, if any, challenges to established representation structures. Nevertheless, in recent years unions have widely reported that they are experiencing a higher level of employer resistance to new claims for recognition. This has not been confined to newly established companies. A number of unions have experienced increasing difficulty in mopping up unorganized pockets of workers in strongly organized sectors and a reluctance on the part of unionized employers to extend recognition agreements to newly acquired subsidiaries. The 1986 ACAS *Annual Report* stated that in recognition cases in which ACAS was involved unions found it difficult to make progress in such situations, but 'where recognition was achieved single-union arrangements almost always proved the way forward'.[5] ACAS also noted that single-union recognition had become the rule in organizations which have recognized unions for the first time in recent years.

One result of these developments has been a heightening of competition between unions for recognition. In an attempt to compensate for falling membership some unions have sought recognition in hitherto unorganized areas and/or in, for them, new areas of organization. These unions, to gain sole recognition rights, have been prepared to accept terms which restrict and limit their subsequent role. This has happened on a number of occasions when, in opening a significant new plant, the employer has insisted on what has been described in trade union circles as 'a union beauty contest', in which several unions parade competitively before the employer to seek recognition. Increasing union competition for sole recognition has also resulted in incidents where, when there were objections to the recognition of one union by an employer from other unions, that employer has delayed granting recognition or preferred to remain, or go, non-union.

However inter-union competition for recognition needs to be kept in perspective. Experiences reported by unions presents a mixed picture. Many unions have not found inter-union competition a serious problem in the recognition sphere. These tend to be public sector unions or those which organize only specific groups of employees in a particular industry based on clear demarcation lines accepted by employers and unions alike. Some unions consider that the real problem of recognition derives not so much from inter-union competition but from the existence of a growing body of employers who are determined to avoid recognizing any union on any terms. The serious inter-union competition difficulties are largely confined to manufacturing, the private services and other sectors.

Single-union agreements: union difficulties

The trade union movement is not opposed as a matter of principle to single-union agreements. As we have seen, the controversy within the movement is over the terms on which some trade unions are prepared to enter into such arrangements. A number of unions have specific policies on single-union agreements and the role of the arbitration in gaining recognition. The AEU is not prepared to enter such deals if the price includes compulsory, 'binding' pendulum arbitration linked to a hard clause prohibiting industrial action. The EETPU, in contrast, in return for sole recognition accepts 'binding' pendulum arbitration (initiated jointly by either side) as part of a wider package including single status for staff and manual employees, a system of employee communication and participation, labour flexibility backed up by effective training and re-training, a consensual style of management, and a final procedural stage of 'binding' pendulum arbitration. In the case of the MATSA section of the GMB, the recognition package also includes provision for a unilateral reference to binding arbitration but to be preceded by a joint commitment to change through discussion or agreement, and followed, if unsuccessful, by conciliation. Also included is a joint commitment to the prosperity of a company and its employees; to employment policies which are equitable, fair and safe; strong advice from the employer to its employees to join MATSA; and recognition of MATSA.

It is against the background of union competition for recognition that union attitudes to single-union agreements have to be considered. This is linked with the policy of many of those employers being prepared to recognize unions on new sites only on the condition that it is on a 'single-union' basis. The concluding of single-union agreements has caused particular differences between unions where they:

1. *Exclude other unions who may have some membership in the unit covered by the agreement or exclude unions which previously held recognition or bargaining rights.* This was illustrated in March 1984 when Hitachi bought out GEC's share in GEC–Hitachi TV Ltd to form Hitachi Consumer Products (UK) Ltd. At the time five unions – EETPU, AUEW, UCATT, APEX and TASS – were recognized at the company's Hirwaun establishment. The unions were told that the company intended to introduce new personnel philosophies and operational changes, that they should understand that a fundamental principle of the change would be the creation of single-status conditions and that such conditions required a single-union with sole bargaining rights.

   The company considered that the union representing the interests of the clear majority of existing employees was the EETPU and that that union would be invited to discuss the creation of an agreement giving them sole bargaining rights. The company invited the other unions to join the EETPU in negotiating the new agreement so that they could at least have some influence on the future terms and conditions of their membership. The EETPU agreed to begin discussions on a single-union agreement.

   The 'rejected' unions offered the company discussions towards the changes they required through a joint negotiating committee. Management rejected this proposal and concluded an agreement with the EETPU. The 'ousted' unions complained to the TUC about the electricians' union behaviour. A TUC Dispute Committee commented that the EETPU should not have signed the sole recognition and negotiating agreement until the inter-union claims had been resolved including if necessary by TUC adjudication.[6]

2. *Exclude other unions who, while having no members in the unit concerned, have recognition agreements in other UK units operated by the same employer.* An example of this situation occurred in January 1988 when the EETPU signed a single-union agreement with Caledonian Paper, a subsidiary of the Finnish forestry products group, Kymmene, to cover the 300 manual workers it planned to employ at its £215 million high tech paper mill at Irvine in the West of Scotland. Four unions – TGWU, AEU, EETPU and SOGAT (82) – competed for recognition at the plant but the company only negotiated fully with the last two. When Caledonian Paper decided upon the EETPU, SOGAT (82), which represented the company's employees at two of its other mills – Star Paper and Wolvercote – said it would not accept the agreement. They reported the EETPU's behaviour to the TUC and, in September 1988, made a formal complaint to the Scottish

Trade Union Congress and urged other TUC-affiliated unions to 'black' the company's products.

A further example of inter-union conflict arising from unions being excluded from new establishments that are opened by a company, in whose other establishments those unions had membership, occurred with Christian Salvesen. A major distribution company, Christian Salvesen, had agreements at all its warehouses and depots covering warehouse workers and drivers with the TGWU, GMB and USDAW. When in 1988 its Saltstream division opened depots at West Cross and Warrington, the EETPU, without consulting the other unions, signed single-union agreements with the company. The three other unions complained to the TUC that their interests had not been considered. They were supported by the TUC Disputes Committtee which awarded that all unions should meet and make a common approach to the company for recognition with the TGWU to represent drivers, the TGWU/GMB/USDAW to represent warehouse workers, as at all other Christian Salvesen plants, and the EETPU to represent maintenance workers. The electricians were recommended to terminate the single-union agreements but they refused to comply with this award.

3. *Represent an intrusion by one union into areas considered to be the province of an industrial union, or the exclusion by an industrial union of unions representing particular occupations.*

4. *Are agreed by one union, where another has been previously campaigning for membership, perhaps, over a long period.* A good example of this occurred when Orion Electrics established a factory on the Kenfig Industrial Estate at Port Talbot in 1986.[7] After the company had rebuffed approaches for recognition from a number of unions the TGWU began recruiting members. They pressed the management with little success for talks on recognition. Over a few months, however, they recruited 38 members out of a workforce of just over 100 and organized a petition which was signed by 79 workers, who represented a majority of the workforce. The TGWU involved ACAS to help reach an agreement with the company. The EETPU did not have a single member in the firm but despite this, management granted the EETPU sole facilities for recruitment and signed with them a single-union deal.

After hearing full details of the case from both the EETPU and the TGWU, the TUC Disputes Committee decided in 1988 that the electricians, in signing the agreement, had not considered the position of the TGWU as they were required. It, therefore, recommended that the EETPU withdraw from the agreement and join with the TGWU in formulating a common approach to the company for joint recognition and negotiating rights and to work together at Orion Electric to eliminate competition for members. They did not comply with this recommendation and the EETPU's behaviour at this firm, together with that at Christian Salvesen, led to their suspension from the TUC in July 1988 and to their expulsion from membership by the September 1988 Trades Union Congress.

5. *Lead unions to compete with each other for employers' approval which encourages dilution of trade union standards and procedures.* Some trade unions have expressed concern at what others have been willing to offer in return for sole recognition terms that dilute industry norms for pay, hours and holidays, etc. An example of this was the EETPU behaviour at Wapping in 1986. However charges that unions have 'sold out' to gain recognition can be difficult to prove when taken case by case because no-one else can be sure that they would have achieved recognition on better terms. However, this has not prevented inter-union conflict about the offer by unions to employers, in return for sole recognition, of agreements which, by usually employing compulsory arbitration, make official industrial action a breach of an agreement. It is not known how many of these so-called 'no-strike' agreements exist, but they have been particularly controversial when unions have offered compulsory arbitration to gain recognition in what other unions regard as being outside that union's traditional spheres of organization. The majority of trade unions in the TUC are strongly opposed to the imposition of restrictive, compulsory arbitration arrangements as a condition of securing single-union agreements.

6. *Enable employers to secure their wish to 'escape' from agreements which cover other plants in the UK.* The classic example of this situation was the Ford Company proposed investment at Dundee in Scotland.[8] In October 1987 the AEU announced that it had reached a single-union agreement with Ford covering its planned new electronic component plant in Dundee and which was to start production in 1989. The AEU pointed out that the new plant would be a wholly-owned subsidiary of Ford (USA) and quite separate from Ford (UK). The new plant was to operate, therefore, outside the 'Blue Book' national agreement applying to other Ford operations in the UK. Ford had told the AEU that it would only locate in Dundee if it were able to operate under such arrangements. The company committed itself to pay wage rates in the upper quarter of those applying throughout the electronics industry in Scotland. The AEU Executive endorsed the agreement in the interests of securing jobs for Dundee but did so reluctantly accepting the difficulties that would arise for other unions recognized in other Ford plants.

However, other unions with members in Ford, eg TGWU and MSF, compared the proposed Dundee situation with the Ford's spark plug plant in South Wales at Treforrest. This is part of Ford's diversified products division, reporting directly to the USA, but operating under traditional Ford (UK) bargaining arrangements. Ford insisted that the Dundee plant was an electronics operation, quite separate from Ford car manufacturing, that a single-union agreement outside the 'Blue Book' was the only way that the plant could be viable, and that they would *only* proceed on the basis of a single-union agreement. In March 1988, when it was clear that the issue of union organization at the proposed Dundee plant could not be resolved, Ford announced it would not be going ahead with the project.

Consultation with empoloyees

Those trade unions concerned about what they regard as restrictive conditions for recognition in many contemporary single-union agreements have also been perturbed that the employees to be covered are denied the choice of membership of their appropriate union, or a say in whether they wish to be represented by the union gaining sole recognition status. The EETPU has expressed support for the idea of satisfaction ballots of employees in companies which sign single-union agreements so as to ascertain the level of support for such arrangements after a period of their operation.[9] The GMB holds to the basic principle that unions should have the procedural aspects of agreements confirmed by the workforce in whose name they are signed, and that every agreement which explicitly surrenders the right to take strike action should contain a clause establishing a review at specified intervals. However, little information is known as to what arrangements unions make for consulting the workforce as to which union they prefer to represent them when approaching appropriate employers for recognition prior to new plants being opened.

The TUC Special Review Body

Throughout its history the TUC has sought to promote cooperation between affiliated unions and avoid, but if necessary resolve, inter-union rivalry by discussion, conciliation and arbitration (via a Disputes Committee recommendation). This has never been easy but, by and large, rivalries have been contained through the operation of the TUC *Disputes Principles and Procedures* (commonly known as the Bridlington rules). A fundamental principle is that no union should commence organizing activities at any establishment or undertaking in respect of any grade or grades of workers, in which another union has the majority of workers employed and negotiates wages and conditions, unless by arrangement with that union. A second is that no affiliated union should take into membership a member of another affiliate without first investigating the reason why the member wishes to change unions.[10]

These Disputes Principles are highly relevant to the question of single-union agreements. Following the decision of Congress in 1985,[11] the principles were amended to require that no union should enter into a sole negotiating agreement or any other form of agreement in any circumstances (including a takeover or change of ownership or some other reason) where other unions would be deprived of their existing rights of recognition or negotiation, except by prior consultation and agreement of the other unions concerned. Where agreement cannot be reached through consultation between the unions concerned, the issue should be referred to the TUC for advice and conciliation, and if necessary, a Disputes Committee adjudication. In any adjudication by a Disputes committee full account is taken of the existing practices and agreements of the industry.

The implementation of this Principle has already led to TUC Disputes Committees instructing unions to cancel single-union agreements made on existing sites with employers and to seek joint recognition arrangements with the other unions who have been excluded. Some employers will not act on Disputes Committee Awards with the result that when the union cancels the agreement, under a TUC recommendation, no new recognition agreement can be made. In most of these incidences the employer becomes non-union.

However by 1987 it was clear that the Bridlington procedures were being strained by inter-union competition to secure recognition in new areas. This was one reason why the 1987 TUC Congress agreed to the establishment of a Special Review Body (SRB).[12] At the outset the SRB identified four key areas for examination:

1. The need to review the problems of securing recognition, the terms on which recognition is gained, the pressure arising from inter-union competition, and the role of the *TUC Disputes Principles and Procedures* – linked to an assessment of employer attitudes.

2. Public perceptions of unions and the promotion of trade unionism generally as well as among specific groups.

3. The need to give further emphasis to consolidating membership and building organization in the light of the labour market trends in order to protect and to expand the 'frontiers of trade unionism'.

4. The role of union and TUC services and the scope for their coordination, expansion and development.

The SRB's first report, entitled *Meeting the Challenge*, was published in August 1988 and was accepted at the 1988 Congress.[13] The report proposed immediate action on an extended role for the TUC in regulating inter-union relations through a Code of Practice governing unions' approaches to seeking recognition from employers. It also proposed a change to Disputes Principle 5.

The Code of Practice[14]

The Code is intended to operate in conjunction with the TUC's existing Bridlington principles for a trial period from 1 October 1988 to 31 March 1989 and is to be reviewed by the SRB and possibly by a consultative conference of TUC-affiliated unions in early 1989. The Code covers prior notification, no-strike clauses and arbitration, inward investment, and general levels of terms and conditions. Affiliated unions are expected to observe the Code and its provisions will be taken into account by TUC Disputes Committees.

(i) *Prior notification*
A union in the process of making a single-union agreement should, at the initial stage of discussion, notify the TUC General Secretary of the fact and supply as many relevant details as possible on a standard form. On receipt of these details the TUC will tender guidance within two weeks. It will not normally circulate the standard form to any other union but it is possible that the TUC in giving its guidance may suggest that the union making the agreement discusses the matter with another union or unions. In providing guidance the TUC will take into account factors such as whether another union had a significant membership at the site, eg 10 per cent, or whether another union was recognized by the same employer for similar groups of workers elsewhere.

(ii) *No-strike clauses and arbitration*
The Code requires that when unions are making recognition agreements they should not make arrangements which specifically remove, or are designed to remove, the basic democratic lawful right of a trade union to take industrial action in advance of the recruitment of members and without consulting them. This has been described in the press as a 'ban' on no-strike provisions. This is not so because the Code goes on to legitimize a no-strike clause by stating 'this is not meant to deter unions using arbitration, pendulum or otherwise, at the request of one or both parties'. If unions are faced by circumstances where the procedures insisted upon remove the right to take industrial action, the Code requires that the union should consult the TUC at the earliest opportunity.

(iii) *Inward investment*
Some companies opening new plants have been encouraged to locate in a new area by a range of inward investment authorities, eg the Scottish and Welsh Development Agencies. There can be advantages for unions in seeking constructive relationships with inward investment authorities which provide information to unions about incoming plants. The Code makes provision that unions will be expected to cooperate with any procedures which have been approved by the TUC General Council and which are operated by the TUC, STUC, Wales TUC or TUC Regional Councils in relation to inward investment authorities.

(iv) *General level of terms and conditions*

This part of the Code is designed to deal with situations where an employer seeks to 'escape' from agreements which cover other plants in the UK as the price for granting recognition. The Code provides that when negotiating recognition agreements which have implications for substantive factors, unions should pay attention to the general level, and terms and conditions of employment which are already the subject of agreement with the company concerned (or which have been set through recognized arrangements) and take all possible steps to avoid undermining them.

Principle 5

In addition to the Code of Practice, the 1988 Congress also accepted an amendment to the *TUC Disputes Principles and Procedures* to clarify that, where a union has an agreement with an employer but few members, other unions are not prohibited from seeking to organize the workers concerned. This is significant for unions in the context of the reputedly low level of membership achieved by the AEU and the EETPU from the single-union agreements to which they are a party.[15]

Employer Interest in Single-union Agreements

Employers have an interest in unions finding some way of working jointly in given industries or establishments rather than competing with each other for membership. This already happens in many places at the domestic factory level where joint works committees function satisfactorily without too much regard to individual union affiliations. Although from an employer's point of view this may not be as satisfactory or tidy as a single-union agreement, it is a workable arrangement. A degree of discipline and authority is needed in joint committees. Many employers have commented on the need for unions to find ways of recognizing such joint bodies within their overall structures and preventing them from flying apart in pursuit of sectional interest when they are put under stress. One employer has gone as far to say,

'. . . it is no longer possible for British employers to try to satisfy the separate interests and ambitions of half a dozen unions when their competitors only have to deal with one. I don't think the unions have ever fully understood how predisposed employers would be to accept a joint union view, if only they could rely upon it. What they can't be expected to cope with is a series of claims from different unions, none of which can be reconciled with the others.

This is one reason why employers prefer a single-union deal and why, indeed, they even make it a condition of opening up a greenfield site.'[16]

However, single-union agreements are particularly attractive to employers who operate in industries where technology changes rapidly (if not even daily) and in product markets which are highly competitive, particularly if the competitors include firms from low cost Far East countries. They become even more attractive when they can be combined with measures designed to eliminate production disruption, eg pendulum arbitration. It is not surprising, therefore, to find that most of the known 'new style agreements' are in such companies as Nissan, Hitachi and Komatsu.

Single-union agreements offer a number of advantages to employers by removing obstacles to greater efficiency:

They minimize recognition difficulties.

They allow for greater flexibility and mobility of the workforce between jobs and duties within the company and departments.

They make it easier to introduce changes in production processes and working practices and thereby respond quickly and flexibly to changes in demand for the company's product.

They facilitate the correction of imbalances in labour flows since having only one union with which to deal makes it easier to get the workforce to accept training, re-training and re-deployment.

If they are accompanied by single status between manual and non-manual employees then concepts such as teamwork and quality consciousness are more easily achieved.[17]

However success does not depend on the wording of an agreement. It depends on the underlying management philosophies and working practices which that philosophy generates. No matter how good the agreement might be a poor management will fail. Conversely, a good management will succeed against the odds.

Multi-union Plants

Companies opening new plants (greenfield sites) are often seeking to establish a competitive edge over existing ones and single-union flexibility agreements contribute to this. They are able to escape from multi-unionism and the process of dealing with separate unions which they may regard as difficult and time consuming. In so far as employers with 'traditional' multi-union bargaining arrangements perceive that they are at a competitive advantage in comparison with single-union or non-union competitors, there will be pressures on union organization in these areas.

In the 1980s de-recognition of unions has been rare, although not unknown, but there is now growing interest in employer circles in the concept of the 'single bargaining' table. Union influence is, however, being challenged from other management trends, such as the increasing emphasis on winning the commitment of the individual employee and the continuing de-centralization of collective bargaining. Indeed, in some areas of collective bargaining there are signs of employers seeking to move away from joint regulation towards joint consultation and 'communications' strategies and to narrow the range of matters subject to bargaining. These pressures are not confined to the private sector. Many are also evident in the public sector where there is considerable pressure to weaken national pay bargaining and collective bargaining more generally.

From a workers' viewpoint one effect of multi-unionism can be a denial of training and promotion opportunities and an obstacle to self-development. It can also be a significant obstacle to presenting a united front to an employer and to building up trade union influence on key company decisions. In an attempt to offset the pressures on union organization from employers who perceive a loss of competitiveness from operating multi-union arrangements relative to those enjoying single-union arrangements, the TUC has recognized that a possible option is to make the best of existing trade union structures by developing strong, single-channel bargaining at company and plant level.[18] It envisages company level committees which can take decisions on matters relevant to that company and joint union machinery for particular sectors which can shape policy and take decisions for those sectors. This major issue is to be dealt with in the TUC Special Review Body's second report.

References

1. See Trades Union Congress *Meeting the Challenge*, August 1988
2. Millward N and Stevens M (1986) *British Workplace Industrial Relations 1980–1984*, Gower
3. Gregory M 'The No strike deal in action' *Personnel Management*, December 1986
4. In September 1988 the EETPU was expelled from the TUC for failing to abide by two decisions of the TUC Disputes Committee. As a result TUC membership fell to 8.8m
5. ACAS *Annual Report 1986* (1987) HMSO
6. See *TUC Report 1985* para 5 pp 6–8
7. For a more detailed account of the Christian Salvesen and Orion Electric cases see *TUC Report* 1988 paras 18 & 19 pp 13–14
8. For a detailed account of this episode see 'TUC facing a cliffhanger today over its creditability' *Financial Times* 23 March 1988, and the *TUC Report 1988* para 50 pp 28–29
9. See 'EETPU supports ballots on single-union deals' *Financial Times* 11 January 1988
10. The TUC Disputes Principles and Procedures were agreed at the 1939 TUC which was held at Bridlington in Yorkshire. Although the broad disputes principles have remained virtually unchanged, developments and refinements have taken place over time. For example, they were amended in the mid-1970s to deal with inter-union problems stemming from unions achieving sole negotiating rights and union membership agreements
11. This was the result of a successful motion from APEX who had lost, along with other unions, its bargaining rights at Hitachi in South Wales to the EETPU

12. The Special Review Body is undertaking a wide ranging review of promoting trade unionism and union organization and is to make regular reports, including where appropriate to the General Council and subsequently to a full Congress. The membership of the Special Review body is 20 members of the General Council plus the TUC General Secretary and Deputy General Secretary
13. See Trades Union Congress *Meeting the Challenge: First Report of the Special Review Body*, August 1988
14. The Code is published as an annex to the TUC Disputes Principles and Procedures
15. It was reported that in late 1986 the density of AEU membership at Nissan was 15 per cent. See 'Nissan: a catalyst for change?' *Industrial Relations Review and Report* No 397 November 1986. However, it has recently been reported that the density of membership has now fallen to 7 per cent. On average the EETPU has peformed little or no better in terms of membership gained from the single-union agreements it has signed
16. James McFarlane 'Change or Decay – Management and Unions' *The Fourth Annual Strathclyde Lecture on Industrial Relations* Strathclyde University Dept of Industrial Relations, June 1988
17. See 'Komatsu – the first year of a new start' *Industrial Relations Review and Report* **No 391** May 1987; Peter Wickens, 'Nissan: the thinking behind the union agreement' *Personnel Management* August 1985 pp 18–21 and Tracy Pegge 'Hitachi: Two Years On' *Personnel Management*, October 1986 pp 42–7
18. See Trades Union Congress *Meeting the Challenge*, August 1988 p 22 para 175

Part Three
The Law in Industrial Relations

Chapter 13

Changes in the Law since 1979: an Overview

Karl J Mackie

Law as Strategy: Reforming the UK Industrial Relations Culture

Much of the thrust of government policy since 1979 has been aimed at undermining the industrial relations culture which has dominated union, business, public and government thinking, arguably for most of this century, and certainly from 1945 onwards. Within this change effort, trade union and employment laws have played a central part as targets, and instruments, of change. The question of the rights and wrongs of these changes, and their permanence, are matters for political judgement and evaluation, and are touched on in the conclusion of this chapter on likely futures for employment law in Britain. However, the primary aim of this chapter is to set out the legal objectives and mechanisms of the changes made in this period.

What were the elements of the British industrial relations culture which came under attack? Its most favoured concept as far as lawyers of British industrial relations were concerned was that of *voluntarism* or abstentionism; the notion that it was, in Kahn-Freund's words:

'. . . the policy of the law to allow the two sides by agreement and practice to develop their own norms and their own sanctions, and [to abstain] from legal compulsion in their collective relationship.'

The clearest expression of this policy was in the area of the statutory 'immunities' for industrial action, the provisions which protected British trade unions from legal actions for which the common law (judges) would have otherwise made them liable. It was a system which was effectively in place by 1906 and gave formal political approval to the legality of trade unions and their methods, but in the simple form of a shield rather than an arsenal of legal rights. The voluntarist system has always had both its exceptions (for example, in emergency powers or Wages Councils' authority) and its tensions – it was subject to amendment during both World Wars and after the 1926 General Strike, but otherwise became the 'norm' of practice in British industrial relations.[1]

However, the strains arising from unchecked industrial action became pronounced again in the 1960s, with concern over the impact of industrial action on the economy and a lengthy debate about how to reform the

'British disease'. A variety of ideas for legal measures were canvassed in the period (most especially in the Donovan Royal Commission Report and the Labour government's proposals in *In Place of Strife*), culminating in an attempt by a Conservative government to restructure industrial relations law completely in the 1971 Industrial Relations Act. The attempt was widely recognized as having failed[2] and the Labour government which came to office in 1974 restored, in an amended form, the traditional approach, while maintaining and extending some of the new legal provisions affecting employers, such as unfair dismissal. The period since 1979, following the re-election of a Conservative government, has seen a return yet again to an attempt to re-regulate British industrial relations. This chapter aims to outline and analyse the nature and extent of this attempt.

The Elements of Change

Although one can set the legal changes descriptively within sophisticated academic debates around issues of voluntarism or interventionism in British industrial relations,[3] the central strategic objective behind government legislative policies since 1979 has been a simple one: *to shift the balance of power from trade unions to employers.*

The government campaign on this issue in the 1979 election repeatedly referred to the need to restore a proper balance of power between employers and trade unions. The trade unions were said to have abused their privileged position, exercising industrial pressure regardless of the country's social or economic interests. In the re-election campaigns of 1983 and 1987, the same theme was prominent, although by then the message to the electorate was a warning not to endanger the achievements of the government in restructuring the industrial relations culture of the country. Also, talk of 'balance' had given way to statements merely stressing the need to prevent a return to the abuses of union power.

The immediate concerns expressed in the 1979 campaign were consequent on the 'winter of discontent' of 1978–79 with its examples of extensive secondary picketing and secondary industrial action, and of trade unions which were ready to confront both employers and government to achieve their industrial objectives.

An important element of the changes since 1979, therefore, has been the reform of law affecting *industrial action*. This has entailed re-regulation, first, to create a legal structure which constrains industrial action to within more narrowly defined boundaries, principally disputes between workers and their own employer. A second, related set of regulations has been devised to support this framework by means of legal controls on *union organization and activities* – union membership agreements, elections, political funds and other aspects of union internal affairs.

Although industrial action and forms of union organization are distinct issues, the government's view was that they were linked facets of the 'union problem'. If one were to represent the Conservative view at its most basic, it ran something along the following lines: industrial action was initiated by unrepresentative and politically-motivated activists or militants inside the unions, leaders who were often unanswerable to the members at large; this leadership then used their power to invoke industrial action for wider industrial or political ends, relying in particular on the institution of the closed shop to control dissident members with threats of expulsion and therefore loss of job.

This line of reasoning helps to explain why a government party which claimed to be committed to 'deregulation' could be so ready to turn to *increased* regulation of the unions beyond merely outlawing certain forms of action. The regulations were regarded as a necessary component of freeing employers and government from what was viewed as illicit exercise of union power.

Underpinning the desire to set union conduct within a more constrictive legal framework, lies a government drive to ensure business competitiveness and 'free market' conditions, unhampered by the exercise of trade union power as an obstacle to the development of a culture of wealth-creation and enterprise. For the same reasons, the government has therefore altered legal constraints on *employer power* – industrial relations legislative policies moving in a contrasting direction of freeing employers from some of the earlier regulations which determined or set minimum standards on *employer-employee* relations, with the aim of giving employers more flexibility in their management of labour (at a time, as other chapters document, when economic conditions and employer policies have in any case induced a significant shift to more 'flexible' work patterns of, and in, employment).

One must also, however, acknowledge the existence of contradictory or countervailing forces to this simple analysis of the legal reforms since 1979 as representing merely a power-realignment strategy. That is, there is evidence also of *increased* regulation of employers. The sources of this can be traced to at least three factors:

> The desire of the government to limit public spending has, in certain circumstances, led to a shift of responsibility for social security payments from administration by government to administration by employers, as in the case of sickness and maternity benefits.

> The influence of membership of the EEC and other European bodies has continued to make itself felt in, for example, the imposition on employers of new duties to employees on the transfer of undertakings, or the extended coverage of sex discrimination and equal pay claims.

> There are occasions where the government has continued to accept an 'encouragement' role for regulation of employer-employee relations in

areas that generally match their policies, requiring employers to provide facilities for trade union workplace ballots in certain circumstances, requiring statements in company annual reports of measures adopted to encourage employee involvement, providing improved taxation treatment for share-owning or profit-sharing schemes.

Law as Tactics: Effecting Change

The above is an outline of the regulatory policies which have reshaped British industrial relations law since 1979. In understanding these changes, one must also take account of two further emphases. First, the nature of the law-in-action is not merely a matter of the substantive principles of law, the rights and obligations created. The law's effectiveness is also determined by questions of procedure, legal remedies, ease of access to adjudication, and by the alternative means of control available to the parties in dispute. These remain vital factors in understanding the impact of law and changes in the law.

One of the principal features of an earlier Conservative government's attempt (in the 1971 Industrial Relations Act) to achieve the same objective of increased restraint on union/worker conduct, was the failure of the legal measures to make a sufficient impact on the practices of employers and unions. There are aspects of this evident in the post-1979 legislation. However, it is also widely acknowledged that these measures have been far more successful in achieving their aims. While this success must be in part attributed to the presence of a more chastening economic climate, it is also a measure of a more sophisticated approach to legislative control.

The 1979 government was at pains to emphasize the need for a 'step-by-step' approach to removing union 'abuses'. Thus, the legislation whose content is described below, is the outcome of a series of measures, in particular a major Act passed every two years of the Conservatives' period of office – the Employment Acts 1980, 1982, the Trade Union Act 1984, the Wages Act 1986 and the Employment Act 1988.

Alongside this important 'gradualist' approach, building on changing attitudes and experience (of public, government and legal drafting), the nature of the procedures and remedies made available by the Acts have helped to sidestep some of the resistance tactics of the unions to the Industrial Relations Act. First, the legislation has been drafted to help to avoid the direct clashes between the trade unions and government (or special institutions created for the purposes of the legislation) which were typical of the earlier Act, such as over registration of unions or 'cooling-off' periods to be called by the Secretary of State for Employment. Second, the legislation has built on existing rights rather than created special new ones – for example, merely narrowing down the traditional 'immunities' rather than creating direct statutory prohibitions, thus returning industrial action to scrutiny by traditional common law principles; attacking the closed shop through the medium of unfair dismissal claims and compensation rather than declarations of unlawfulness for the practice. In a similar fashion the legislation has relied on established institutions – industrial tribunals, Certification Officer, High Court – rather than creating new ones.

This step-by-step approach has also been evident in the case law around the legislation, although here there is more of an element of chance. While employers generally were hesitant to test the new rights in relation to their 'domestic' unions, other significant and well-publicized cases emerged from outside the mainstream, cases where an employer was in a less close relation with a union (as in the *Stockport Messenger* case). The success and publicity attaching to such cases provided other employers with the confidence and example to apply to the law where they might have hesitated before (and the unions with examples which diminished confidence among officials and members). In this way, change in conduct (for example in relation to use of ballots before industrial action)[4] has been a clear outcome of the legislative programme.

Finally, the re-emergence in law of the liability of trade unions *as organizations* has allowed the courts when seeking to enforce judgements to cause severe economic damage to unions concerned, rather than imposing martyrdom on individual officials. (The same process was apparent through the miners' strike of 1984–85 but in that dispute the main cases involved were member complaints against their union, actions derived under traditional common law rules rather than the new statutory rules.) This has had the consequence of eroding the initial union refusal to recognize the validity of the laws, thereby gradually establishing the legitimacy of legal intervention in a way which had never been wholly successful under the 1971 Act. The fact that this legitimacy has also been given an opportunity to establish itself over three terms of Conservative government office is, of course, a final factor in consolidating the legitimacy of the new laws as a new 'Queensberry Rules' in industrial relations.

Space does not permit an adequate analysis of case law developments (judicial interpretation of legislation) over the period since 1979, but this aspect of the tactics of legal intervention is a crucial one, quite separate from the issue of the nature of the new legal rules. It is also worth commenting on the fact that not only has judicial attention continued to play a significant part in the interpretation of the survived remnants of the pre-1979 legislation, but that the miners' strike of 1984–85 has created a body of case law within the common law which is likely to be highly significant for some time in the future.

In line with the earlier analysis of the regulatory objectives of the governments of the period, a more detailed discussion of the main changes in the law is set out in the rest of this chapter under three headings: employer-employee relations; industrial action; trade union organization and activities. A final section provides an evaluation of the significance of recent legal changes, and speculates briefly on possible future directions.

Before discussing the legal changes in more detail, it is useful to demonstrate the extent of legislation enacted by the Conservative government since 1979 by a summary of the changes made in these substantive areas. (Discussion of pensions law, health and safety and taxation law developments has had to be limited. The other items listed in the following chart are intended as an *aide-mémoire* rather than as a precise description of legal provisions.)

Labour Law: Main Changes Since 1979

Employer-employee relations

INDUSTRIAL TRIBUNAL PROCEDURES
Pre-hearing assessments introduced with warning on costs and possibility of awarding costs on grounds of unreasonable as well as frivolous or vexatious claims.

*Summary judgements** possible.

Equal pay procedures with 'independent expert' to conduct job evaluation where 'equal value' claim.

Non-union members given *right to join union* and other workers before tribunal where individual dismissed or victimized for non-union membership; right to claim *interim relief*;† *compensation* made significantly higher than ordinary dismissal claims for dismissals on relevant union or non-union grounds.

UNFAIR DISMISSAL
Length of service requirement increased to two years.

Reasonableness. Equal burden of proof rather than employer to prove; 'size and administrative resources' factor to be taken into account.

Fixed-term contracts. One-year period sufficient for employee to agree to waive rights to claim unfair dismissal or redundancy.

Compensation amendments (loss of minimum basic award; conduct other than that contributing to dismissal can be taken into account; higher minimum basic award and 'special award' system for dismissals for non-union/union reasons).

---

* ie reasons for decision may be written in summary form in most cases (although parties may request full reasons).
† ie a special procedure for obtaining rapid relief by way of re-employment or continuation of contract until a full hearing is held.

Dismissals for *industrial action*. Employer immunity extended.

Dismissals or victimization of *non-union member* unfair. Legal support for the closed shop ended.

Protection where *transfer of undertakings*, unless reasonable dismissal for 'an economic, technical or organizational reason entailing changes in the workforce'.

REDUNDANCY
Employer rebates withdrawn unless fewer than 10 employees.

TERMS AND CONDITIONS
Wages Councils' powers. Abolished powers of setting wage levels for workers under 21 years, non-wage conditions and above-minimum differentials. Powers restricted to setting minimum adult hourly rate and overtime rate/live-in accommodation payment maximum.

Wages Councils' structures. Simpler abolition or variation powers for Secretary of State; more independent members, small employer representatitves; three-year term of office; statutory requirement to have regard to effect of order on employment levels in the industry, in particular regional areas of low employment.

Cashless pay. Truck Act restrictions abolished for new contracts.

Truck Acts repealed. New right for all workers to go to tribunal for unlawful deductions from pay (where non-statutory, no prior written notification in contract or written agreement); one-tenth limit on deductions in any one pay day for retail workers (where cash shortages/stock deficiencies).

Fair Wages Resolution rescinded.

Repeal of 'comparable terms and conditions' arbitration procedure ('recognized' terms in collective agreements or 'general level' claims).

Statutory Sick Pay introduced to replace direct state benefit for up to 28 weeks.

Statutory Maternity Pay to replace maternity allowance.

Transfer of undertakings require transfer of contracts and collective agreements in appropriate cases.

Duty on employers to respond promptly to *employee request to terminate union subscription check-off from pay or to vary check-off deduction amount where employee contracts out of union political levy.*

Repeal of legislation on women's hours of work.

Pension transfers across employments improved.

MATERNITY RIGHTS
Right to reasonable *time off for ante-natal care* with pay.

Right to return to work. Introduction of extended written notice requirements to retain right to return to work. If not reasonably practicable for employer to offer old job back, can offer suitable alternative or, in the case of employer with five or fewer employees, can refuse to take back.

SEX DISCRIMINATION
Equal pay for work of equal value introduced where not in the same or similar job as the comparator man in the same employment.

Sex Discrimination in relation to *retirement* provisions. Unlawful in relation to dismissal, demotion, promotion, transfers, and training.

Eligible employment extended. Right to claim sex discrimination in relation to employment in private households or for small employers.

EMPLOYEE OR TRADE UNION INVOLVEMENT OR CONSULTATION
Employers required to state in *Annual Reports* what consultation and employee involvement measures have been introduced.

Share ownership and *profit-related pay* tax incentives.

Right for union to claim *recognition* from employer abolished.

Union (or non-union) labour only or union recognition/consultation clauses in commercial contracts void; unlawful to discriminate against or victimize contractors on these grounds.

Reduced minimum period of trade union *consultation on redundancies.* Thirty days where 10–99 employees/new right to *consultation on transfer of undertakings.*

Pension scheme consultation requirements with employees and trade unions.

Data protection safeguards for personal information held about individuals on computer. Rights of access to, and amendment of, data.

Industrial action

Trade union liability for damages. Can be sued for unlawful industrial action where called by 'responsible person'.

Trade dispute definition narrowed to disputes between workers and their employer, for action 'wholly or mainly' related to industrial relations issues.

Selective dismissals and re-engagement simplified.

Social security benefits for strikers' dependents subject to a 'deemed' union strike payment.

Secondary and sympathetic action unlawful unless employer has contract with primary employer.

Ballots required for any union-supported action.

Industrial action to enforce union membership made unlawful.

Union membership and subcontractors. Industrial action to compel union membership (or non-membership) or union recognition/consultation by other employers made unlawful.

Secondary picketing unlawful.

Trade union organization and activities

Ballots required: before *industrial action* made official; every five years or less for union *principal executive committee* members and presidents and general secretaries; every 10 years or less to maintain a *political fund*.

Candidates in elections must be given the opportunity to have *election addresses* sent out.

Qualified *independent scrutineers* must be appointed to supervise election and political fund ballots.

Public funds available to pay certain postal ballot expenses.

Right to use employers' premises for certain ballots.

Register of members' names and addresses must be maintained.

Broader and updated definition of 'political objects' when political fund necessary.

Rights for union members

- *to prevent industrial action without a ballot*
- *not to be 'unjustifiably disciplined'* (for not supporting industrial action or for making assertions that the union is acting unlawfully)
- *to inspect union accounts*
- *to prevent misuse of union funds* to indemnify unlawful conduct or use of union property by trustees for unlawful purposes
- *to pursue grievances against the union in the courts* after six months of internal procedures.

Commissioner for the Rights of Trade Union Members appointed to assist members to enforce certain statutory rights.

Right for individuals to claim *unreasonable expulsion/exclusion from union membership* where UMA (union membership agreement) exists.

Employer-employee Relations

The main policy emphasis in this area has been the stress on 'deregulation' in order to allow the labour market to work more freely and to allow employers to concentrate on the question of the production of goods and services rather than on external systems of rules and legal diversions. Many of the legal changes reflect this philosophy. However, in other respects this has been an area of reform and modification rather than deregulation. In addition, other burdens have fallen on employers where other elements of government policy – European legal requirements, transfer of aspects of public spending on to employers' shoulders – have overridden the search for deregulation. Finally, it is worth making the point that 'deregulation' merely replaces rule by statutory provision with the older 'common law regulation' of the contract of employment (or, more frequently than before 1979, contracts for 'self-employment' arrangements).

It was of course the inadequacy of the earlier protection which led to the addition of modern statutory controls. However, a return to the older regulation also takes place in a different socio-economic context. Thus, the formalization of contracts, encouraged by the statutory requirement of written statements of terms and conditions, and a more legalistic (and more white-collar) environment, may perhaps mean a greater number of disputes will take place around the contract of employment than was once the case for personnel managers. The effect, however, is probably relatively insignificant compared with the impact of the statutory rights. Even within these rights, the question of individual contract remains important, for instance, in terms of the factors which go into assessments of 'reasonableness' in unfair dismissal or of constructive dismissal claims, in terms of questions of suitable alternative employment in redundancy and maternity rights cases, and in calculation of compensation by industrial tribunals.

The interlinking of contract and collective agreements has always been one of the curious features of British industrial relations law, the courts managing to recognize the collective bargain without giving it any legal status or intent in its own right, by finding it incorporated (in appropriate cases) into individual contracts of employment. This was one area which the 1971 Act completely misjudged, seeking to establish a system of legally binding agreements but allowing a disclaimer clause which was universally used. Despite this issue rumbling on in government circles from 1979, it has remained one the government has thought better to avoid (perhaps because the 'balance' of advantage in a legally binding agreement is not entirely clear?). However, collective aspects of employer-employee relations inevitably find their way into a number of elements of law in employer-employee relations and the amendments to these since 1979 are also discussed below.

Industrial tribunals and unfair dismissal*

The sphere of individual employee rights has been the most consistent sector of government policy since the 1960s when statements of contract and redundancy payments were first introduced. These established the industrial tribunals as the primary 'labour court' in the country, their presence already familiar to employers as an appeal body from industrial training levy decisions. Their work expanded with the explosion of regulation in the 1970s into unfair dismissals, maternity rights, sex and racial discrimination cases and equal pay, alongside issues of victimization and dismissal of union members and activists, claims for time off and other rights. Their jurisdiction is now extensive.

However, the tribunals have still not been given any powers to deal with general employment disputes, even those arising over contracts of employment (the power to extend their jurisdiction into this area remains: s 131 of the Employment Protection (Consolidation) Act 1978); they are limited to the specific provisions of the statutes. Further, the vast majority of claims they deal with concern unfair dismissal, suggesting a reticence by employees to tackle their employers in such a forum until their relationship has been severed. The 'severed relationship' factor is also an important element in the fact that only a minuscule number of cases lead to

---

* See Chapter 15 for a more detailed treatment of the law on unfair dismissal.

re-employment, although the orders for reinstatement and re-engagement were once intended to be the primary remedy of the tribunals.[4] This fact and the associated aspect that tribunals cannot enforce such orders but merely increase the compensation element if the employer refuses re-employment has remained a sore point with trade union critics of the system.

For their part, employers prior to 1979 were apt to stress the 'unrealistic' nature of tribunal decisions and (especially small employers) the interference and expense involved in spending time away from their business. It was these claims which the Conservatives stressed in emphasizing the need to induce a sense of realism and proportion in the regulation of employee rights. However the period since 1979 has been less one of deregulation of the elements of tribunal jurisdiction (although there are important elements of that) than one of technical amendments and procedural points. Employers have for the most part learned to live with tribunals and many acknowledge, at least in private, that the dismissals legislation has helped employers to become more professional about matters of discipline and dismissal.

The government's emphasis on its desire to reduce the burden of employment legislation on employers led primarily to amendments directed at unmeritorious applicants. The rule on costs in tribunals, that they would not normally be awarded except against cases brought or conducted 'frivolously or vexatiously', was extended to include those who acted 'otherwise unreasonably'. To reinforce this, a new interim procedure was introduced at the same time, the Pre-Hearing Assessment, where a party who had a *prima facie* weak case could be warned that a costs award might be made against them at the full hearing should they lose their case, although they were entitled to continue to a full hearing by a separate tribunal. This procedure has deterred many applicants, although of those who did continue despite the warning, it appears that a sizeable minority (of around 13 per cent) still win their case. A suggestion by the government in 1986 that in addition a £25 fee for all tribunal claims (refunded if successful) could be charged to deter unfounded applications was dropped after widespread opposition to the proposal, but returned in 1988 with consultations over a £150 refundable deposit procedure. Finally, the tribunals can now if they wish, issue their decisions in summary form in most cases, rather than full, reasoned judgements, although parties may request the fuller statement.

Other reforms were directed at the main category of complaint before the tribunals (ie unfair dismissals) but again were for the most part relatively limited in effect. The test of unfair dismissal remains that of 'reasonableness' in all the circumstances, but now includes an additional phrase that the circumstances include the 'size and administrative resources' of the employer's undertaking. Again intended to assist small employers, this amendment appears merely to have confirmed existing practice in the tribunals rather than to have altered their approach. Similarly, there is little evidence of any effect from the change in the onus of proof which now requires the tribunal to find that the dismissal was reasonable (or not) rather than requiring the employer to show that it was reasonable. (The employer is still required to show he has a relevant reason for dismissal.) These amendments were accompanied by a number of adjustments to the system of compensation in ordinary cases, for example the ending of a system of a minimum entitlement of two weeks' pay as a basic award (the part of compensation based on length of service with a company calculated in a similar manner to statutory redundancy payments), and the widening of the circumstances tribunals could take into account in reducing compensation because of an employee's conduct. There was, however, a more drastic review of the compensation system in relation to dismissal of non-union (and union) members. The reforms in this area are outlined in the section below on collective relations in employment.

The most significant deregulation element of the changes since 1979 has been the gradual raising of the qualification period for claiming unfair dismissal, from six months (to which the Labour government had gradually reduced it by 1979) to two years. The rationale for this is to allow employers time to assess their need for an employee (and his or her acceptability). (For a short period, this rationale led to a difference in qualification periods for large and small employers, the latter allegedly needing more freedom from such legal restraint in order to establish themselves or to grow. On similar grounds, the government proposed at one stage that they would raise the weekly hours of service required over the two years from 16 to 20.) The research evidence in this field has consistently indicated that employment legislation is a long way from most employers' minds as a business problem, and the limited deregulation introduced by the government suggests an acknowledgement of this. Employers in this area, as in the field of industrial action, tend to look for stability in their environment so that they can get on with their main interests. However, on the union side, there is concern about the growing army of temporary and part-time workers not protected by any effective employment legislation.

As regards the case law of tribunals, there has also not been much for employers to become indignant about. The general test behind most tribunals' assessments – 'Is this decision within the range of responses of a reasonable employer?' – has provided limited scope for tribunals to be idiosyncratic or to set advanced standards, while experience in personnel departments and the assistance of a growing army of experts on employment law, briefing documents, legal insurance schemes etc has provided employers with more than a measure of guidance on how to avoid liability. The number of successful applicants before tribunals has therefore tended to decline (to below 30 per cent of those who reached a hearing, by 1984) alongside union enthusiasm for the system. Related to this, the value of being represented, especially being represented by a lawyer, also seems borne out by the statistics. Many employers still settle, however, rather than face the costs, time and doubts of going to a full hearing, or settle because by this stage they have been informed that they have a weak case.

Terms and conditions of employment

The impact of other aspects of government policy has in most cases been more significant than the hue and cry over the tribunal system of the 1970s. Thus, one may contrast the limited degree of deregulation of tribunal rights (which, after all, still affects only limited numbers of employers at any one time) with the government's readiness to 'privatize' the cumbersome administration of Statutory Sick Pay on to the shoulders of all employers in the interests of seeking savings on public sector manpower costs. An element of reimbursement of employer administrative costs as well as of the basic sickness payment was introduced after protests from employers over the original scheme, but the scheme is likely to remain something of a headache for small employers (and an uncertainty for employees).

A repeat run of this is to take place over Statutory Maternity Pay, introduced in April 1987. This latter reform combines with earlier reforms (more complex written requirements for women to claim maternity leave; rights to time off for maternity care) to make 'maternity management' a sophisticated element of personnel practice.

More central to the government's ideology have been the reforms affecting payment systems. One of the earliest measures to be repealed as inappropriate to free market conditions was schedule 11 of the Employment Protection Act 1975 (itself an extension of an earlier Act), which had provided trade unions with a form of access to unilateral arbitration for claims based on 'recognized' or 'general level' terms and conditions for comparable workers. A similar rationale led to the Fair Wages Resolution (covering employment terms and conditions of contractors on government department contracts) being rescinded. Also repealed some time later were the Truck Acts which had required manual workers to be paid in the current coin of the realm. The Wages Act 1986 removes this right unless it is part of the employee's contract (an element giving some cause for confusion in relation to existing employees' rights), freeing employers from the costs and constraints of payment in cash. The provisions in the Truck Acts providing safeguards for employees against fines and deductions from their pay, have been replaced with new legal rights against unauthorized deductions, and maximum limits on deductions from the pay of retail workers for cash shortages or stock deficiencies.

Similarly, the government has been unhappy with the effects on the labour market of Wages Councils (which set legally binding minimum terms and conditions in sectors of employment which have traditionally had limited degrees of union organization), particularly their impact on the 'rigidity' in young workers' earnings. Although the option of abolishing the Councils was considered, and their numbers reduced, the government opted for surgery rather than abolition in the 1986 Act, although it was fairly severe surgery. The power of Wages Councils to set any rates for workers under the age of 21 was abolished. For adult workers, the Wages Councils were restricted to setting one minimum hourly rate (compared to a range of rates in recognition of differentials) and one overtime rate. Their powers to set other conditions (eg holidays) were repealed (apart from setting a maximum level of payments made by workers for living accommodation). Also, the constitution of Wages Councils was revised to add more independent members (for shorter terms of office), more small employer representatives, and a requirement imposed on Councils to have regard to the effect of their orders on employment levels in an industry, in particular regions with low levels of employment. (This latter aspect relates to a wider initiative of the government to increase flexibility in payment systems, and especially to loosen the hold of 'national bargaining' processes.)

An added regulation in the field of payment systems in 1983 provided unwelcome news for employers, with the finding of the European Court that the UK government was in breach of European law (not for the first or last time) over the Equal Pay Act 1970. The result was a complex set of regulations (the Equal Pay (Amendment) Regulations 1983) providing women (or men) effectively with the right to claim a job evaluation exercise if they claimed that their work was of equal value to a man (woman) in the same employment doing a different job. Although the case law has proved this area is also a minefield for applicants, it still represents something of a slowly-ticking time bomb under many payment systems if one assumes that pay differentials in many parts of industry represent long-held but now unlawful assumptions about 'women's work' (for example, canteen assistants, clerical workers, paramedical professions). (One must also make the assumption that the tribunals and 'independent experts' appointed to report on these cases will be able to detect this through job evaluation techniques.) Recognition of the difficulties of protracted hearings over individual cases have led some employers and trade unions to opt for collective bargaining to seek to arrive at more stable pay structures.

Similarly, employers have had to rethink their treatment of men and women approaching retirement, following from the Sex Discrimination Act 1986, which incorporated the results of the *Marshall* case in the European Court, declaring it unlawful to discriminate between the sexes in age of compulsory retirement (or in a range of other retirement-linked aspects of employment such as opportunities for promotions, transfers, access to training, etc). In the same Act the government were for once usefully able to combine sex equality with deregulation, by provisions phasing out the existing restrictions on women's hours of working.

Collective relations in employment

Many aspects of employment relations are linked to collective issues and these, too, have been subject to scrutiny in an attempt to root out what were regarded as undesirable statutory requirements, but with other requirements again added, however, in pursuit of other policy aims. The provisions (ss 11–16 of the 1975 Employment Protection Act) allowing trade unions to claim recognition from an employer by means of ACAS conciliation, investigation and recommendation, were repealed. A similar distaste for the unnecessary extension of trade unionism other than by the voluntary wish of the workers directly involved, or their employer, led to the 1982 Employment Act (ss 12, 13) depriving employers of any legal right to require other employers (or those seeking to tender for contracts) to recognize, consult or negotiate with trade unions, or to employ union labour only. In the interest of strict equality, the latter rule applies also to attempts to extend non-unionization.

The concern for protecting individual freedom against union and/or employer coercion into membership led in the 1980 and 1982 Acts to an extension of the protection for non-union members against dismissal or victimization, and the extension of the circumstances where non-members could claim unfair dismissal or victimization in the closed shop. In particular, the earlier limited grounds of conscience (genuine religious objection to being a member of any trade union) were broadened to grounds of conscience or deeply held conviction against trade unions or any particular trade union(s).

In an early signal of the government's intention to extend balloting in trade union affairs, came the additional requirement in the 1980 and 1982 Acts that, for an employee to defend himself against unfair dismissal or victimization claims, a closed shop had to receive high levels of approval in a secret ballot (80 per cent of those entitled to vote or 85 per cent of those voting, the latter level only valid in ballots reviewing an existing closed shop arrangement to be held every five years or less). Even then a vote in favour did not apply to those who had been non-union members before the day of the ballot. It was not specified who should hold the ballot but some additional protection for employees was provided in allowing the employer or complainant to join the union or others who had induced the dismissal/victimization by threats of industrial action, for the purpose of the tribunal apportioning compensation (s 7 of the 1982 Act). However, by 1988 the government felt confident enough, despite evidence of some employer support for such agreements (and despite the fact that a majority of ballots held did meet the high level of support required), to dispense with the remaining legal support for the closed shop. The Employment Act 1988 (s 10) made unlawful industrial action to enforce union membership practices and repealed (s 11) the remaining legal support for dismissal or victimization for non-union membership in the limited circumstances where closed shop agreements had applied. (The joinder provisions remain applicable to all dismissals or victimization for non-union membership reasons.)

The 1982 Act recognized the ineffectiveness of current compensation levels in achieving re-employment offers from employers, by dramatically increasing the compensation available for unfair dismissals for reasons of non-union membership (and by extending the interim relief procedure to claims of dismissal for non-union membership). A new minimum basic award was to apply, currently £2,520 (compare the earlier repeal of the two-week minimum payment for claimants generally). Further, where the unfairly dismissed employee asked for re-employment, a payment of 104 weeks' pay was to apply (£12,550 minimum) if the tribunal did not order it, and 156 weeks' pay (minimum £18,795) if it did but the employer refused to take the employee back (unless the employer proved it was not practicable to do so). Again in the interests of equality these provisions applied to protect union members where they were dismissed by reason of becoming or remaining union members or because of their union activities (at an appropriate time).

European requirements led to extended consultation rights for workers and trade unions in the limited cases (outside share purchase takeovers) where the new Transfer of Undertakings (Protection of Employment) Regulations 1981 applied. Further encouragement of consultation was approved by the government in imposing a requirement in the 1982 Act for annual reports of companies with more than 250 employees to state what action had been taken with regard to informing, consulting with or involving employees in company issues. A similar desire to encourage employee identification with the company led in the Finance Acts to new tax benefits for share purchase and profit-related pay schemes. On the other hand, the lower time limit required for consulting with trade unions about intended redundancies (60 days where 10–99 workers) had been halved to 30 days in 1979. In 1986, when most of the 'labour shake-out' in traditional manufacturing industry had taken place, the government ended the entitlement of employers to a rebate (then 35 per cent) on their statutory redundancy payments, with the exception of employers with less than 10 employees.

Industrial Action

The restoration after 1974 of the traditional immunities for trade unions and for industrial action did not create any stable political consensus on the issue. In particular, the major national disputes in the 'winter of discontent' around Labour government incomes restraint gave the Conservatives a popular electoral platform on which to condemn a system which offered such opportunities for disruption of business and public life, although the public were perhaps less concerned with the subtle nuances of the immunities system than with the fact of social disruption as such.

Conservative and employer complaints about the legal framework focused especially on two aspects of this disruption. First, the extent to which trade unions were involving other employers and workers (through picketing and sympathy or secondary action) to add to pressure on the employer in dispute. This was seen to be harming other businesses and members of the public who were not immediately concerned with the issues in the dispute nor necessarily in a position to influence their outcome. Second, there was concern that trade unions were exercising the power they held over members, through closed shop agreements in particular, to rally support for action from unwilling members who would not have wished to be involved.

The post-1979 reforms have therefore attempted to single out these practices for reform, by making secondary action and picketing unlawful in most circumstances, and by providing a requirement that trade unions adopt secret ballots in order to show they have the backing to authorize or endorse (lawful) industrial action. The effectiveness of these measures in terms of their impact on practice is discussed elsewhere in this book, but their significance in terms of an attack on the traditional legal framework, alongside the other measures outlined below, is profound.

Trade dispute

The 'golden formula' underlying immunity from tort actions in industrial disputes covered acts taken 'in contemplation or furtherance of a trade dispute'. This formula still applies to protect those actions by individuals or trade unions which are not otherwise declared outside its scope by the reforms of secondary action, action without ballots etc. In line with the government's intent to narrow the extent of the immunities system, the scope of this formula has also been narrowed by s 18 of the 1982 Act. It now covers only a dispute 'between workers and their employer' over industrial matters rather than disputes between workers and workers or workers and employers generally, or a trade union and an employer independent of employee support.

Thus, the new definition requires a specific employer focus in a dispute rather than being action taken against employers generally, or a dispute between workers such as a demarcation dispute. Also, the dispute must be 'wholly or mainly related to' one or more of the industrial relations issues listed in the Trade Union and Labour Relations Act 1974 s 29 rather than, as in the older formula, be merely 'connected with' them. The significance of this change was demonstrated in the Mercury case, where the refusal of telecommunications workers to link up a new telecommunications competitor to the telephone network, as part of a campaign against privatization and fear of loss of jobs, was suggested not to be wholly or mainly related to the loss of jobs but primarily political in intent and therefore outside the protection. The new rules also limit the occasions when a trade dispute can exist in relation to matters outside the UK. This will only apply if the persons involved in this country are 'likely to be affected' with respect to their terms and conditions or other industrial relations matters listed in the 1974 Act, s 29.

Secondary action

This was declared (s 17 of the 1980 Act) outside the bounds of immunity protection except in certain detailed circumstances. Action by employees of an employer (outside the parties to a primary dispute) loses immunity unless its purpose is directly to prevent or disrupt the supply of goods or services between the secondary employer and the employer in dispute (on the basis of an existing contract between the employers), and it is likely to have such an effect. (Associated employers who step in to substitute for the employer in dispute in respect of goods and services and their immediate contractors are treated as also within the bounds of lawful secondary action.) The fact that the workers involved might have no knowledge of the commercial arrangements involved (ie whether there is or is not a contract between the relevant employers) is irrelevant to the loss of immunity, although a genuine, but false, belief that there was, would presumably affect the level of any damages awarded. Where the commercial arrangements ensure that there is no direct contract, the case law suggests that the courts will not intervene to pierce the 'corporate veil', even in circumstances where this situation arises more out of company law formalities rather than any essential difference of employer involved (see, for example, the *Dimbleby* case). 'Sympathy' action, ie action taken to express support for fellow workers or union members (eg to show solidarity with a pay claim by the nurses), is of course subject to the same tests and in most cases unlikely to meet the requirements.

Secondary picketing

It was natural to ally the question of secondary picketing to the restrictions on secondary action, although in fact the provisions go much further. Section 16 of the 1980 Act redefined s 15 of the 1974 Act to restrict lawful picketing to a person attending at or near his own place of work. 'Place of work' is generally seen as implying a restriction to one's normal working premises, ie it would not extend to other plants or sites of one's employer even where there is a common dispute across sites, let alone to another employer's premises (whether or not any of the tests of lawful secondary action would apply to action taken by workers on that site). There are exceptions: for mobile workers or workers who find it impracticable to picket their place of work (who can picket any premises from which they work or from which their work is administered); for union officials who are accompanying members whom they represent; and for employees dismissed in connection with a trade dispute (who may picket their former place of work).

Although the section does not deal directly with the problem of 'mass picketing', guidelines in a Code of Practice issued by the Secretary of State for Employment suggest that six pickets at any one entrance is a reasonable number, a figure stressed in some of the cases arising from the miners' dispute and in subsequent disputes.

Ballots

The introduction of a requirement to hold secret ballots in connection with official industrial action, in s 10 of the 1984 Trade Union Act (as amended by the Employment Act 1988), marked a significant stage in the government's growing confidence in the effectiveness of its legal reforms. The provision was intended to moderate calls for strikes or other industrial action by the requirement to show majority support among those to be involved (an intention also evident in the requirement that the ballot paper mention without qualification that the action may be in breach of the contract of employment). Failure to hold a properly conducted ballot leads to a loss of immunity where the union authorizes or endorses the action. The detailed requirements of the Act ensure that this is a likely source of much litigation on technical grounds, although most employers are likely to be more concerned with the substantive question and result.

In addition to the possibility of employers or their suppliers or customers pursuing actions in tort, the 1988 Act (s 1) provided a statutory right for individual members (who are likely to be induced to take part) to go to court for an order preventing union support of industrial action where a valid ballot was not held. The Act also adds to the legal technicalities surrounding industrial action ballots by imposing a requirement of separate workplace ballots except where the workers across the sites have a distinct occupational factor or factors in common. (This provision is intended, according to government claims, to prevent manipulation of ballot results by use of artificial constituencies, but may also be a 'step' towards a more general requirement in future legislation.)

There is growing evidence that ballots are becoming an accepted part of union practice in industrial disputes, although their moderating influence is less evident than their use as part of the standard negotiating tactics in a dispute.[5] The majority of ballots on industrial action result in support for the action, although in many cases this is merely a signal to employers to re-open negotiations on their last offer.

Trade union liability

One of the most important reforms in the law for the success of the government's legislative efforts to restructure the balance of power in industrial disputes, has been to restore trade union liability for tortious acts (ie civil wrongs such as inducing a breach of contract etc). Section 14 of TULRA, going back to the reforms of the 1906 Act, had given trade unions as organizations blanket immunity from actions in tort (with some exceptions outside the field of industrial relations). The immunity given by the traditional 'in contemplation or furtherance' formula mainly applied therefore on behalf of individual union officials who were alleged to be acting unlawfully. Trade unions as such were protected from most tort actions. Section 15 of the 1982 Employment Act removed this general immunity to make trade unions open to legal actions where they acted outside the new restricted range of immunities. By this means, litigants and the courts were able to avoid 'martyring' individual officials (although this route is still the only option in the event of unofficial action). Orders of the court (injunctions) and actions in damages could be awarded against the union and its funds, although the Act specified limits on the amount of damages claimed, according to the membership size of the union. This change in the law was particularly important in undermining the unions' campaign of opposition to the new laws, as unions which disobeyed court orders found themselves liable to penalties for contempt of court which exceeded the limits on damages laid down in the Act. In the case of repeated disobedience, not only could the fines multiply but sequestration of union assets (receivership in the case of the miners' union) followed in a number of cases, facing unions with a choice of compliance or of eventual major losses of members' funds, if not bankruptcy.

Experience of such clashes led the government, in the Employment Act 1988, to introduce new statutory rights for union members to go to the courts where union funds are being used to indemnify individuals for criminal offences or contempt of court (s 8), or where trustees are permitting or carrying out unlawful application of union funds.

Industrial action and trade union recognition

Another area where immunity was lost relates to attempts to influence the union practices of subcontractors or other employers. In keeping with its other measures to prevent the practice of 'secondary unionization', by employers requiring other employers to employ union labour only (or non-union labour) or to recognize, negotiate or consult with unions, immunity was withdrawn from industrial action with these purposes. Section 10 of the Employment Act 1988 went even further, withdrawing immunity from industrial action intended to enforce a closed shop with one's own employer.

Dismissals/strike benefit

Finally, two other reforms confirmed the government's readiness to add to the pressure on workers to avoid industrial action. First, s 9 of the 1982 Act amended the rules relating to dismissals taking place during industrial action. The previous rules in the 1978 Act (s 62) had given the tribunals jurisdiction to hear claims of unfair dismissal only in cases where there were selective dismissals or selective re-engagement offers among any employees taking part in the action. A leading case on this section had decided that the measure of selection applied in respect of all workers who had taken part in the action, even where a number had returned to work (*Stock v Frank Jones (Tipton) Ltd*). The amendments ensured that:

The criterion of selection only applied at the date of the dismissal and did not include those who might have participated earlier but had since returned to work.

The test was only applicable at one establishment and did not require an 'all or none' approach across all sites affected.

There was a limited time period (three months from the dismissals) during which the 're-engagement offer' discrimination test applied.

A second change in the law sought to reduce the state 'support' for industrial action, by reducing social security benefits to strikers' dependents by an amount representing a 'deemed' union payment to the striker. (The individual taking part in industrial action was already ineligible for such benefit.)

Trade Union Organization and Activities

Much of the legislation on trade unions since 1979 has reflected a government belief (supported by opinion polls of union members) that union actions did not reflect a true level of support by members for many of the activities in which trade unions and trade union leaders engage. This has accompanied concern at the pressure individual members may face to participate in industrial action, or the pressures exerted on non-unionists to join the union.

The legislation in this area has therefore broadly sought to emphasize the 'voluntary' aspect of trade unions as organizations, to give individuals rights to opt out of membership and other activities or to express without interference or pressure their views on key affairs of the union. This programme was phrased both in terms of the rights of the individual over the organization and in terms of the need to support the workings of democracy in union affairs – the need to 'hand the unions back to their members'.

A somewhat different approach was taken to union recognition by employers, repealing an earlier measure which gave trade unions a right (normally following an inquiry and ballot of workers by ACAS) to require an employer to recognize their authority to negotiate on behalf of employees. (And in the celebrated case of GCHQ, the government as employer withdrew established union membership and recognition rights on the ground of threat to national security.)

Trade union recognition

The attempt to establish a legal procedure (ss 11–16 of the Employment Protection Act 1975) whereby trade unions could seek recognition from an employer on the basis of a degree of employee support was repealed by the 1980 Employment Act. The repeal was justified on the grounds that none of the parties, including ACAS which was responsible for the first stage of investigation and recommendation, had found the previous procedure satisfactory. A number of employers had disliked the outside intervention and challenged details of the procedure in the courts, initially with considerable success; trade unions had found it slow and often ineffective, and raising awkward issues of inter-union rivalries; ACAS had been unhappy at the effect on its conciliation work of its involvement in a quasi-compulsory capacity. Whatever the merits of such arguments they were in tune with the inclinations of the incoming government to repeal rather than seek to amend or improve the statutory provision.

In retrospect, with the cutbacks in traditional areas of union membership to follow and the trends to non-unionism and withdrawal of union recognition in some sectors, it seems likely that many in the trade unions must now doubt the wisdom of their stance. More broadly, future policy makers are left with the question of the inequity of legislative policies advancing the argument of 'extending democracy' in union affairs, while effectively abolishing one of its significant manifestations (the right for employees to decide who should speak for them) as between employees and their employer.

Secondary recognition and unionization

The traditional practice of trade unions exerting pressure on their own employer to ensure that other employers with whom he contracts use union labour or recognize, negotiate or consult with trade unions has been another object of the government's attention. Section 14 of the 1982 Act removed any immunity from industrial action taken against employers with these purposes. Immunity is therefore not saved in this particular instance merely because a worker is in dispute with his or her own employer, nor is it relevant that the other workers may be working on the same site, or haulage contractors may be entering or leaving the site. Thus, it is more appropriate to dub this restriction as one of 'secondary unionization' rather than one of secondary action. (The section also prohibits secondary 'non-unionization' although this was inserted more on the grounds of equality of treatment rather than on any widespread campaign by employees or employers to compel others to be non-unionists.)

The restrictions on secondary unionization (and non-unionization) are also extended to common employer practices with the same purposes. Sections 12–13 of the Act make it a breach of statutory duty for one employer to terminate a contract or discriminate against others in seeking or awarding tenders etc, where these practices are one of the reasons for so doing. Finally, this same philosophy is applied to contractual provisions. The Act makes void any term in a contract with the same effects.

A final element in the government's restrictions on means to extend union membership is its various amendments to the legislation on dismissal or victimization of non-union members, particularly in closed shop situations. These are discussed below.

Union membership and union membership agreements

From its entry into office in 1979, the Conservative government has never concealed its dislike for the closed shop or 'union membership agreement' (UMA) as the law terms it. Nevertheless it sufficiently recognized its extent, its support among many employers (on the ground of orderly collective bargaining), and the fact that it could be continued informally even when formally repealed, not to seek its outright abolition initially. It used other legal tactics in the 1980 and 1982 Acts to restrict its scope to a point where its effective legal validity was more tenuous. In addition, other factors such as the decline of employment in traditional strongholds of unionism and the difficulties raised by the law for employers contemplating new UMAs have contributed to a decline in its extent.[6] Thus, the possibility of ending legal support for the closed shop was realized in the Employment Act 1988, in the sense of making industrial action to enforce a closed shop unlawful and repealing the earlier provisions which made it fair to dismiss (or take action short of dismissal against) a non-union member where there was a valid UMA.

Further measures to discourage trade unions and employers from enforcing union membership are found in other remedies made available to the tribunals. First, applicants and/or employers may 'join' trade unions (ie sue them as well as the employer in the tribunal action) and others as respondents where they claim the employer was induced to dismiss (or take action short of dismissal) by reason of industrial action or threats to that effect. If the tribunal finds the dismissal unfair they may make any compensation, or any part of it, payable by the joined party. Second, a special system of remedies has been created for dismissals for non-union membership. This system of relief has been in part inspired by, and extended to dismissals on union grounds also (membership or union activities at an appropriate time), although the compensation elements were largely in response to non-unionist dismissals. The dismissed employee may claim interim relief (formerly only available to trade union members who produced a certificate from a union official saying he had reason to believe the dismissal was because of union grounds). This allows an early award of re-employment or continuation of contract with the employer. Also, compensation levels have been increased considerably to add to the pressure on respondents to re-employ, or not to dismiss in the first place (see p 281).

Individual rights against the union

A series of measures other than those already outlined have been introduced to protect union members (and in some instances non-members) from union actions, and to allow individual members to control or monitor union affairs. Most of these were introduced by the Employment Act 1988. One of the most significant innovations in the Act was the creation of a Commissioner for the Rights of Trade Union Members, who may provide assistance (by way of legal advice or representation or paying legal costs) to union members who are considering legal action against their union in relation to a number of the statutory rights.

Section 1 of the Act gives to union members, who are likely to be induced to take part in industrial action, a right to take their union to court where action has been authorized or endorsed without a valid secret ballot (see below). Section 3 of the Act at the same time prevents unions from disciplining individuals who fail to take part or support industrial action or who indicate opposition to it, whether or not a ballot has been held. The section also protects individuals from being so 'unjustifiably disciplined' where the discipline is taken because of a member making assertions that the union or its officers are acting unlawfully or in breach of union rules, or because of a member consulting the Certification Officer or the new Commissioner for the Rights of Trade Union Members. Complaints of unjustifiable discipline can be taken to the industrial tribunals, with a separate later claim necessary (to a tribunal or the Employment Appeal Tribunal, depending on whether or not the union has responded to a tribunal declaration) where compensation is sought.

Other rights provided by the 1988 Act include: a right to pursue a grievance against a union through the courts after six months of internal procedures have elapsed (whatever union rules or court practices there may be to the contrary) (s 2); a right to inspect a union's accounting records and be accompanied by an accountant for this purpose (s 6); a right to prevent deduction of union subscriptions by the employer as soon as the employee notifies the employer of his resignation (s 7); a right to prevent union funds being used to indemnify individuals in respect of criminal offences or for contempt of court, and to prevent union trustees applying union property for unlawful purposes (ss 8, 9).

An earlier right for an individual to claim unreasonable exclusion or expulsion from a trade union was created by s 4 Employment Act 1980. It only applies where the applicant is in, or seeking employment in, an area of employment where a UMA applies. A two-stage procedure is used, with the need first to obtain a declaration from a tribunal, followed by a further application to a tribunal or the Employment Appeal Tribunal for compensation where compensation may be assessed according to whether the union admitted or re-admitted the applicant to membership in the intervening period. Compensation is based on unfair dismissal levels. Reasonableness is decided on the merits of the case and not solely by the union rules.

Secret ballots

State Funding

The government made a cautious attempt to encourage wider use of secret ballots in trade unions in 1980 (s 1 of the Act and the regulations made thereunder) by offering a refund from public funds for a range of important ballots if those ballots were postal ballots and the trade unions applied for reimbursement for basic postal costs from the Certification Officer. (Section 2 of the Act also provided a legal right to request the use of an employer's premises for similar ballots.) The scheme was boycotted initially by the TUC and its affiliates but this eventually broke down after pressure from some of its members who used postal ballots extensively and because of the increasing range of areas of union activity in which a legal requirement to ballot was becoming necessary. The scheme covers ballots on industrial action, employer offers, union amalgamations or rule changes, national officer or national executive elections, political fund ballots.

Union Membership Agreement Ballots

The provisions for these in the 1980 Act were repealed by the 1988 Employment Act.

Industrial Action

This requirement, introduced in Part II of the 1984 Act (as amended by the 1988 Act), has also been described above. Like the other ballot requirements of the 1984 Act, this was a more direct intervention in union affairs and one with greater impact than the UMA ballots. The Act also specified in much greater detail the conditions which had to be satisfied for the ballot to attract immunity (assuming the intended action was otherwise lawful):

Allowing voters to vote in secret and without interference.

Balloting only those whom it was reasonable to believe would be called on to take action and no others.

Holding a ballot no more than four weeks before the industrial action and giving support only after the ballot and within four weeks of it.

Asking separate questions for a strike or other industrial action (and specifying that these may be in breach of the contract of employment).

Informing constituents as soon as reasonably practicable of the detailed results.

Trade unions could use either a postal ballot or a workplace or semi-postal ballot, not aggregating the votes from separate workplaces unless there was a genuine occupational factor (or factors) common to those voting.

Principal Executive Committee Elections
Part I of the 1984 Act required that voting members of union principal executive committees be elected at least every five years by secret ballot (postal, workplace or semi-postal) of members or defined constituencies of members. Detailed conditions were again laid down (including maintaining a register of members' names and addresses) and members could complain of non-compliance to the Certification Officer or the High Court. The latter could issue an enforcement order against the union, specifying steps to be taken to remedy the non-compliance.

A number of reforms to these provisions were enacted in the Employment Act 1988, reflecting government concern at the slow pace of reform in union rules, the lack of cases being taken by members to the High Court, continuing controversies over the reliability of some election results, and the fact that major union influence could be exerted by certain national officials who nevertheless had no vote on their union's executive committee. The 1988 Act therefore extended the balloting requirement (with effect from mid-1989) to all members of a Principal Executive Committee (including those attending other than in a purely informatory or advisory capacity) and to the positions of union president and general secretary (s 12). Election candidates were given the right to prepare an election address and have it distributed with ballot papers (s 13). Ballots were to be postal ballots only and to be supervised by a qualified independent scrutineer (ss 14, 15). The Act also gives the Secretary of State power to issue Codes of Practice on election procedures (and on political and industrial action ballots) (s 18), and of course the new Commissioner for the Rights of Trade Union Members will be able to support any individual claims to the High Court over the conduct of election ballots.

Political Fund Ballots
Secret ballots to establish a fund to be used for political purposes (support for political parties and political candidates) had been established by the 1913 Trade Union Act. In part III of the 1984 Act, the government extended this legislation. In future authorization for the use of political funds was required to be subject to ballots at least every 10 years. The trade

unions who had established such funds many years earlier were given one year from the Act's commencement date to hold such a review ballot. Members could complain to the High Court if a union continued to collect contributions after a resolution to have a political fund ceased to have effect. Also, stricter rules were laid down with regard to the management of the funds and the occasions when proposed expenditure required the establishment of a political fund. The round of ballots which followed the Act delivered something of a rebuff to the government, every union (including some without such a fund previously) receiving a majority vote in favour of holding such a fund (see Chapter 14).

Conclusion

Working to legal rules: a revolution in industrial relations?

It is difficult to evaluate the labour law of the 1970s or 80s without acknowledging the importance of politics and political beliefs. Both decades have demonstrated in different ways the remarkable extent to which political beliefs, underpinned (more or less systematically) by theories of economics and industrial relations, can inform the legal rules which adjust power balances in industrial relations.[7] More open to question in the earlier period of the 1970s was the extent to which laws can act as a primary force to change social attitudes or to move resistant social forces such as employers or trade unions. Yet both the 1970s and 80s show that legal rules can foster significant changes in the exercise of power in industrial relations.

The 1970s first established the legal notion that an employer ought to have a reason, and be able to demonstrate the reasonableness of its application in dismissing a worker; that he should have equal rates of pay for men and women doing similar work; that he should offer women workers the right to return to their work after maternity leave. One can argue about the exact impact of such developments, in particular whether they achieved all that was hoped for them (and in most cases they did not). However, they still constituted a revolution of a kind in past employer practice which recent Conservative governments have both eroded and in some instances extended, certainly not yet reversed. However, they did reverse much of the 1974–79 (and earlier) gains of trade unions in extending legal support for collective bargaining – recognition claims, fair wages arbitrations, extended Wages Council powers.

The other changes in the law since 1979 also constitute their own kind of revolution, this time setting new boundaries on the flexibility of conduct by trade unions. The latter revolution, however, is perhaps of more significance not only in having a longer period to consolidate the legal rules as the new 'Queensberry Rules' of industrial relations but also because there had been greater doubts as to whether the trade unions, by their nature as collective organizations or by tradition, could as easily be made to conform as employers to legislative norms in the areas of industrial action or internal affairs. That they have to a great extent done so, testifies as much to the changing nature of trade unions and their members as to the skilled crafting of the law.

Of course there are other social factors, such as unemployment, which have assisted the legislation in making the impact it has, particularly the failure of the unions to mount the campaign of opposition to the post-1979 legislation which they mounted against the 1971 Industrial Relations Act. Until there is a revival of conditions of full employment (and there are some who would argue that this is beyond the capacity of the modern economy), it is difficult to assess the long-term hold of the new legal framework without knowing the exact weight of the different contributory factors.

Nevertheless, the later period suggests one should not underestimate the power of the forces of law nor the changing attitudes of union members to law and to union practices. Law can be a primary as well as a secondary force in altering human conduct. In the changed climate of the late 1980s, it is easy to forget the difficulties the government faced after the experiences of 1978–79 and the campaign of resistance to the 1971 Act, in wondering whether it had the capacity this time to overcome union resistance in well-rooted areas such as the closed shop, secondary action and picketing, union internal procedures.

Nor should one underestimate what can be done *tactically* in the way legal change is approached and legal rules framed – one of the main lessons the Conservatives had gleaned from the Industrial Relations Act experience. The legislation since 1979 has been remarkable in the care given to its phasing (step-by-step) and to the drafting of the rules and procedures necessary to achieve its objects, down to the detail of specifying that a ballot paper on industrial action should inform the worker that industrial action may be in breach of contract. Even those parts of the legislation which have been condemned by the courts as so obscure as to leave the players baffled as to the rules of the game (such as s 17 of the Employment Act 1980 dealing with secondary action), have been rationalized by government spokesmen – why worry about the rules of the game appearing complex when one would prefer the sport (of industrial action) to stop? (It is a moot point whether the same philosophy lies behind the complexities of the regulations dealing with workers' rights on transfer of undertakings, or equal pay for work of equal value.)

The return of industrial action and picketing into the arms of the common law, combined with trade union liability for official industrial action, was a particularly significant move in the step-by-step approach to reform, relying on those employers who were more able and/or more willing to take on the power of the unions to establish the effectiveness of the reforms, supported by the financial penalties exacted by the courts for contempt of court where injunctions were resisted. The legal actions by some union members in the miners' strike on the basis of common law principles (the contract between the union member and his union/fellow members) were also significant in contributing to a more legalistic culture and to the political objectives underlying the legal rules and have in turn provided experience for some of the detailed statutory regulation of union internal affairs provided by the 1988 Employment Act.

Similarly, the government has tackled the statutory reform of internal union affairs on the basis largely of areas of union activity – leadership elections, strike ballots, the political fund, the closed shop – where the political groundwork had already been laid to make it difficult for trade unions to make a popular political case even among their own members.

The assumption in the voluntarist tradition that a major social group was best left to set its own rules proved too simplistic in the face of wider political undercurrents of 'public interest' in debates on 'democracy', 'individual freedom' and 'industrial disruption'. The traditions (sceptics called them 'privileges') of trade unionism proved no more popular in this wider domain than those of the legal profession (although the latter's version of self-government mechanisms has perhaps been more delicately handled by the government). Hence the attack on the closed shop on the basis of individual freedom, despite evidence of support among many employers for its operation; hence the use of the term 'democracy', a concept itself so much part of union tradition, to win support for a formalized, uniform system of balloting procedures among trade unions which had had a variety of traditional methods of interpreting accountability to members.

The political impact of the legislative goals and reforms revealed the complacency of tradition in the unions rather than its values. The fact that the extent of change in union practices in these areas is still more patchy in reality than the legal rules might lead one to expect, should not detract from a recognition of the extent and direction of the changes towards a legal rule-bound industrial relations culture which have been set in process.

Industrial relations law in the future?

To compliment the government on the cleverness of its approach to legal intervention since 1979, however, should not be the sole measure of judgement on the current legal rules or the likely future of the policies. There are some cautionary notes to add, not only because a future government may seek to readjust the balance, nor because improvements in the economy, with a reduction in unemployment or skills shortages, may again enhance union power and influence, but also because of question marks hanging over the objectives of the current policies. What role for trade unions do such policies envisage? Does the present legislation provide an adequate framework for effective industrial relations? Is the balance of power the right one?

Some suspect that the drift of government policies is towards the step-by-step emasculation of trade unions as an independent social force. Certainly, many free market economists see trade unions simply as an obstacle to the workings of the market. Whether the government embraces such an extreme view may be judged by how much further it seeks to proceed with restrictive legislation. If one were to try to characterize the image of appropriate trade unionism which can be implied from the legislation so far enacted, one comes close to a concept of trade unionism as 'enterprise', or 'domestic unionism' as the goal of government policies. Trade unions can speak for employees to their own employer, and in doing so can encourage traditional pressure via industrial action so long as sufficient members individually demonstrate support for them in this.

However, even this is an inexact picture. Secondary action is outlawed, but the right to some disruption of goods and services produced or supplied by other employers is retained (so long as other complex legal tests are answered). Secondary picketing on the other hand, while outlawed, is outlawed not as measured against a test of employment, but of place of work. Even in one's own place of work and against one's own employer, it is unlawful to take industrial action with the purpose of ensuring that other employers he deals with recognize trade unions or employ union labour only (even where that labour comes on one's own site). By 1988, the government had moved further to outlaw even industrial action which was aimed at ensuring the form of organization of trade unionism in one's own workplace (the closed shop), and to prevent trade unions disciplining members who felt unable to follow majority ballot votes in favour of industrial action or who campaigned against such action.

It is difficult to find any clear coherence of principle in such provisions, other than a sense of dislike for industrial action as a form in which to exercise power. Yet if industrial action is the problem – and undoubtedly it forms the major basis for the resentment against trade unions and trade union power – why stop at secondary action? (Tentative proposals to exclude industrial action in 'essential service' industries were at one stage voiced but later dropped, apparently because of the complications in political and legal measures this entailed.)

There is plenty of evidence that, despite the restrictions placed on some forms of action, trade union members are still willing to engage in industrial action against their own employers. This is particularly the case in the public sector where major strikes by miners, teachers and civil servants have taken place. Even in the private sector, the evidence suggests that industrial action is far from dead, and that the obstacle of strike ballots has not prevented unions from receiving support in the majority of instances.

Of course, these are disputes between workers and their own employer, therefore not the target of the post-1979 legislation. Nevertheless, one suspects that the government wished to achieve more in relation to union power than to prohibit merely the particular weapon of secondary action which became a politically pre-eminent issue of the 1970s (although the 'winter of discontent' had been essentially a matter of 'primary' industrial disputes). If that is the case, the legislation will in the long run prove ineffective, even by the government's own standards, and it will be forced back on further legislation or on other routes to avoiding industrial action. There is, in other words, still a substantial gap between the current political claims for industrial relations legislation and its actual or likely long-term outcomes. (The provisions of the 1988 Act protecting individuals who defy majority ballot results, and the part-requirement of separate workplace ballots, are of course further steps towards the attempted erosion of the effectiveness of industrial action. Their significance has yet to be tested.)

The limits to the legislation, in terms of its achievement of the underlying political objective of a reduction in union power, are also apparent in the area of union internal affairs. The use of the flag of 'democracy' to justify secret ballots on industrial action, the political fund and union leadership elections, proved a potent political symbol for reform and touched a sensitive nerve in the practice and ideology of trade unionism. In this area, the legal reforms may in substance have the greatest chance of surviving a future change of government (as did the requirement in the 1913 Trade Union Act of a secret ballot for a political fund), as unions have been forced to acknowledge that their members like the opportunity of participating in ballots.

However, the success of union campaigns in the political fund review ballots (in some instances to set up a new fund) and in industrial action ballots, and the few complaints made to date by union members with regard to election ballots (apart from other evidence suggesting that ballots do not always result in 'moderate' outcomes), suggest that the government may have misjudged the impact of its reforms in the complex world of union-member relations.[7] While the government has hit on the right note that workers like to influence directly decisions which will affect them, it would be absurd to consider that they join trade unions to practise the art of democracy. More fundamental interests are at stake and it is the trade unions' capacity to fulfil these interests which will determine the popularity and extent of union membership.

Once again, therefore, one returns to the position that, given economic conditions favourable to the trade unions, it is possible that the issue of industrial action and union power may again confront the government, as it has bedevilled many other governments which equally sought to 'correct the imperfect market' but by incomes policies rather than public spending limits and legal control of trade union actions. Public sector employees in particular, where stability of employment and union membership is still strong, will continue to provide difficulties in relation to industrial action. The government will therefore be faced again with whether it wishes to correct further 'abuses' going to the heart of industrial action as a legitimate method of pressure or to take other policy initiatives. Of course there are other more indirect legislative routes to undermining the strength and confidence of trade unions in the public sector, such as privatization measures or fragmentation of bargaining units, and there is some evidence of such policy emphases now emerging.

At this point one comes to the heart of the 1980s legislation: questions of the redistribution of power. The legislation has tackled some of the obvious *symptoms* of the traditional culture of union-employer conflict which typified Britain and the British disease, but has it done sufficient to tackle the causes of this problem? Here one comes back full circle to the question of what legal forms are provided, or are needed, to represent workers' interests?

Most managers would assert that they have the interests of their workers at heart, and this assertion and the need for a highly motivated and quality workforce are at the root of an upsurge in talk of employee involvement and consultation, of 'human resource management' practices which have followed the 'macho management' styles that rooted out many traditional union powers (and employees) in the traditional manufacturing industries in the early 1980s.

For their part, trade unions would argue that representation of workers' interests to employers and state remains their fundamental role and the reason why the technical reforms to their procedures will make life more complex, but certainly not alter the fundamentals of union-employer conflicts and the trade union role in them. Hence the new emphasis on recruitment drives and on extending union organization to groups such as part-timers that were previously on the margins of union activity.

However, whether or not it is correct to argue that the power of the unions in society is likely to recur again as an issue of the 1990s, a social critic's view of the future role of law in the distribution of social power must also encompass the question of the representation of employees' interests within the employment relationship (perhaps even more so if trade union power declines). Is the balance right? The critic is likely to ask whether, given a decline of voluntarism as the cornerstone of legal approaches to the employment relationship, one can justify the continuation of a legal framework which is dominated largely by the contract of employment and the machinery of unfair dismissal. Neither looks entirely satisfactory in the long term from this perspective; particularly with the growth in the economy of part-time and short-term labour. The contract of employment remains for most individual workers a formalization of unequal bargaining power, while unfair dismissal provides only a minimum level of protection in this respect, offering little in respect of other grievances. Similarly, the effect of hierarchy in employment is sufficient to ensure that most employers underestimate the extent of workers' disaffection with aspects of their employment.

But how far should such claims of unequal power or occasional inequity justify outside intervention and the use of law? Managers would of course argue, as they did against the employment protection legislation of the 1970s, that such legal intervention wasted time which could be spent on the business and that they were perfectly capable of looking after employees' interests. Just so did union leaders argue they were perfectly capable of looking after their members' interests, until the legislation proved there was popularity in the individual having a say, however much a token vote. Claims of a new era of employee commitment and involvement in the 1980s and 90s based on management initiative may come to prove as short-lived as the many previous motivation fads, from Taylorism and work study through the human relations movement of the 1930s to the job enrichment and 'quality of working life' fashions of the 1960s and 70s.

It may be that if the wider public interest element in 'sensible' industrial relations is to be guided by basic legal rules (as discipline and dismissal came to be), then critics of current policies will begin to look for more robust, more 'political' notions of employment grievance-mediation rules in the way that legal 'democracy' rules have appealed to union members. Hence the new emphasis among some for a 'positive rights' approach to replace the traditional immunities approach to collective power relations, although whether this would extend to industrial democracy concepts will have to await the complexion of future governments.

A legal requirement for a secret ballot among employees to elect a company chief executive may seem a weird fantasy of the 21st century, but if employee involvement and commitment to the enterprise is to become a legal rather than a voluntarist notion, and industrial action is to be diminished as an element of employee behaviour, questions of legal rules which seek to help to cure employee grievances, as well as tackle the symptoms of the British disease, may be in order.

The present government has opted for the carrot approach in terms of encouraging share ownership and profit-sharing pay participation. There are many other options, however, for grievance-handling rule structures: supervisory boards with worker-directors; statutory works councils; industrial tribunals with jurisdiction to hear contract of employment cases or industrial action disputes; agreements which guarantee mediation/ arbitration. (In the context of this discussion, one can begin to see the source of popularity for 'no-strike' agreements, which rests on the strength of their rules of procedure for handling disputes as much as on the more controversial issues of their prohibition of industrial action or the single-union recognition element.)

In the present climate, the macho-manager or macho-trade unionist may react to such futuristic suggestions with more than disbelief. On the management side, there may be anticipated no end in sight of the current road to free market fulfilment, while the macho-trade unionist may trust in the history of the 'inevitable' march to trade unionism and collectivism that has been apparent since the 19th century.

Nevertheless, if one starts from the lessons of the 1970s and 80s for trade unions that they need to find more creative ways to handle disputes than the unpopular and blunt weapon of industrial action; and if managers are going to accept that employee commitment to enterprise must ultimately mean some degree of check on managerial prerogative (perhaps the simplest way to define 'democracy' in the context of employment); then proposals such as these may merit more debate than either would be willing to admit. The increased trend to 'Europeanization' of law after 1992 may be a further factor in suggesting new directions in employment law mechanisms.

The problem for would-be governments and for lawyers drafting future industrial relations law will be to find a new vocabulary and new visions which will adequately describe the range of forms and objects of intervention that the employment relationship of the future will merit in terms of control of the exercise of social power in the 'public interest'. And, of course, no government starts with a clean slate in law or in industrial relations, although post-1979 governments have done their best to work their way back towards one. If the period of reform since 1979 has demonstrated anything for the future of British industrial relations law, its success in undermining much of the attitudes and practices of social consensus and voluntarism in British industrial relations has surely indicated at least that, given the will and the right legal tactics, anything is now possible.

References
1. Mackie K J 'The Changing Role of Law in British Industrial Relations' *Industrial Relations Journal* **10** 4, Winter 1979–80, pp 57–65
2. Weekes B, Mellish M, Dickens L and Lloyd J *Industrial Relations and the Limits of the Law: the Industrial Effects of the Industrial Relations Act 1971* (1975) Blackwell, Oxford.
3. For a sense of the different emphases, see Lewis R (ed) *Labour Law in Britain* (1986) Blackwell, Oxford, Ch 1; and Wedderburn Lord *The Worker and the Law* 3rd Edition (1986) Penguin, London, ch 1
4. For a recent survey of the operation of industrial tribunals, see Dickens L, Jones M, Weekes B and Hart M *Dismissed: A Study of Unfair Dismissal and the Industrial Tribunal System* (1985) Blackwell, Oxford
5. See *Annual Report 1986* ACAS, March 1987
6. Millward N and Stevens M *British Workplace Industrial Relations 1980–1984* (1986) Gower, London
7. See Wedderburn, op cit
8. Undy R and Martin R *Ballots and Trade Union Democracy* (1984) Blackwell, Oxford

Chapter 14

Ballots, Picketing and Strikes

Derek Fatchett MP

For students of industrial relations, conflict is seen as a central motivating characteristic of the system. Mostly that conflict will be latent rather than manifest, subject to control through joint procedures and regulation. The ability to influence the outcome of these regulatory processes will depend upon the power of the parties and their ability to mobilize that power. The pursuit of outcomes, however, through the exercise of power, has itself been subject to further regulation by the state: an intervention which can be interpreted in contrasting ways, either with the state as the benign impartial umpire, or as the supporter of one side in the conflict.

This chapter will be mainly concerned with aspects of open, often dramatic, conflict; but it will, in relation to the question of ballots and picketing, analyse a context in which, especially under the Conservative government first elected in 1979, the State has sought to influence the means by which, and the extent to which, trade unions are able to mobilize support.

Ballots

Ballots have always formed an important aspect of trade unionism. Their use has been wide and varied: at branch level, for the election of branch officers; at the workplace, to offer support or guidance to wage negotiators, or to demand or sanction industrial action; at all levels, to elect members of a union's national executive committee, or, in certain cases, to elect the union's full-time officials.

As the subject of balloting can be extensive, so can the means by which the ballot is conducted; from a show of hands at a branch meeting, or at a packed factory gates meeting, to the more formal provision of a postal ballot.

Despite the trade unions' considerable formal commitment to the use of ballots, there can be little doubt, from the mid-1960s onwards, with a gathering pace in the 70s, that questions of internal union democracy assumed a greater salience in the broader political context. The main reasons for this were twofold:

1. There was often articulated a feeling that trade union leaders, be they elected or appointed, were out of touch with their members, thereby forcing the rank-and-file members into a more militant stance than they would otherwise have sought.
2. There was detailed criticism of particular approaches to balloting, either because it was felt that the expression of choice was circumscribed by pressure or intimidation, or because it was asserted that particular approaches would enhance turnout rates, with a consequent greater degree of democracy and reliability in the result.

It is certainly open to a good deal of debate as to whether these particular arguments could be supported by strong factual material. That, however, became almost irrelevant; perceptions and political pressures moved inexorably in that direction which demanded a greater scope for a more formalized balloting system.

The most significant changes were introduced by the 1984 Trade Union Act, which set out the requirements for balloting in relation to the election of members of a union's principal executive committee, to the conduct of industrial disputes and to the endorsement of a union's political role through the continuation of its political fund. The changes have been further reinforced by the provisions of the 1988 Employment Act.

It was the political fund change which initially attracted so much controversy as, with the available evidence showing the sharp loss of support by the Labour Party in the 1983 election, it appeared more than possible that the vast majority of unions would vote to discontinue their political funds and hence, to sever their links with the Labour Party. The conditions imposed by the Trade Union Act made it difficult, if not impossible, for a union to bypass the balloting requirements: any member would be able to take action to declare the collection of political funds ultra vires, if an affirmative ballot had not taken place within the previous 10 years. As the 37 political fund-holding unions had not held a ballot within the specified timescale, all were caught within the net imposed by the 1984 Act.

Although the 1984 Act did not set out a specific form for the ballots to follow, along with the provisions of the 1913 Trade Union Act, it did provide the Certification Officer with sufficiently firm guidance to ensure that a definable pattern emerged; in broad terms, voting at geographical branch meetings was excluded, while workplace and individual postal balloting were regarded with considerably greater favour. The 1988 Employment Act now excludes the possibility of a workplace ballot: Section 14 states that ballots held for deciding on political funds must be postal. Perhaps this development can best be construed as largely ideological, as evidence, referred to later in this chapter, seems to support a greater potential for participation in workplace, rather than postal ballots.

In many respects, the change involving internal union elections introduced by the 1984 Act was more significant in terms of relationships between unions and the State than the provision concerning the political funds. Since the *Osborne* case[1] and the consequent 1913 Act, the state had set down ground rules against which unions must conduct their political role. No such ground rules had previously existed as far as internal union elections were concerned; a union could organize itself to satisfy its own formal requirements and those of its members. Indeed, the composition of union executive committees varied substantially: some unions operated systems of indirect election whereby, following election to a subordinate committee, members of that committee elected their representative on to the union's executive body; others, very much a minority, conducted their election on the basis of individual postal ballots. The differences reflected a variety of factors: the skilled-unskilled origin of the union, its current spread of membership, and the way in which the union's present structure had emerged as a result of merger and takeover.

The historical splendour of that diversity was immediately put at risk by the 1984 Act: balloting would now have to conform to a pattern which allowed direct elections and equality of access for each individual member. Unions would be forced into change, or face the risk of every election being declared invalid. The 1988 Employment Act takes the process of state prescription a stage further, by, in Section 14, insisting that the election for members of a trade union governing body, including non-voting members, should be held on a postal ballot.

The 1984 Act also confronted a third area of balloting, relating to industrial action. The rationale for change in this context could not have been made more explicit: no longer, it was argued, was it acceptable for a union to call out its members for industrial action without a ballot, which was secret and conducted without intimidation. The workplace mass meeting was no longer acceptable, and the penalty for not conforming to the Act's requirements was substantial. Although the 1980 and 1982 Employment Acts had severely curtailed the scope of the immunities previously enjoyed by the unions, the 1984 Act made these immunities conditional upon holding a ballot on the question of industrial action.

The unions defended their existing practices, especially against those accusations which suggested that union leaders or rank-and-file activists simply forced their members into industrial action. It was pointed out, for instance, as we shall see later in this chapter, that many strikes assume the character of spontaneous reactions to managerial decisions, thereby making more formal processes of balloting less appropriate. In addition, the argument was made that it is extremely difficult, if not impossible, to maintain or to spread a dispute without the consent of those involved. Three separate provisions included in the 1988 Employment Act will further restrict the ability to strengthen or to spread a strike. Section 1, for instance, gives a right to a union member to obtain a Court Order to require his or her union to withdraw authorization of a strike given without the backing of a properly conducted ballot, while Section 3 gives a right to continue working during a strike without fear of union discipline. Furthermore, in the context of a closed shop, even one approved by the requisite ballot, dismissal on the grounds of non-union membership is deemed unfair.

Although experience under the 1984 Act is inevitably somewhat limited, certain conclusions can be drawn. First, there can be little doubt that the 1984 Act has changed trade union practice and thinking. Unions have been forced, often with a great deal of disquiet, to change the way in which they conduct ballots. In addition, and maybe more importantly, unions have started to accept that ballots will continue to form a part of this behaviour. This was well illustrated during the debate at the 1986 TUC Congress when the joint Labour Party/TUC document, 'People at Work; New Rights, New Responsibilities',[2] was discussed.

The TUC General Secretary, Norman Willis, explained the provision in the document which granted to individual union members a right to have a secret ballot on decisions relating to strikes. 'Balloting is here to stay,' he said, 'because our members favour it. We are committed to making the trade union movement even more representative and more democratic because that way we will be stronger and more effective.'[3] It is difficult to imagine quite the same form of words from a TUC General Secretary a few years earlier.

Second, and somewhat ironically given the character of previous debates, trade union experience of ballots under the 1984 Act has been rather encouraging. On strike ballots, the 1985 Annual Report of ACAS offered the following information:

'At the end of the year the service had become aware of 94 cases in which ballots had been organized, involving no fewer than 37 trade unions. Of these 68 resulted in a majority vote for industrial action and 25 against, with one tie. In 38 of the cases where voting was in favour of action, stoppages or other industrial action took place and 23 resulted in no action. It is not clear whether all ballots had complied with the strict terms of the Act. In 15 cases we were aware that injunctions had been sought by employers in the courts, either because no ballot had taken place before industrial action began, or because they considered that ballots which had been held did not meet all the requiremnets of the Act.'[4]

From the ACAS figures, it is not unreasonable to conclude that industrial action ballots have not, in themselves, been particularly damaging to trade unions. In over 70 per cent of the cases, members had supported industrial action. Furthermore, it is worth noting that ballots had taken place in no more than 12 per cent of reported disputes: in 1985, there were 813 officially recorded stoppages, but only 94 ballots. The provisions of the 1984 Act have hardly been all-consuming in practice.

If the experience of industrial action ballots has been less damaging than feared by the trade unions, the results of political fund ballots exceeded the unions' wildest dreams. During the 12 months from April 1985 to March 1986, 37[5] balloted, and with, by the standard of union elections, a reasonably high turnout of 51 per cent, only two unions failed to achieve an affirmative level of support of less than 70 per cent of those voting. Indeed, in 21 out of the 37 unions, the vote in favour of maintaining a political fund exceeded 80 per cent.[6] These were quite remarkable results, especially against a background of early opinion poll evidence which suggested that the number of unions likely to record a 'yes' vote could be counted on one hand. As with industrial action, the fear of ballots, so deep in the rhetoric of union debate, if not in practice, may have been misplaced. The notion that a silent moderate majority would automatically surface, thereby preventing the more radical and militant options, proved illusory and chimerical. When the union leadership, at whatever level, campaigned for their case, without taking the members' support for granted, the members, on the whole, seemed to respond.

Another aspect of interest emerged in relation to the political fund ballots. It has often been asserted that individual postal ballots will invariably guarantee a turnout higher than other methods of voting. The case for this has more often rested upon optimism and prejudice rather than hard facts. While an analysis of postal, as against geographical branch, ballots will mostly, but not always, come out in favour of the former, when compared against workplace ballots the evidence is considerably more mixed. This was certainly the case with the political fund ballots, where the requirements of the 1913 and 1984 Acts virtually ensured that union executives had little alternative but to opt for a postal or a workplace ballot, or a mixture of both. For comparison purposes, it is unfortunate that only four unions adopted a full postal ballot. This, however, did not prevent Leopold feeling able to conclude that; 'those unions which conducted their ballot in the workplace had turnouts on average 30 per cent higher than those using postal ballots.'[7] It is doubtful as to whether it is valid to come up with generalizable conclusions based on the political fund ballot experience, but it is reasonable to assume that the evidence on turnout gained from that experience will enable trade unionists to respond more confidently to the argument that only postal ballots secure high turnouts.

In many ways, the debate about ballots has recently taken place on false ground, with the impression being given that the trade unions are by nature hostile to ballots and often, by extension, to democracy itself. Several sustainable conclusions show that such assertions, while valuable debating points, may bear little relevance to the facts. Unions have always extensively employed ballots; the main argument has been about the method of balloting, and not the principle itself. That argument has now moved on: the unions have found both in relation to industrial action and the political funds that they have been able to secure support. The demand now is, given that ballots have come to be regarded as an integral part of union decision-making, they must be so organized as to maximize participation. For the TUC, workplace ballots offer the most effective means of encouraging involvement. Willis reflected this viewpoint in his speech to the 1986 TUC congress: 'We want ballots with proper facilities, polling stations at the workplace, meetings in working time.'[8]

The government soon rejected the TUC proposals for greater facilities for workplace balloting; for the government the need was to extend the subject matter of balloting, and to introduce, in certain contexts, mandatory postal balloting.

As for the subject matter, the government, in its consultative document of February 1987,[9] and in its subsequent Employment Act, 1988, have established two further areas in which balloting should take place.

The 1984 Trade Union Act restricted the benefit of immunities to those strikes which had been endorsed by a ballot. As we have seen from the earlier quoted ACAS figures, unions have not felt that it was invariably necessary to conduct a strike ballot. Now, through Section 1 of the Employment Act, the government seeks to enforce ballots by imposing upon the union a duty to its members not to authorize industrial action without obtaining majority approval from those likely to take part. Through this method, it is hoped that a ballot would become the inevitable practice. However, with the existence of many short strikes, it is unlikely that the hope will ever become the invariable rule.

Second, while the 1984 Act, as we have seen, provided for direct balloting for the election of the union's principal executive committee, the provision did not extend to non-voting members of the executive. The government came to see this as a loophole, perhaps largely because of the decision of the NUM to deprive their president and general secretary of a vote on the union's executive. For this reason, it was argued that:

'. . . the sensible course seems now to be to extend the requirements to include all general secretaries, presidents and executive members whether elected or appointed. In this way the members themselves would be given a direct say in the appointment of all members of the union's governing body. Only then could there be any strong certainty that officials who speak for the union (and may be seen in some sense by the public as being the union itself) fully represent those for whom they speak.'[10]

The government's suggested course was given statutory backing in the 1988 Employment Act. In addition to the wider scope for ballots, the government also envisaged a further push towards postal balloting. The justification offered for this course of action mainly rested upon the assertion that pressure could be applied upon individual members in the context of a workplace ballot.

> 'Because of the scope for subtler forms of pressure in a workplace ballot, however, there is a real question whether such ballots can ever be totally free from suspicion. Having ensured that individuals have a right to participate in ballots the government is determined to ensure that they are able to do so without constraint and that all the votes cast are properly reflected in the result. If necessary, therefore, because of their greater degree of security the government is prepared to take the further step of insisting on postal ballots for executive elections and for political fund ballots.'[11]

These proposals will help to ensure that balloting will remain on the broader political agenda, with the trade unions emphasizing their commitment to, and practice of, democracy, and arguing for the statutory provision of the necessary facilities to secure workplace ballots, and with the government stressing the rights of the individual union member and placing their faith in postal ballots. As we have already noted, this proposal now forms Section 14 of the 1988 Employment Act.

Picketing

In relation to industrial action, ballots have always offered one means of mobilizing support. Another method, not necessarily mutually incompatible, involves picketing fellow workers, in order to persuade them to take steps which might be sympathetic to the objectives of those initiating the industrial action. The persuasion, implicit in the picketing, could vary from encouraging others to take industrial action, to asking workers not to handle the goods of the employer involved in the dispute, or to service that employer in other ways. These attempts, through picketing, to broaden the base and the scope of industrial action have inevitably always formed part of trade union activity. Equally, they have always been activities fraught with difficulty as far as the relationship between the individual picket and the law is concerned.

Before commenting on aspects of the law, it might be worthwhile reminding ourselves of the nature of picketing. For a variety of reasons, the impression gained by many people in recent years, especially during the 1984–85 miners' strike, is that picketing always involves large numbers, with the attendant risk of violence. Associated with these images is the belief that a police presence, again in large numbers, forms a normal, indeed integral part of the plot.

In contrast to these perceptions, we must recognize that in any one year there will be hundreds, if not thousands, of strikes with the vast majority involving some form of picketing, and usually taking place without the presence of any police officers. Overwhelmingly, picketing is peaceful: conclusion supported by Kahn and her colleagues[12] and by Evans.[13] And even in the 1984–85 miners' strike, which has been held up as characteristic of all that is wrong with unions in general, and picketing in particular, the National Council for Civil Liberties was confident enough, on the basis of its analysis of the strike, to conclude that: 'contrary to the impression inevitably created by media concentration on incidents of mass picketing and violent confrontation, most of the picketing during the strike has been orderly and on a modest scale.'[14]

Liability for the picket can arise through both the civil and criminal law. Consistent with the attitude of the common law towards trade unionism and industrial action, picketing was regarded as both a criminal offence and a civil wrong. This liability was first restricted by the 1875 Conspiracy and Protection of Property Act; and after further judicial intervention which opened up the loopholes which Parliament considered that it had closed by the 1875 Act, s 2 of the 1906 Trade Disputes Act provided a framework which, with alteration, has carried forward into the 1980 Employment Act.

Section 16 (1) of the 1980 Employment Act now sets out the current legal parameters for picketing:

'1. It shall be lawful for a person in contemplation or furtherance of a trade dispute to attend (a) at or near his own place of work, or (b) if he is an official of a trade union, at or near the place of work of a member of that union whom he is accompanying and whom he represents, for the purposes only of peacefully obtaining or communicating information, or peacefully persuading any person to work or abstain from working.

2. If a person works or normally works (a) otherwise than at any one place, or (b) at a place the location of which is such that attendance there for a purpose mentioned in subsection (1) is impracticable, his place of work for the purposes of that subsection shall be any premises of his employer from which he works or from which his work is administered.'

Further, subsection (3) permits the definition of his own place of work to extend to a worker whose contract of employment has been terminated in relation to a trade dispute, or whose dismissal was a cause of the trade dispute; and subsection (4) defines the scope of trade union officials.

A number of significant points emerges. First, while the Act talks of certain action being lawful, characteristically of English labour law, the Act does not provide a legal right to picket. As with other aspects, immunities are provided in relation only to those actions which are in contemplation or furtherance of a trade dispute. This means that, given the action would have to fall within the definition of a trade dispute, picketing in the context, say, of a boycott of South African goods, or similar activities which may be regarded as political and therefore being outside the scope of the definition,

ered; nor would the immunity be extended to picketing in
ent context, such as by tenants outside the offices of their

munity provides only for picketing at or near one's place
his might appear a somewhat specific point, it is worth
noting that the provision does not allow employees to occupy, to sit in or to
work-in at a place of work. These forms of industrial action, usually
associated with attempts to resist closures and redundancies, cannot be
regarded as picketing. Liability, for instance, in relation to the civil law of
trespass, would almost invariably be present in the circumstances of an
occupation of a workplace.

Third, the definition of place of work assumes relevance in a number of
respects. For some workers, such as the classic example of lorry drivers, the
place of work is not easy to define or locate. In this context the 1980 Act
referred specifically to premises from which an employee may work, or
from which his work may be administered. For others, while the immediate
place of work may be self-evident, the employer may operate from a
number of interrelated locations; increasingly, in practice, in separate
companies forming part of an overall, interdependent organization. Often,
for such employees the need to spread the dispute to other sections of the
organization is quite pressing, and vital to the successful prosecution of the
dispute. However, given the interpretation of a place of work adopted by
the courts, there appears to be little room for doubt that lawful picketing
can take place only at the immediate workplace, and not at other
workplaces in the group; a conclusion which was reinforced in the bitter
Stockport Messenger newspaper group dispute[15] in which work was
transferred between companies in the same group, and in which picketing
by displaced employees at other workplaces in the group, was deemed to be
unlawful.

Section 16 of the Employment Act, then, can be considered as severely
restricting the ability to picket, especially in relation to secondary or
sympathetic action. Attempts to extend disputes in order to gain the
support of other workers through sympathetic action has always formed
part of the trade union response. Even though the practice of secondary
action attracted widespread publicity in the 1970s, its historical respectabil-
ity can scarcely be questioned. The 1980 Act, however, ensures that for the
present, sympathetic action enjoys immunities only in the following
contexts: when pickets at their own place of work persuade other workers,
employed by another company, not to cross the picket line; and when
workers at their own place of work organize picketing in support of other
workers who are involved in a trade dispute. The practice, therefore, of
workers from the primary dispute sending pickets to other workplaces, on
the pattern, say, of the miners picketing the power stations, would not
enjoy immunity under Section 16.

In addition to the statutory immunities, the law of picketing become more complex because of the powers of the police, in relation to what are normally described as public order offences. A picket may be behaving in such a way as to fall within the scope of Section 16 yet still be committing a criminal offence. Some of these offences may, in fact, be clearcut; an assault would most often fall into that category. There are, however, grey areas, such as aspects of threatening behaviour, obstructing the police in the course of their duty, or obstructing the highway, which can give rise to argument and, in the context of a dispute such as the 1984–85 miners' strike, a great deal of controversy. As the statistics of the Home and Scottish Offices indicate, it was these offences which were most used by the police during the miners' strike. Of some 10,000 charges brought, over 4,000 were for threatening words and behaviour, over 1,500 for obstructing the police, 1,000 for criminal damage, and 640 for obstructing the highway.

These offences illustrate the widespread powers of the police in relation to any picket or, indeed, any demonstration. It is not too great an exercise of licence to suggest that pickets are always at the mercy of the police, although, as we know, picketing is mostly tedious and without a police presence. Certain cases illustrate the width of the police powers.

In order to illustrate that a judicial restrictiveness dates back a number of years and is not just a characteristic of recent years, it might be worthwhile to point to the case of *Piddington* v *Bates* (1961) IWLR 162. In that case, a police officer felt that two pickets only were necessary at the back entrance of an employer's premises. A third person attempted to join the pickets, refusing to accept the police officer's determination that two were sufficient. A conviction for obstructing the police officer was upheld, because it was concluded that the police officer had reasonable grounds for believing that there might have been a breach of the peace unless he restricted the number of pickets to two.

It was the miners' strike which brought into sharp public focus the extent of police powers; and in no way more so than in the willingness of the police to prevent miners travelling to those pits which were still working. At its most dramatic, this power was used to prevent Kent miners travelling through the Dartford tunnel on their way to the Nottinghamshire coalfield. It would appear from *Moss and others* v *McLachlin* (1985) IRLR 76, that the police can rely upon roadblocks and arrests to prevent pickets gathering as long as they have reasonable grounds for believing that a breach of the peace is likely to occur. The reasonable grounds can arise out of what has already happened at picket lines, or what, from other information, including newspaper reports, can be reasonably anticipated to happen.

At this stage, a word about mass picketing may be appropriate. In many ways, mass picketing is a modern phenomenon, made possible by extensive access to private travel, and popularized by its implied success during the 1972 miners' strike at the Saltley power station. In relation to that dispute, it is always necessary to assess coolly the contribution made by mass picketing

f the strike; other factors, particularly the dramatic shift in
:s, can be considered as of greater significance. Effective
of the mass picket has been pursued in other contexts,
n numerous occasions.

nass picketing is such that it might be seen more as a
demonstration. The dividing line may not always be easy to establish, but
there is one defining characteristic of a mass picket: the action is designed to
persuade or to prevent others from carrying out their contract of
employment. Such an intention, it is suggested, would not be present in
relation to a demonstration.

Judicial comment on mass picketing *per se* is somewhat limited, but from
Thames and others v *NUM South Wales* (1985) IRLR 136, it is safe to
conclude that a mass picket will be regarded as unlawful because it will be
associated with unreasonable harassment. And, from *obiter dicta* by Lord
Reid in *Broome* v *DPP*, it would appear that mass picketing is likely to
constitute the criminal offence of wilful obstruction of the highway.
According to Lord Reid: 'it would not be difficult to infer as a matter of fact
that pickets who assemble in unreasonably large numbers do have the
purpose of preventing free passage. If that were the proper inference then
their presence on the highway would become unlawful.'[16]

Given the controversy and the complexity surrounding the existing law
on picketing, it is scarcely surprising that there have been both attempts to
clarify acceptable practice and to argue for reform. In relation to practice,
the most important document is the Department of Emnployment Code on
picketing.[17] Three aspects of that code are worthy of further comment: the
number of pickets, the organization of picketing, and the provision of
essential goods and services. Before looking at these detailed areas, it is
necessary to point out that the code in itself has no direct legal effect,
although it is clearly persuasive in evidential terms.

In relation to numbers, *Piddington* v *Bates* has already indicated the
extent of police powers in determining the acceptable number of pickets.
As for the Code: 'the main cause of violence and disorder on the picket line
is excessive numbers.'[18] Without denying that excessive numbers can be a
cause of disorder, it would be presumptuous to read too much into that
general statement, given that large numbers are not normally associated
with picketing. However, having defined the problem in these terms, the
Code goes on to offer the following advice: 'pickets and their organizers
should ensure that in general the number of pickets does not exceed six at
any entrance to a workplace; frequently a smaller number will be
appropriate.'[19] The conditions in which that smaller number would be
appropriate are not stated, nor is the reasoning which leads to the
conclusion that six pickets should be the maximum number. The Code
would offer greater practical assistance if these issues had been adequately
addressed.

A key role is, therefore, accorded to the picket organizer, who is seen by the authors of the Code as an experienced person, preferably a trade union official. That person should be authorized by his union, and be mainly responsible for liaison, and negotiation with the police. In addition to that pivotal task, the Code sets out five other areas of responsibility for the picket organizer:

1. To ensure that pickets understand the law and the provision of the Code and that picketing is conducted peacefully and lawfully.

2. To be responsible for distributing badges or armbands, which authorized pickets should wear so that they are clearly identified.

3. To ensure that employees from other places of work do not join the picket line and that any offers of support on the picket line from outsiders are refused.

4. To remain in close contact with his own union office, and with the offices of other unions if they are involved in the picketing.

5. To ensure that such special arrangements as may be necessary for essential supplies or maintenance are understood and observed by the pickets.[20]

This is an exhaustive and onerous set of responsibilities, with the duties in relation to essential supplies and services being strongly emphasized, partly as a result of the public sector strikes during the so-called 'winter of discontent' in 1978–79. The Code is clear as to responsibility: 'pickets should take very great care to ensure that their activities do not cause distress, hardship or inconvenience to members of the public who are not involved in the dispute.'[21] The list of essential supplies and services is itself lengthy, covering all those activities which provide, in a public context, for the young and the elderly, and which can also be seen as intrinsically related to public health and safety. While that list may not give rise to controversy, even though the pay and conditions for those providing the services may be a source of serious dispute, the overall phrase used in the Code about not causing distress, hardship or inconvenience to members of the public, may be of little value. In certain disputes, for instance in public transport, it is an inevitable consequence of an industrial dispute that public services are adversely affected. Similarly, referring once more to disputes in the coal industry, the ability to disrupt the supply of electricity has always offered the miners a potent weapon. The inability to threaten electricity supplies was central to the weakness of the miners during the 1984–85 strike.

Defining a list of essential services may be none too difficult or controversial; giving such a provision legal substance may be much more hazardous.

In addition to the three aspects to which attention has been drawn in some detail, the Code also comments on the role of the police: 'It is not the function of the police to take a view of the merits of a particular trade dispute.'[22] This statement of police neutrality would earn widespread approval. Yet, in practice, the law seems to work in such a way as to lessen the chances of the police being regarded as impartial. While on the one hand, there is clearly a duty to make it possible for people to go to work if they so wish, there is no corresponding duty to allow individuals to picket. This flows from the legislation itself which gives no legal right to picket, and from the fact that the law was drafted more than 100 years ago. At that stage, it was impossible to envisage coaches full of strike breakers, or lorries loaded with basic materials for a factory speeding through a picket line. When that happens the opportunity to persuade and to inform peacefully does not exist.

The problem posed by the practical restriction on the exercise of the right to picket was addressed by the then government in 1975 with clause 99 of the Employment Protection Bill. The clause sought to allow pickets the ability, 'to persuade any other person (whether in a vehicle or not) to stop for the purpose of peacefully obtaining or communicating information from or to that other person or peacefully persuading him to work or abstain from working.'[23]

Quite what clause 99 would have achieved is unclear. The government held it to be a 'declaratory' provision, not changing the law but making explicit what they felt to be implicit in s 15 of the 1974 Trade Union and Labour Relations Act, that pickets had a right to seek to persuade others not to enter their place of work. The clause was, however, defeated, with the Conservative opposition members of the Standing Committee objecting on the grounds that the proposed clause would, in effect, confer a right to stop vehicles; and with the government's own supporters feeling that the declaration contained in clause 99 was of no value.

As a further illustration of that viewpoint, a government backbencher, Jeff Rooker, proposed an amendment to the clause which would have allowed pickets to stop any lorry, and which would have made any lorry driver driving through the picket line guilty of breaches of the peace. For Rooker, 'the ideal of picketing, . . . is not so much to prevent people or vehicles entering a factory as to put the strikers' case, so that people may be persuaded not to enter a particular factory.'[24] The amendment would aim not just to make it possible to stop vehicles, but would, in Rooker's view, overcome some of the causes of mass picketing: 'the reason we have mass picketing . . . , is that it is realized that the only chance strikers have of even stopping a vehicle is to have mass picketing.'[25]

While the Rooker amendment was defeated, it can be argued that it sought to tackle the main difficulty inherent in the current law of picketing. Buses and lorries can be driven through picket lines, thereby effectively eliminating the possibility of peaceful persuasion, while in practice, both casting the police in such a role as to be seen as sympathetic to the employer and the strike breakers, and at the same time, inflaming passions and the feeling of impotence on the part of the pickets. That scenario can only be changed by achieving a more effective legal balance between those picketing and those wishing to cross the picket line.

For the current government, however, the desired balance must always lean towards those trying to exercise the right to work. This much is clear from the arguments used by government ministers during the course of industrial disputes. It is further reinforced by a proposal contained in 'Trade Unions and Their Members' published in February 1987:

> 'The government believes that a decision to take industrial action should be a matter for the individual. Every union member should be free to decide for himself whether or not he wishes to break his contract of employment and run the risk of dismissal without compensation. No union member should be penalized by his trade union for exercising his right to cross a picket line and go to work.'[26]

From this assertion, it is argued that the powers exercised by unions to discipline members who refuse to join in strike action should be severely curtailed. All of which scarcely suggests that both the necessary balance between the right of strikers and non-strikers, and the impartiality of the role of the police, are about to be achieved. But, without that balance, and given the complexity of the existing law, it is not unreasonable to conclude that picketing will continue to be a hazardous pursuit.

Strikes

Picketing and ballots often, but not invariably, form part of industrial action; strikes constitute but one form of industrial action. Works to rule, go slows, and overtime bans are all collective actions, usually in breach of the individual contract of employment, which seek to impose pressure upon an employer with the objective of seeking benefit or securing redress for employees. Strikes will virtually always be prosecuted as a last resort measure, as it will be in the interest of workers, who will lose financially as a result of the strike, to adopt approaches through collective bargaining and the threatened imposition of sanctions, which might provide beneficial results at little or no cost.

Before turning to the extent and causes of strikes, it would be useful to differentiate between different types of strike action. The usual categories in this respect are official and unofficial; and constitutional and unconstitutional. The distinction between official and unofficial reflects not upon the merits of a particular dispute, but upon the attitude of the union towards the stoppage. An official strike will simply be a dispute which has been officially sanctioned by the appropriate body in the union, usually the national executive committee. By definition, it follows that an unofficial dispute will not have received that sanction. However, it would be naive and misleading to conclude from this that the union officially looks askance at such disputes. Mostly, strikes are short in duration and arise more or less spontaneously from issues which have occurred at the place of work; in these circumstances they are usually resolved before a national union committee has an opportunity to meet and either to approve or disapprove. Furthermore, the fact that the strike remains unofficial can provide a full-time union official with a useful bargaining lever: while distancing the union from the action which has been taken, the official may be able to argue that his influence with his striking members will only be enhanced if management were to make an improved offer. Then, of course, he might feel in a strong enough position to advocate a return to work.

While the official/unofficial category relates to decisions which are internal to the union, the constitutional nature of strike action refers to the established industrial relations procedures for a particular firm or industry. In all collective bargaining contexts, two sets of agreements will emerge: those relating to substantive issues, such as pay and conditions, and which are subject to periodic renegotiation; and those relating to procedural matters, which are rarely changed and which provide a framework in which industrial conflict can be controlled and managed. It is against these procedural arrangements that the constitutionality of a strike is judged.

Those procedure agreements usually offer a series of steps, typically initially from the workplace to an eventual final step outside the immediate firm. Going through all these procedures can take some time, often months, and there is a great temptation or need on occasions to speed up the resolution of the dispute by taking industrial action, which would then be regarded as unconstitutional. Indeed, characteristic of strikes in the 1950s and 60s was the so-called wildcat strike: often likely to last for no more than two shifts, not sanctioned by the union, and in breach of the procedural agreements. It was this type of strike which gave rise to so much political debate in the 1960s and which was one of the main reasons for the creation of the Donovan Commission between 1965–86.

By the mid-1960s unofficial and unconstitutional strikes accounted for about 87 per cent of all workers involved in strikes, and 69 per cent of the working days lost through strike action. As Table 14.1 indicates, during the 1960s the recorded level of stoppages was regularly between 2,000 and

Table 14.1: *Recorded number of industrial stoppages 1960–1969*

1960	2832	1965	2354
1961	2686	1966	1937
1962	2449	1967	2166
1963	2068	1968	2350
1964	2524	1969	3116

Source: Department of Employment *Gazette* (various issues)

3,000 per year. The economic boom of that period, with low levels of unemployment, gave workers the ability to mount effective short strikes. From the mid 1970s, however, the pace of economic decline quickened, especially during the early years of the Thatcher government. Whether unemployment was deliberately used as a means of reducing trade union power is open to political debate; the impact of unemployment on trade union power, however, is clear. As one would anticipate, the willingness to take industrial action, given the knowledge that high unemployment often enables the employer to resist effectively, has been reduced. The pattern of a falling number of strikes emerged slowly at first, but gained pace in the 1980s with 1985 recording no more than one-third of the stoppages experienced in 1975 (see Table 14.2).

It is, of course, not just unemployment alone which has transformed the pattern of strikes in this country. Also taking place has been a significant restructuring of the economy, characterized by the decline of traditional industries in which unionization was high and in which there was a markedly above average propensity to strike; and by a growth in the service sector, which exhibits the constraining features of low unionization and a deep reluctance or little ability to take strike action. These changes, combined with the effects of high unemployment, may ensure that the experience of the 1960s with its preponderence of short unofficial strikes may not be repeated, at least, not in the near future.

Emphasis for this change has been placed upon economic factors. For some, this may be surprising given the legal constraints imposed by the Employment Acts of 1980 and 1982, and by the Trade Union Act 1984. Perhaps the legal risks are in the minds of those taking and organizing industrial action. Nevertheless, it is reasonable to suggest that in relation to the law two other factors are of more relevance: first, most people organizing and participating in industrial action expect any strike to be over in days rather than weeks; and second, there is a feeling that, even though there are well publicized cases of legal intervention in disputes, it will not happen in your case with your employer. After all, it is only a small minority of cases in which the courts are asked to intervene.

Table 14.2: *Recorded number of industrial stoppages in progress 1975–1985*

1975	2332	1980	1348
1976	2304	1981	1344
1977	2737	1982	1538
1978	2498	1983	1364
1979	2125	1984	1221
		1985	903

Source: Department of Employment *Gazette* (various issues)

Alongside the declining number of strikes, the last 20 years have experienced a re-emergence of the official strike. While unofficial action will tend to be localized, involving relatively small groups of workers, the official strike will in contrast involve more workers, often a whole industry or firm. In other words, official strikes, while remaining few in number, will influence the calculation of days lost through strike action simply because of their likely duration and numbers involved, and they will most likely attract public attention. For instance, in 1984, 27.13 million working days were lost, about seven times the annual average for the 1960s, mostly caused by the dispute in the coal industry.

Again, the most powerful explanation for this re-emergence of official strikes can be found in economic factors:

> First, because of the falling ability of the economy to afford wage increases, governments have intervened directly in the wage bargaining process, either as an employer itself in the public sector or through some form of incomes policy. The consequence of these interventions has been to restrict the scope for compromise, thereby ensuring that if a dispute takes place, it will be an official confrontation between union and government. In this way, governments have politicized industrial relations, and the traditional role of the State as umpire has been overtaken by the State as active participant.

> Second, again because of incomes policies, employers have found themselves unable to make a wage offer which may be regarded as appropriate for the particular firm's circumstances. This again is likely to produce a context in which official strike action becomes a response.

> Third, given the squeeze upon profits resulting from the economic recession and the often perceived requirement to shed labour, employers have found it necessary both in the public and the private sector to define disputes much more in principled terms rather than subject to the normal possibilities of compromise. These factors have combined to reactivate the official strike, often with an impact upon days lost, if not on the number of strikes.

The 1980s, then, can be seen as a decade in which the number of strikes was falling; but, in which because of a few lengthy official strikes, the number of days lost through industrial action would vary considerably, but would often be very high in comparison with earlier decades.

Conclusion

From the viewpoint of trade unionists, the most often expressed wish in relation to the law and the courts is that they should keep out of industrial relations practices. Sometimes that view is put forward because it is felt that lawyers possess little understanding of what happens in a factory, shop or office. On other occasions, the argument is couched in stronger terms, asserting that the courts are intrinsically anti trade union.

Regardless of whether judges reflect only the views of the narrow social class background from which they overwhelmingly originate, English law will almost inevitably appear to be against the trade unions, as the fundamental doctrine of the legal system is based upon the individual and the primacy of contract, and not upon collective interest and collective action. For this reason, the common law was never able to develop concepts out of which could have been built a set of collective rights, such as the rights to organize, to picket and to strike.

Parliament also has never intervened to shift the balance from the individual to the collective. Parliament has only felt sufficiently strong to provide immunities from the legal consequences of certain collective action. Nevertheless, that approach provided, for more than half a century, an acceptable and tolerable framework, and assisted the development of voluntarism which was so much the cornerstone of the industrial relations system.

But now it is possible to argue that the previous consensus has been destroyed, leaving little but fear and the naked parameters of an imbalance of power. The government has enthusiastically assisted in the destruction of the old consensus: by legislation which restricts immunities; by the extension of individual rights as against collective rights; and by action as employer often showing a ruthless determination not to bargain with employees. Private sector employers have been encouraged to join in; so, too, it could be argued, have the courts, which have noted not just the detail of change, but the climate of change, as well. All of this plus the government's decisions to ban union membership at its own General Communications Headquarters and to suspend the right to bargain for teachers, reflects a new philosophy of individualism.

It is that doctrine and its implementation which could challenge the basic assumptions of a pluralist society. Pluralism depends not only upon their legitimacy and viability. An approach which emphasizes the individual as against the collective threatens the very legitimacy of trade unionism, since for trade unionists, it is through collective action and strength that the individual can enhance his life chances, thereby extending freedom and opportunity. By questioning the legitimacy of collective action and interest, there is, by extension, a risk that one of the key actors in a pluralist democracy is similarly questioned. That contention is made stronger if that same key actor, the trade union, is significantly reduced in power through economic pressure and legal constraint. If the consequence of that is to be found in the inability of trade unions to deliver, the risk is that there develops in society a class whose values and interests are substantially alienated from decision-making and the sources of power.

Part of the trade union response to such a depressing scenario should be found in a vigorous campaign to gain wider acceptance of the need for collective values and action. Such a campaign would emphasize the link between the individual interest and the broader collective approach. As part of this, it may be necessary for the unions to give more thought to the legal embodiment of a right to strike. In that way, industrial action may be seen less as a deviant and subversive activity, and more as a necessary and manageable part of a pluralist democracy.

References
1. The case of the *Amalgamated Society of Railway Servants* v *Osborne* (1910) AC 87 prevented unions from financing political activity out of general funds. For this reason, the 1913 Trade Union Act developed the concept of a separate political fund, out of which political activities could be financed.
2. TUC/Labour Party 'People at Work: New Rights, New Responsibilities' London 1986
3. As reported in *The Times* 2 September 1986
4. *Annual Report* ACAS, 1985, p 15
5. See Fatchett D 'Trade Unions and Politics in the 1980s' (1987) Croom Helm, London; and Fatchett D 'Trade Union Political Funds' *Industrial Relations Journal* **15** 3, Autumn 1984
6. Reference is made to 37 unions with membership in the UK. In addition, the Scottish Carpet Workers Union also held a successful ballot
7. Leopold J 'Trade Unions Political Funds: A Retrospective Analysis' *Industrial Relations Journal* **17** 4, Winter 1986
8. As reported in *The Times* 2 September 1986
9. 'Trade Unions and their Members' Cm 95, HMSO, February 1987
10. *Ibid* para 5.29
11. *Ibid* para 5.14
12. Khan P, Lewis N, Livock R and Wiles P *Picketing – Industrial Disputes, Tactics and the Law* (1983) Routledge and Kegan Paul, London
13. Evans S 'Picketing under the Employment Acts' in Fosh P and Littler C (eds) *Industrial Relations and the Law in the 1980s. Issues and Future Trends* (1985) Garner Alenshurst
14. National Council for Civil Liberties, *Civil Liberties and the Miners Dispute; first report of the Independent Inquiry* London 1984
15. *Messenger Newspapers Group Ltd* v *NGA* (1984, IRLR 397)
16. (1974), ICR 84 90
17. 'Picketing' Code of Practice, Department of Employment, 1980
18. *Ibid* para 29
19. *Ibid* para 31
20. *Ibid* para 34
21. *Ibid* para 37
22. *Ibid* para 26
23. Minutes of Standing Committee F, 17 July 1975, col 1488
24. *Ibid* col 1488
25. *Ibid* para 2.22
26. *Ibid* para 2.22

Chapter 15

Unfair Dismissal and Tribunals

Paul Lewis

The aim of this chapter is to provide industrial relations practitioners, whether managers or union officials, with a description of the essential requirements of the law on unfair dismissal in order to help them to avoid being caught up in tribunal cases. The chapter relates to the law as at 1 August 1988.

Purposes of the Legislation

The law on unfair dismissal was first introduced by the Industrial Relations Act 1971, and has been in operation since the end of February 1972. It currently appears as Ss 54–80 of the Employment Protection (Consolidation) Act 1978 (EP(C)A). At the level of the individual, the aim is to provide employees with a measure of job security. Thus, the emphasis in the statute is upon reinstatement as a remedy if the employee is found to have been unfairly dismissed. The legislation also has its purposes as far as collective labour relations are concerned. At this level the aims are to reduce the number of strikes over dismissals and to encourage the parties to collective bargaining to develop and improve voluntary procedures. The mechanisms for achieving the latter are the ACAS Code of Practice* and the provision for good voluntary agreements to be substituted for the legislation through ministerial exemption Orders.†

The Law in Practice‡

We do not know how many dismissals occur each year but a government committee estimated that there were three million, including redundancies, in the late 1960s.[1] Since the number of unfair dismissal applications

---

* *Disciplinary Practice and Procedures in Employment* ACAS, 1977, HMSO, London. ACAS has also produced an advisory handbook on discipline. This complements the Code but has no legal status. *Discipline at Work* (1987), ACAS, London.
† Employment Protection (Consolidation) Act 1978 c 44, s 65.
‡ The statistics in the text are taken from *Employment Gazette* October 1987, pp 498–502, HMSO, London, and relate to 1986–87, the most recent year for which figures are available.

disposed of in a year (1986–87) is only 29,392 the likelihood of a dismissed employee or a dismissing employer being involved in a tribunal application is quite small. Even if they are so involved there is more likelihood of a withdrawal or a conciliated settlement than an appearance at a tribunal hearing. In 1986–87 the 29,392 applications were disposed of in the following ways: withdrawn, 8,866 (30 per cent); agreed settlement, 10,459 (36 per cent); decided by tribunals, 9,287 (32 per cent); disposed of otherwise, 780 (2 per cent).

Thirty-four per cent of applicants obtained findings of unfair dismissal in the cases decided by tribunals in 1986–87. Of these 3,129 successful applicants only 103 secured reinstatement or re-engagement,* although there were 749 cases in which the remedy was left to the parties to sort out themselves and the outcome is unknown. Past experience suggests that only a few of these will result in reinstatement or re-engagement. The main reason for this appears to be that by the time a hearing is held – typically three to four months after the dismissal† – the applicant is not keen on going back to his former employer. The passage of time and the adversarial nature of the proceedings harden attitudes and result in irreparable damage being done to the parties' relationship.[2] It has also been alleged that tribunals are reluctant to award the re-employment remedy, although no direct evidence exists on this point.[3] The average (median) level of compensation in 1986–87 was £1,805. Outcomes in the agreed settlements followed a pattern similar to that of the tribunal-decided cases. Few cases result in re-employment. The usual outcome is a cash settlement, the median level being lower than the average tribunal award.

There is no means by which the law can force an employer to re-employ an unfairly dismissed employee. In the event of an employer's failure to abide by a tribunal's re-employment order the only remedy available to the applicant is increased compensation.

The contract of employment

Although the law on unfair dismissal is provided for by Act of Parliament the role played by the judicially-decided common law is also significant. It is so in three ways.

First, the essence of the employment relationship in law is still the contract, written or unwritten, between the employer and the individual employee. The distinguishing feature of the contract is that the employee

---

* Reinstatement means that the employee is treated in all respects as if he had not been dismissed, while re-engagement allows some difference in the terms and conditions on which the employee returns, including in the job itself. Re-employment is a generic term covering both of the above.

† In 1984–85, 59 per cent of cases took under 12 weeks from receipt of application by regional offices of industrial tribunals to the date of a (first) hearing. *Annual Report of the Council on Tribunals 1984–85* House of Commons Paper No 54, HMSO, London, p 22.

agrees to work for wages or salary, in exchange for the employer agreeing to pay wages or salary for the work that is done. Thus, every employee has a contract of employment even though no Act of Parliament decrees this.

Second, the terms of the contract, including implied terms* inserted historically by the judiciary, will have an important bearing on such matters as the duties of the employee and the place and hours of work. Thus, although the issue to be decided may be whether or not the dismissal is fair, in practice it may turn on the terms of the contract and what rights the employer or employee has. For example, whether an employee can refuse to obey an order from the employer will depend largely on whether the order is legitimate as part of the contract. Similarly, an employer who wishes to move an employee to another site within the company will have to look at whether or not the employee's contract specifies one particular place of work. Such contractual considerations will heavily influence the question of whether or not a dismissal is fair because employers can operate freely within the contract, but in theory contractual changes need to be agreed. In practice, however, employers can often change the contract terms unilaterally, dismiss employees who refuse to accept the change and still avoid a finding of unfair dismissal by arguing that the change was 'in the interests of the business'. In effect, the courts have decided that the employee has an implied contractual duty to cooperate in change.

Third, to some extent the institutions operating the legislation have defined important concepts with ideas based on contract. For example, the test for a constructive dismissal† is contract-based. Moreover, there is a redundancy if fewer employees are required to do not that particular job but the jobs that could be done under the terms of the contract.

Clearly, unfair dismissal law involves an interplay of statutory provision and common law. It should not, however, be confused with the common law concept of wrongful dismissal, which means that dismissal has not been in accordance with the terms of the contract. All other things being equal, a dismissal with less notice than that specified in the contract would be a wrongful dismissal, as would be a dismissal before the expiry of a fixed-term contract which had no provision for termination by notice. By contrast, a dismissal is unfair if it fails to meet the statutory tests, even though common law contract influences, as we have seen, may be at work. Employees will generally find the unfair dismissal provisions to be more useful than a claim for wrongful dismissal. However, wrongful dismissal may be relevant to

---

* These are terms which courts and tribunals treat as being part of the contract of employment, but which were not expressly stated by the parties. The aim of the courts is to decide what the parties intended in the absence of express agreement (see Chapter 16, p 354).

† A constructive dismissal is termination by the employee, with or without notice, in circumstances where the employee is entitled to terminate the contract without notice because of the employer's conduct.

those not covered by the unfair dismissal law, and may be preferred by high earners, especially if they are on fixed-term contracts or have long notice periods, and find the statutory maximum compensation to be restrictive.

Exclusions

The coverage of the legislation is much more limited than many people believe. The following are excluded:

Anyone who is not an employee.

Anyone who is employed for fewer than 16 hours a week (but see below).

Anyone who has reached normal retiring age. Where there is a normal retiring age and it is the same for men and women, that age applies even if it is different from 65. In any other case 65 will apply.[4]

Anyone with less than two years' employment with their present employer if that employment started on or after 1 June 1985. (Anyone who started their employment on 31 May 1985 or earlier will already have sufficient qualifying employment.)

Anyone who is the subject of a certificate excepting them from the legislation in the interests of national security or confirming that they have been dismissed for that same reason.

Anyone in a number of specified occupations, namely registered dock workers, the police, the armed forces and share fishermen.

Those who ordinarily work outside Great Britain.

Those with contracts for a fixed term of one year or more who have agreed in writing to waive their rights.

Those covered by a dismissal procedure which is exempted from the legislation by ministerial Order.

Anyone who has made an agreement to refrain from complaining to a tribunal 'where a conciliation officer has taken action'.[5] Normally an agreement to exclude unfair dismissal rights is void. A mutual termination by consent, to avoid the act of dismissal, was such an agreement, and was therefore void, according to the Court of Appeal, in *Igbo* v *Johnson Matthey Chemicals Ltd*.

Anyone whose employment contract has an illegal purpose (eg to defraud the Inland Revenue). An unknowingly illegal contract may not restrict statutory rights.[6]

It should be noted that the legislation does apply to Crown Servants, and to House of Commons staff. An employee is defined as, 'an individual who has entered into or works under (or, where the employment has ceased, worked under) a contract of employment'. A contract of employment means 'a contract of service or apprenticeship'.[7]

Unfortunately this does not get us very far, since the critical question – 'How is it to be decided if the worker is employed under a contract of service?' – is left unanswered. In fact the common law of contract provides some tests to be applied, although no single test is generally conclusive. The issue is whether the worker is an employee, working for an employer under a contract of employment (or service), or a person in business on his own account providing services for a customer under a contract for services. Tribunals are likely to consider the following:

Who has the right to control the manner of work?

Is the worker integrated into the structure of the organization?

Whose business is it – who takes the risks, who takes the profits?

Who provides the tools, instruments and equipment? (However, some employees by custom provide their own tools.)

Is the employer entitled to exclusive service?

Are there wages, sick pay and holiday pay? If yes, who pays them? A fixed payment for a specified period suggests a contract of employment. Payment by task argues for a contract for services, but not conclusively.

Who has the power to: select and appoint; dismiss; fix the place and time of work; fix the time of holidays?

Is PAYE deducted?

Is there a mutual obligation – the employee to work, the employer to provide it? (*Nethermere (St Neots) Ltd* v *Gardiner and Taverna*.)

Until recently the question was one of fact for the tribunal to decide, and could be appealed only if there was an error of law (*O'Kelly* v *Trusthouse Forte Plc*). This includes a tribunal coming to a conclusion that no reasonable tribunal could have come to on the evidence before it. The House of Lords has ruled, however, that whether a person is an employee is a matter of law (*Davies* v *Presbyterian Church of Wales*). The tribunal will examine and decide the real nature of the relationship on the facts even if the parties have themselves agreed, for example, that the worker is self-employed (*Oyston Estate Agency Ltd* v *Trundle*).

The hours qualification arises out of the legal definition of continuous employment.[8] An employee must either be employed for 16 hours or more per week, or work under a contract which normally involves employment for 16 hours or more. Those with five years' continuous employment enjoy continuity if the contract is for eight or more hours per week. Continuity is also preserved where there are gaps in the employment contract because of incapacity, a temporary cessation of work (*Ford* v *Warwickshire County Council*), custom or arrangement and pregnancy or confinement. However, separate contracts with the same employer cannot be aggregated to obtain sufficient hours and therefore sufficient continuous qualifying employment (*Surrey County Council* v *Lewis*). There is no continuous employment qualification if the dismissal is for reason of race, sex, trade unionism or non-unionism, and the qualification is one month where the dismissal is on medical grounds specified in Schedule 1 of the EP(C)A. It should be noted that continuous employment begins when the contract of employment commences, rather than when the employee actually starts to do the work (*The General of the Salvation Army* v *Dewsbury*).

Meaning of dismissal

Deciding whether or not there has been a dismissal is a matter of fact for tribunals (*Martin* v *MBS Fastenings (Glynwed) Distribution Ltd*). Dismissal is defined as:

Termination of the contract by the employer with or without notice.

The expiry of a fixed-term contract without renewal.

Constructive dismissal (see p 338).

Failure to permit a woman to return to work after confinement.

The effective date of termination (EDT) is when any notice expires or, if there is no notice, the actual date of termination. Oral notice starts on the day after it is given (*West* v *Kneels Ltd*). A distinction can be drawn between wages in lieu of notice and situations where notice is given but the employee is not required to work it. In the latter case termination is on the expiry of the (unworked) notice (*Adams* v *GKN Sankey Ltd*). Even when an appeals procedure has been followed the termination will normally conform to the above rules (*Savage* v *J Sainsbury Ltd*) unless the contract of employment provides for continuation until the procedure is exhausted, in which case the dismissal prior to appeal is conditional (*Greenall Whitley Plc* v *Carr*). The EDT was on conclusion of the appeal in *Lang* v *Devon General Ltd*. In *British Railways Board* v *Batchelor* the appeals procedure was part of the contract of employment, but the words 'dismissal with immediate effect' meant that the EDT was prior to the appeal, even though the dismissal might have involved a breach of contract.

Where notice given by the employer is less than the statutory minimum, the EDT (for the purposes of qualifying employment for unfair dismissal and written reasons claims, and the calculation of the basic award) becomes the date on which the statutory minimum notice would have expired. In constructive dismissals the EDT is at the end of whatever period of notice the employer would have had to give if he had dismissed on the date of the employee giving notice or terminating (whichever applied). None of the above removes the employer's right to dismiss summarily (ie without notice or wages in lieu of notice) for gross misconduct. What constitutes gross misconduct is a matter of fact for tribunals to decide (*Dalton* v *Burton's Gold Medal Biscuits Ltd*). For the woman refused her right to return to work the dismissal is taken as having effect on the notified day of return.

It should be noted that sometimes the contract of employment can end because one party is no longer capable of performing it in the way the parties envisaged. This is called 'frustration'. The circumstances are likely to be external, unforeseen and not the fault of either party (*Paal Wilson & Co v Partenreederei*). Long-term illness is an example. Recently a borstal sentence was frustration in *F C Shepherd & Co Ltd v Jerrom*. The contract may be said to be frustrated after the passage of time. The significance of frustration is that it is not a dismissal, therefore no question of unfair dismissal or redundancy would arise. The expiry of a fixed-term contract is itself a dismissal. Such a contract must have definite starting and finishing dates, although there may be provision for termination by notice within its period (*BBC v Dixon*). This contrasts with a 'task' contract which is discharged by performance. Its expiry does not constitute a dismissal (*Wiltshire County Council v NATFHE and Guy*).

Remedies other than an unfair dismissal claim

Before looking at the essence of unfair dismissal law, it should be noted that a person who is dismissed might have a remedy under public law. Where a person's rights are affected by a decision made by 'someone empowered by public law' judges may enforce duties or quash decisions if they are, for example, illegal, irrational or procedurally deficient (*Associated Provincial Picture Houses Ltd v Wednesbury Corporation; Council of Civil Service Unions and others v The Minister for the Civil Service*). Such 'judicial review' has an advantage over unfair dismissal law for the dismissed person, in that it allows the dismissal to be reversed. The general rule is that this remedy is available only where there is no other means of challenging the decision in question. Exceptionally, however, courts will depart from this rule, as in *Calveley and ors v Merseyside Police*, where decisions to dismiss were quashed by the Court of Appeal.

Finally, the courts will exceptionally grant an injunction restraining dismissal. Such cases are rare because it is not thought desirable to order specific performance of a contract against the wishes of one of the parties. Special circumstances need to apply, as they did in *Hill v C A Parsons & Co* in 1971. Recently, there is some evidence that the courts may be more willing to grant such injunctions. In *Irani v Southampton and South-West Hampshire Area Health Authority* there were again special grounds: there was still confidence between employer and employee, a disputes procedure was available, and damages would not have been adequate as a remedy. An injunction was also granted in *Powell v London Borough of Brent*. The injunctions in *Hill*, *Irani* and *Powell* were all temporary.

When is a Dismissal Fair?

The two-stage process
The essence of the law on unfair dismissal is the right of the employee not to be unfairly dismissed by his employer. The employee has this right

regardless of whether or not he is in a union. In deciding cases, industrial tribunals go through a two-stage process. They ask: has the employer established a fair reason for the dismissal? did the employer act reasonably or unreasonably?

The starting point is to ask when a dismissal is fair, rather than when it is unfair. This is because the statute defines fairness rather than unfairness. The fair reasons for dismissal – the first stage of the process – are:

1. The capability or qualifications of the employee.
2. The conduct of the employee.
3. The employee was redundant.
4. The employee could not continue in his work without contravention of a statutory duty or restriction.
5. Some other substantial reason (SOSR).

If an employer cannot establish a fair reason his case will fall. On the other hand, if a tribunal is satisfied that one of these reasons has been shown, it must then decide whether the employer acted reasonably or unreasonably in treating it as a sufficient reason for dismissal. The second stage of the process, therefore, is a test of reasonableness. The statute says little about reasonableness except that tribunals must take into account, 'the size and administrative resources of the employer's undertaking', and decide the issue, 'in accordance with equity and the substantial merits of the case'.[9]

The onus of proof for establishing a fair reason lies with the employer. The employee may, however, wish to bring evidence and put arguments in order to challenge the reason put forward. On reasonableness the onus of proof is neutral. Both parties will need to present arguments and evidence on this point. If the act of dismissal itself is denied the employee will be responsible for establishing dismissal within the meaning of the Act. The employee will also be responsible for proof of loss for compensation purposes.

The fair reasons

Capability

It is fair to dismiss an employee on the grounds of capability or qualifications, but subject to the test of reasonableness. Capability refers to 'skill, aptitude, health or any other physical or mental quality'. Qualifications means any 'degree, diploma or other academic, technical or professional qualification'.[10] In practice, dismissals on the grounds of capability fall into two categories: those involving incompetence or lack of skill; those arising from ill-health.

In cases of incompetence, where the poor performance is something over which the employee himself has control, there should be warnings and a chance to improve. Employers must ensure that adequate training has been provided, and that the employee knows the standard that is required of him. Evidence of the employee's incompetence will be needed, although obviously quantitative measures will not always be possible. Loss of confidence in an employee, more likely in a management position, can amount to incompetence. Dismissal of a probationary employee is less likely to come before the tribunals because of the two-year qualifying period for claimants. The employer will generally find he has a greater freedom to dismiss in such cases, although warnings and evidence will still be required.

In ill-health dismissals much depends on the context. A dismissal in a small firm will often be fair, while in a larger firm, where the work can be 'covered', it may well be unfair. The nature of the job will be a consideration too: is it a relatively low level job which can be covered, or a senior position which is difficult to fill except by permanent replacement? At some stage, provided a proper procedure has been followed, an ill-health dismissal is likely to be fair. The procedural necessities were set out in *East Lindsey District Council* v *Daubney*. The employer should:

> Discuss the situation with the employee to establish what the illness is and when the employee will be fit to return to work.

> Obtain medical evidence about the employee's condition.

> Look for, but not necessarily provide alternative work.

Alcoholism, as opposed to drunkenness or drinking at work, ought to be dealt with as sickness rather than misconduct. The medical position and prospects for rehabilitation will need to be investigated.

Conduct
This is probably the most common reason put forward for dismissal, and ranges from the mundane (clocking offences, theft, drunkenness, fighting) to the more unusual (having long hair, not wearing a tie properly, and even losing the company cat). The EAT has set out what it considers is the correct approach for tribunals to take. Known as the *British Home Stores* v *Burchell* test and endorsed by the Court of Appeal in *W Weddel & Co Ltd* v *Tepper*, it requires the tribunal to ask:

> Did the employer have 'a reasonable suspicion amounting to a belief' that the employee had committed the misconduct, at the time the dismissal decision was taken?

> Did the employer have reasonable grounds for this belief?

> Did the employer carry out a reasonable investigation?

These three requirements – belief, reasonable grounds and reasonable investigation – are widely applied by tribunals. As a result there is a duty imposed upon employers to handle misconduct cases with some care, although they will not be expected to establish an employee's guilt 'beyond all reasonable doubt' as would be necessary in the Crown Court.

Certain offences normally attract the label 'gross misconduct'. These include theft, physical violence, drunkenness, breach of confidence and refusal to carry out a legitimate order. Negligence on the part of the employee does not necessarily amount to gross misconduct (*Dietmann* v *London Borough of Brent*). The penalty of summary dismissal is often attached to gross misconduct. However, this does not mean that proper procedure can be dispensed with; an opportunity to explain will be necessary in most cases (*W & J Wass Ltd* v *Binns*). There should always be a full investigation and a chance for the employee to put his case.

Typically, the employee will have been sent home following the misconduct. A period of suspension therefore can be used to gather the facts, hear the employee's side of the story and arrive at a decision. That decision would not be at risk, if the employee's misconduct is criminal, simply by virtue of an acquittal in the Crown Court. The Court and the tribunal are deciding different issues, and different degrees of proof are necessary. An employee may be not guilty, but the employer may still have dismissed fairly, and vice versa. What is considered 'gross misconduct' should be stated clearly in the rules, and if dismissal is automatic for any offence this should be made known. Ultimately, however, a tribunal will apply the test of reasonableness, so the rules themselves need to be reasonable. Some cases of theft, for example, may be relatively minor and may not justify dismissal.

In cases of physical violence employers will not only need to apply the *BHS* v *Burchell* criteria but also make sure that there is fairness of treatment between the offending parties. The degree of violence involved, the location of the fight, and the previous records of those involved need to be taken into account. Drunkenness or drinking is another common form of misconduct. Here the *BHS* v *Burchell* test directs the employer to ask:

Is the employee unfit for work?

Have I reasonable grounds for that belief?

Have I carried out a reasonable investigation?

If there is any doubt a warning or suspension may be more appropriate. On the other hand, if there is no doubt, and the person is a danger to himself or others, or commits some other serious offence while drunk, a tribunal is likely to consider a dismissal fair. Again, though, the rules need to be clear and drawn to the attention of employees. If it can be shown that management often turned a 'blind eye' to this sort of occurrence there may be doubts about their reasonableness in dismissing.

Another form of misconduct is breach of trust. A typical example is working part-time for a competitor. This would be a breach of contract on the part of the employee, but the dismissal, it is submitted, should still be subject to the second-stage test of reasonableness. The same applies to the refusal to carry out a legitimate order from management, that is, one within the terms of the contract of employment. Here, the important issue for both employers and employees is the content of the contract. Employers may, however, be able to change the contract terms unilaterally (see SOSR).

Not all misconduct is gross. 'Good' disciplinary rules and procedures will carefully distinguish, by examples, between gross misconduct (usually subject to dismissal) and other misconduct. An employee's record and length of employment should be taken into account. Absence will have to be either persistent or excessive. The employee should keep the employer informed of developments (eg reason for absence and how long it is likely to last), but in any case the employer ought to initiate contact early on, and maintain it regularly. Management should also make clear what level of absence is tolerable, and what can happen to those who exceed it. Warnings should be used, with a chance to improve.

Some misconduct outside the workplace may justify dismissal. It will usually have to be of a serious, criminal nature, and even then it may not justify dismissal. It will have to be shown that the misconduct damaged the basis of trust between the employer and employee, or harmed the employer's reputation. For those in manual jobs in large companies it may be difficult to sustain such arguments. If, however, there is some degree of relevance between the offence and the job the employee performs, a dismissal may indeed be justified. The seriousness of the offence, and the employee's record, however, are of importance.

In the absence of clear evidence of rejection of works rules by employees or their representatives the rules will become part of the contract of employment. Silence is consent. Breach of rules will be difficult to defend, especially if the employer has evidence (eg signature for receipt) that a rulebook was given to the employee. The assumption is that the employee will have read the rules. Nevertheless, employees may argue that the rules are not enforced in practice, or that they are unclear or unreasonable. Occasionally they may succeed with the argument that a rule was not known.

Redundancy
Redundancy is defined in the EP(C)A as a dismissal which is 'attributable wholly or mainly to':

> An actual or intended cessation of business, either generally, or in the place in which the employee is employed

or

> An actual or expected diminution in the requirements of the business for employees to carry out 'work of a particular kind', either generally, or in the place in which the employee is employed.[11]

The expiry of a fixed-term contract could be dismissal for redundancy if redundancy was the reason for non-renewal. A properly carried out dismissal by reason of redundancy will be a fair dismissal, although the employee, if qualified, may be entitled to a statutory redundancy payment (see Chapter 16). Properly carried out in this context means that the dismissal passes the general test of reasonableness, and in addition satisfies the selection requirements laid down in the statute. These are that selection must not be: because of the employee's proposed or actual union membership or activities; because of union non-membership; in contravention of a customary arrangement; in contravention of an agreed procedure.

If the selection fails on any of these points the dismissal is automatically unfair, and the Stage 2 test of reasonableness is not applied. Otherwise, reasonableness must be judged, and this can include selection criteria (*Bessenden Properties Ltd* v *Corness*). In examining whether there has been a breach of customary arrangement or agreed procedure it should be noted that such a breach is permissible if there are 'special reasons' justifying it.

In practice, employers will have to substantiate any arguments they put forward for special reasons by, for example, reference to the needs of the business. Employees, on the other hand, will need to provide evidence to establish a customary arrangement. Agreed procedures will normally apply only in unionized workplaces. If there is no customary arrangement and no agreed procedure, the employer has a free hand in selection, subject to the general test of reasonableness.

In the context of a dismissal for redundancy, reasonableness is governed in part by the 1972 Industrial Relations Code of Practice. This states, among other things, that responsibility for deciding the size of the workforce rests with management.[12] Moreover, case law has established that redundancy is essentially a management prerogative, and in the absence of bad faith there will normally be no challenge to it (*Moon* v *Homeworthy Furniture (Northern) Ltd*). The fact of needing fewer employees is what matters; once this has been established few tribunals will put the reasons under a microscope. The statutory rights of unions in this field are limited to advance warning and consultation; there is no legal right to a share in decision-making.

More generally on the question of reasonableness the Code of Practice states that, 'as far as is consistent with operational efficiency and the success of the undertaking management should . . . seek to avoid redundancies' by, for example, restricting recruitment, reducing overtime, using short-time working and transferring people to other work. If redundancy becomes necessary there should be consultation with employees or their representatives (see *Graham* v *ABF Ltd*). In non-union workplaces, it may be deemed unreasonable if the employee is not consulted and given some advance warning. An employee called in to the manager's office at 9.20 am, told for the first time of his redundancy, and departing at 9.30 am the same morning may be unfairly dismissed. Reasonableness will also include an investigation of the possibility of alternative work. The larger the organization, the more demanding will be the tribunal's requirements on this point, but ultimately there is no obligation to provide alternative employment (*MANWEB* v *Taylor*).

Reasonableness will include method of selection. Last in, first out (LIFO) would be reasonable. Tribunals will want to identify the candidates for redundancy and to know the criteria used for selecting between them. They will also want to know how the selection was operated, and by whom. In general, they will look for an objective approach, which includes taking into account length of employment. It may be however that a tribunal will apply the 'any difference' test to deficiencies such as lack of consultation and failure to investigate alternative employment prospects (*British United Shoe Machinery Co Ltd* v *Clarke*). The difference may be perceived as simply a postponement of the redundancy. This would give rise to a finding of unfair dismissal with compensation limited to the period during which the redundancy would have been delayed. The 'any difference' test should not be applied to the question of whether or not the dismissal is unfair, but may legitimately affect the compensation (*Polkey* v *A E Dayton Services Ltd*).

In 1982 the EAT laid down some guidelines in *Williams and others* v *Comp Air Maxam Ltd*. These comprised the need for advance warning, consultation, objective selection criteria, fair selection process and examination of possible alternative work. Subsequent decisions make it clear that the absence of one or more of these will not necessarily lead to a finding of unfair dismissal.

Contravention of statutory duty or restriction

This reason is likely to apply, for example, to people who drive on the public road as part or the whole of their job. Loss of licence means that they cannot do this job without a breach of law. Or does it? The employer should check that there would in fact be a breach of statute and seek expert advice if there is any doubt. Second, can the job be done by that person in any other way, for example, by using public transport? If driving is only a small part of the job this may be feasible. Moreover, the general Stage 2 test of reasonableness applies: has the employee been warned of the risks of losing his job if he loses his licence? Has the employer looked at the possibility of alternative work? Has proper procedure been invoked? Are there mitigating factors such as a good record and long 'service'?

Some other substantial reason (SOSR)

The dismissal of a temporary replacement for someone on maternity leave or someone suspended on medical grounds specified in Schedule 1 of the EP(C)A would be a dismissal for SOSR if the replacement was informed in writing at the outset that they would be dismissed on the return of the absent employee. A dismissal for economic, technical or organizational reasons arising out of a transfer of undertaking is also a dismissal for SOSR.

The main application of SOSR, however, is where the employer seeks to change employees' terms and conditions of employment unilaterally as a result of some form of reorganization. The justification for doing this, which is usually accepted by tribunals, is the need for business efficiency or financial saving (*Hollister* v *National Farmers' Union*). The financial problems facing firms in the 1980s have greatly influenced tribunals in this respect but management will need to show a 'sound business reason' for introducing the change, and evidence of some advance consultation with employees. Moreover, anyone dismissed for not agreeing to the change will need to be given due procedural rights – investigation of their circumstances, warnings, right to put their case, right of appeal etc. In other words, the test of reasonableness will have to be satisfied.

It is possible that an employee may justifiably resign as a result of the employer's actions, and claim constructive dismissal. A finding of constructive dismissal may result, but it will not necessarily give rise to an unfair dismissal (see p 338). Where the reorganization leads to a requirement for fewer employees this will be a redundancy. The employee who is confronted by an imposed change in terms and conditions of employment (eg a wage reduction) may of course invoke common law procedures in order to obtain remedy. In the light of the employer's repudiation of contract the employee may continue working and sue for damages for the breach (*Ferodo Ltd* v *Rigby*). Changing terms by terminating existing contracts and offering re-engagement on new terms opens the door to successful unfair dismissal claims as in *Gilham and ors* v *Kent County Council*.

The expiry of a fixed-term contract can be SOSR. The employer will need to show: that he had a genuine need for a fixed-term contract in the first place; why that reason has ceased to operate. The dismissal would then have to stand the test of reasonableness. As noted earlier, a dismissal as a result of the expiry of a fixed-term contract could be for reason of redundancy rather than SOSR.

SOSR could include the dismissal of people with personal characteristics that are unconventional or socially unacceptable. Such people have little protection unless the characteristics have no bearing at all on the work situation. In fact, employers will nearly always argue that such factors do have a bearing because, for example, of the effect on relationships with other employees and/or customers. Because of this it remains to be seen whether the dismissal of AIDS virus carriers will be unfair, as the Employment Minister seems to think.[13] The dilemma for people with 'something to hide' is that hiding it will help them obtain a job, but after discovery by the employer the deceit will count against them in any unfair dismissal claim. The Rehabilitation of Offenders Act 1974 offers protection to some of those who have criminal records. Another issue assuming prominence is the introduction of rules prohibiting smoking at the workplace. Such rules will need to be introduced in a reasonable way, including the provision of adequate notice. A tribunal has recently found that an employee's resignation, because such a rule was to be introduced, did not constitute constructive dismissal (*Rogers* v *Wicks and Wilson Ltd*). There was no implied contractual term giving a right to smoke. The company was carrying out its duties under the Health and Safety at Work Act 1974. The consequences of breaking a no-smoking rule will have to be made clear to employees, and any dismissal will be subject to the general test of reasonableness.

Reasonableness

The ACAS Code on Disciplinary Practice and Procedures in Employment, and a wealth, if not a surfeit of case law, provide a clear indication of what is meant by reasonable. In short it means:

Following proper disciplinary procedure, including carrying out a reasonable investigation.

Being consistent in the application of discipline.

That the disciplinary action taken needs to be appropriate for the particular case or, to borrow a phrase from criminal law, the punishment must fit the crime.

Taking into account any mitigating circumstances (eg long service, good record, provocation).

The standard of proof required is that facts need to be established on the balance of probabilities.

The ACAS Code

This was issued under the Employment Protection Act, 1975, and has been in operation since 1977. A failure to observe the Code does not render anyone liable, but in tribunal proceedings the Code is admissible and, where relevant, must be taken into account by the tribunal.

The Code deals with both rules and procedures. The former set standards of conduct at work, the latter provide means of dealing with a failure to meet those standards. On rules the Code states that: they should be reasonable; they should be readily available; management should do all it can to ensure that employees know and understand them; management should make employees aware of the likely consequences of breaking any particular rule. Faced with an industrial tribunal management will want to be able to give positive answers on these points. From the employee's point of view, however, each of the above provides a potential mitigating factor to be offset against their breach of discipline.

The Code states that procedures should be speedy and in writing. They should indicate the range of disciplinary action and specify which levels of management have authority to take particular action. Immediate superiors should not have power to dismiss without reference to senior management. The Code goes on to detail a number of requirements which have become quite prominent in the deliberations of industrial tribunals:

The employee has a right to know the charges against him, and to have an opportunity to state his case – principles derived from the concept of 'natural justice'. See *Pritchett and Dyjasek* v *J McIntyre Ltd*, however, in which these requirements were not met but the dismissal was nevertheless judged to be fair.

He has a right to be accompanied by a union representative or some other person.

Except for gross misconduct there should be no dismissal for a first offence. Instead, a system of oral and written warnings should be used. A warning, however, is not just a general exhortation to improve. It spells out the offence and indicates what will or may happen if it recurs, or if there is no improvement.

There should be a careful investigation before any disciplinary action is taken.

The reasons for the choice of disciplinary penalty should be explained to the employee.

The employee should be given a right of appeal, and told of this right, and how to exercise it.

The Code distinguishes between suspension with pay while an alleged breach is being investigated, and the use of suspension without pay as a disciplinary penalty. Criminal offences outside employment should not be taken as automatic reasons for dismissal. The main consideration is whether it makes the employee unsuitable or unacceptable in his employment. Records of disciplinary breaches should be kept, as should details of warnings (including oral ones) and disciplinary penalties. Although records may be kept, the 'slate' ought to be wiped clean after a period of satisfactory conduct. The length of the period is not specified in the Code.

Case law

The Code distinguishes the punitive aspect of a procedure from its role in encouraging an improvement in conduct. Tribunals have, in fact, added the chance to 'make good' or improve to the questions they are likely to ask of an employer. They have also been influenced by the principles of 'natural justice' (see above). These include the requirement that nobody should be a judge in their own interest. This is significant particularly in relation to appeals. It prevents those taking the original decision from being involved in any subsequent appeal against that decision. An appeals body should act in 'good faith' (*Khanum* v *Mid-Glamorgan Area Health Authority*). Refusal to grant a right of appeal which is part of the contract of employment may lead to a finding of unfair dismissal (*Tipton* v *West Midlands Co-operative Society*; but see *British Railways Board* v *Batchelor*).

The reference in the statute to 'equity' has been taken as the basis for the need for consistency of treatment as part of reasonableness (*The Post Office* v *Fennell*). In practice, some degree of inconsistency may be reasonable if the facts of different individual cases can be distinguished, as in *British Steel Corporation* v *Griffin*. Taking into account the 'size and administrative resources of the . . . undertaking' may affect such factors as the offering of alternative work, but is not an excuse for the absence of a proper investigation.

Although the tribunals and appeal courts have been active in determining the principles of good disciplinary practice there has nevertheless been a tendency – especially during the latter half of the 17 years in which the legislation has been operative – for breaches of good practice to be more leniently viewed. In the early days the maxim applied in some cases was that a breach of disciplinary procedure made an otherwise fair dismissal automatically unfair. Since then appeals have produced the doctrine that breach of procedure is an important factor to be taken into account, but does not necessarily make an otherwise fair dismissal unfair. It may or may not do (*Tipton* v *West Midlands Co-operative Society*). The approach to be adopted, as laid down by the appellate courts, is as follows:

> The tribunal should not put itself in place of the respondent and say what it would have done if it, the tribunal, had been the employer.
>
> Rather, it should note that for any disciplinary offence there will be, among employers, a range of reasonable responses (*British Leyland (UK) Ltd* v *Swift*).
>
> The tribunal should ask itself if the response of the employer before it falls within that range.
>
> If it does, the employer has behaved reasonably.
>
> If, on the other hand, no reasonable employer would have behaved in that way, the employer before it has behaved unreasonably.

Until recently, a further complication in the approach to the question of reasonableness had been the operation of the 'any difference' test (*British Labour Pump Co Ltd* v *Byrne; W & J Wass Ltd* v *Binns*). If there has been a breach of procedure this test asks whether the proper application of procedure would have made any difference to the outcome. For example, would dismissal have been averted if the applicant had had an opportunity to state his case, or if a warning had been given? Often the answer has been that it would have made no difference, or at best that it would have delayed the dismissal (eg pending fuller investigation). As a result of the House of Lords' ruling in *Polkey*, however, the application of the 'any difference' test may be restricted to questions of compensation. The substantive matter of the fairness or otherwise of the dismissal will be decided according to the statutory tests, ie a fair reason and reasonableness. Exceptionally, perhaps, an employer may be able to dispense with the procedural niceties on 'no difference' grounds and still be reasonable.

The *Polkey* decision should restore to procedural propriety some of its former importance. As the Court of Appeal noted in one of the cases arising out of the 1984–85 Miners' Strike, not even a heated industrial dispute is an excuse for serious procedural flaws (*McLaren* v *National Coal Board*).

In *W Devis & Sons Ltd* v *Atkins* it was decided that post-dismissal evidence not connected with the reason which the employer gave for the dismissal could not be admitted except in the determination of compensation. Similarly, the test of reasonableness is to be applied to the employer's behaviour at the time of the dismissal, on the basis of the facts that he had at his disposal, or should have had if a reasonable investigation had been carried out. However, post-dismissal facts which emerge during any internal appeal can be taken into account in deciding reasonableness (*Tipton* v *West Midlands Co-operative Society*). Ultimately, reasonableness is a question of fact for the tribunal to determine (*Union of Construction, Allied Trades and Technicians* v *Brain*).

Special Cases

We have stressed the two-stage process of unfair dismissal law involving the establishing of a fair reason, and the satisfying of the test of reasonableness. We now have to add the fact that some dismissals are not subject to this process because the statute provides specifically for them.

Automatically unfair dismissals

In certain cases the statute instructs that dismissals are to be regarded as automatically unfair once the reason for dismissal is established. This applies to:

Dismissals on grounds of proposed or actual trade union membership or activity, or proposed or actual non-membership. (Prior to the operation of the Employment Act 1988, the dismissal of a non-unionist in a 'closed shop' could sometimes be fair.[14])

Unfair selection for redundancy (already described, pp 329–30 above).

Dismissals on grounds of pregnancy.

Dismissals on grounds of union activity or membership or non-union membership are not subject to the requirement for qualifying employment nor to the usual age limits. If the applicant has the normal qualifying employment the onus of proof lies with the respondent (*Shannon* v *Michelin (Belfast) Ltd*). Otherwise it lies with the applicant (*Smith* v *The Chairman and other councillors of Hayle Town Council*). Even in the former circumstances however the applicant will have to adduce evidence that the reason for dismissal was trade unionism, as well as rebutting the employer's reason.

It is not surprising that trade union dismissals are difficult to prove, and that the success rate for applicants is well below the average for all unfair dismissal claims.[15] A factor in this has been the restrictive interpretation of trade union activity by the courts, as in *Chant* v *Aquaboats Ltd*. The statute says that union activities must be at the 'appropriate time' if they are to be protected – namely, outside working hours, or in working hours with the employer's agreement or consent – but does not say what constitutes such activities. The courts have ruled, for example, that these activities do not include the actions of the union itself (*Therm-A-Stor Ltd* v *Atkins and others*) or the acts of a union member not done formally within the union's responsibility (*Drew* v *St Edmundsbury Borough Council*). The protection is given to employees. It does not cover the recruitment process in the way that the Sex Discrimination Act 1975 does. The person refused employment because of a union record or union membership therefore has no remedy.

A non-unionist has the right not to be dismissed for refusing to make a payment (eg to a charity) in lieu of a union subscription.

In pregnancy dismissals the employer has the following defences:

At the date of termination of employment the employee could no longer do her work adequately.

That she could not have continued working after termination of employment without contravening a statute (eg The Health and Safety at Work Act 1974).

Even if one of the above applies, the employer or successor must still offer suitable alternative employment, if there is any, on terms which 'are not substantially less favourable to her'. The onus of proof will be upon the employer to show that he made a suitable offer, or that there was no suitable available vacancy. Selection for redundancy on grounds of pregnancy will automatically be unfair dismissal following the House of Lords' ruling in *Brown* v *Stockton on Tees Borough Council*, and in any case opens up the prospect of a claim on grounds of sex discrimination (*Hayes* v *Malleable Working Men's Club*).

In addition to the automatically unfair dismissals mentioned above there are some further 'special cases'. These are: dismissal of strikers; constructive dismissals; failure to permit a woman to return to work after confinement; dismissals associated with transfers of undertakings.

Dismissal in connection with industrial action

Dismissal in connection with a lock-out, strike or other industrial action is largely excluded from unfair dismissal law. It is explicitly put outside the jurisdiction of the tribunals unless certain features apply. These features relate to selectivity of treatment of those taking the action. If everyone is treated the same, no complaint of unfair dismissal can be heard by the tribunal. If, however, some are dismissed and others are not, there is a possible unfair dismissal claim. The selectivity must apply, however, at the time of the complainant's dismissal, rather than from the beginning of the strike. Thus, if 100 people go on strike, and all are still on strike a month later, the dismissal of the six strike leaders will give rise to unfair dismissal claims. The dismissal of all 100 will not. Moreover, if 40 people had returned to work after a month, the dismissal of the remaining 60 would not give rise to claims, since there was no selectivity among those on strike at the time of the dismissal.

Where all strikers are dismissed, but only some are re-engaged, the critical factor will be the time interval between the dismissal of those re-engaged and their re-engagement. If this period is three months or more, none of the people who have not been re-engaged will have a claim. It can be seen that the employer can be selective in dismissing strikers without giving rise to any unfair dismissal claims. Whether a person is taking part in industrial action is a matter of fact for the tribunal to decide (*Coates and Venables* v *Modern Methods and Materials Ltd*). The law regards a strike as breach of contract (*Simmons* v *Hoover*).

Constructive dismissals

Constructive dismissals were mentioned earlier when we looked at what was meant by a dismissal. It is important to note not only that the onus of proof will be upon the applicant, but also that the two-stage process does not apply. Instead, the test is whether there has been a breach of contract (*Western Excavating (ECC) Ltd* v *Sharp*). In other words, the judicial bodies have replaced the statutory test with a traditional, common law test. This, however, establishes only the fact of dismissal, and not its fairness or otherwise.

It has to be stated that, perhaps surprisingly, constructive dismissals are not automatically unfair (*Savoia* v *Chiltern Herb Farms Ltd*; see also *Vose* v *South Sefton Health Authority*). The employer may argue that it was necessary to change the contract of employment unilaterally in the interests of the business. This would have special weight if the business was 'in trouble' or had to make specified savings. Other breaches would be less easy to defend, for example, breach of trust (an implied contractual term; *Woods* v *W M Car Service (Peterborough) Ltd*), abusive language, failure to provide proper safety arrangements or reducing an employee's pay and/or status. Of course (as noted earlier, p 332) the employee does not have to resign and claim constructive dismissal (ie accept the employer's repudiation of contract). He can affirm the contract, either accepting the change, or rejecting it but carrying on working and suing for damages (*Ferodo Ltd* v *Rigby*).

Refusal of right to return to work after confinement

Next, there is the position of the woman who is refused her right to return to work after confinement. We noted earlier that this was part of the statutory definition of dismissal. It will not be treated as dismissal, however, if: the employer has five or fewer employees; and it was not reasonably practicable to allow her to return to work or offer her alternative employment on 'terms not substantially less favourable to her'. Nor will it be a dismissal, irrespective of the size of firm, if it is not reasonably practicable to take her back, but she is offered alternative employment which she unreasonably refuses. The onus is upon the employer to show that there was no dismissal.

*Dismissals in connection with transfers of undertakings**

Finally, there is the question of dismissals in connection with the transfer of undertakings. Regulations issued under the European Communities Act 1972, apply where there is a legal change of owner, but not where there is simply a change in the ownership of share capital. Undertaking includes 'any trade or business . . . in the nature of a commercial venture'.[16] Contracts of employment automatically transfer with the business, as do rights and duties under the contract, including continuity of employment. Dismissals arising out of the transfer are automatically unfair, unless there is some economic, technical or organizational reason for them 'entailing changes in the workforce'. Such a reason, including redundancy, would constitute SOSR. Thus, the mere change of identity of the employer does not give an employee the right to resign and claim unfair dismissal or redundancy. However, a detrimental and substantial change to the employee's working conditions will give a right to claim unfair dismissal.

Industrial Tribunals

Industrial tribunals are statutory judicial bodies. They were first established under the Industrial Training Act of 1964 to hear employers' appeals against levies made by the various training boards that were set up under the Act. Since then the tribunals have been given the task of deciding many other types of disputes, typically those between individual employees and their employers. In addition to handling unfair dismissal cases, tribunals deal with disputes about whether an employee is receiving the amount of redundancy pay to which he is entitled, claims for equal pay between men and women, time off for union representatives, allegations of race and sex discrimination in the employment field and other issues put within their

* See also Chapter 16, pp 352–53.

jurisdiction by various statutes. Unfair dismissal complaints account for about three-quarters of the tribunals' caseload.

Tribunals currently operate as a result of the Employment Protection (Consolidation) Act 1978,[17] with most of the procedural details set out in regulations issued under that Act.[18] Except in rare cases tribunals comprise three people: one from a panel nominated by the unions, one from a panel nominated by the employers, and a legally-qualified chairman. The chairman is appointed by the Lord Chancellor (Lord President in Scotland), while the two other members are appointed by the Secretary of State for Employment. At the end of March 1985 there were 66 full-time chairmen, 132 part-time chairmen and 2,053 lay members. All the lay members are part-time. The purpose of having a combination of lay members and a lawyer is to get a blend of legal knowledge and industrial experience. A majority decision suffices, but in all except a handful of cases the decision is unanimous.

The tribunal process is triggered off by an individual who thinks he has been unfairly dismissed completing an originating application form, known as an IT.1, and sending it to the Central Office of the Industrial Tribunals (COIT) within three months of the effective date of termination. An application may arrive later than this if it was not reasonably practicable to apply within three months but in practice tribunals enforce the three-month rule quite strictly. The individual may or may not have already exercised his separate legal right to request and obtain from his former employer a written statement of the reasons for the dismissal. This right is given to those who had six months* or more continuous employment with their employer prior to termination. The claim for compensation for failure to give written reasons is usually put on the same IT.1 as the unfair dismissal claim itself, and must be at COIT within three months. The respondent employer has 14 days in which to reply to the request for written reasons. An unreasonable failure to comply will result in a tribunal making a penalty award of two weeks' pay. The two weeks' pay is gross, and since the right to have written reasons is separate from the right not to be unfairly dismissed there is no percentage deduction for any contributory fault. The award will usually be made at the end of the hearing of the substantive unfair dismissal claim.

Regardless of whether a request for a written statement of reasons has been made, the respondent employer will need to reply to the originating application. A copy of the IT.1 will be sent to him, and a form IT.3 on which the reply can be made. The IT.3, known as the Notice of Appearance, should be returned to the specified regional office (or sub-office) within 14 days. This act secures for the respondent the right to take part in any hearing which might ensue. A copy of the IT.3 is sent to the applicant. The regional office of the industrial tribunals then sets in train the arrangements for a hearing. A brief questionnaire is sent to the parties asking about representation at the hearing, and about the number of witnesses they will

* This is likely to be increased to two years as a result of what will become the Employment Act, 1989.

be bringing. Finally, the regional office will fix a date for a hearing and notify the parties.

The above description constitutes the minimum of what might happen. There may be more. First, COIT will notify an applicant if it looks as though the case is not within the tribunals' jurisdiction, and will indicate that the case may be struck out unless the applicant confirms in writing that he is determined to go ahead. Second, the regional chairman may decide that a full hearing of the case should not go ahead until there has been a pre-hearing assessment (PHA). This device was introduced in order to prevent meritless cases being pursued. It can be requested by either party, or ordered by the chairman of his own volition. A PHA involves the full tribunal in a brief, perhaps 30-minute hearing, at which the arguments are put, but little or no evidence is given. The regulations say that the tribunal may consider the IT.1, the IT.3, any representations in writing and any oral argument. If the tribunal considers that a party's case has 'no reasonable prospect of success', it may warn that party of the possibility of costs being awarded against it if it continues. The outcome of a PHA therefore is either a 'costs warning' or no such warning. The working of the PHA system during 1986–87 shows that 80 per cent of those applicants given a costs warning subsequently withdrew or settled. Only 15 per cent of those given a costs warning who continued through to the full hearing were successful, and almost two-fifths of the 85 per cent who lost had costs actually awarded against them. In any particular case, the tribunal dealing with the PHA will have a different membership from that dealing with any subsequent hearing.

A Department of Employment *Consultation Paper on Industrial Tribunals* in May 1988 stated that PHAs had not worked as well as had been expected.[19] It proposed their abolition, with replacement by a pre-hearing review conducted by a tribunal chairman. In a case which had no reasonable prospect of success, or was frivolous, vexatious or otherwise unreasonable, the chairman would have the power to require a deposit of up to £150 from that party. The deposit would be returned unless that party lost at the tribunal hearing and had costs awarded against it. The consultation paper also proposed a more investigative role for tribunals, and the payment of interest on awards. These changes are likely to be effected by what will become the Employment Act, 1989. The latter is provided for by the Employment Act 1982, but has not been activated.[20].

Irrespective of whether or not the case involves a PHA there may be a preliminary matter to settle before a full hearing of the case is considered. Such matters usually concern eligibility:

Is the applicant an employee?

Was the IT.1 received in time?

Has the employee the requisite length of qualifying employment?

Is the applicant under normal retiring age?

If there is no PHA, and there is no preliminary matter to decide, the parties will not meet the tribunal until the full hearing. They might, however, meet the chairman if there are any procedural difficulties. Such difficulties might arise if the parties choose to implement the interlocutory procedure. This procedure allows the parties to deal with each other, requesting and providing information, and exchanging documents. Ultimately there may be an agreed bundle of documents. In the event of a refusal to cooperate by one of the parties, a tribunal order may be sought by the other.

The tribunal regulations allow orders for discovery and inspection of documents, and for further particulars of the grounds of the case. Discovery means finding out what documents the other side is relying upon, while inspection is the right to see one or more of those documents. If the other party refuses, it will be necessary to make out a case to the regional chairman, and a hearing in Chambers (ie in the chairman's room) will be held at which his decision will be given. The other members of the tribunal are not present. The same process will be necessary if the other party refuses to provide further particulars of their case.

The tribunal may also compel witnesses to attend. Application for witness orders is made to the chairman. If the orders are granted they will be sent to the party requesting them and that party serves them on the witnesses. (The tribunal serves them in Scotland.) Failure to abide by tribunal orders is a criminal offence punishable by fine.

There is an important role for ACAS. Copies of the papers – the IT.1 and the IT.3 – are sent to the regional office of ACAS. The purpose of this is to allow ACAS to perform its statutory duty, which is to conciliate. The duty is: 'to endeavour to promote a settlement of the complaint without its being determined by an industrial tribunal'.[21] The duty to conciliate applies if ACAS is requested to do it by the parties, or in the absence of such a request, if the conciliation officer considers that there is 'a reasonable prospect of success'. Where it is sought by the applicant, and where it is 'practicable', the conciliation officer must try to promote re-employment rather than a cash settlement.

ACAS defines conciliation in the way that the process is commonly understood. The essential features are that the outcome (ie the agreement) is a joint decision of the two parties, the employee and the employer, and that the conciliator does not impose nor even recommend what the particular outcome should be. In 1984 almost half of unfair dismissal applications resulted in agreed settlements, although these were nearly all in the form of cash compensation rather than re-employment. The tribunal may promulgate the agreed decision.

Any information conveyed to a conciliation officer is privileged – it cannot be admitted in evidence at the hearing without the permission of the person who communicated it. Moreover, it should be noted that once ACAS has conciliated and an agreed settlement has been reached, the right to pursue the case through to a tribunal hearing is lost. The same is not true if the settlement is agreed without ACAS. The ACAS role can continue until all questions of liability and remedy have been decided (*Courage Take Home Trade Ltd* v *Keys*). This means that ACAS could be used to conciliate over compensation if the tribunal decides unfair dismissal but leaves it to the parties to settle compensation.

Since settlements tend to be in the form of a sum of money, it is useful to have some idea of what a tribunal might award. In most cases tribunal awards comprise two elements, namely:

1. *A basic award* calculated in the same way as a statutory redundancy payment (RP), ie according to age, length of employment and earnings, but with the one-twelfth reduction operating from the age of 64 in the case of both men and women, unlike RPs where the ages are different (64 and 59). (But see Chapter 16 p 346.) The maximum basic award from 1 April 1989 is £5,160.*

2. *As compensatory award* arrived at by establishing the applicant's net loss as a result of the dismissal. The maximum possible under this head from 1 April 1989 is £8,925.

It may be more difficult for the respondent to do this calculation, since only the applicant will know the detail of his own losses, and in any case future loss is something of an imponderable. Nevertheless, a rough estimate will inform the bargaining process.

The parties may represent themselves or be represented by a person of their own choosing. Because legal representation is not compulsory, legal fees can be avoided. Legal advice is available under the Legal Aid and Advice Scheme, but legal aid (including representation) is not. The normal legal rule under which the loser pays the victor's costs does not apply. Costs will be awarded only if a party acts frivolously (ie pursues a hopeless case), vexatiously (ie pursues a case in order to inconvenience the other party) or behaves unreasonably in some other way.

Legal procedure is used. This means that the representative will proceed by examining witnesses (ie asking them questions). Each witness is examined first by the representative of the party for whom he, the witness, is appearing. Then he will be examined by the representative of the other 'side' (ie cross-examined). At this stage the tribunal may well ask some questions. Finally, the witness may be re-examined by the representative of his own 'side'. Representatives will need to be familiar with the substance of the law and with the procedure of industrial tribunals.

* In dismissals on grounds of union membership or non-membership there is also a minimum basic award. From 1 April 1989 this is £2,520.

References

1. '*Dismissal Procedures' Report of a Committee of the National Joint Advisory Council*' Ministry of Labour, HMSO, London, 1967

2. Lewis P 'An Analysis of why legislation has failed to provide employment protection for unfairly dismissed employees' *British Journal of Industrial Relations* **XIX** 3, November 1981, The London School of Economics and Political Science, pp 316–26
3. Dickens L, Jones M, Weekes B and Hart M *Dismissed* (1985) Basil Blackwell, Oxford, p 114
4. Sex Discrimination Act, 1986 c 59, s 3
5. EP(C)A, s 140(2)(e)
6. Wedderburn Lord *The Worker and the Law*, 3rd edition (1986) Penguin Books, Harmondsworth, p 235
7. EP(C)A, s 153
8. EP(C)A, Schedule 13
9. EP(C)A, s 57(3)
10. EP(C)A, s 57(4)
11. EP(C)A, s 81
12. 'Industrial Relations Code of Practice' HMSO, London, 1972, para 44 (pp 11–12)
13. *The Guardian* 25 November 1986, p 3
14. Employment Act 1988 c 19, s 11
15. Wedderburn, p 313
16. The Transfer of Undertakings (Protection of Employment) Regulations, Regulation 2, SI 1981/1794, HMSO, London, 1981
17. EP(C)A, s 128
18. The Industrial Tribunals (Rules of Procedure) Regulations, SI 1985/16, HMSO, London, 1985
19. See para 2 of *Consultation Paper on Industrial Tribunals* Department of Employment London, 16 May 1988. The contents of the paper became embodied in an Employment Bill in November 1988.
20. Employment Act 1982 c 46, Schedule 3, para 7
21. EP(C)A, s 134

Chapter 16

Other Individual Rights

Paul Lewis

In the main this chapter is concerned with the rights of the individual employee or worker. From time to time, however, we shall make a departure to deal with the rights of trade union members (in relation both to employers and their own unions) and sometimes the rights of unions as given to their officials. As we noted in Chapter 15, the common law contract of employment is still the essence of the employment relationship, therefore we shall examine contractual as well as statutory rights.

We provide a broad survey of the legislation at the expense of much detail. In particular, little space is devoted to legislation the essential character of which is unchanged (eg redundancy payments) or which has had minimal usage (eg the law on itemized pay statements). Instead, space is devoted to areas which have been the subject of substantial change (eg equal pay; payment of wages) or caused difficulty of interpretation (eg transfers of undertakings). Social security law (including pensions, sick pay and maternity pay) and data protection are excluded. The chapter relates to the law as at 1 August 1988.

Statutory Employment Rights

Redundancy[1]

An employee dismissed by reason of redundancy (see definition in Chapter 15 p 329) may be entitled to a statutory redundancy payment (RP). To qualify the employee must have been continuously employed by the employer (or an associated employer) for two years or more and be under 65 years old (60 years for women) but see below. Employment before the age of 18 does not count towards continuous employment. Those working under a contract for less than 16 hours per week are excluded, unless there have been five or more years of continuous employment at eight or more hours. Share fishermen, registered dockworkers, Crown Servants, NHS employees, most merchant seamen and certain other miscellaneous categories are also excluded.

A redundancy payment is calculated by taking the number of years' employment in each of the age ranges in Table 16.1 and multiplying by the

Table 16.1: *Formula for computation of RPs*

Age	No of weeks' pay
under 22	½
22–40	1
41 and over	1½

appropriate number of weeks' pay. No employment beyond 20 years is counted, so the maximum payment is $20 \times 1\frac{1}{2} = 30$ weeks' pay. There is a maximum level of weekly pay which is counted. From 1 April 1989 this will be £172. Where a week's pay varies with the amount of work done an average hourly rate is to be calculated over the last 12 weeks of employment. In such circumstances overtime hours are to be included, but must be treated as if paid at the non-premium rate. This can give rise to the anomaly of those working overtime having a lower hourly rate for RP (and unfair dismissal basic award) purposes than those who do not work overtime (*British Coal Corporation* v *1. Cheesbrough 2. Secretary of State for Employment*).

The RP is reduced by one-twelfth for each month beyond the age of 59 (women) and 64 (men). However, in *Hammersmith & Queen Charlotte's Special Health Authority* v *Cato* the EAT ruled that such a provision in the NHS redundancy scheme was a contravention of European Law. On 29 October 1987 the government announced that the age limit for Statutory RPs would be set at 65 for both sexes, unless there was a lower, non-discriminatory normal retiring age (NRA). The reduction of one-twelfth would start at 64 or one year before NRA (whichever applied) for both sexes.*

An employee has six months in which to claim an RP by applying to an industrial tribunal or writing to the employer. The employee will lose any right to an RP, however, if the employer offers 'suitable' alternative employment and the employee 'unreasonably' refuses it. Where the terms of the new employment differ from those of the old there is a requirement for a 'trial period' of at least four weeks to establish whether the employment is suitable, without loss of entitlement to claim the RP.

An employee may claim a payment, or any unpaid part of it, direct from the Redundancy Fund after taking all reasonable steps (other than legal proceedings) to recover the payment from the employer, or when the employer is insolvent. An employer with fewer than 10 employees, who meets an RP claim for an eligible employee, is entitled to a rebate from the Fund equal to 35 per cent of the statutory RP.[2]

An employee given notice of dismissal by reason of redundancy may be entitled to a reasonable amount of time off before the expiry of that notice

* This is likely to be given effect by what will become the Employment Act, 1989.

in order to look for new employment or make arrangements for training for future employment.

Maternity

There is no minimum qualifying employment for the right to ante-natal time-off.[3] The woman must have an appointment. For any second or subsequent appointment she must provide a medical certificate as proof of pregnancy, and evidence of the appointment (eg an appointment card).

The right to return to work applies until the end of the period of 29 weeks beginning with the week in which the child is born, although it may be extended in certain circumstances.[4] The qualifying period of employment is two years at 16 or more hours, or five years at eight or more, up to the eleventh week before the expected week of confinement, as medically certified. The woman must continue to be employed, but does not necessarily have to be at work, up to the eleventh week before confinement. She must inform the employer of her intention to return, and her expected (or actual) week of confinement. This must be done in writing at least 21 days before maternity absence, or as soon as it is reasonably practicable. If requested by the employer she must produce for inspection the medical certificate showing the expected week of confinement. The employer has the right to send a written request within 49 days from the notified date of the beginning of confinement asking for confirmation of intention to return. He must explain that a failure to give written confirmation within 14 days (or as soon after as is reasonably practicable) will lose her the right to return. She must in any case notify the employer in writing of her proposed date of return at least 21 days beforehand.

The right to return will not apply if there has been a redundancy and there is no suitable alternative work, or an offer of such work is unreasonably refused. Similarly, if the employer can argue that it is not reasonably practicable to take the woman back in her original job, but that he has offered suitable alternative work which she has unreasonably rejected, the right to return will be lost. An employer with five or fewer employees can argue that it was not reasonably practicable to take her back nor to offer her suitable alternative work. Suitable means that the terms, conditions and location are not substantially less favourable than those of her employment prior to maternity absence.

Access to medical reports

The Access to Medical Reports Act 1988 c 28 is operational from 1 January 1989. Its relevance will be where an employer requests a medical report from a medical practitioner in respect of an employee or prospective employee. The individual's consent is needed and the individual can have access to the report. He may veto it or arrange for its amendment. A major uncertainty is whether the act will apply to company doctors as well as to the individual's own GP. Actions will lie in the County Court.

Time off for public duties[5]

An employee is entitled to time off for duties arising out of holding one of the following public positions: JP; local government councillor; member of a statutory tribunal; member of a health authority or family practitioner committee; member of a water or river authority. The amount of time off is what is 'reasonable in all the circumstances'. There is no obligation upon an employer to pay for the time off.

Payment of wages

This is an area which has been radically altered by the Wages Act, 1986.[6] There is now a general restriction on deductions from wages which applies to both manual and non-manual workers. There is no qualifying period of employment or minimum number of hours of work, and the rights extend to Crown employees and workers in the NHS. A deduction from wages may not be made unless it is authorized by Statute, or by a relevant provision of the worker's contract, or by the worker himself in advance, in writing.

A copy of the appropriate contractual term, or notification of it in writing, must be given to the worker in advance of any deduction. Neither contractual changes nor the worker's agreement can be used to authorize deductions retrospectively.

The term 'wages' includes weekly and monthly pay, and includes salaries. It includes any holiday pay, commission, bonuses and other pay, whether contractual or non-contractual as well as statutory sick and maternity pay and various statutory payments such as guarantee pay and pay for time off. It does not include advances of wages, payments of expenses, pensions, *ex gratia* payments, redundancy payments or payment to the worker otherwise than in his capacity as a worker. Payments or benefits in kind are excluded from wages, except for vouchers with a fixed monetary value (eg luncheon vouchers) which are capable of being exchanged for money, goods or services.

Certain deductions from wages are not subject to the above rules, such as deductions to obtain recovery of overpayment of wages (although this will not necessarily be lawful), agreed deductions payable to third parties (eg a union), deductions arising from industrial action.

In addition to the general restrictions on deductions, there are special restrictions applicable to retail employment. This includes not just shop assistants but many others handling money, for example bus conductors, drivers who collect fares, cashiers, ticket clerks. These apply to deductions for cash shortages or stock deficiencies, including those arising from the dishonesty or negligence of the worker. The deduction is limited to 10 per cent of gross wages on any pay day, although there is no limit at the termination of employment. Deductions, or the first of a series of deductions, must be made within 12 months of the employer's discovery of the shortage or deficiency, or from any earlier date when the employer ought reasonably to have made the discovery.

Both the general and the special retail rules governing deductions apply equally to employers' demands for payments. The employer may take the usual steps for recovery providing that within the 12-month period he made a written demand, on a pay day, showing the employee's total liability. The right of application to an industrial tribunal replaces the worker's right to go to the County Court over the matters contained in the Wages Act.

An unresolved question is whether the Wages Act can be used by workers to recover monies which have not been paid at all (eg wages, holiday pay) as well as deductions. The information available suggests that tribunals are restricting themselves to a literal interpretation of the word 'deductions', and are avoiding straying into the area of contractual debts (*Shepperd* v *Saxon Home Heating*; *Jenks, Jenks and Jenks* v *Meltstore Ltd*). (Provision was made in 1978 in s 131 of the Employment Protection (Consolidation) Act for tribunals to judge contractual matters, but this section has not been activated.)

The repeal of the Truck Acts means that manual workers no longer have a statutory right to be paid in cash. The issue will be subject entirely to matters of employment contract and union-employer negotiation. It may well be that those employees paid in cash have an implied term in their contracts that cash will be the method of payment. The imposition of cashless pay, therefore, could result in claims for damages for breach of contract. For employees starting on or after 1 January 1987 employers are likely to insist on cashless pay as part of the contract, unless unions can persuade them otherwise. The repeal of the Truck Acts has no bearing on the frequency of pay (ie weekly or monthly), which remains a matter of contract and collective bargaining.

The Wages Act 1986 does not affect the employee's right under the 1978 EP(C)A to have an itemized pay statement.[7]

Minimum wages

There is no general minimum laid down by law. There are, however, minimum levels laid down for certain industries through the medium of Wages Councils.* Originally, trade boards, under the Trade Boards Act of 1909, they were to afford protection to employees in industries which were low paid, and where trade union organization was weak. They now operate under the Wages Act, 1986.[8] A Wages Council consists of equal numbers of employers' and workers' representatives appointed by their respective organizations, and up to five independent members, one of whom is the

* See Chapter 1, p 9.

chairman. Small business interests are specifically required to be represented on the employer's side. Wages Orders are enforceable as implied terms of the contract of employment, and implementation is monitored by a Wages Inspectorate. In fixing minimum rates Wages Councils must consider the possible effect on levels of employment. The Orders cannot be retrospective. A period of 28 days exists for objections to the proposed rate.

A worker may sue for arrears for up to six years, but the Wages Inspector can in fact institute civil proceedings on behalf of a worker. If the Wages Inspector instigates criminal proceedings the worker may obtain up to two years' arrears, and the employer may face fines of up to £400, or £2,000 if false records are kept or false statements made. Just over two million workers are covered by the Wages Council system in industries such as clothing manufacture, catering, hairdressing, toy manufacture, retail distribution and laundries. A notice of the current Wages Order must be displayed and home-workers notified. The employer must keep records. Orders may fix a single minimum rate of remuneration for basic hours and a minimum overtime rate, and set a limit on deductions in respect of living accommodation. The Orders do not apply to anyone under the age of 21. Underpayment may allow an employee to resign and claim unfair constructive dismissal. Any redundancy payment must be based on a figure no less than the statutory minimum, otherwise an application may be made to a tribunal to establish the proper amount of the payment.

Guarantee pay

The Employment Protection (Consolidation) Act of 1978 provides for a daily guarantee payment where the employer is unable to provide any work at all during a day when the employee would normally be required to work.[9]

Medical suspension

Under the EP(C)A an employee, or someone in Crown employment, who is suspended on medical grounds under one of a limited number of sets of regulations specified in Schedule 1 to the Act, has a right to be paid for up to 26 weeks.[10]

Notice periods

The EP(C)A lays down minimum notice periods.[11] The right is given to those employees with one month or more of continuous employment, and is as follows: if the continuous employment is less than two years, one week's notice; one week's notice per year of continuous employment from two years to 12. The minimum legal notice to be given where length of employment exceeds 12 years is still 12 weeks. The minimum notice which has to be given by the employee to the employer is one week. This does not increase with length of employment.

Written particulars[12]

Not later than 13 weeks after the commencement of employment the employer must give the employee a written statement of the main terms of his employment. Registered dock workers, Crown Servants (including NHS employees) and employees who normally work outside Great Britain are excluded, as is anyone working under 16 hours a week (or under eight if they have five years or more continuous employment).

The statement must identify the employer and employee, the date when the employment began, and whether any employment with a previous employer counts as continuous employment and, if so, when the continuous employment began. The following particulars have to be given:

Scale or rate of pay or method of calculating it.

Interval of payment.

Any terms and conditions relating to: hours of work; holiday pay, sufficient for holiday pay entitlement to be calculated; sick pay; pensions.

Length of notice on both sides.

The title of the job the employee is employed to perform.

If there are no terms under any of these headings the statement should say so. An additional note should specify disciplinary rules* and grievance procedures, and whether a pensions contracting-out certificate is in force.

The above details do not have to be actually provided in the statement. The statement can simply refer the employee to other documents containing the details (eg works rules, collective agreements).

Insolvency rights[13]

Insolvency rights fall into two categories: some debts are made preferential; some debts (including any unmet preferential debts) can be paid out of the Redundancy Fund.

The preferential debts are:

Wages and salaries.

Guarantee payments.

Remuneration payable on suspension on medical grounds.

Payment for time off for union duties or to look for work or arrange training on being made redundant.

Remuneration payable under a protective award.

* Small firms are likely to be exempted from this by the Employment Act, 1989.

Payment for time off for ante-natal care.

Statutory sick pay.

Certain accrued holiday pay.

The debts which may be claimed from the Redundancy Fund include arrears of pay for up to eight weeks, holiday pay for up to six weeks, notice pay, unfair dismissal basic award and statutory RP.

Transfer of undertakings[14]

The Transfer of Undertakings Regulations 1981, reverse the normal common law position that a change in ownership automatically terminates the contract of employment. Instead, the regulations state expressly that the contract of employment will continue. Thus, the mere change of identity of the employer does not give an employee the right to resign and claim an RP. The regulations apply where there is a legal change of owner, but this does not include changes in control which arise simply from changes in share ownership. The regulations apply to undertakings which are 'in the nature of a commercial venture'. Deciding what is a commercial venture is a matter of first impression for the industrial tribunal (*Woodcock and ors v 1. The Committee for the time being of the Friends School, Wigton 2. Genwise Ltd.*)

The employee's statutory rights are transferred by virtue of the Employment Protection (Consolidation) Act 1978. Maternity rights are also transferred. Liability for tortious acts (eg negligence) committed in relation to an employee also appear to transfer (see *Secretary of State for Employment* v *Spence and ors* on this general question). Criminal liabilities do not transfer, and occupational pension schemes are expressly excluded from automatic transfer. Liability for unfair dismissal or redundancy does not transfer as was thought in the early cases. In *Spence* the Court of Appeal made it clear that responsibility here would be with the transferor if the effective date of termination (EDT) predated transfer, and with the transferee if it postdated it. There might be difficulties if the transfer itself spans a period of time.

Nothing in the regulations removes the individual's right to resign and claim breach of contract, either for unfair dismissal or common law damages purposes. However, this right is circumscribed to a degree by the wording of the regulations which says that either: 'a substantial change is made in his working conditions to his detriment', or; the change in identity of the employer itself is 'significant' and 'to his detriment'.

A dismissal before or after the transfer will be automatically unfair if the reason is the transfer itself or·something connected with it. Automatic means that the second stage test of 'reasonableness' does not apply. There is, however, what appears to be a very wide exception, although recent case law may have narrowed it. The exception is that the dismissal can be justified as fair if it is for an economic, technical or organizational reason (ETO) entailing changes in the workforce. This constitutes some other substantial reason (SOSR) under dismissal law, and requires the normal second stage (ie the test of reasonableness) to be entered. The onus of proof for ETO lies with the employer. The Court of Appeal has ruled, in *Berriman* v *Delabole Slate Ltd*, that changes in the workforce mean a deliberate change in the numbers and functions of employees. This narrows ETO and was not the case in *Berriman*. It was the case, however, in *Gorictree Ltd, v Jenkinson* which also showed that dismissal for ETO can simultaneously be dismissal for redundancy giving rise to entitlement to a redundancy payment. If redundancy is the reason for dismissal, the statutory provisions relating to unfair selection will apply. Straightforward changes in terms and conditions will, it seems, not constitute ETO. In *Wheeler* v 1. *Patel* 2. *J Golding Group of Companies* the EAT held that an ETO must relate to the conduct of the business.

Collective agreeements also transfer automatically, but unless specifically provided otherwise in the agreement, these will not be legally enforceable. However, the collective agreement terms may be incorporated into individual contracts, which can be enforced (*Marley* v *Forward Trust Group Ltd*). Occupational pension schemes are again excluded from automatic transfer. Trade union recognition transfers automatically if the union is independent. Any redundancy agreement will have been transferred automatically, so in the event of a redundancy this will be relevant to the question of unfair selection. The employer has a duty to inform and consult union representatives.

The regulations are complex and a certain amount of difficulty has been encountered in operating them. For example, in *Banking, Insurance & Finance Union* v *Barclays Bank plc* a union complaint that the company failed to consult them about a transfer was dismissed because transfer of the staff and the business separately meant that no transfer had occurred for the purposes of the regulations. Also, the various rights conferred by the regulations depend on the employee being employed at the time of the transfer. There have been difficulties in deciding when a transfer occurs. In *Kestongate Ltd* v *Miller* the EAT opted for the period between exchange of contracts and completion. More recently, however, the EAT held, in the *Wheeler* case, and in *Brook Lane Finance Co* v *Bradley*, that transfer occurred on completion.

Contractual Rights

Although statute limits to some extent what can be agreed between the parties much of the substance of the employment relationship stems from express and implied contractual terms, works rules, custom and practice and, where applicable, collective agreements between unions and employers. Like the statute-imposed terms the implied terms are of particular importance because they lay down some ground rules for all employment contracts. The following obligations are prominent:

Employer	*Employee*
To pay wages for work done.	To obey the employer's lawful commands.
To take reasonable care for the employee's safety.	To take reasonable care and skill in going about the work.
	To give faithful and honest service.
	Not to act manifestly against the employer's interest.

In general, a breach of a major term will amount to a repudiation of contract which the other party may accept and treat as grounds for ending the contract. Alternatively, that party may affirm the contract and insist on its further performance (*W E Cox Toner (International) Ltd* v *Crook*). The remedies for the breach would be a claim for compensation for constructive dismissal or suing for damages. It may also be possible to affirm the contract while standing on the original terms and sue for the breach. Thus, in *Ferodo Ltd* v *Rigby* a worker continued the employment contract but sued for the damages arising out of a wage reduction imposed by the employer.

The contractual rights exist despite a body of statute law containing statutory rights, and are not replaced by them. They give rise to claims for damages for either breach of contract, or in tort – the committing of a civil wrong. The most prominent type of case is an employee's claim for damages for injuries arising out of the employer's negligence. The employer's biggest advantage in contract is the legitimacy given to his commands and the fact that many terms become part of the contract by imposition because employees fail to challenge rules or changes – 'silence is consent'.

The courts may, in any dispute about the terms of a contract, imply a term. The approach taken is that such a term should be so obvious that the parties did not feel a need to state it expressly. In practice, of course, it is difficult in the absence of express provisions, to decide what was intended by the parties. Sometimes evidence can be found in the terms of collective agreements, or in custom and practice. The former may be incorporated into the contract either expressly or by implied means. Thus, although a collective agreement is not itself legally enforceable, its terms nevertheless may be enforceable because of the process of incorporation into individual contracts of employment.

Courts will generally enforce contract terms without reference to their fairness to the respective parties, providing that the contract itself is not illegal, the terms are not made void by Statute and the contract was entered into willingly. However, in *Electronic Data Systems Ltd* v *Hubble* the Court of Appeal set aside (pending trial) a judgment of the High Court that the employee should pay a refund of training costs because he left within a specified time. This term had been contractually agreed but may be in restraint of trade.

The interplay between contract law and unfair dismissal was alluded to in Chapter 15 and we noted the granting of injunctions to prevent dismissal, albeit perhaps temporarily. It should be added that there have been a number of cases recently where employees have sought injunctions for purposes other than preventing dismissal. For example, in *Hughes and ors* v *London Borough of Southwark* social workers obtained an injunction to stop their employer transferring them to a different type of work. On the other hand, the High Court would not grant an injunction in *MacPherson* v *London Borough of Lambeth* to stop the employer withholding pay because the employees would not operate a new computer. The employees were not able and willing to perform their contractual duties.

The development of industrial action based on partial performance of duties has given prominence to another aspect of the employment contract. Can an employer deduct some, or perhaps all, of the employee's pay if there is a partial withdrawal of labour, as there was, for example, in the long-running teachers' dispute? In *Miles* v *Wakefield Metropolitan District Council* the House of Lords held that an employer may refuse to accept partial performance and may withhold all of the pay. However, if partial performance is accepted by the employer, only part of the pay may be withheld (*Wiluszynski* v *London Borough of Tower Hamlets*). A different view (but with the same effect) is that where partial performance is accepted full wages are payable, but with an amount set-off to cover the breach (*Sim* v *Rotherham Metropolitan Borough Council*).

A different aspect of contract was relevant in *Dietmann* v *London Borough of Brent*. Here the dismissal was wrongful because the disciplinary procedure had not been used, but was part of the contract of employment.

Many employees faced with a repudiatory breach of contract by an employer will prefer the simpler, quicker and cheaper route of claiming constructive unfair dismissal to processing a claim for damages. This may, perhaps, be less true where a claim for damages is compatible with continued employment, and where the legal services of a trade union are available (both of these applied in *Ferodo*). In practice, many employees will probably reluctantly accept the employer's imposed change because of the need to keep their job. Many employers will prefer a dismissal, which can be defended as fair by using a mix of contract and statute arguments, to a claim for damages against the employee. Obtaining injunctions may have important advantages for both employers and employees.

Equal Opportunities

Equal pay

The legislation operates by inserting an equality clause in the contract of employment. This means that there should be equality where a man and a woman are employed: on 'like work' – work of the same or a broadly similar nature; or on 'work rated as equivalent' – work of equal value under a non-discriminatory job evaluation scheme which must be analytical (*Bromley and ors* v *H & J Quick Ltd*); or on work which is of equal value.

The British legislation states that equal value claims are permitted only if neither 'like work' nor 'work rated as equivalent' claims are possible. In *Pickstone and ors* v *Freemans Plc*, however, the House of Lords held that this was a restriction of the wider European right to pursue an equal value claim. Thus, the present domestic law is deficient and complainants can rely on the wider European interpretation. This means, for example, that the existence of a man doing work that is the same as the complainant's does not preclude an equal value claim.

In 1982 the European Court had decided that the British Equal Pay Act was not sufficient to meet the requirements of the EEC Directive on Equal Pay[15] (*Commission of the European Economic Communities* v *UK*). A woman must be able to claim equal pay for work of equal value, hence the 1983 Regulations, operative from the beginning of January 1984 and issued under the European communities Act 1972.[16] These mean that equal pay can be claimed irrespective of the jobs being completely different, provided that the demands made (under such headings as effort, skill and decision) are of equal value. The House of Lords has rejected the argument that the whole remuneration package has to be considered, rather than just pay. The basic rate must be the same regardless of other contractual benefits (*Hayward* v *Cammell Laird Shipbuilders Ltd*).

The Act does not apply solely to pay. It extends to other terms. It also applies to both men and women. The comparator has to be in the 'same employment' as the claimant.[17] This means employed by the same (or an associated) employer at the same establishment, or at a different establishment if there are common terms (see *Leverton* v *Clwyd County Council*). It will be for the applicant to establish like work, equally rated work and the same employment. Conversely, these issues will provide a basis for the employer's defence.

If the applicant succeeds in establishing the comparison, the employer may then argue that the variation in male/female terms is nothing to do with sex. The equality clause does not operate if the variation is 'genuinely due to a material factor'. This can include economic and other factors as well as individual differences such as skills, qualifications, age and experience (*Rainey* v *Greater Glasgow Health Board*). Different pay structures may be a material factor, as in *Leverton*, and in *Reed Packaging Ltd* v *Boozer and Everhurst*. The onus of proof is on the employer to show a material factor. Such factors must be justifiable, ie caused by a real need on the part of the understaking, appropriate to meet that need and necessary (*Bilka-Kaufhaus GmbH* v *Weber*).

There appears to be no time limit for complaints made by individuals to industrial tribunals, nor, by inference, for applications by employers (*British Railways Board* v *Paul*). The Secretary of State may also take cases to the tribunals, either while the complainant is still employed or within six months of leaving. Where the claim is successful the remedies are damages, and up to two years' arrears of pay. A special procedure operates for equal value claims. First, the tribunal may dismiss the claim if it is not based on reasonable grounds,[18] or if the employer establishes a material factor defence at the outset (*Forex Neptune (Overseas) Ltd* v *Miller and ors*). Second, if the case progresses, an expert (from a panel drawn up by ACAS) will be called in to do an assessment of the value of the respective jobs, and present a report to the tribunal.

The Act is comprehensive in its application. Few occupations are excluded and there are no hours or length of employment qualifications for making a claim. It applies to those who are 'employed', which is a category wider than employees (see *Quinnen* v *Howells*).[19] It is not provided under the Act, however, for comparison with a 'notional' man, ie to argue that a man doing the same job *would* have been paid more. Until recently, equality of retirement and death provisions was excepted, apart from access to pension schemes. The Sex Discrimination Act 1986, however, considerably narrowed the exemption so that pay provisions relating to retirement and concerning demotion, dismissal, promotion, transfer or training must not be discriminatory.[20]

Race and sex discrimination

It is unlawful in relation to employment to discriminate against a person because of their sex, because they are married, or on grounds of colour, race, nationality or ethnic or national origins. Discrimination takes the following forms:[21]

Direct. Treating a person 'less favourably' than another person is or would be treated, on one of the prohibited grounds (eg colour). This includes segregation on racial grounds.

Indirect. Applying a 'requirement or condition' which is or would be applied equally (eg to women and men) but which is such that the proportion of one group (eg women) who can comply with it is 'considerably smaller' than the proportion outside that group who can comply.

Victimization. Treating a person less favourably because they have, or are suspected of having used the legislation, or because they intend to use the legislation, or have properly alleged breaches of the legislation.

The legislation referred to is the Sex Discrimination Act 1975, the Equal Pay Act 1970 and the Race Relations Act 1976. The Equal Opportunities Commission and the Commission for Racial Equality are charged with overseeing the working of the legislation, and have issued Codes of Practice for their respective areas.[22] The Race Relations Code of Practice encourages ethnic monitoring. The Court of Appeal has recently given support to this practice, and to the use of the results of monitoring for evidential purposes when claims are brought (*West Midlands Passenger Transport Executive* v *Singh*).

We have noted that the Equal Pay Act applies to terms of employment. By contrast the two other discrimination Acts apply to:

Recruitment and selection arrangements (eg a discriminatory interview as in *Brennan* v *Dewhurst Ltd*).

The terms on which jobs are offered.

Refusals to offer employment.

Opportunities for promotion, transfer or training, or access to any other benefits, facilities or services.

Dismissal or any other detriment.

The Race Relations Act additionally contains terms of employment, conferring a right equivalent to that contained in the Equal Pay Act for women.

Both Acts allow discrimination where it is a 'genuine occupational qualification'.[23] This means that a person of a particular sex, race, nationality etc can be chosen for a job because of their sex, race, nationality etc. The circumstances are limited, and there are differences between the two Acts.

There is, in addition to discrimination, a series of other unlawful acts, including discriminatory advertising, instructing or putting pressure on others to discriminate, and aiding or assisting in the committing of unlawful acts.

Remedies are obtained by applying to an industrial tribunal within three months of the act which is the subject of complaint. The tribunal may make a declaration of rights, an order for compensation and a recommendation that the respondent take a particular course of action. The maximum compensation is the same as the compensatory award for unfair dismissal. From 1 April 1989 this is £8,925. However, in a sex discrimination case involving a breach of European law, an industrial tribunal felt that it could substantially exceed the limit because the British Statute did not provide the adequate remedy required by European law (*Marshall* v *Southampton and South-West Hampshire Area Health Authority*). Some recent decisions under the Race Relations Act have emphasized that compensation can be awarded for injury to feelings and may include aggravated damages which compensate for the manner of or motive for the discrimination. Exemplary damages can also be awarded in order to punish the offender and deter others from similar unlawful conduct (*Alexander* v *The Home Office*; *Noone* v *North West Thames Regional Health Authority*; *Pratt* v *Walsall Health Authority*).

Discriminatory provisions in collective agreements and works rules are void, but discrimination in relation to death and retirement is permitted except for retirement provisions which affect promotion, demotion, dismissal, training and transfer.

Rights of Trade Unionists and Non-unionists

Action short of dismissal[24]

Employees are given a right not to have action short of dismissal taken against them by their employer: because of their actual or proposed membership of an independent trade union; because of their actual or proposed union activities; or to compel them to join a union. In addition, the non-unionist must not have action short of dismissal taken against him if he refuses to make some other payment (eg to a charity) instead of a union subscription.

It appears that paying a wage increase to members of one union, but withholding it from members of another can constitute action short of dismissal for union reasons (*Ridgway and Fairbrother* v *National Coal Board*).

Time off for union officials and members

These rights give a 'reasonable' amount of time off during working hours, and are of two types:

Paid time off for union officials for duties concerned with industrial relations between the employer and his employees, or for training for such duties.*

Time off with no obligation to pay, for union members for union activity regardless of whether or not it is related to the employer.

The term 'official' means any union representative elected in accordance with the union's rules to represent some or all of the members in a particular company or workplace. The duties which attract time off with pay are those which are carried out by the official performing his role in jointly agreed

* These rights are likely to be limited by the Employment Act, 1989.

procedures or customary arrangements for consultation, bargaining and grievance handling.[25]

Redundancy consultation

These are rights given to union officials under the Employment Protection Act 1975.[26] The union must be recognized by the particular employer, and be independent. In fact, the right is given to the 'trade union representative', which means 'an official or other person authorized to carry on collective bargaining with the employer in question by that trade union'. The employer must actually be proposing redundancy rather than just considering it if the Act is to apply. Consultation rights extend to non-unionists of the same description as the members represented by the union.

Consultation must begin 'at the earliest opportunity'. More specifically:

Where the employer proposes to make redundant 100 or more employees at one establishment within 90 days or less, the consultation must start at least 90 days before the first dismissal.

Where the number is 10 employees or more in one establishment within 30 days or less, it must start at least 30 days before the first dismissal.

The employer must also notify the Secretary of State for Employment within the above time periods. Failure to do so could result in a reduction in redundancy rebate or a fine.

The consultation process itself comprises the employer disclosing in writing to trade union representatives the whole of the following:

The reason for his proposals.

The numbers and descriptions of employees whom he proposes to dismiss.

The total numbers of such description(s) employed at that establishment.

The proposed method of selection.

The proposed method of carrying out the dismissals, having regard to any agreed procedure, and the period over which they are to take effect.

The employer must consider any representations made by the union representatives, and reply to them, stating reasons if any of them are rejected. An employer may argue that there were 'special circumstances' for failing to comply with one or more of the statutory provisions. If a tribunal finds an infringement of the statute, it must make a declaration to that effect, and may also make a 'protective award'. This is an award that the employer shall pay the employee remuneration for a protected period. An employee whose employer fails to pay him during the protected period may apply to a tribunal within three months of the last day of non-payment, and the tribunal may order the employer to pay.

Disclosure of information[27]

This is another right given to the 'trade union representative', defined in the same way as in the redundancy consultation rights. Again, the union must be independent and recognized. Union representatives have a right to information about the company which is both: information without which they would 'be to a material extent impeded' in their bargaining; and is information which it is good industrial relations practice to disclose.

An ACAS Code of Practice[28] sets out good practice as including disclosure of information on pay and benefits, conditions of service, manpower, company performance and company finance. An employer does not have to disclose information in certain circumstances, including when disclosure would cause 'substantial injury' to the company (apart from through any effect on collective bargaining).

If a union considers that an employer has failed to disclose the required information it may make a complaint to the Central Arbitration Committee. The Committee may ask ACAS to conciliate, but if that fails it will hear the complaint. If the complaint is upheld, the Committee will specify the information to be disclosed, and a period of time in which disclosure must take effect. A failure to disclose then gives the union a right to apply again to the Committee, this time for an award of improved terms and conditions. If the Committee make such an award it has effect as part of the individual employees' contracts of employment, and is enforceable.

Individuals' rights in relation to trade unions

These rights are a mixture of common law and statute. On joining a union the individual (regardless of whether they are an employee or, for example, an unemployed person) enters into a contract of membership with the union. The essence of the contract is a subscription in exchange for the provision of benefits and services. The terms of the contract are to be found in the rulebook. Thus, a member may use the ordinary courts to prevent a union breaching its own rules. A claim that the union was in breach of contract by not representing a member properly may fail because of the absence of a term in the contract on which the action could be based (*Iwanuszezak* v *General Municipal Boilermakers and Allied Trades Union*). However, a claim in tort for negligence might be possible in these sorts of circumstances.

Union rules will not reign supreme if they involve a breach of the principles of 'natural justice'. In particular a person must be told the charge against him, and be given an opportunity to put his case. Nobody hearing the appeal should have a vested interest in the decision. Nor will rules reign supreme if they conflict with a statutory provision. There is now a substantial amount of statute law governing the internal functioning of trade unions. Here we concentrate on the rights given to individuals in connection with exclusion or expulsion from unions, under the Employment Act 1980, and upon new rights conferred by the Employment Act 1988.[29]

A person unreasonably refused admission to or unreasonably expelled from a trade union in a closed shop may make a complaint to an industrial tribunal within six months of the refusal or expulsion. A tribunal will decide the matter 'in accordance with equity and the substantial merits of the case', taking into account the DE's Code of Practice on Closed Shops.[30] The matter to be decided is whether the trade union acted reasonably or unreasonably. Acting in accordance with its rules is not conclusive evidence of reasonableness, nor is acting in breach of them conclusive evidence of unreasonableness. If the tribunal upholds the complaint it will make a declaration to that effect. The individual may then make a claim for compensation after four weeks have elapsed, but within six months of the date of declaration.

More generally, the Courts have frequently granted injunctions against unions to stop them disciplining members who have refused to take part in industrial action. As a result of the operation of the Employment Act 1988, there is now a statutory right given to union members and ex-members not to be unjustifiably disciplined. This includes the right not to be disciplined for failing to participate in industrial action and applies even if the majority of members have voted in favour of the action in a ballot. The member may complain to an industrial tribunal. The act also provides that union members seeking to exercise their legal rights shall not be denied access to the courts. Moreover, the act establishes a Commissioner for the Rights of Trade Union members to help members take cases against their own unions. Members are also given rights of access to their union's detailed accounts and have the right to be accompanied by a professional adviser. Members may seek court orders if union funds are used to indemnify individuals against penalties arising from criminal offences or contempt of court, and if trustees make unlawful use of union property. There is also a right to stop employers deducting union subscriptions once union membership has been terminated.

Right to hold a ballot on the employer's premises[31]

In firms with over 20 employees an independent, recognized union has a right to hold one of the various ballots which attract public funding (eg on industrial action, NEC elections, amending rules, amalgamations) on the employer's premises. The employer must comply if it is 'reasonably practicable' to do so.

Health, Safety and Welfare

Here again is a mixture of statutory and common law rights. The main common law right arises from a term in the contract of employment which imposes upon the employer a duty of care towards the employee. A breach of this duty, coupled with detriment suffered by the employee (eg through an accident) provides the basis of a claim in tort for damages for negligence. The processing of such claims constitutes a major trade union activity.

In this area, however, unlike many others within the employment field, there is also a long history of statutory provision. The keystone of this today is the Health and Safety at work etc Act 1974, which imposes upon employers a general duty 'to ensure, so far as is reasonably practicable, the health, safety and welfare at work' of all their employees.[32] The general duty includes health and safety in relation to the:

Provision and maintenance of plant and systems of work.

Arrangements for use, handling, storage and transport of articles and substances.

Maintenance of the place of work and access to and egress from it.

Working environment.

It includes the duty to provide:

Adequate welfare facilities.

Necessary information, instruction, training and supervision.

'Reasonably practicable' involves weighing risks against the costs of prevention. Unions and employers may adduce evidence about the risks and costs involved, so influencing what is 'reasonably practicable'.

We noted that the employee had a common law duty to go about his work with reasonable care. This is supplemented by the 1974 Act which lays upon the employee a statutory duty of care and a statutory duty to cooperate with the employer or any other person in meeting the statutory requirements. The Act and other statutes are enforced by the Health and Safety Inspectors. Thus, neither individual employees nor employers can actually enforce the Act except through the Inspectorate.

Regulations under the Act allow a recognized trade union to appoint safety representatives, with specified functions:

To investigate potential hazards, dangerous occurrences and the cause of accidents.

To investigate and process members' complaints about health and safety at work.

To deal with management over general questions of health and safety.

To carry out workplace inspections.

To represent members in discussions with Inspectors.

To receive information from the Inspectors.

A Code of Practice and Guidance Notes give further detail.[33]

Safety representatives are the appropriate people to receive information from the Inspectors about particular occurrences in the workplace, and any action that Inspectors take or propose to take. The Safety representatives are given a right to time off in order to perform their functions, and also for training. A separate Code of Practice covers time off for training.[34]

Firms with five or more employees must have a written safety policy, which must be brought to the attention of employees.

References

1. Employment Protection (Consolidation) Act (EP(C)A) 1978, c 44, ss 81–120
2. Wages Act 1986, c 48, s 27. Rebates are likely to be abolished by what will become the Employment Act, 1989.
3. Employment Act 1980, c 42, s 13
4. EP(C)A, ss 45, 56
5. EP(C)A, s 29
6. Wages Act, ss 1–11
7. EP(C)A, s 8
8. Wages Act, ss 12–16
9. EP(C)A, s 12
10. EP(C)A, s 19
11. EP(C)A, s 49
12. EP(C)A, s 1
13. EP(C)A, ss 122–27; Insolvency Act 1985, c 65; Insolvency Act 1986, c 45
14. The Transfer of Undertakings (Protection of Employment) Regulations SI 1981/1794. These were issued under the European Communities Act 1972, c 68
15. No 75/117 under Article 119 of the Treaty of Rome
16. Equal Pay (Amendment) Regulations SI 1983/1794. These were issued under the European Communities Act 1972, c 68
17. Equal Pay Act (EqPA) 1970, c 41, s 1(2)
18. Equal Pay (Amendment) Regulations 1983, Regulation 3
19. EqPA, s 1(6)
20. Sex Discrimination Act (SDA) 1986, c 59, s 2
21. Sex Discrimination Act 1975, c 65, ss 1, 3, 4; Race Relations Act (RRA) 1976, c 74, ss 1–2
22. *Race Relations Code of Practice* Commission for Racial Equality, London, 1983; *Sex Discrimination Code of Practice* Equal Opportunities Commission, Manchester, 1985
23. SDA 1975, s 7; SDA 1986, s 1(2); RRA 1976, s 5
24. EP(C)A, s 23
25. *Time off for trade union duties and activities* ACAS Code of Practice 3, London, 1977
26. Employment Protection Act 1975, c 71, s 99
27. Employment Protection Act, s 17

28. *Disclosure of information to trade unions for collective bargaining purposes* ACAS Code of Practice 2, London, 1977
29. Employment Act 1980, ss 4–5; Employment Act 1988, c 19, Part I
30. *Closed Shop Agreements and Arrangements* Department of Employment Code of Practice, London, 1983. The Government has said that it will produce a consultation document in the spring of 1989 proposing that the closed shop be outlawed.
31. Employment Act 1980, s 2
32. Health and Safety at Work etc Act 1974, c 37, s 2(1)
33. *Safety Representatives and Safety Committees Regulations* SI 1977/500
34. *Code of Practice on time off for the training of safety representatives* Health and Safety Commission, London, 1978

List of Cases Cited

Adams v *GKN Sankey Ltd* EAT (1980) IRLR 416

Alexander v *The Home Office* (1988) IRLR 190

Associated Provincial Picture Houses Ltd v *Wednesbury Corporation* (1947) 1 KB 233

Banking, Insurance & Finance Union v *Barclays Bank plc* 32146 (1986)

Banking, Insurance & Finance Union v *Barclays Bank plc* EAT (1987) 347 IDS Brief 16

Banking, Insurance & Finance Union v *Barclays Bank and ors* EAT (1987) 479

BBC v *Dixon* CA (1979) IRLR 114

Berriman v *Delabole Slate Ltd* CA (1985) ICR 546

Bessenden Properties Ltd v *Corness* NIRC (1974) IRLR 338

Bilka-Kaufhaus GmbH v *Weber* ECJ (1986) IRLR 317

Brennan v *Dewhurst Ltd* EAT (1983) IRLR 357

British Coal Corporation v (1) *Cheesbrough* (2) *Secretary of State for Employment* CA (1988) IRLR 351

British Home Stores v *Burchell* EAT (1978) IRLR 379

British Labour Pump Co Ltd v *Byrne* EAT (1979) IRLR 94

British Leyland (UK) Ltd v *Swift* CA (1981) IRLR 91

British Railways Board v *Batchelor* CA (1987) IRLR 136

British Railways Board v *Paul* EAT (1988) IRLR 20

British Steel Corporation v *Griffin* EAT (1986) 316 IRLIB 10–11

British United Shoe Machinery Co Ltd v *Clarke* EAT (1977) IRLR 297

Bromley and ors v *H&J Quick Ltd* CA (1988) IRLR 249

Brook Lane Finance Co Ltd v *Bradley* EAT (1988) IRLR 283

Brown v *Stockton-on-Tees Borough Council* HL (1988) IRLR 263

Calveley and ors v *Merseyside Police* CA (1986) IRLR 177

Chant v *Aquaboats Ltd* (1987) ICR 643

Coates and Venables v *Modern Methods and Materials Ltd* CA (1982) IRLR 318

Commission of the European Economic Communities v *UK* ECJ (1982) IRLR 333

Council of Civil Service Unions and ors v *The Minister for the Civil Service* HL (1985) ICR 14; ECHR 323 IRLIB 15

Courage Take Home Trade Ltd v *Keys* EAT (1986) 334 IDS Brief 2–3

Dalton v *Burton's Gold Medal Biscuits Ltd* NIRC (1974) IRLR 45

Davies v *Presbyterian Church of Wales* HL (1986) IRLR 194

Dietman v *London Borough of Brent* High Ct (1987) IRLR 259; CA (1988) IRLR 299

Drew v *St Edmundsbury Borough Council* EAT (1980) IRLR 459

East Lindsey District Council v *Daubney* EAT (1977) IRLR 181

Electronic Data Systems Ltd v *Hubble* CA (1987) IDS Brief 1.

FC Shepherd & Co Ltd v *Jerrom* CA (1986) IRLR 358

Ferodo Ltd v *Rigby* HL (1987) IRLR 516

Ford v *Warwickshire County Council* HL (1983) ICR 273

Forex Neptune (Overseas) Ltd v *Miller and ors* EAT (1987) ICR 170

Gilham and ors v *Kent County Council* CA (1986) IRLR 56

Gorictree Ltd v *Jenkinson* EAT (1984) IRLR 391

Graham v *ABF Ltd* EAT (1988) IRLR 90

Greenall Whitley Plc v *Carr* EAT (1985) IRLR 289

Hammersmith & Queen Charlotte's Special Health Authority v *Cato* EAT (1988) ICR 132

Hayes v *Malleable Working Men's Club* EAT (1985) IRLR 367

Hayward v *Cammell Laird Shipbuilders Ltd* HL (1988) IRLR 257

Hill v *C A Parsons & Co* (1971) 3 All ER 1345

Hollister v *National Farmers' Union* CA (1979) IRLR 238

Hughes and ors v *London Borough of Southwark* High Ct (1988) IRLR 55

Igbo v *Johnson Matthey Chemicals Ltd* CA (1986) IRLR 215

Irani v *Southampton and South-West Hampshire Health Authority* High Ct (1985) IRLR 203

Iwanuszezak v *General Municipal, Boilermakers and Allied Trades Union* CA (1988) IRLR 219

Jenks, Jenks and Jenks v *Meltstore Ltd* IT (1987) 358 IDS Brief 1

Kestongate Ltd v *Miller* EAT (1986) ICR 672

Khanum v *Mid-Glamorgan Area Health Authority* EAT (1978) IRLR 215

Lang v *Devon General Ltd* EAT (1986) 319 IDS Brief 3–4

Leverton v *Clwyd County Council* CA (1988) IRLR 239

MacPherson v *London Borough of Lambeth* High Ct (1988) 377 IDS Brief 2–3

MANWEB v *Taylor* High Ct (1975) IRLR 60

Marley v *Forward Trust Group Ltd* CA (1986) IRLR 369

Marshall v *Southampton and South-West Hampshire Area Health Authority* (No 2) IT (1988) IRLR 325

Martin v *MBS Fastenings (Glynwed) Distribution Ltd* CA (1983) IRLR 198

McLaren v *National Coal Board* CA (1988) IRLR 215

Miles v *Wakefield Metropolitan District Council* HL (1987) IRLR 193

Moon v *Homeworthy Furniture (Northern) Ltd* EAT (1976) IRLR 298

Nethermere (St Neots) Ltd v *Gardiner and Taverna* CA (1984) IRLR 240

Noone v *North West Thames Regional Health Authority* CA (1988) IRLR 195

O'Kelly v *Trusthouse Forte Plc* CA (1983) ICR 728

Oyston Estate Agency Ltd v *Trundle* EAT (1986) 337 IDS Brief 5–6

Paal Wilson & Co v *Partenreederei* HL (1983) AC 854

Pickstone and ors v *Freemans Plc* HL (1988) IRLR 357

Polkey v *A E Dayton Services Ltd* HL (1987) IRLR 503

Powell v *London Borough of Brent* CA (1987) IRLR 466

Pratt v *Walsall Health Authority* IT (1988) 376 IDS Brief 20

Pritchett and Dyjasek v *J McIntyre Ltd* CA (1987) IRLR 18

Quinnen v *Howells* EAT (1984) IRLR 227

Rainey v *Greater Glasgow Health Board* HL (1987) IRLR 26

Reed Packaging Ltd v *Boozer & Everhurst* EAT (1988) IRLR 333

Ridgway and Fairbrother v *National Coal Board* CA (1987) IRLR 80

Rogers v *Wicks & Wilson Ltd* IT (1988) 366 IDS Brief 11–13

Savage v *J Sainsbury Ltd* CA (1980) IRLR 109

Savoia v *Chiltern Herb Farms Ltd* CA (1982) IRLR 166

Secretary of State for Employment v *Spence and ors* CA (1986) IRLR 248

Shannon v *Michelin (Belfast) Ltd* CA (1981) IRLR 505

Shepperd v *Saxon Home Heating* (1987) 362 IDS Brief 16

Sim v *Rotherham Metropolitan Borough Council* High Ct (1986) ICR 897

Simmons v *Hoover Ltd* EAT (1977) QB 284

Smith v *The Chairman and other Councillors of Hayle Town Council* CA (1978) IRLR 413

Surrey County Council v *Lewis* HL (1987) IRLR 509

The General of the Salvation Army v *Dewsbury* EAT (1984) IRLR 222

The Post Office v *Fennell* CA (1981) IRLR 221

Therm-A-Stor Ltd v *Atkins and ors* CA (1983) IRLR 78

Tipton v *West Midlands Co-operative Society* HL (1986) 2WLR 306

Union of Construction, Allied Trades & Technicians v *Brain* CA (1981) IRLR 224

Vose v *South Sefton Health Authority* EAT (1986) 314 IRLIB 12

W and J Wass Ltd v *Binns* CA (1982) IRLR 283

W Devis & Sons Ltd v *Atkins* HL (1977) IRLR 314

W E Cox Toner (International) Ltd v *Crook* EAT (1981) IRLR 443

Western Excavating (ECC) Ltd v *Sharp* CA (1978) IRLR 27

West v *Kneels Ltd* EAT (1986) IRLR 430

West Midlands Passenger Transport Executive v *Singh* CA (1987) IRLR 351

Wheeler v (1) *Patel* (2) *J Golding Group of Companies* EAT (1987) IRLR 211

Williams and ors v *Comp Air Maxam Ltd* EAT (1982) IRLR 83

Wiltshire County Council v *National Association of Teachers in Further & Higher Education and Guy* CA (1980) IRLR 198

Wiluszynski v *London Borough of Tower Hamlets* High Ct (1988) IRLR 154

Woodcock and ors v (1) *The Committee for the time being of the Friends School, Wigton* (2) *Genwise Ltd* CA (1987) 346 IDS Brief 18–19

Woods v *WM Car Services (Peterborough) Ltd* EAT (1981) IRLR 347

W Weddel & Co Ltd v *Tepper* CA (1980) IRLR 96

Useful Addresses

Advisory, Conciliation & Arbitration Service (ACAS)
Head office 27 Wilton Street, London SW1X 7AZ Tel 01–210 3000

Scotland
  Franborough House, 123–157 Bothwell Street, Glasgow G2 7JR

Wales
  Phase 1, Ty Glas Road, Llanishen, Cardiff CF4 5PH Tel 0222 762636

London Region
  Clifton House, 83–117 Euston Road, London NW1 2RB

Midlands Region
  Alpha Tower, Suffolk Street, Queensway, Birmingham B1 1TZ Tel
  021–631 3434
  Nottingham Office, 66–72 Houndsgate, Nottingham NG1 6BA Tel 0602
  415450

Northern Region
  Westgate House, Westgate Road, Newcastle upon Tyne NE1 1TJ Tel
  091–261 2191

North West Region
  Boulton House, 17–21 Chorlton Street, Manchester M1 3HY Tel
  061–228 3222

South East Region
  Clifton House, 83–117 Euston Road, London NW1 2RB Tel 01–388 5100

South West Region
  Regent House, 27a Regent Street, Clifton, Bristol BS8 4HR Tel 0272
  744066

Yorkshire and Humberside Region
  Commerce House, St Albans Place, Leeds LS2 8HH Tel 0532 431371

British Institute of Management (BIM)
Africa House, Kingsway, London WC2 Tel 01–405 3456

Central Arbitration Committee (CAC)
1 Abbey Garden, Great College Street, London SW1P 3SE Tel 01–222 8571–5

Certification Office for Trade Unions and Employers' Associations
15–17 Ormond Yard, Duke of York Street, London SW1Y 6JT Tel 01–210 3733

Commission for Racial Equality (CRE)
Elliot House, Allington Street, London SW1E 5EH Tel 01–828 7022

Birmingham Alpha Tower (11th Floor), Suffolk Street, Queensway, Birmingham B1 1TT Tel 021–632 4544

Leeds Yorkshire Bank Chambers (1st Floor), Infirmary Street, Leeds LS1 2JT Tel 0532 434413/4

Leicester Haymarket House (4th Floor), Haymarket Shopping Centre, Leicester LE1 3YG Tel 0533 517852

Manchester Maybrook House (5th Floor), 40 Blackfriars Street, Manchester M3 2EG Tel 061–831 7782/8

Commonwealth Trade Union Council (CTUC)
Congress House, Great Russell Street, London WC1B 3LS Tel 01–631 0728 *or* 636 4030 ex 290

Confederation of British Industry (CBI)
London Centre Point, 103 New Oxford Street, London WC1A 1DU Tel 01–379 7400

Eastern 14 Union Road, Cambridge CB2 1HE Tel 0223 65636

East Midlands 17 St Wilfrid Square, Calverton, Nottingham NG14 6FP Tel 0602 653311

Northern 15 Grey Street, Newcastle upon Tyne NE1 6EE Tel 091–232 1644

Northern Ireland Fanum House, 108 Great Victoria Street, Belfast BT2 7PD Tel 0232 226658

North Western Emerson House, Albert Street, Eccles, Manchester MS0 0LT Tel 061–707 2190

Scotland Beresford House, 5 Claremont Terrace, Glasgow G3 7XT Tel 041–332 8661

South Eastern Tube Hill House, London Road, Sevenoaks, Kent TN13 1BX Tel 0732 454040

Southern Bank Chambers, 10a Hart Street, Henley on Thames, Oxon RH9 2AU Tel 0491 577838

South Western 8–10 Whiteladies Road, Bristol BS8 1NZ Tel 0272 737065

Wales Pearl Assurance House, Greyfriars Road, Cardiff CF1 3JR Tel 0222 32536

West Midlands Hagley House, Hagley Road, Edgbaston, Birmingham B16 8PS Tel 021 454 7991

Yorkshire & Humberside Arndale House, Station Road, Crossgates, Leeds LS15 8E4 Tel 0532 644242

Department of Employment
Caxton House, Tothill Street, London SW1H 9NA Tel 01–213 3000

Scotland Pentland House, 47 Robb's Loan, Edinburgh EH14 1UE Tel 031–443 8731

Northern Wellbar House, Gallowgate, Newcastle upon Tyne NE1 4TP Tel 091–232 7575

Yorkshire & Humberside City House, New Station Street, Leeds LS1 4JH Tel 0532 43832

London Eastern (North) Arena House, Bridge Road, Wembley, Middlesex HA9 0NF Tel 01–903 1414

London Southern Union House, 28 Elmfield Road, Bromley, Kent BR1 1NX Tel 01–464 6418

South Western The Pithay, Bristol BS1 2NQ Tel 0272 273755

Midlands 2 Duchess Place, Hagley Road, Birmingham B16 8NS Tel 021–456 1144

North Western Sunley Buildings, Piccadilly Plaza, Manchester M60 7JS Tel 061–832 9111

Wales 4th Floor, Companies House, Crown Way, Maindy, Cardiff CF4 3UW Tel 0222 388588

Engineering Employers' Federation (EEF)
Broadway House, Tothill Street, London SW1 Tel 01–222 7777

Employment Appeal Tribunal (EAT)
St James's Square, London SW1 Tel 01–210 3000

Equal Opportunities Commission (EOC)
Overseas House, Quay Street, Manchester M3 3HN Tel 061–833 9244

European Trade Union Confederation (ETUC)
Rue Montagne Aux Herbes Potagères 37, 1000 Brussels, Belgium Tel 010 322 219 1090

European Trade Union Institute (ETUI)
Boulevard de L'Imperatrice 66, 1000 Brussels, Belgium Tel 010 322 512 3070

General Federation of Trade Unions (GFTU)
Central House, Upper Woburn Place, London WC1H 0HY Tel 01–387 0852

Health and Safety Commission
Baynards House, 1 Chepstow Place, Westbourne Grove, London W2 4TF Tel 01–229 3456

Incomes Data Services (IDS)
193 St John Street, London EC1 Tel 01–250 3434

Industrial Injuries Advisory Committee
157–168 Blackfriars Road, London SE1 8EU Tel 01–703 6380

Industrial Participation Association
85 Tooley Street, London SE1 Tel 01–403 6018

Industrial Relations Services (European)
18 Highbury Place, London N5 Tel 01–354 5858

Industrial Society
41 Charles Street, London W1 Tel 01–493 8899

Industrial Training Boards (ITB)
Agricultural Training Board (ATB) Bourne House, 32–34 Beckenham Road, Beckenham, Kent BR3 4PB Tel 01–650 4890

Clothing and Allied Products Industry Training Board (CAPITB) Tower House, Merrion Way, Leeds LS2 8NY Tel 0532 441331

Construction Industry Training Board (CITB) Radnor House, London Road, Norbury, London SW16 4EL Tel 01–764 5060

Engineering Industry Training Board (EITB) 54 Clarendon Road, Watford, Herts WD1 1LB Tel 0923 38441

Hotel and Catering Industry Training Board (HCITB) Ramsey House, Central Square, Wembley, Middx HA9 7AP Tel 01–902 8865

Offshore Petroleum Industry Training Board (OPITB) Forties Road, Montrose, Angus, Scotland Tel 0674 72230

Plastics Processing Industry Training Board (PPITB) 950 Great West Road, Brentford, Middx Tel 01–568 0731

Road Transport Industry Training Board (RTITB) Capitol House, Empire Way, Wembley, Middx HA9 0NG Tel 01–902 8880

Industrial Tribunals
London and North 19 Woburn Place, London WC1 Tel 01–278 2380
England and Wales 93 Ebury Bridge Road, London SW1 Tel 01–730 9161

Institute of Directors (IOD)
116 Pall Mall, London SW1Y 5ED Tel 01–839 1233

Institute of Personnel Management (IPM)
IPM House, Camp Road, Wimbledon, London SW19 4UW Tel 01–946 9100

International Confederation of Free Trade Unions (ICFTU)
Rue Montagne aux Herbes Potagères 37/41, 1000 Brussels, Belgium Tel 010 322 217 8085

International Labour Organisation (ILO)
CH-1211, Geneva, Switzerland Tel 010 4122 99 6111

Labour Relations Agency
Windsor House, 9–15 Bedford Street, Belfast BT2 7NU Tel 0232 221442

Labour Research Department
78 Blackfriars Road, London SE1 8HF Tel 01–928 3649

Local Authorities Conditions of Service Advisory Board (LACSAB)
41 Belgrave Square, London SW1X 8NZ Tel 01–235 6081

Local Government Information Unit (LGIU)
1–5 Bath Street, London EC1V 9QQ Tel 01–608 1051

Low Pay Unit
9 Upper Berkeley Street, London W1H Tel 01–262 7278

National Economic Development Council
Millbank Tower, Millbank, London SW1P 4QX Tel 01–211 3000

National Institute of Economic and Social Research (NIESR)
2 Dean Trench Street, Smith Square, London SW1P 3HE Tel 01–222 7665

Northern Ireland Committee, Irish Congress of Trade Unions (ICTU)
1–9 Castle Arcade, Belfast BT1 5DG Tel 0232 241452

Trades Union Congress (TUC)
Congress House, Great Russell Street, London WC1B 3LC Tel 01–636 4030

Scotland 16 Woodlands Terrace, Glasgow G3 6ED Tel 041–322 4946

Wales Transport House, 1 Cathedral Road, Cardiff CF1 0SD Tel 0222 372345

Northern Ireland Committee (ICTU) 1–9 Castle Arcade, Belfast BT1 5DG Tel 0232 241452

National Education Centre 77 Crouch End Hill, London N8 8DG Tel 01–341 6161

Regional Councils

Northern 3rd Floor, Scottish Provident House, 31 Mosley Street, Newcastle upon Tyne NE1 1YF Tel 0632 616934

Yorkshire and Humberside Leeds Trades Council Club, Saville Mount, Leeds LS7 3HU Tel 0532 622872

North West Caxton Hall, 88–92 Chapel Street, Manchester M3 7AY Tel 061–832 2091

West Midlands 10 Pershore Street, Birmingham B5 4HU Tel 021–622 2050

East Midlands 61 Derby Road, Nottingham NG1 5BA Tel 0602 472444

East Anglia 119 Newmarket Road, Cambridge CB5 8HA Tel 0223 67691

South East Congress House, Great Russell Street, London WC1B 3LS Tel 01–636 4030

South West 1 Henbury Road, Westbury on Trym, Bristol BS9 3HH Tel 0272 506425

Trades Union Congress Affiliated Unions

Amalgamated Association of Beamers, Twisters and Drawers (Hand and Machine) 27 Every Street, Nelson, Lancashire BB9 7NE Tel 0282 64181

Amalgamated Engineering Union 110 Peckham Road, London SE15 5EL Tel 01–703 4231

Amalgamated Society of Textile Workers and Kindred Trades Foxlowe, Market Place, Leek, Staffordshire ST13 6AD Tel 0538 382068

Amalgamated Union of Asphalt Workers Jenkin House, 173a Queens Road, Peckham, London SE15 2NF Tel 01–639 1669

Associated Metalworkers' Union 92 Deansgate, Manchester M3 2QG Tel 061–834 6891

Associated Society of Locomotive Engineers and Firemen 9 Arkwright Road, Hampstead, London NW3 6AB Tel 01–431 0275

Association of Cinematograph, Television and Allied Technicians 111 Wardour Street, London W1V 4AY Tel 01–437 8506

Association of First Division Civil Servants 2 Caxton Street, London SW1H 0QH Tel 01–839 7406

Association of Professional, Executive, Clerical and Computer Staff 22 Worple Road, London SW19 4DF Tel 01–947 3131

Association of University Teachers United House, 1 Pembridge Road, London W11 3HJ Tel 01–221 4370

Bakers, Food and Allied Workers' Union Stanborough House, Great North Road, Stanborough, Welwyn Garden City, Herts AL8 7TA Tel 07072 60150

Banking, Insurance and Finance Union Sheffield House, 17 Hillside, Wimbledon, London SW19 4NL Tel 01–946 9151

British Actors' Equity Association 8 Harley Street, London W1N 2AB Tel 01–636 6367, 637 9311

British Air Line Pilots Association 81 New Road, Harlington, Hayes, Middlesex UB3 5BG Tel 01–759 9331

British Association of Colliery Management BACM House, 317 Nottingham Road, Old Basford, Nottingham NG7 7DP Tel 0602 785819

Broadcasting and Entertainment Trades Alliance 181–185 Wardour Street, London W1V 3AA Tel 01–439 7585

Card Setting Machine Tenters' Society 36 Greenton Avenue, Scholes, Cleckheaton, West Yorkshire BD19 6DT Tel 0274 670022

Ceramic and Allied Trades Union Hillcrest House, Garth Street, Hanley, Stoke on Trent ST1 2AB Tel 0782 272755

Civil and Public Services Association 215 Balham High Road, London SW17 7BN Tel 01–672 1299

Civil Services Union 5 Praed Street, London W2 1NJ Tel 01–402 7451

Communication Managers' Association Highes House, Ruscombe Road, Twyford, Reading, Berkshire RG10 9JD Tel 0734 342300

Confederation of Health Service Employees Glen House, High Street, Banstead, Surrey SM7 2LH Tel 07373 53322

Educational Institute of Scotland 46 Moray Place, Edinburgh EH3 6BH Tel 031–225 6244

Electrical, Electronic, Telecommunication and Plumbing Union Hayes Court, West Common Road, Bromley BR2 7AU Tel 01–462 7755

Engineers' and Managers' Association Station House, Fox Lane North, Chertsey, Surrey KT16 9HW Tel 09328 64131

Film Artistes' Association 61 Marloes Road, London W8 6LF Tel 01–937 4567

Fire Brigades Union Bradley House, 68 Coombe Road, Kingston upon Thames KT2 7AE Tel 01–541 1765

Furniture, Timber and Allied Trades Union Fairfields, Roe Green, Kingsbury, London NW9 0PT Tel 01–204 0273

General, Municipal, Boilermakers and Allied Trades Union Thorne House, Ruxley Ridge, Claygate, Esher, Surrey KT10 0TL Tel 0372 62081

General Union of Associations of Loom Overlookers Overlookers Institute, Jude Street, Nelson, Lancashire BB9 7NP Tel 0282 64066

Greater London Staff Association 150 Waterloo Road, London SE1 8SB Tel 01–633 5573

Health Visitors' Association 36 Eccleston Square, London SW1V 1PF Tel 01–834 9523, 821 0310

Hospital Consultants and Specialists Association The Old Court House, London Road, Ascot, Berkshire SL5 7EN Tel 0990 25052

Inland Revenue Staff Federation Douglas Houghton House, 231 Vauxhall Bridge Road, London SW1V 1EH Tel 01–834 8254

Institution of Professional Civil Servants 75–79 York Road, London SE1 7AQ Tel 01–928 9951

Manufacturing, Science and Finance 79 Camden Road, London NW1 9ES Tel 01–267 4422

Military and Orchestral Musical Instrument Makers Trade Society 2 Whitehouse Avenue, Borehamwood, Hertfordshire WD6 1HD

Musicians' Union 60–62 Clapham Road, London SW9 0JJ Tel 01–582 5566

National and Local Government Officers' Association 1 Mabledon Place, London WC1H 9AJ Tel 01–388 2366

National Association of Colliery Overmen, Deputies and Shotfirers Simpson House, 48 Netherhall Road, Doncaster, South Yorkshire DN1 2PZ Tel 0302 68015

National Association of Co-operative Officials Saxone House, 56 Market Street, Manchester M1 1PW Tel 061–834 6029

National Association of Licensed House Managers 9 Coombe Lane, Raynes Park, London SW20 8NE Tel 01–947 3080

National Association of Probation Officers 3–4 Chivalry Road, London SW11 1HT Tel 01–223 4887

National Association of Schoolmasters/Union of Women Teachers 22 Upper Brook Street, London W1Y 1PD Tel 01–629 3916, 629 3917

National Association of Teachers in Further and Higher Education 27 Britannia Street, London WC1X 9JP Tel 01–837 3636

National Communications Union Greystoke House, 150 Brunswick Road, London W5 1AW Tel 01–998 2981

National Graphical Association (1982) Graphic House, 63–67 Bromham Road, Bedford, Bedfordshire MK40 2AG Tel 0234 51521

National League of the Blind and Disabled 2 Tenterden Road, London N17 8BE Tel 01–808 6030

National Union of Domestic Appliances and General Operatives Imperial Buildings, Corporation Street, Rotherham, Yorkshire S60 1PB Tel 0709 382820, 362826

National Union of Hosiery and Knitwear Workers 55 New Walk, Leicester LE1 7EB Tel 0533 556703

National Union of Insurance Workers 27 Old Gloucester Street, London WC1N 3AF Tel 01–405 1083

National Union of Journalists Acorn House, 314–320 Gray's Inn Road, London WC1X 8DP Tel 01–278 7916

National Union of Lock and Metal Workers Bellamy House, Wilkes Street, Willenhall, West Midlands WV13 2BS Tel 0902 66651, 66652

National Union of Marine, Aviation and Shipping Transport Officers Oceanair House, 750–760 High Road, Leystonstone, London E11 3BB Tel 01–989 6677

National Union of Mineworkers St James' House, Vicar Lane, Sheffield, Yorks S1 2EX Tel 0742 766900

National Union of Public Employees Civic House, 20 Grand Depot Road, London SE18 6SF Tel 01–854 2244

National Union of Railwaymen Unity House, Euston Road, London NW1 2BL Tel 01–387 4771

National Union of Scalemakers 1st Floor, Queensway House, 57 Livery Street, Birmingham B3 1HA Tel 021–236 8998

National Union of Seamen Maritime House, Old Town, Clapham, London SW4 0JP Tel 01–622 5581

National Union of Tailors and Garment Workers 16 Charles Square, London N1 6HP Tel 01–251 9406

National Union of Teachers Hamilton House, Mabledon Place, London WC1H 9BD Tel 01–388 6191

National Union of the Footwear, Leather and Allied Trades The Grange, Earls Barton, Northampton NN6 0JH Tel 0604 810326

Northern Carpet Trades' Union 22 Clare Road, Halifax HX1 2HX Tel 0422 60492

Pattern Weavers' Society New Field End, Hill Top, Cumberworth, Huddersfield HD8 8YE Tel 0484 892547

Power Loom Carpet Weavers' and Textile Workers' Union Callows Lane, Kidderminster, Worcestershire DY10 2JG Tel 0562 3192

Prison Officers' Association Cronin House, 245 Church Street, Edmonton, London N9 9HW Tel 01–803 0255

Rossendale Union of Boot, Shoe and Slipper Operatives 7 Tenterfield Street, Waterfoot, Rossendale, Lancashire BB4 7BA Tel 07062 15657

Scottish Prison Officers' Association 21 Calder Road, Saughton, Edinburgh EH1 3PF Tel 031–443 8105

Screw, Nut, Bolt and Rivet Trade Union 368 Dudley Road, Birmingham B18 4HH Tel 021–558 2001

Sheffield Wool Shear Workers' Union 50 Bankfield Road, Malin Bridge, Sheffield, Yorkshire S6 4RD

Society of Civil and Public Servants 124–130 Southwark Street, London SE1 0TU Tel 01–928 9671

Society of Graphical and Allied Trades '82 Sogat House, 274–288 London Road, Hadleigh, Benfleet, Essex SS7 2DE Tel 0702 554111

Society of Shuttlemakers 31 Moorside Avenue, Intack, Blackburn BB1 2BA Tel 0254 60272

Society of Telecom Executives 102–104 Sheen Road, Richmond, Surrey TW9 1UF Tel 01–948 5423

Spring Trapmakers' Society Bellamy House, Wilkes Street, Willenhall, West Midlands WV13 2BS Tel 0902 66651, 66652

TASS Park House, 64–66 Wandsworth Common north side, London SW18 2SH Tel 01–871 2100

Tobacco Mechanics Association 16 Clifton Terrace, Whitley Bay, Tyne and Wear NE26 2JD Tel 0632 513254

Transport and General Workers' Union Transport House, Smith Square, Westminster, London SW1P 3JB Tel 01–828 7788

Transport Salaried Staffs' Association Walkden House, 10 Melton Street, London NW1 2EJ Tel 01–387 2101

Union of Communication Workers UCW House, Crescent Lane, London SW4 9RN Tel 01–622 9977

Union of Construction, Allied Trades and Technicians UCATT House, 177 Abbeville Road, Clapham, London SW4 9RL Tel 01–622 2442

Union of Shop, Distributive and Allied Workers Oakley, 188 Wilmslow Road, Fallowfield, Manchester M14 6LJ Tel 061–224 2804

United Road Transport Union 76 High Lane, Manchester M21 1FD Tel 061–881 6245

Wire Workers' Union Prospect House, Alma Street, Sheffield, Yorks S3 8SA Tel 0742 21674

Writers' Guild of Great Britain 430 Edgware Road, London W2 1EH Tel 01–723 8074

Yorkshire Association of Power-Loom Overlookers 20 Hallfield Road, Bradford BD1 3RQ Tel 0274 727966

The Training Agency
Moorfoot, Sheffield S1 4PQ Tel 0742 753275
Employment Division
Wales and South 236 Grays Inn Road, London WC1X 8HL Tel 01–278 0363

South East 4th Floor, Telford House, Hamilton Close, Basingstoke, Hants RG21 2UL Tel 0256 467111

South West The Pithay, Bristol BS1 2NQ Tel 0272 273710

Wales Companies House, Crown Way, Maindy, Cardiff CF4 3UU Tel 0222 388588

Midlands Alpha Tower, 8th Floor, Suffolk Street, Queensway, Birmingham B1 1UR Tel 021–631 3555

Scotland and North 9 St Andrew Square, Edinburgh EH2 2QX Tel 031–225 8500

Northern Broadacre House, Market Street, Newcastle upon Tyne NE1 6HH Tel 0632 326181

Yorkshire and Humberside Jubilee House, 33–41 Park Place, Leeds LS1 2RJ Tel 0532 446299

North West Washington House, New Bailey Street, Manchester M3 5ER Tel 061–833 0251

Northern Ireland Employment Service, Department of Economic Development, Netherleigh, Massey Avenue, Belfast BT4 2JP Tel 0232 63244

World Federation of Trade Unions (WFTU)
Namesti Curieovych 1, 11688 Prague 1, Czechoslovakia Tel Prague 67856

Index

The following abbreviations are used in this index:

ACAS – Arbitration, Conciliation and Advisory Service
CBI – Confederation of British Industry
AEU – Amalgamated Engineering Union
EETPU – Electrical, Electronic, Telecommunication and Plumbing Union
GCHQ – Government Communications Headquarters
GMB – General, Municipal, Boilermakers and Allied Trades Union
SOGAT– Society of Graphical and Allied Trades
TGWU – Transport and General Workers Union

absence, and dismissal, 329
ACAS
  on ballots, 303
  Disciplinary Code, 141–4, 211
    and dismissal reasonableness, 333–4
  in disciplinary procedures, 145–6
  in health and safety, 150
  and tribunals, 342–3
  in negotiations, 108–9, 137–9
  on pay harmonization, 244–5
  small firm recruiting guide, 202
  on trade union decline, 1
Access to Medical Records Act 1988, 347–8
AEU and inter-union conflict, 26, 27–8
  at Dundee, 254–5
AIDS, 332
alcoholism, 144
annualization, 5

ballots in unions, recent law on, 11, 284, 290–2,
    300–6
  for closed shops, 280
  impact of, 11–12
  and industrial action, 10, 302–3
  for internal elections, 301–2
  new proposals on, 305–6
  opinions on, 303
  for political funds, 11, 12, 291, 301, 304
  pre-1984 criticism, 300–1
bargaining power in negotiations, 101
Bridlington Principles, 27
  and single-union agreements, 255–6
    amendment, 258
British Institute of Management, 185–6
British Steel worker directors, 174
British Telecom
  Mercury connection dispute, 282–3
  privatization, union review, 47
Bullock Committee, 173

CAD/CAM, 59, 62
Caledonian Paper, EETPU agreement, 252–3
car trade trends, 3–4
cashless pay, 349
Cassells report, 49
CBI, new technology union negotiations, 69–70
Christian Salvesen, EETPU agreement, 253
closed shops
  ballots, legislation changes, 280
  individuals' rights, 362
collective agreements, 112–31
  content, 115–18
  format, 114–15
  the future, 129–30
  legal enforcement, 114
  levels of, 118–22
    corporate, 121
    establishment, 121
    national, 119–21
    sub-establishment, 121–2
  trends
    in content, 127–9
    decline of importance, 122–5
    in form, 125–6
    in level of bargaining, 127
  union recognition and, 113–14
collective bargaining
  global, and new technology, 67
  government intervention 1979–88, 7–8
  public sector, 36–8
Commission for Racial Equality, 190
company cars, 193
comparability, public sector, 44
competitive tendering, 47–8
constructive dismissal, 338
contracts of employment
  legislation, recent, 274–5
  and unfair dismissal, 320–2
    tests for existence of contract, 323

contractual rights, 353–6
cost-effective management
  flexibility of labour, 85–7
    contractual arrangements, 87
    working time arrangements, 86–7
  vs. socially aware management, 83–4

decertification, GCHQ, 12, 39
deductions from pay of retail employees, 348–9
deregulation, 274
Direct Consensus Method, 240
disciplinary procedures, 141–6
  ACAS in, 145–6
  alcoholism, 144
  appeals, 143–4, 145
  elements in, 141–2
  misconduct
    gross, 142–3
    less serious, 143
  warnings, 143
discrimination
  race, 357–9
  sex, 357–9
    in management, 189–90
    new law, 272
dismissal in small firms, 211–12
  see also unfair dismissal
Disputes Principles, see Bridlington Principles
Donovan Commission, 34, 266
driving licence loss and dismissal, 331
drunkenness, 144
  and dismissal, 328
Dundee Ford plant, 29, 254–5

early retirement of managers, 188
education, management, 184–6
EETPU
  inter-union conflict, 26–8
  single-union agreements
    acceptance conditions, 251
    Caledonian Paper, 252–3
    Christian Salvesen, 253
    Hitachi Consumer Products Ltd, 85–6, 252
    Orion Electric, 253–4
  TUC expulsion, 254
employee participation, 159–80
  conflict of interpretations, 159
  forms of, 160–1
  joint consultation, 169–73
    factors in success, 170–1
    organization details, 171–2
  legislative pressure, 162
  profit sharing/share ownership, 176–8, 229–33
  quality circles, 167–9
    factors for success, 168
    problems, 168–9
  team briefing, 163–6
    benefits, 163–4
    principles, 164

  problems, 165–6
  trend towards, 161
  worker directors, 173–6
    British Steel, 174
    Bullock Committee, 173
    Post Office, 175
    private sector, 174
    Vredeling Directives, 175–6
employment
  public sector, 45–6
  structural changes in, 4–6
  flexible work, 5–6
  see also unemployment
Employment Act 1980, on picketing, 307–8
Employment Act 1982
  on employee participation, 162
  and unionization, 280
Employment Protection Act 1975, 278
  Disciplinary Code, 333–4
  and government intervention, 7–8
  on picketing, 312
  on redundancy consultation, 360–1
Employment Protection (Consolidation) Act
  1978, 350
  and tribunals, 340
employment rights, statutory, 345–53
  and insolvency, 351–2
  and maternity, 347
  medical records, access to, 347–8
  on medical suspension, 350
  on notice periods, 350
  on pay, 348–50
  on redundancy, 345–7
  on time off, 348
  and transfer of undertakings, 352–3
  on written particulars, 351
equal opportunities
  pay, 356–7
  race/sex, see under Discrimination
Equal Opportunities Commission, 190, 241
Equal Pay Act 1970
  and job evaluation, 240–1
  European Court decision on, 279, 356
Equal Pay (Amendment) Regulations 1983, 279
Equal Value (Amendment) Regulations 1983,
  240
European Law
  decision on UK Equal Pay Act, 279, 356
  sex discrimination, UK statute inadequacy,
  358–9

First Division Association, and GCHQ union
  ban, 12
flexibility of labour, 5–6
  in collective agreements, 117
  and cost-effectiveness, 85–7
    contractual arrangements, 67
    working time arrangements, 86–7
  and new technology, 60

flexitime, 86
Ford Dundee plant, 29, 254–5
Fraser, Munro, interview grading system, 204
fringe benefits, 193
'frustration' as dismissal, 325

GCHQ union ban, 12, 39
GMB
   small firm recruitment, 213
   TGWU merger, 24
government intervention 1979–88, 6–13
   and ballots, impact, 11–12
   collective bargaining, 7–8
   future assessment, 14
   GCHQ union ban, 12, 39
   individual employment rights, 7
   industrial action 9–11
   miners' strike, 12–13
   pay bargaining, 13
   pay regulation, 8–9
   union organization and ballots, 11
graduate recruitment, 183–4
grievance procedures, 139–41
   elements in, 139–40
   in small firms, 212
gross misconduct, and dismissal, 142–3, 327–8

harmonization of payment structures, 242–5
   benefits, 243
   costs, 243–3
   and pay, 244
   pressures towards, 242–3
   questions for organizations, 244–5
Hay Guide Chart Profile Method, 240
'headhunters', 183
Health and Safety at Work etc Act 1974, 148, 363–4
Health and Safety Executive, 150
health, safety and welfare, 363–4
   procedures, 148–53
      consultation *vs.* negotiation in, 151–2
      elements in, 148–50
      safety representatives, 152–3
Hitachi Consumer Products Ltd
   EETPU agreement, 252
   and job flexibility, 85–6
homeworking and new technology, 62–3

ill-health, and dismissal, 327
In Place of Strife, 266
individualization of labour, 87–8
induction in small firms, 205
industrial action
   ballots and, 10, 302–3
   and dismissal fairness, 337–8
   individuals' rights, 362
   and legislation, future, 295–7
   legislation since 1979, 9–11, 281–6
      ballots, 284, 290–1

dismissals, 285–6
   secondary action, 283
   secondary picketing, 283–4
   strike benefit, 286
   'trade dispute', 282–3
   union liability, 284–5
   and union recognition, 284–5
Industrial Training Act 1964, 339
industrial tribunals, *see* tribunals
information technology, *see* new technology
insolvency rights, 351–2
interviewing plans, 203–4
'intrapreneurial' ventures, 188

Japanese business success, 64
'Japanization', 6
Jacques' time-span of discretion method, 240
job evaluation, 233–42
   in collective agreements, 116–17
      decline of, 129
   'equal value' implications, 240–1
   limitations, 241–2
   methods, 233–40
      factor comparison, 238–9
      grading, 235, 237
      paired comparisons, 234–5
      points rating, 237–8
      ranking, 234
   trend towards, 245–6
joint consultation, 169–73
   factors in success, 170–1
   organization details, 171–2
joint safety committees, 149–50

Labour Party
   finance, 12
   and union strategy, 23
legislation since 1979, 265–99
   analysis and the future, 294–9
      and employee commitment, 298
      industrial action, 295–7
      union power, 297–8
   analysis of impact, 292–4
   on collective relations, 280–1
   effecting change, 268–70
   on employer–employee relations, 274–81
      contracts of employment, 274–5
      and deregulation, 274
      industrial tribunals/unfair dismissal, 275–8
      terms/conditions, 278–9
   on industrial action, 281–6
      ballots, 284
      dismissals, 285–6
      secondary action, 283
      secondary picketing, 283–4
      strike benefit, 286
      'trade dispute', 282–3
      union liability, 284–5
      and union recognition, 284–5

labour law changes, 270–4
  consultation, 272
  individual rights, 270–2
  union restrictions, 273–4
  and payment harmonization, 243
  regulatory objectives, 266–8
  on union organization/activities, 286–92
    ballots, secret, 290–2
    and individual rights, 289–90
    membership, 288–9
    recognition, 287
    secondary recognition/unionization, 287–8
  voluntarism attacked, 265–6
  see also employment rights, statutory;
    government intervention 1979–88
LIFO in redundancy, 146–7
localization of labour, 88–9

McCarthy review, 37
management, 81–94
  cost-effective approach
    flexibility of labour, 85–7
    vs. socially aware management, 83–4
  education, 184–6
  individualization, 87–8
  localization, 88–9
  of new technology, 58–65
    and flexibility, 60
    homeworking, 62–3
    and poverty, 61
    and R and D, 59
    strategies, 64
    structures, 63
  perspectives, 93–4
  union recognition/collective agreements,
    113–14
  of unions, 89–92
    bargaining unit restriction, 91–2
    employee communication, 90–1
    and shop stewards, 92
    strategies, 89–90
managerial/professional staff, 181–96
  appraisal, 186–7
  career blockages, 187–8
  definitions, 181
  economic rewards, 190–4
    job evaluation/salary structure, 191–3
    public sector and privatization, 193–4
    remuneration package, 193
  education, 184–6
  equal opportunities, 189–90
  mobility, 184
  recruitment, 182–3
    graduates, 183–4
  redundancy, 188–9
  selection, 183
  unionization, 194–5
manufacturing decline, 3–4

maternity
  rights, 272, 347
    after confinement, 339
  Statutory Maternity Pay, 271, 278
MATSA, and single-union agreements, 251
medical records, right of access to, 347–8
medical suspension, statutory rights, 350
Meeting the Challenge, 256
Megaw Committee, 44
Mercury telecommunications dispute, 282–3
mergers, and union survival, 24
merit pay, managerial, 192
method study, 222
'milk round', 183
miners' strike 1984–85, 50
  cases involved, 269
  financial penalties, 10
  government intervention, 12–13
  picketing in
    offence statistics, 309
    police powers, 309
    and violence, 306–7

National Association of Local Government
  Officers, and privatization, 47
negotiations, 95–111
  adjournments in, 106–7
  analysis models, 97–8
  dynamics, 98–9
    breakpoints, 99
  the future of, 110
  in health and safety, vs. consultation, 151–2
  personal relationships in, 109–10
  preparation for, 99–103
  procedures, 135–9
  purposes, 95
  sanctions in, 107–8
  stages of, 103–6
  third parties in, 108–9
  training for, 110
  trust in, 109
  uniqueness in industrial relations, 96–7
new technology, 55–77
  in collective agreements, 117
  and individualization, 88
  management, 58–65
    and flexibility, 60
    homeworking, 62–3
    and poverty, 61
    and R and D, 59
    strategies, 64
    structures, 63
  and part-time employment, 57–8
  and payment harmonization, 242–3
  process innovation, and unemployment, 56–7
  and service employment, 57
  and unions, 65–74
    CBI negotiations, 69–70
    collective bargaining, global, 67

new technology agreements (NTAs), 68–9,
71–4
new technology agreements (NTAs), 68–9
analysis, 71–4
newspaper industry, and new technology, 62, 66
NHS dispute 1982, 39
Nissan/AEU agreement, 27
North Sea oil/gas and manufacturing decline, 4
notice periods, statutory rights, 350
National Union of Mineworkers, *see* miners'
strike
see also Union of Democratic Mineworkers

Orion Electric, EETPU agreement, 253–4

part-time work, 86
legislation protection, 277
new technology and, 57–8
Paterson's decision band method, 240
pay/payment systems, 217–47
choice of system, 220
classification, 217–19
payment by results, 217–18
time rate, 218–19
and equal opportunities, 356–7
expectations, 219–20
government intervention, 13
harmonization, 242–5
benefits, 243
costs, 243–4
and pay, 244
pressures towards, 242–3
questions for organizations, 244–5
implementation, 220–1
and job evaluation, 233–42
'equal value' implications, 240–1
limitations, 241–2
methods, 233–40
legislation, recent, 278–9
measured daywork, 224–6
industrial relations implications, 225–6
objectives, 219
output-related, 221–4
control limitations, 224
decay, 223–4
pre-conditions, 223
standard setting, 221–2
variations, 222–3
plant/enterprise-wide, 226–9
advantages, 227
limitations, 227–9
profit sharing schemes, 176–8, 229–33
public sector
bargaining, 36–8
determination, 40–5
managerial, and privatization, 193–4
in small firms, 207–8
bargaining, 208
statutory regulation, 8–9

statutory rights, 348–50
terminology, 219
trends, 245–7
and job evaluation, 245–6
pay disparities, 246–7
see also managerial/professional staff;
economic rewards
picketing, 306–13
Code, Department of Environment, 310–12
goods/services supply, 311
number of pickets, 310
organizer's role, 310–11
police role, 311–12
Employment Act 1980 on, 307–8
mass, 309–10
miners' strike, 306–7
offence statistics, 309
police powers, 309
recent law on, 10
and 'right to work', 313
secondary, legislation since 1979, 283–4
and vehicles, 312–13
piecework, 221
Plessey Control, pay harmonization, 244
police and picketing, 306–7
powers, 309
role in, 311–12
political funds, union, 52
ballots for, 11, 12, 301, 304
legislation since 1979, 291
future government intervention, 14
Post Office
dispute 1985, 40
worker directors, 175
poverty, 61
privatization, 46–7
economic effects, 3
and salaries, managerial, 193–4
unions and, 46–7
procedures, 132–58
checklist, 153–4
disciplinary, 141–6
ACAS in, 145–6
alcoholism, 144
appeals, 143–4, 145
elements in, 141–2
gross misconduct, 142–3
less serious misconduct, 143
warnings, 143
grievance, 139–41
in small firms, 212
health and safety, 148–53
consultation *vs.* negotiation in, 151–2
elements in, 148–50
safety representatives, 152–3
meaning/extent, 132–3
merits/limitations, 133–5
negotiating, 135–9
arbitration/conciliation, 137–9

elements in, 135–6
legal enforceability, 137
peace clause, 136
redundancy, 146–8
trends/developments, 154–7
last-offer arbitration, 156
statutory forces, 155–6
productivity agreements, 117
Professional and Executive Recruitment
Agency, 183
see also managerial/professional staff
Profile Method, 240
profit sharing, 176–8, 229–33
public sector, 34–54
competitive tendering, 47–8
decentralization trend, 48–9
employment in, 45–6
joint procedures, 36–40
pay
bargaining, 36–8
determination, 40–5
privatization, 46–7
economic effects, 3
and salaries, managerial, 193–4
unions and, 46–7
strikes, 49–52
structural features vs. private sector, 35

quality circles, 167–9
factors for success, 168
problems, 168–9

race discrimination, 357–9
Commission for Racial Equality, 190
Race Relations Act 1975, 358
Royal College of Nursing, and industrial action,
51–2
Reagan, Ronald, on negotiations, 107
recession, and payment harmonization 243
recruitment
of graduates, 183–4
of managerial/professional staff, 182–3
in small firms, 202–5
interviewing, 203–4
personal recommendation, 203
redundancy
and collective agreements, 117–18
fairness, 329–31
law changes since 1979, 271, 281
of managers, 188–9
procedures, 146–8
elements of, 146–7
statutory rights, 345–7
to consultation, 360–1
references, 204
retail employment and pay deductions, 348–9
retirement
early, of managers, 188
Sex Discrimination Act 1986 and, 279

Robens Report, 151
Rodger, Alec, interviewing plan, 203–4
Rooker, Jeff, on picketing 312
Rucker Plan, 227

safety representatives, 149–50, 364
procedural arrangements, 152–3
see also health, safety and welfare
salary structures, managerial, 191–3
see also Pay/payment systems
Scanlon Plan, 227
secondary picketing, 1979, 283–4
secondment of managers, 188
selection
of managers, 183
testing, 204
self-employed, as union target, 24–5
sex discrimination, 357–9
law changes since 1979, 272
on retirement, 279
Sex Discrimination Act 1975, 358
Sex Discrimination Act 1986, and retirement,
279
share ownership, 176–8
for managers, 193
shift work, 86
shop stewards, changing role, 92
Sick Pay, Statutory, 271, 278
see also ill-health, and dismissal
single-union agreements, 248–61
advantages, 249
Code of Practice, 257–8
Disputes Principles strained, 255–6
elements of, 249–50
and employee consultation, 255
employer interest in, 258–60
extent, 249
and inter-union conflict, 26–8, 251–5
recognition problems, 250–1
small firms, 197–216
communications, 209–10
definitions, 198–9
employing people, 200–8
human resource plan, 201–2
induction, 205
pay, 207–8
problems exaggerated, 200–1
recruiting, 202–5
training, 206
low priority employee relations, 200–1
rules/regulations, 210-12
dismissal, 211-12
grievances, 212
staffing limit, 214
systematic approach, 215
unions in, 212–14
smoking rules, and dismissal fairness, 332–3
SOGAT, membership policies, 25
'some other substantial reason' (SOSR), 331–3

Statutory Maternity Pay/Sick Pay, 278 ·
  introduction, 271
strikes, 313–16
  benefit, legislation since 1979, 286
  categories of, 313
  constitutionality of, 314
  economic factors, 315
  official strike, recent re-emergence, 316
  public sector, 49–52
  and unemployment, 315
  see also industrial action

teachers' disputes, 51
Teachers' Pay Act 1987, 51
team briefing, 163–6
  benefits, 163–4
  principles, 164
  problems, 165–6
technology, *see* new technology
TGWU
  GMB merger, 24
  small firm recruitment, 213
total quality management (TQM), 167
Trade Boards Act 1909, 349
trade deficit/surplus trends, 3–4
Trade Disputes Act 1906, 9
Trade Union Act 1984, and industrial action,
  9–10
trade unions
  decline, 1, 15–22
    explanation, 20–2
    finances, 17, 20
    membership/density, 15–17
    response strategies, 22–6
  and flexible work, 5–6
  GCHQ ban, 12, 39
  and legislation since 1979, 286–92
    ballots, secret, 290–2
    collective bargaining, 7–8
    and individual rights, 289–90
    membership, 288–9
    recognition, 273–4, 287
    secondary recognition/unionization, 287–8
  for managers, 194–5
  managing, 89–92
    bargaining unit restriction, 91–2
    employee communication, 90–1
    and shop stewards, 92
    strategies, 89–90
  members' rights, 359–62
    action short of dismissal, 359
    ballots, workplace, 362
    individual rights, 280–1, 361–2, 317–18
    to information disclosure, 361
    redundancy consultation, 360–1
    time off, 259–60
  membership, and unfair dismissal, 336–7
  and new technology, 65–74
    CBI negotiations, 69–70

collective bargaining, global, 67
New Technology Agreements (NTAs),
  68–9, 71–4
political funds, 52
  ballots for, 11, 12, 291, 301, 304
  future government intervention, 14
positive trends, 14
and privatization, 46–7
prospects, 28–31
public sector density, 36
recognition and collective agreements, 113–14
in small firms, 212–14
team briefing oppositions, 165–6
transfer of undertaking, statutory rights, 1981,
  353
see also ballots in unions; industrial action;
  picketing; single-union agreements; strikes

see also by specific union
training
  and collective agreements, 118
  of graduates, 183
  for negotiations, 110
  in quality circles, 167
  in small firms, 206
  for team briefing, 165
transfer of undertakings, statutory rights, 352–3
Transfer of Undertakings Regulations 1981, 281,
  352
tribunals, 339–44
  ACAS in, 342–3
  awards, 343
  composition of, 340
  in equal pay claims, 357
  originating application, 340
  pre-hearing assessment, 341
  procedure changes since 1979, 270
  representation, 343
  and unfair dismissal, 275–8
    compensation, 277
    pre-hearing assessment, 276
    qualification period, 277
Truck Acts repeal, 271, 278
TUC
  membership review body, and single-union
    agreements, 248
  Special Review Body, 256
    Code of Practice, 257–8

unemployment
  and new technology, 56
    process innovation, 56–7
  and strikes, 315
  trends, recent, 2–3
unfair dismissal, 7, 319–44
  automatically unfair, 336–7
  compensation and union membership, 281
  constructive dismissal, 338
  deciding fairness/unfairness, 325–36

case law, 334–6
fair reasons, 326–33
reasonableness, 333–6
and industrial action, 10–11, 285–6, 337–8
industrial tribunals and, 275–8
law changes since 1979, 270–1
law on
    contract of employment, 320–2
    definitions, 324–5
    exclusions, 322–4
    public law remedies, 325´
    purposes, 319
    statistics, 319–20
rights after confinement, 339
and transfer of undertakings, 339
Union of Democratic Mineworkers recognition, 51
see also Trade Unions

Vredeling Directives on employee participation, 175–6

Wages Act 1986, and cash pay, 278
Wages Councils, 9, 349–50
law changes since 1979, 271
restrictions, 278–9

wages, *see* pay/payment systems
Wapping dispute, 66
water industry, pay bargaining, 36–7
Willis, Norman
    on ballots, 303
    on revival strategies, 25
winter of discontent, 266
    and union immunity, 281–2
women
    employment trends, 4–5
    equal pay legislation 1983, 279
    homeworking and new technology, 62–3
    law changes since 1979, 272
    managers, 189–90
    rights, 7
    as union target group, 24
    see also maternity; sex discrimination
work measurement, 222
work study, 221–2
worker directors, 173–6
    British Steel, 174
    Bullock Committee, 173
    Post Office, 175
    private sector, 174
    Vredeling Directives, 175–6
Workplace Industrial Relations Survey 1984, 249